CW01368296

AMERICAN
JEWISH
HISTORY

EIGHT VOLUME SET ISBN 0-415-91933-9

VOLUME 1: ISBN 0-415-91920-7
  VOLUME 2: ISBN 0-415-91921-5
  VOLUME 3: ISBN 0-415-91943-6 (SET)
    VOL 3, PART 1: ISBN 0-415-91922-3
    VOL 3, PART 2: ISBN 0-415-91923-1
    VOL 3, PART 3: ISBN 0-415-91924-X
  VOLUME 4: ISBN: 0-415-91925-8
  VOLUME 5: ISBN 0-415-91944-4 (SET)
    VOL 5, PART 1: ISBN 0-415-91926-6 (SET)
    VOL 5, PART 2: ISBN 0-415-91927-4
    VOL 5, PART 3: ISBN 0-415- 91928-2
  VOLUME 6: ISBN 0-415-91945-2 (SET)
    VOL 6, PART 1: ISBN 0-415-91929-0
    VOL 6, PART 2: ISBN 0-415-91930-4
  VOLUME 7: ISBN 0-415-91931-2
  VOLUME 8: ISBN 0-415-91932-0

AMERICAN JEWISH HISTORY

A EIGHT-VOLUME SERIES
Edited by Jeffrey S. Gurock

SPONSORED BY
The American Jewish Historical Society

CONTENTS OF THE SET

1.
AMERICAN JEWISH HISTORY:
THE COLONIAL AND EARLY NATIONAL PERIODS, 1654-1840

2.
CENTRAL EUROPEAN JEWS IN AMERICA, 1840-1880:
MIGRATION AND ADVANCEMENT

3.
EAST EUROPEAN JEWS IN AMERICA, 1880-1920:
IMMIGRATION AND ADAPTATION
(THREE PARTS)

4.
AMERICAN JEWISH LIFE, 1920-1990

5.
THE HISTORY OF JUDAISM IN AMERICA:
TRANSPLANTATIONS, TRANSFORMATIONS,
AND RECONCILIATIONS
(THREE PARTS)

6.
ANTI-SEMITISM IN AMERICA
(TWO PARTS)

7.
AMERICA, AMERICAN JEWS, AND THE HOLOCAUST

8.
AMERICAN ZIONISM: MISSION AND POLITICS

AMERICAN JEWISH HISTORY: VOLUME 4

AMERICAN JEWISH LIFE, 1920-1990

Edited by Jeffrey S. Gurock

Routledge
Taylor & Francis Group
LONDON AND NEW YORK

Preface, selection, organization, and index copyright © 1998 by American Jewish Historical Society.

Individual articles are protected by separate copyrights. Permissions statements are included on the title page of each article.

Library of Congress Cataloging-in-Publication Data

American Jewish life, 1920-1990 / edited by Jeffrey S. Gurock.
    p. cm.— (American Jewish history ; 4)
  Includes bibliographical references and index.
  ISBN 0-415-91925-8 (lib. bdg. : alk. paper)
    1. Jews—United States—History—20th century. 2. Jews—United States—Social conditions. 3. United States—Ethnic relations.
I. Gurock, Jeffrey S., 1949– . II. Series.
E184.J5A554   1998
973'.04924—dc21   97-23848

Published in 1998 by
Routledge
2 Park Square, Milton Park, Abingdon, Oxon OX14 4RN
52 Vanderbilt Avenue, New York, NY 10017

Routledge is an imprint of the Taylor & Francis Group, an informa business

All rights reserved. No part of this book may be reprinted or reproduced or utilised in any form or by any electronic, mechanical, or other means, now known or hereafter invented, including photocopying and recording, or in any information storage or retrieval system, without permission in writing from the publishers.

Notice:
Product or corporate names may be trademarks or registered trademarks, and are used only for identification and explanation without intent to infringe.

ISBN 13: 978-0-415-91925-8 (hbk) (Vol. IV)

Case design: Helene Benedetti

Contents

Introduction to the Series vii
Preface xiii

1. The Midpassage of American Jewry, 1929–1945, *Lloyd P. Gartner* 1
2. A "Golden Decade" for American Jews: 1945–1955,
   Arthur A. Goren 17
3. Jewish Migration in Postwar America: The Case of Miami
   and Los Angeles, *Deborah Dash Moore* 35
4. The German-Jewish Community of Washington Heights,
   Steven M. Lowenstein 51
5. The Impact of Holocaust Survivors on American Society:
   A Socio-Cultural Portrait, *William B. Helmreich* 61
6. The Sephardim of the United States: An Exploratory Study,
   Marc D. Angel 75
7. Occupational Patterns of American Jews I, *Nathan Goldberg* 137
8. Occupational Patterns of American Jews II, *Nathan Goldberg* 159
9. Occupational Patterns of American Jews III, *Nathan Goldberg* 185
10. The Postwar Economy of American Jews, *Barry R. Chiswick* 215
11. Investing in Themselves: The Harvard Case and the Origins of
    the Third American-Jewish Commercial Elite, *Henry L. Feingold* 233
12. The Impact of Feminism on American Jewish Life,
    Sylvia Barack Fishman 257
13. Rage and Representation: Jewish Gender Stereotypes
    in American Culture, *Riv-Ellen Prell* 317
14. Value Added: Jews in Postwar American Culture,
    Stephen J. Whitfield 337

Index 355

AMERICAN JEWISH HISTORY

Introduction to the Series
Jeffrey S. Gurock

Americans have been writing about the Jewish experience in this country for more than one hundred years. But, the academic examination of this minority group's saga in the United States did not really begin until the 1950s. Until that time, Jewish amateur historians were the primary chroniclers of American Jewish history. They wrote to extol Jewish achievements and to romanticize that people's affinity for the American way of life. Motivated by their desire to answer anti-Semitic critics who, beginning the 1880s, questioned the role Jews played in the rise of this country, these undaunted authors documented the antiquity of the Jewish presence on these shores and their consistent allegiance to all that was good in America. To prove their point beyond all reasonable doubt, these authors focused on the Colonial and Early National periods of American Jewish history (ca. 1654–1840) and attempted to cite all examples of Jewish presence in the thirteen colonies, every story of Jewish courage and heroism in defense of their adopted land, and each instance where Judaic teachings seemed to inform the great documents of American freedom. Sometimes, Gentile friends and neighbors helped them in their communal-directed labors. Together, these apologists did the job they set out to do. By the 1950s, no similar-size contingent of Jews had been as well chronicled as the 2,000 or so souls who made up the first Jewish communities in what became the United States.

Still, when professional, academically trained historians began to study the American Jewish experience some forty-five years ago, they recognized that for all of these amateurs' earnest efforts, work still needed to be done in the area of early American Jewish history. Their predecessors' spade work needed to be synthesized. Aspects of the Colonial experience that were intentionally ignored, like instances of Jewish loyalist allegiances, had to be examined. Issues that the discipline's founding writers overlooked, such as the problems that Jews faced in maintaining their identities in a country that accepted them, had to be scrutinized. In addressing these questions, writers since the 1950s have broadened the scope of early American Jewish history. They have worked well in reusing the materials that were assembled early on.

However, the rewriting of the amateurs' work did not preoccupy those who upgraded this field. Rather, they have been largely concerned with describing and interpreting the other chronological periods and central historical themes that previously were accorded scant attention. For example, as late as the 1950s, only the general contours of the era of Central European migration and settlement (ca. 1840–1880) had been documented and analyzed. Much more needed to be known, for example, about the concert of forces that brought Jews to the United States from European homes and the variety of experiences that awaited the newcomers in this country. Similarly, American Jewry's earliest writers had little access to, or affinity for, the history of mass East European migration (ca. 1880–1920). They did not read the foreign languages of the new immigrants and were often insensitive to their travails and triumphs. But, since the 1950s, the story of those who came here during this period has interested more historians than any other time-frame in American Jewish history. The first generation of professionally trained historians and their students, some of whom were scions of East European Jewish stock, have examined closely why "Russian" Jews came to America, how they found homes and jobs and ultimately become entrepreneurs, consumers, and leaders in America even as they struggled to maintain their religious and ethnic identities.

In the last few decades, professional historians have also critically explored how Jews managed and matured as an American minority group after America in the early 1920s closed its gates to East European migration. Some of these amateur chroniclers lived through the so-called inter-war period. But they wrote little about their contemporary experiences. Fortunately, some of the first sociologists American Jewry produced did study the 1920s–1940s community. Academic historians built upon these ground-breaking works as they examined the processes of acculturation, identification, and the integration of second generation children of immigrants. In recent years, scholars have also begun to explore the assimilation patterns of post-war Jewry as the experience of third and fourth generation Jews—those who were born and grew to maturity between the 1950s and the 1970s—has begun to intrigue historians.

The fears of American Jewry's first historians that public discussion of anti-Semitism would injure the status of Jews in America deterred them from taking long, hard looks at the historical roots of prejudice and discrimination. Their Gentile friends and neighbors who dabbled in Jewish history also had no desire to speak about this blot on America's record. Similarly, the Jewish amateurs' apprehension that some unsympathetic Americans might misconstrue the story of Jewish support for Zionism and accuse them of "dual loyalty" contributed to their reluctance to examine the course of the Jewish national movement in America. Today, the history of discrimination against Jews and the saga of Jewish and American interaction with Israel are but two of the more important aspects of the Jewish experience that attract professional historians anxious to compose a comprehensive picture of how they, and all other minority groups, have lived in this country. Thus, the course of Jewish inter-group relations, the instances of cooperation among minority and ethnic groups and more often, the occurrences of tensions, racism, and anti-Semitism that have separated Jews from their fellow Americans, have all been accorded significant scholarly consideration. Similarly, the role of Zionism and the State of Israel, both as a prime force in promoting Jewish identification and as a factor in American and Jewish political and diplomatic life, has also received intense scholarly scrutiny.

The history of Judaism in America, the story of how, from the seventeenth century on, different expressions of a traditional faith, transported from Europe, changed and survived under the conditions of freedom is another historical issue that has received, in recent decades, a lion's share of scholarly attention. To be sure, American Jewry's first chroniclers did display some interest in the story of Jewish religious life. But, their focus was narrow, limited to biographies of well-known rabbis and cantors and anecdotal histories of famous congregations. Contemporary historians look carefully both at congregational elites and lay constituents. They consider, among other themes, how congregants understood and acted upon the ideological and theological statements that their rabbis made. They also look closely at the confluence of American familial, cultural, economic and social realities that have brought Jews into, and separated them from, their synagogues and communities.

The understanding that American Jewish history is part of, and is informed by, a larger and more inclusive American social and ethnic history is implicit in all the professional work that has, since the 1950s, restructured and redefined this field. The amateur first writers of American Jewish history labored in almost complete isolation from students of other groups and from scholars of Jewish history. Today, avant-garde American Jewish historians display a keen awareness of new methodological approaches and historical perspectives that have become part of their general academic discipline. They ask the same types of questions that all other historians do and they look for comparable answers. To note just two prime examples:

Over the last twenty-five years, the use of quantification in the writing of American history has opened up additional scholarly vistas. Through the use of census materials, business records, school registry lists, etc., it has often become possible to gain access to the lives of the poor and the inarticulate whose stories could not be documented otherwise. American Jewish historians have become attuned to these techniques and typically have used these once-unconventional sources to chart the rise of the German Jewish peddler-businessmen, to compare immigrant Jewish mobility within different turn-of-the century communities, or even to determine the socio-economic status of members of congregations who, in the nineteenth century, debated whether their synagogue should retain or reform their religious rituals.

The stories of American women have also found their proper historical place over the past several decades. American Jewish history has followed suit and, arguably, some of the best new works have retold the immigrant saga through the lens of the female experience. Equally important, studies of American Judaism increasingly have become concerned with the position of women within the synagogue and religious society, a reflection in part of contemporary developments within the late twentieth century Jewish community itself.

Finally, when American Jewish history has been written in recent years, its best authors have been sensitive to indicate how individual experiences here and group developments in this New World compare to Jewish history elsewhere in the modern world. For example, studies of American Zionism or of anti-Semitism in this country or of religious life in the United States are now carefully placed against the backdrop of modern Jewish history of which they clearly are a part.

This thirteen-volume series brings together 211 of the best articles written by professional historians over the past forty years in American Jewish history. These are among the pathbreaking, insightful studies that did the job of transforming this field from a bastion of apologetics to a respected academic discipline. Together these volumes make conveniently available the essential articles that inform all contemporary interpretations of American Jewish history.

Readers will immediately note that nine of the thirteen volumes in this series focus on but four themes and periods in American Jewish history. That is because most of the best work that has been published since the 1950s has been in the specific areas of American Judaism, the saga of East European migration and settlement and anti-Semitism—including the troubled history of America and American Jewry during the period of Nazism and the Holocaust. These are the fields where American Jewish historians have most often utilized the newest methodological approaches, shown sensitivity to what colleagues were doing in cognate fields of American immigration and ethnic history, and dealt most often with the issues that have concerned students of modern Jewish history.

The remaining four volumes include the most important articles on the Colonial and Early National periods, the era of Central European migration, American Zionism, and the economic fate and social status of inter-war and post-World War II Jewry. Here, too, new methodologies and perspectives abound as the story of the early periods has been rewritten, as the evolution of Jewish nationalism as a force in the life of Americans and Jews has been explicated, and as the history of our own contemporary era has begun to be told.

Finally, readers should be aware that even in a compendium as large as this, difficult choices had to be made about what to include. I chose those studies that told the story of American Jewry well while effectively relating its history to that of other Americans or to Jews worldwide. In addition, in organizing my 211 choices into series volumes, I decided to group articles dealing with religion, anti-Semitism, and Zionism into their own volumes, even if a particular article in these three fields dealt with a narrow chronological period. This was done in appreciation of the breadth of work being done within these major genres of American Jewish historiography.

A reader who works assiduously through these thirteen volumes, guided by this general introduction and the prefaces to each of the eight titles, will emerge with a clear understanding of the central themes, periods, and historical questions that define and inform American Jewish history today. The student will, likewise, gain a sense of the quality of the writing and the interest of the major writers who have brought coherence and an ever broadening scope to this still relatively young academic discipline.

# Preface
Jeffrey S. Gurock

Until the 1920s, the story of East European Jews in America was primarily the saga of immigrant encounter and adaptation to a new environment. After the United States closed its doors to most foreigners in the early 1920s, the issues for American Jews increasingly became those of minority group members who shared this country's social and cultural values but who wanted to maintain an ethnic identity even as they sought to overcome the limitations placed upon their full participation in society. After the Second World War, the themes of assimilation, integration, and ethnic group persistence continued to loom large in American Jewish life, but with one fundamental difference. While the most pressing question for Jews of the inter-war period (ca. 1920–1941) was whether they could overcome the anti-Semitism that retarded their integration, the basic communal dilemma for post-war and contemporary Jews has been how to survive in an American environment so favorable to assimilation.

The historiography on the last seventy-five years in American Jewish life has reflected the changing bases of Jewish communal concerns. While some pathbreaking work has been done on the religious and communal life of Jewry in the 1920s and 1930s, the majority of studies of that era focus on anti-Semitism. Important histories of inter-war social and political discrimination speak not only about limitations imposed on individual Jews' lives but also serve as starting points for understanding the insecurity Jewish leaders felt in approaching America's government on behalf of Jews who were endangered overseas. Conversely, while historians have not ignored manifestations of post-war anti-Semitism, many more treatments of Jewish life in our own day have looked at the problem of disaffection from Judaism and how synagogues and rabbis and other communal institutions and leaders have attempted to cope with assimilation.

But, even as more should be known about synagogues, rabbis, and identification in the 1920s and the 1930s, and while the story of American anti-Semitism has not been told completely, other dimensions of Jewish life have to be explored for a complete picture of the period from the 1920s to the 1990s. Jewish economic progress through Depression, war and post-war booms and busts needs to be comprehensively evaluated. Intra-city demographic changes and patterns of cross-country migration still have to be charted. Though New York City was America's largest Jewish metropolis in 1920 (and remains so in 1997), other cities in the South, Midwest and Far West have in recent decades absorbed masses of Jews. There Jews built communities in social environments that were very different from New York City and the nature of Jewish life in these locales requires analysis. Jewish cultural creativity and its shifting impact upon American society in the inter-war and post-war years has to be chronicled. Similarly, the way changing American cultural mores have impacted upon Jewish consciousness over the last three generations must be understood. Once these and other monographic examinations are completed, a comprehensive picture may be composed fully depicting the experiences of second, third and fourth generation American Jews.

The fourteen articles in this volume include a sampling of the valuable work that has been done on the Jewish economic, demographic, and cultural life of the descendants of East European Jews and examples of worthy first efforts to provide synoptic overviews.

The three lead articles are excellent guides to understanding the textures of Jewish life among the children and grandchildren of East European immigrants both before and after World War II. Lloyd Gartner's work identifies and analyzes the problems which, during the Depression and the war, undermined the Jewish community's confidence in itself, as it sought to solve its own social and economic dilemmas and attempted to influence foreign events.

According to Arthur Goren, the period from 1945 to 1955 was a golden decade for American Jewry. It was then, he explains, that a more self-assured and self-assertive community joined other Americans on the road to suburbia. At that turning point, Jews found social acceptance greater than ever before as the anti-Semitism of the past became no longer fashionable. At the same time, Goren also notes that as group allegiance increasingly became a matter of personal choice—Jews were really no longer forced to associate with their own kind—thoughtful and prescient leaders began to acknowledge that assimilation would be the greatest future challenge to communal survival. In other words, for Goren, the first post-war decade witnessed the patterns of Jewish progress and problematics that continue to this day.

Deborah Dash Moore's study complements Goren as she introduces the background, goals, and outcomes of Jewish migration from the older cities of the East and Midwest to the Sun Belt areas of the South and Far West. She isolates the factors that created new types of Jewish communities and culture as these Jews integrated rapidly and had to deal with questions of group survival.

The next three articles remind us that American Jewish history of the last seventy-five years is more than just the story of the descendants of East European Jews. German Jewish refugees of the 1930s and 1940s and Holocaust survivors of the 1940s and 1950s also have their unique histories as do the American Sephardim. Lowenstein's work focuses on the transplantation of elements of the Frankfurt on the Main community. Helmreich looks at the achievements of survivor groups, while Angel offers an overview of Sephardic life in different American locales. Each study, in its own way, sets an agenda for further explorations.

The striking contrast in the economic profile of pre-war and post-war periods is quantified and illuminated in the articles by sociologists Nathan Goldberg and Barry Chiswick. Both successfully extrapolate data from government and private sources to document the dimensions of Jewish mobility. While not contesting the reality that Jews have done much better in the most recent decades, historian Henry Feingold's study suggests that the paths Jews took toward contemporary economic success can be traced back to the 1920s. Feingold posits a somewhat positive evaluation of the Jews' lot during the 1920s and the 1930s.

The next two studies look at how changing American cultural mores affected the life of the integrated post-war American Jew. Sylvia Barack Fishman offers a survey of the pervasive influence feminism has had on Jewish communal life. Riv-Ellen Prell looks at how changing forms of humor and stereotypes about Jewish women underscore the conflicts Jewish men feel about their place within an evolving American culture and society. The concluding essay in this volume by Stephen Whitfield is a useful starting point for gauging the dimensions of the Jewish contribution to American cultural life in the contemporary period.

AMERICAN JEWISH HISTORY

American Jewish Life, 1920–1990

The Midpassage of American Jewry, 1929-1945

Lloyd P. Gartner

Zurich, August, 1929. The reconstruction of the Jewish world after World War I came to fullness when, after years of negotiation, non-Zionist notables entered into the "Pact of Glory" with the Zionist movement to found the Jewish Agency for Palestine. The agreement was joyously made official at the Zionist Congress, held as usual in Switzerland. Then, after a few heady days, began the rapid, steep, and almost uninterrupted descent. Louis Marshall, the recognized head of American Jewry and main negotiator with Chaim Weizmann, fell ill after the Jewish Agency assembly and was dead in three weeks. As Marshall lay dying, a bloody onslaught by Arabs on the Jewish National Home exposed its physical weakness, and made clear a depth of Arab hostility that few had reckoned with. Great Britain started its long retreat from the promise of the Balfour Declaration and the stipulations of the Palestine Mandate. The disturbing summer of 1929 ended with the first massive crack in the United States stock market, and other cracks followed until the securities market lay in ruins. Unemployment and business failures increased monthly, while banks collapsed and the world's financial system came into peril. The international dimensions of the economic crisis gave point to the alarming reports being received from Germany over the rising power of the Nazi movement.

The new agenda of American Jewry was outlined during that summer and autumn of 1929, while the death of Marshall symbolized the weakening of its patrician leadership. Depression in America on a scale never known before had to turn the concerns even of prosperous American Jews to making a living and holding on to what they had. The world depression helped the Nazis into power in 1933, and the hideous

---

Originally published as *The Fifth Annual Feinberg Memorial Lecture*, University of Cincinnati, 1982. Reprinted by permission of the Department of Judaic Studies, University of Cincinnati and the author.

twelve years' chronicle of European Jewry began. Where lay hope? It was not a propitious time to wager on America's liberal democracy. Soviet Russia, many urgently argued, was the future and it worked. Depression in America, Nazism in Germany, the Jewish National Home and the sinking fortunes of East European Jewry became the agenda of American Jewry after 1929, and a hesitant, uncertain leadership had to cope with it all. Fifteen years earlier, in 1914, it is hard to imagine anyone foreseeing even a small part of this agenda. Fifteen years after it ended, in 1960, did not many sense that their world was so different that what had happened between 1929 and 1945 was a nightmare, or some portion of it a matter decent enough for nostalgia? So different had the times become, and that much had the public affairs of American Jewry changed. Historians generally stress continuity beneath the surface of change, but we had better look upon these years as a time of abrupt and drastic alterations in the regularities and tempo of American Jewish life. It is not only that the events of these years were stark, horrifying, and sometimes thrilling. In 1929, American Jewry was still dominated by its immigrant experience, the end of which had been decreed only four years earlier by the Johnson Act. Yiddish in its varied uses, Jewish trade unions, and *landsmanshaften* all reflected publicly the kind of life led in thousands of Jewish households. Thousands more studiously kept apart from the immigrant milieu in which they had grown up, or rebelled against it. Sixteen years later, in 1945, the immigrant world was shrivelled or gone, and so was the complex of attitudes towards it. The years when this happened were American Jewry's eventful, trying midpassage.

How can we recount what happened to the Jewish people between 1929 and 1945 without seeking the wrath of Amos, the grandeur of Isaiah, the despair of Jeremiah? There is no hope I can do this. Let me attempt something modest by comparison: what lay before American Jews in their country? How did they attempt to cope with their public agenda? And how did their domestic affairs influence their foreign activities?[1]

During the first thirty years of the 20th century American Jews had progressed materially to an astonishing degree. Neither the foreignness of most of them as East European immigrants nor xenophobia nor anti-Semitism kept them from improving their lot with the general prosperity of the age, marked only by brief setbacks. The Jews quit the Lower East Side and its counterparts in practically every city and moved to better neighborhoods. They left proletarian occupations and peddling to become shopkeepers, petty entrepreneurs, and white collar workers. Those who remained garment workers were fortified in strong unions. There were high hopes for the economic advance of the children. A good many Jews were teachers, accountants, lawyers, and physicians. From 1929 all that changed. As large enterprises laid off their workers en masse and small firms closed down, unemployment rose to levels never imagined: in major industrial cities like Pittsburgh, Cleveland, and Detroit it ranged between 30% and 35% of the labor force, besides those who could find only part-time work. Unemployment also struck the Jews hard. With the cessation of building in the boom city of Los Angeles, "two hundred Jewish carpenters cannot find work, or to put it in milder terms sixty per cent of the Jewish carpenters belonging to this group have been out of employment . . . for many, many months." We learn of a man with a wife and three young children who was "working as a presser irregularly, averaging $3.50 per week."[2] Jewish needle workers' unions could do nothing against their employers going out of business or cutting back severely. The old days of sweatshops and piece work seemed to be returning as wages and hours fell back to what they had been twenty-five years before. Voluntary wage cuts and industry-wide strikes accomplished little before the New Deal's programs. Many dispossessed shopkeepers and men out of work took to door to door peddling, which underwent a revival owing to the desperate efforts of men to support themselves. Ruined businessmen presented an "insistent and increasing demand" for relief to Jewish agencies:

> Our Jewish people have asked help later because they are tradesmen. They will buy and sell as long as there are those to trade with. Coming to us now in increasing numbers [in 1931] are the small merchant, the builder and real estate dealer. In fact, a new clientele is being created—the so-called "white collar" class.[3]

The Jewish merchant could hold out longer, but to return to business was harder than for the worker, who needed no capital but only a job. Jewish institutions suffered harshly as contributions dwindled. Perhaps the worst off were schools, especially those with ambitious programs whose following was mainly among the Orthodox, then the least prosperous segment of the Jewish community. Tuition could not be collected and other income was scarce. For the unfortunate teachers there were frequent payless paydays, and months of waiting for even partial payment of arrears of salary.

A generation inured to the psychic trials of prosperity might be reminded of those which came from proverty:

> . . . a period such as we are passing through takes its toll in various forms of physical illnesses, particularly that of undernourished children, to say nothing of mental conflict and mental illness, depression and despondency and the increasing number of problems of delinquency.[4]

And a veteran social worker sighed:
> As I observe the young people in this fourth year of the depression [1934] I am appalled by their cynical acceptance of things as they are, They are not avid for tools of understanding: they reject opportunities for vocational preparation, seeing, as they do, that fitness is no guarantee of work . . .[5]

Young people went to college but with faint prospect of employment. Alfred Kazin's mood was typical: "One hot afternoon, in June, 1934, deep in the depression, I had just completed my college course for the year and was desolately on my way home to Brooklyn . . . ."[6] Early in the Depression it was possible to declare, as did the director of a Jewish employment bureau, that "We should face our employment situation as a people and solve our problems within the group,"[7] in the spirit of the apologetic pride that "Jews take care of their own". However, the dimensions of the problem became so huge that Jews no longer even made the attempt. Until the New Deal made the relief of unemployment a Federal responsibility, there were sad and sometimes stormy scenes in Jewish agencies which, like other private charities, were the funnel through which state unemployment relief appropriations were doled out to recipients.[8] The New Deal unemployment programs relieved Jewish and private charities of an impossible burden. Even in 1938 there was heavy Jewish unemployment, said to be 14.7% of the Jewish labor force in Pittsburgh, 5.2% in Buffalo, and 8.8% of experienced Jewish workers in San Francisco; in Detroit three years before it had stood at 14.7%.[9] In the New York metropolis, the percentage was 12%-13% in 1935-1937. The rapid shifting of Jewish neighborhoods which accompanied upward mobility lessened or ceased.[10]

So shattering was the Depression and the wave of economic anti-Semitism it released that the economic future of the Jews in the United States seemed in question:
> . . . unlike Americans as a whole, the Jewish group does not possess a balanced economic distribution which allows economic gains and losses, strains and tensions, to be spread evenly among their number. Jews are not represented on the farms or in manual jobs. The needle trades have employed large numbers, although even here other nationalities have been supplanting them in recent decades. The heavy industries engage few Jews either among employers or workers. Banking, stock brokering, moving pictures and other forms of amusement, real estate, and the distributive trades account for most of our Jewish wealth. The professions, small business and white-collar oc-

cupations yield our large Jewish middle class.[11]
The middle class, and precisely its mercantile and white collar segment in which Jews sought their place, seemed the most endangered in the long range, although, as it happened, it was rather less afflicted by unemployment than was unskilled and proletarian labor. Thus, unemployment among Jews was proportionately less severe. Perhaps, it was argued, Jews were "overrepresented" in trade and the professions, and their youth should be directed to become farmers, technicians, and skilled craftsmen. By no means was it clear when representation became overrepresentation. More or less it meant fields where there were many Jews or against which anti-Semites complained. These proposals for vocational shifts, in retrospect, were attuned more to public relations than to economic realities. Young Jews disregarded them, and continued going to college with an eye on independent business and the professions, preparing without realizing it for the opportunities which opened wide in the 1940s.

What disturbed Jews deepest was not the high unemployment and economic insecurity they shared with the American population at large, but the dangerously anti-Semitic atmosphere fostered by the Depression which might last many more years. Father Charles E. Coughlin broadcast nationally from Detroit, and his anti-Semitism became more explicit with each weekly talk. At street corner meetings in upper Manhattan hatred of Jews was spewed and in subway stations beneath they could be assaulted. The Nazis of the German-American Bund sought to carry on like their mentors in Germany.[12] There was a plethora of anti-Semitic organizations. All the time American Jews had in mind the ravage of the Jews in Germany, like themselves educated, acculturated, patriotic, economically successful. *It Can't Happen Here* was the ironic title of Sinclair Lewis' popular novel of 1935 which imagined how "it" did happen. There was reassurance that the American people largely detested Nazism, yet impossible to suggest any easing of restrictions on the immigration of its Jewish or other victims. President Roosevelt did not choose to try. A proposal for freer immigration was likely to generate a popular counter-proposal to halt all immigration to the United States during a period of mass unemployment.

All Jews knew of the large areas of the labor market which were practically shut to them. They had almost no chance in banks, insurance firms except as brokers selling policies to other Jews, large corporations, department stores, as lawyers in large law firms, as scholars in universities or as physicians in hospitals. To make matters look cleaner, some of these enterprises would hire token Jews who would not be advanced. There were Jewish employers who followed the trend and did not hire Jews. But during a time of desperate job seeking, many employers did not have to bother with excuses—they didn't want Jews working for them. Most private universities, particularly the most distinguished, had quotas on Jewish admissions. Notorious were the medical schools, whose anti-Semitic policies compelled hundreds of Jewish medical students to emigrate to foreign schools, notably Edinburgh in Scotland.[13]

The large cities knew sharp inter-ethnic tensions. In Boston and New York there was friction between Jews and Irish, as the Jews competed hard and often successfully for jobs in which the Irish had long predominated. These included white collar work, positions in the school system, and a share in the control of the Democratic Party machine with its vast job-giving powers, from street cleaners to judges. The dramatic mayoralty of Fiorello H. LaGuardia in New York City meant the decline of Irish municipal power entrenched in Tammany Hall, and the rise of Jews and Italians. Irish anger at the Jewish challenge also had an ideological basis, with the Jews strongly supporting the Spanish Republicans during the Civil War in Spain and the Catholics—meaning mainly Irish, especially at the level of the hierarchy—strong for the insurgents. Jews opposed the Catholic and Irish desire for some religious influence in the public schools. Before Pearl Harbor, the Irish generally opposed aid to their homeland's old oppressor Great Britain, while most Jews advocated aid to Hitler's enemies. Communism rather than Nazism was the great enemy to many Catholics.[14]

Against this bleak setting of economic trouble, anti-Semitism and concern for Jews overseas, the presidency of Franklin Delano Roosevelt held a meaning which was not only tangible and political. Even today, almost fifty years after he entered the White House for the longest, most dynamic and eventful tenure in American history, Roosevelt appears so much more vivid a figure than any of his successors that it is easy to realize what he meant to the electorate which four times sent him to the White House. As William E. Leuchtenburg observes:

> When Roosevelt took office, the country to a very large degree, responded to the will of a single element: the white, Anglo-Saxon, Protestant property-holding class. Under the New Deal, new groups took their place in the sun. It was not merely that they received benefits they had not had before but that they were "recognized" as having a place in the commonwealth.[15]

The New Deal, that vast, quite unplanned aggregation of relief and reform measures, many of which owed something to Jewish economists and social workers, to the Jewish labor movement and the Lower East Side of New York, became part of the fabric of American life. The mass of Jews embraced it enthusiastically. Yet important as they were, these measures were not the reason for the support of Roosevelt which at times surpassed even adoration to become idolatry. This old American Protestant aristocrat, a type Jews have often supported politically, smiling and supremely affable, placed Jews at the political nerve center in his victorious coalition of ethnic urban groups, proletarian workers, Blacks, and deprived farmers. He openly loathed Nazism and Fascism. He appointed Jews to high office, and it was learned with appreciation that he brushed aside the pleas of some prominent Jews not to raise the Jewish political profile in the dangerous year of 1939 and replaced the revered Brandeis on the Supreme Court with Felix Frankfurter. 80% to 90% of the Jews voted for Roosevelt in his four elections, each time in a higher proportion. The lowest was in the 1932 election when many Jews voted Socialist and Communist. The vote for these parties of the left declined with succeeding presidential elections, and the Jews, like most of their other voters, switched to Roosevelt. One might also suggest a kind of Manichean politics. The embodiment of evil, Adolf Hitler, required the embodiment of good against him, and that had to be Franklin Delano Roosevelt, except for those who insisted in seeing the embodiment in Josef Stalin. Roosevelt was supported in New York by such Jewish favorites as Herbert H. Lehman, Robert F. Wagner, and Fiorello H. LaGuardia.

The evident failure of American capitalism in a liberal, democratic state to fulfill the American promise of mass prosperity led to movements leftward and rightward, for abandoning democracy as the right demanded, or for doing away with capitalism as the left demanded. Jews of course gravitated to the left, especially because the far right was anti-Semitic. American literature, including the Jewish writers who were beginning to figure prominently in it, was saturated with the social questions of the time. Jewish writing and thinking moved generally to the left along with American thought and letters at large. The numerous novels of Jewish immigrant life were as a rule autobiographical. They were critical, often harshly so, of the immigrant world and of those who rose within it to worldly success. Now their attitude of rejection extended to the inhospitable social order. One scholar has enumerated seventy radical proletarian novels appearing between 1930 and 1940 by fifty-three authors of whom seventeen appear to be Jewish. Jewish prominence in American literature really begins with these novels of radical protest of which few, to be sure, are good literature.[16]

Social problems were conceived by the intellectual consensus of the time in general social and economic terms, and answers to them were provided in the same frame. There were thus no distinct or specific Jewish problems, and it was unscientific and ethnocentric to assume otherwise. Anti-Semitism had to be regarded as a disease of capitalist society, and the Jews were victims on account of their economic stratification and minority status. Two things were required: a drastic change in capitalism or its abolition, and the participation of the Jews in the forces which were to bring this about, whether these were socialists or communists or the new industrial union movement. It was a specious universalism, for it denied that the Jews constituted a group which, whatever else they were part of, was also whole in itself and merited serious attention as such; whatever society did to solve its problems as a whole would not as an automatic consequence solve the problems of the Jews. The universalist Jews naturally sought their place in universalist social and political movements where they frequently found that quite a high proportion of their fellow-universalists were also Jews. Many were writers and teachers, as well as social workers who were often employed by institutions within the Jewish community.[17]

It was during the 1930s, at a point in time which can not be determined, that the majority of Jews became American born. Moreover, American Jews became an older group as their birth rate continued to decline. The immigrant world and its Yiddish press, speech, synagogues, theatre, and literature was passing, and so was the Jewish character of the trade unions they had built. *Landsmanshaften* were shrivelling, while "Americanization" activities lost their point except to serve the limited number of refugees from Germany. Religious and cultural life was dominated by the quest for an American form of religious tradition and by the effort of maintaining institutions unaided by government or federations of Jewish philanthropies. The characteristic face of Orthodoxy was the post-immigrant neighborhood synagogue, most of whose members were but superficially observant. Major Orthodox leaders arrived from Europe during this time—Rabbis Soloveitchik, Feinstein, Breuer, and Schneerson in chronological order—but their impact was felt only in later years. Reform Judaism, financially better established and long past its adaptation to the American scene, began very tentatively to examine the possibilities of a renewal of religious tradition. It adopted a pro-Zionist policy, but with a forceful anti-Zionist minority in opposition, and also devoted much attention to general social questions. Conservative Judaism was not yet a powerful third force on the religious scene. Yet its Reconstructionist wing, led by Mordecai M. Kaplan, combined theological radicalism with traditional ritual practice, Zionism with the social gospel, and obtained much attention and some influence among rabbis and Jewish communal intelligentsia.

At the level of the organized Jewish community as a whole, except for local Jewish charities fund-raising faded into the background because so little could be raised for overseas needs. The antiseptic words of the *American Jewish Year Book* for 1931-1932 described the situation:

> Economic conditions in the United States during the past year were such as to compel the Jewish community to apply by far the greater part of its energies to the solution of its own domestic problems, including those of continuing the activities and, in some cases, preventing the dissolution of institutions and agencies which had been created by the community in previous years. American Jewry was prevented therefore from taking as active an interest in its sister communities overseas as in former years, especially as far as material aid was concerned.[18]

The Joint Distribution Committee, supported by the older German-Jewish wealth, saw its income shrink from $4,583,000 in 1927 to $1,632,000 in 1929 and to $385,000 in 1932. The disaster of German Jewry brought a great increase, to $1,151,000 in 1933 and to $1,402,000 in 1934. From 1936 the income of the JDC went up steadily, but still lagged far behind the needs.[19] The combined income of the two main funds for Palestine, the Jewish National Fund and the Palestine Foundation Fund, fell even lower than the JDC. From a mere $723,000 in 1930 it sagged to $339,000 in 1933, and then climbed gradually to $3,489,000 in 1939. Hadassah, however, managed to maintain its income fairly well.[20] During the depressed 1930s the permanent overseas aid structure was built. The Jewish National Fund, the Palestine Foundation Fund, and a few smaller bodies joined to form the United Palestine Appeal in 1935. Four years later the financially successful UPA entered into an agreement with the Joint Distribution Committee and the National Refugee Service, renewable annually, to establish the United Jewish Appeal. There was little about the United Jewish Appeal's early years to foretell that after World War II it would become the largest voluntary philanthropy in history. The partners fought one another constantly over the proportionate distribution of UJA funds. The leaders of the Joint insisted that European Jewry required assistance for physical survival, while the Zionists argued that only by developing Palestine could there be a sure and certain solution to Jewish persecution and homelessness which philanthropy could never provide. Individual communities which conducted combined campaigns were vexed by debates over the proportions to be retained for local needs and to be sent for overseas requirements.

The time appeared ripe during the 1930s for power within American Jewry to pass into the hands of the East European stock. Numerically, they constituted the vast majority. They were rising fast in political recognition, thanks especially to the New Deal and its local counterparts. The disillusion with America's political and economic leaders of the 1920s included the affluent stockbrokers, bankers, merchants and lawyers, mainly Republicans of the German-Jewish stock who had controlled the American Jewish community. Louis Marshall, had he lived, would have been out of his element in the 1930s. The old patriciate was vulnerable on other scores. Some of them lost their wealth or much of it, while many patrician heirs were but faintly Jewish when they were Jewish at all. The patriciate had placed its faith in emancipation as the full and sufficient cure for Jewish needs, and in philanthropy, preferably non-sectarian, as their highest expression as Jews. Nazism shattered the first article, while the New Deal made the second expendable. Shorn of their prestige, and in some cases of their wealth and Judaism, their deepest beliefs challenged, it is no surprise that the old leaders hardly led. Their circumspection in Jewish matters domestic and foreign, and their fear and dislike of public agitation ran counter to the eagerness of American Jewry for forceful, passionate demonstration and protest. These were the tactics of the pro-Zionist, pro-New Deal American Jewish Congress, revived in 1930 by Rabbi Stephen S. Wise, and they were deplored by the American Jewish Committee, spokesman of the diminished patriciate. In most local communities Jewish Community Councils were established, functioning as a council of local organizations with a degree of moral suasion but little real power.[21]

Yet the East European stock failed to take over the American Jewish community nationally during the 1930s. They had the numbers but not the money, and men of means are always indispensable in a voluntarily organized community. Perhaps the East Europeans lacked the confidence and the men. Behind the veteran Wise, not an East European himself, one does not find a cadre of potential national leaders of note waiting in the wings, except a few rabbis of whom the most notable was acknowledged to be the brilliant, dominating Abba Hillel Silver of Cleveland. Thus, the old order of the patriciate was gravely weakened during the 1930s, but the newer stock was unable to take over. There was a vacuum of national Jewish leadership at the most critical moment.

It was upon this troubled, hesitant Jewish community of some 5,000,000 souls that war descended in December, 1941. All agreed on the unavoidability of the conflict and the monstrosity of the enemy. The sons and some daughters went into the armed forces, among them refugees from the demonic persecutors they were now to destroy. The 550,000 Jewish soldiers were the first concern of their families, including those devoted to Jewish causes. As to the Jewish community, many of the anxieties of the 1930s continued into the war. True, economic problems shrank and practically disappeared with wartime prosperity and manpower shortages. Job discrimination was reduced, and fair employment practices became a new goal. However, the curve of anti-Semitism rose to a peak in 1944 according to public opinion polls, and Jewish children were so often molested on their way to and from school in New York and Boston that there was serious talk and some reported action of organized self-defense. Jews felt above all that they had to do, and show themselves to be doing, their full duty, whether as soldiers or civilians. This must never appear a "Jewish war", and there were to be no special Jewish requests. There was doubt whether it was right or politic to raise funds in campaigns for particular Jewish needs. Such preoccupations drastically limited what could possibly be done to aid European Jewry during its catastrophe, and Palestinian Jewry in its struggle.[22]

And what was done? A bitter and explicit indictment of the American government, and by implication of American Jewry, has gained wide acceptance. It is argued that American Jews placed their entire trust in Franklin D. Roosevelt, who beguiled them with assurances of his interest and sympathy. However, he knew that he had the Jews in his pocket, and so was not really concerned with their pleas. Overwhelmed with the responsibility for the conduct of the war, he indifferently allowed anti-Semitic State Department officials to withhold knowledge of the Holocaust as long as they could, and then to sabotage rescue efforts. State Department rules were formulated so as to seal the gates of the United States to Jewish immigrant refugees. Jewish leaders were frightened and quiescent. Only after audible discontent in the Jewish community was Henry Morgenthau Jr., Secretary of the Treasury, moved by public pressure, conscience, and perhaps by the efforts of the circle around Peter H. Bergson, to go to the President with a provocatively titled "Report to the Secretary on the Acquiescence of this Government in the Murder of Jews".[23] The War Refugee Board was promptly set up within the Treasury, not State Department, funded by the Joint Distribution Committee, and at last energetic rescue efforts commenced—years late.

This indictment, more properly condemnation, has some basis in fact. However, certain points should be made:

1. The Treasury Department, no less part of the American government than the State Department, was rather liberal in licensing the transfer of funds to Europe in order to finance the Joint's rescue work. They realized that some of the money might reach the Nazis. The conditions of currency transfer were complex but not impossible.

2. The real issue in rescue was not to secure an immigrant visa, find a place on a ship, and cross the Atlantic, but simply to get over some

border and out of Nazi control. There were humane American diplomats in such places as Switzerland and Vichy France who aided fleeing Jews.

3. Rescue depended on money, mainly of the Joint Distribution Committee from American Jews, and there was not enough of it. Twice as much to spend in Europe, or $10,000,000 yearly before 1944, would have probably saved thousands of lives. To be sure, the Joint wasted large amounts on useless agricultural colonies in Latin America.

It is also argued in a similar vein that Roosevelt's repeated assurances of pro-Zionism were bluff, set to naught by the State Department. Actually, American Zionism had long been the despair of the world movement. Since the great days of Brandeis' leadership it had failed to raise big money or to exercise powerful influence in the Jewish community. Aliyah from America was negligible. But during the war, especially after 1943, the Zionists made good their claim to speak for American Jewry as a whole, and from 1944 their political influence was felt in Washington. From this time, the Zionist approach to the American government came from a position of power, and the response had to be serious.[24]

World War II concluded in 1945 with American Jews unharmed except for the 10,500 killed and 24,000 wounded in the war, prosperous as never before, and apprehensive, needlessly as it turned out, of an anti-Semitic revival during the conversion to a peacetime economy. What happened to Europe's Jews was highlighted by pictures in newspapers and newsreels of the eerie horrors found in liberated concentration camps. Self-assurance and militancy, two new emotions, gripped them. The example furnished by the giant mobilization of America's resources to defeat the enemy, in which they had taken part, was now applied in the mobilization of every resource of American Jewry to save the remnant of European Jewry and support Palestinian Jewry. A noted Jewish historian, writing in 1946, believed that "for the first time in many years . . . the mood of utter despondency which permeated large sections of world Jewry is beginning to give way to a new feeling of hopeful expectation."[25] The Depression, New Deal, and World War II, and the often hesitant, fearful responses of American Jewry to overpowering, inscrutable problems came during its mid-passage from immigrant times to a more secure era of affluence, ready assimilation and generous action.

NOTES

I am grateful to Professor Arthur A. Goren who read this work and made valuable suggestions to improve it.

1. Of the library of American history during this period I have used William E. Leuchtenburg, *Franklin D. Roosevelt and the New Deal 1932-1940* (N.Y., 1963); Arthur M. Schlesinger Jr., *The Age of Roosevelt* 3 vols., (Boston, 1957-1960), reaching until 1937; Irving Bernstein, *The Lean Years: A History of the American Worker 1920-1933* (paperback, Baltimore, 1970), dealing mostly with the years after 1929; Lester V. Chandler, *America's Greatest Depression 1929-1941* (N.Y., 1970). No similar work can be cited for American Jewry during this period.

2. Max Vorspan and Lloyd P. Gartner, *History of the Jews of Los Angeles* (San Marino and Philadelphia, 1970), pp. 194-195.

3. Lloyd P. Gartner, *History of the Jews of Cleveland* (Cleveland, 1978), p. 291; see also Selig Adler and Thomas E. Connolly, *From Ararat to Suburbia: The History of the Jewish Community of Buffalo* (Philadelphia, 1960), pp. 358-364; on Jewish labor, see Joseph Brandes, "From Sweatshop to Stability: Jewish Labor Between Two Wars", in *YIVO Annual of Jewish Science*, XVI (1976) ed. Ezra Mendelsohn, pp. 61-104, 110-125.

4. Gartner, *Cleveland*, loc. cit.

5. Walter L. Solomon, quoted in Gartner, *Cleveland*, p. 294; Nettie P. McGill, "Some Characteristics of Jewish Youth in New York City," *Jewish Social Service Quarterly*, XIV (December, 1937), pp. 251-272.

6. Alfred Kazin, *Starting Out in the Thirties* (Boston, 1962), p. 3.

7. Vorspan and Gartner, *op. cit.*, p. 194; note the modest effort in Buffalo, 1934—Adler and Connolly, *op. cit.*, p. 339.

8. Gartner, *Cleveland*, pp. 292-293; Chandler, *op. cit.*, pp. 47-52.

9. Sophia M. Robison with Joshua Starr, ed., *Jewish Population Studies* (N.Y., 1943), pp. 41-42, 98-99, 170-171.

10. Ronald H. Bayor, *Neighbors in Conflict: The Irish, Germans, Jews and Italians of New York City, 1929-1941* (Baltimore and London, 1978) pp. 19-20; Gartner, *Cleveland*, pp. 269-271, 296-297; Thomas Kessner, "Jobs, Ghettoes and the Urban Economy, 1880-1935", *American Jewish History*, LXXI, 2 (December, 1981), pp. 234-237; Stephen Thernstrom, *The Other Bostonians: Poverty and Progress on the American Metropolis 1880-1970* (Cambridge, 1973), pp. 162-175.

11. Ben M. Selekman, "Planning for Economic Welfare", in Robert Morris and Michael Freund ed., *Trends and Issues in Jewish Social Welfare in the United States 1899-1952* (Philadelphia, 1966), p. 346; the selection was drawn from the symposium, "Recent Economic Trends in Relation to Jewish Life", with contributions by I. Lubin, S. Perlman, B.C. Vladeck, D. J. Saposs, and M. R. Cohen, in *Jewish Social Service Quarterly* XI, 1 (September, 1934), pp. 7-27. See the summary statement in The Editors of *Fortune, Jews in America* (N. Y., 1936).

12. Bayor, *op. cit.*, pp. 59-67, 87-108; Leuchtenburg, *op. cit.*, p. 277; Seymour Martin Lipset and Earl Rabb, *The Politics of Unreason: Right-Wing Extremism in America, 1790-1970* (N.Y., 1970), pp. 150-189; Naomi W. Cohen, *Not Free to Desist: The American Jewish Committee 1906-1966* (Philadelphia, 1966), pp. 199-226; John F. Stack, Jr., *International Conflict in an American City: Boston's Irish, Italians, and Jews* (Westport, 1979), pp. 50-56, 56-58.

13. Hardly any historical information exists on what was universally known. Gartner, *Cleveland*, p. 302; I. M. Rubinow, in Morris and Freund, *op. cit.*, pp. 336-340. On Jewish lawyers, see Melvin M. Fagen, "The Status of Jewish Lawyers in New York City", *Jewish Social Studies*, I, 1 (January, 1939), pp. 73-104, and Jerold S. Auerbach, *Unequal Justice: Lawyers and Social Change in Modern America* (N.Y., 1976) pp. 99-100, 125-127, 159, 184-188, and *passim*. As to physicians, see Jacob A. Goldberg, "Jews in the Medical Profession—A National Survey", *Jewish Social Studies*, I, 3 (July, 1939), pp. 327-336, and "Facilities of Jewish Hospitals for Specialized Training", *ibid*, III, 4 (October, 1941), pp. 375-386.

14. Bayor, *op. cit.*, pp. 87, 106, 161-162, 136-137, and *passim*; Stack, *op. cit.*, pp. 59-63, 117-127.

15. Leuchtenburg, *op. cit.*, p. 332. Two eminent American historians, Henry Steele Commager and Richard B. Morris, open this volume of the New American Nation series with their Editors' Introduction which provides a good example of abiding liberal enthusiasm for Roosevelt.

16. Walter B. Rideout, *The Radical Novel in the United States 1900-1954* (Cambridge, Mass., 1956), pp. 295-298. The significant place of Jews may be inferred by their prominent appearance in Richard H. Pells, *Radical Visions and American Dreams: Culture and Social Thought in the Depression Years* (N.Y., 1973) and Daniel Aaron, *Writers on the Left* (N.Y., 1961). Nearly half the contributors to *Proletarian Literature in the United States* (N.Y., 1935) were Jewish. Daniel Aaron, "Some Reflections on Communism and the Jewish Writer", in Peter I. Rose, ed., *The Ghetto and Beyond: Essays on Jewish Life in America* (N.Y., 1969), p. 267.

17. "The Jew and Social and Economic Conditions in the United States—Report of a Committee of Practitioners", Morris and Freund, *op. cit.*, pp. 363-370; Both Zosa Szajkowski, *Jews, Wars, and Communism*, I (N.Y., 1972), pp. 408-417, and Melech Epstein, *The Jew and Communism.... 1919-1941* (N.Y., ca. 1960) have to be used with caution. A distinguished example of the tendency I am describing is Franz Neumann, *Behemoth: The Structure and Practice of National Socialism 1933-1944* (2nd ed., N.Y., 1944), a work written during the 1930s whose first edition was completed in 1941. Anti-Semitism (pp. 106-129) is considered essentially in terms of its meaning and impact on non-Jews. In an appendix (pp. 550-552) written during World War II, the author, a Jewish refugee from Nazism, interprets the mass murder of the Jews in terms of a "spearhead" for Nazi assaults to come on other irritating groups. Thus, Neumann does not consider anti-Semitism or even the Holocaust as sufficient unto themselves; they are required to symbolize something larger and different and more abstract. The left-wing social philosopher Max Horkheimer expressed this outlook to perfection: "Men should become sensitive not to the injustice against the Jews, but to injustice as such, not to the persecution of the Jews but to any and all persecution." (Quoted in George Friedman, *The Political Philosophy of the Frankfurt School* (Ithaca, 1981), p. 94). These were the words of a German Jewish refugee after World War II.

18. *American Jewish Year Book*, vol. 34, *1932-1933* (Philadelphia, 1932), p. 21. The previous year's statement was similar but more moderate—*ibid*, vol. 33, *1931-1932* (Philadelphia, 1931) p. 23.

19. Yehuda Bauer, *My Brother's Keeper: A History of the American Jewish Joint Distribution Committee 1929-1939* (Philadelphia, 1974), pp. 305-306.

20. Samuel Halperin, *The Political World of American Zionism* (Detroit, 1961), Appendix IV facing p. 324.

21. Gartner, *Cleveland*, pp. 306-310; Isaac Franck, "The Community Council Idea", and William I. Boxerman, "Development of a Jewish Community Council", *Jewish Social Service Quarterly*, XX, 4 (June, 1944), pp. 191-210; Mordecai M. Kaplan, *Judaism as a Civilization* (new ed., N.Y., 1967), pp. 541-544.

22. The domestic affairs of American Jewry during World War II have been little noticed. See John Morton Blum, *V Was for Victory: Politics and American Culture During World War II* (N.Y., 1976), pp. 172-181; Gartner, *Cleveland*, pp. 315-319; Louis Kraft and Philip Bernstein in Morris and Freund, *op. cit.*, pp. 437-462; Salo W. Baron, "The Second World War and Jewish Community Life" (1942), *Steeled in Adversity: Essays and Addresses on American Jewish Life* (Philadelphia, 1971), pp. 454-472; Charles Herbert Stember and others, *Jews in the Mind of America* (N.Y.,

1966), pp. 110-170, 246-253 (John Higham), 259-272 (Morton Keller); Stack, *op. cit.*, pp. 129-142.

23. Yehuda Bauer, *American Jewry and the Holocaust: The American Jewish Joint Distribution Committee 1939-1945* (Detroit, 1981), pp. 401 ff. The indictment is synthesized from the works of Henry L. Feingold, Arthur D. Morse, David S. Wyman, Saul S. Friedman, and others; compare James MacGregor Burns, *Roosevelt: The Soldier of Freedom* (N.Y., 1970), pp. 395-397, 441-442.

24. Halperin, *op. cit.*, pp. 61-176, 189-252; Melvin I. Urofsky, *We Are One! American Jewry and Israel* (Garden City, N.Y., 1978), pp. 17-93; N.W. Cohen, *op. cit.*, pp. 249-264, 293-309.

25. Salo W. Baron, "The Year in Retrospect", *American Jewish Year Book*, vol. 49, *1947-1948* (Philadelphia, 1947), p. 122.

A "Golden Decade" for American Jews: 1945–1955

Arthur A. Goren

(COLUMBIA UNIVERSITY
THE HEBREW UNIVERSITY)

Few would deny the proposition that American Jewish life has undergone a radical transformation in the half century since the end of the Second World War. Lucy Dawidowicz, in a synoptic review of American Jewish history, recently captured this sense of major change in two chapter titles. She designated the years 1920 to 1939, "Decades of Anxiety," and the years 1945 to 1967, "The Golden Age in America." "Recovery and Renewal" is how Dawidowicz conceived of the postwar period as a whole.[1]

Remarkably, the essential features of that transformation—the suburbanization of the Jews, the fashioning of a new communal order and the emergence of a collective self-confidence and sense of well-being—were already in place by the mid-1950s. At that point, American Jewry seemed to pause to take stock. The occasion was the yearlong celebration, beginning in the fall of 1954, of three hundred years since the first group of Jews settled on the shores of North America. The flood of tercentenary events intensified group consciousness and pride. The celebrations also encouraged the search for self-definition and self-understanding. Alongside the official and dominant theme of achievement and thanksgiving, a contrapuntal note of disquiet and discontent with the state of American Jewish life was sounded. In this respect, too, the culminating event of the decade set the terms for the years to come. Important publicists and ideologues recognized and debated what Charles Liebman would later pose as the tensions between "two sets of values." In Liebman's formulation, the "ambivalent American Jew" is torn between "integration and acceptance into American society" and "Jewish group survival."[2] Precisely because Jews were fulfilling, at last, their aspiration to integrate into the society at large, identifying with the group and maintaining it were becoming increasingly matters of personal choice. For the most part, Jews responded to their new condition by instinctively adopting a dual construct of identity that aided them in locating and relocating themselves in the volatile pluralism that characterized the nation as well as the Jewish community. This essay seeks to place the first decade of our times, with its new conditions and new perceptions, in historical perspective. It also

3

Originally published in *Studies in Contemporary Jewry* 8 (1992). Reprinted by permission of Oxford University Press.

examines the Jewish community's endeavors to fix its place on the map of the new era and set its future course.

Surely, the subject most discussed among observers of the American Jewish scene in the late 1940s and early 1950s was the exodus of Jews from city to suburb. This was the most concrete expression of the new affluence of the rising Jewish middle class. Entering the professions and the higher levels of entrepreneurship on the wave of postwar prosperity, benefiting from the decline in occupational and social discrimination, integrating culturally both in the workplace and in the classroom and pursuing leisure-time activities similar to those of their social class, the new Jewish suburbanites embraced the tolerant, cosmopolitan image of the suburbs. For the majority of Jews, the creation of an amiable and lenient communal order, religious by definition, went hand in hand with the suburban ethos.[3]

The suburban setting was a far cry from the compact, big-city, middle- and working-class neighborhoods where they had grown up and where some had started their own families during the interwar decades. The Jewish group life in those urban neighborhoods as recalled by the newly arrived suburbanites had contained a multiplicity of synagogues, Jewish secular societies, informal social street settings and "neutral" public institutions that possessed a Jewish ethnic coloration merely by virtue of the high ratio of Jews attending. Less by design than geography, the Jewish neighborhoods had served the broad spectrum of interests, convictions and degrees of Jewish identification both of second-generation Jews and of acculturated immigrant Jews.[4]

The communal order reconstructed during the 1945–1955 decade reflected the new affluence and the rapid pace of social and cultural integration. The synagogue, now including educational and recreational facilities, became the primary guardian of ethnic identity and continuity. The social and educational services of the suburban synagogue expanded enormously when compared with the synagogues of the urban neighborhoods, at the same time as its ritual functions contracted. The years from 1945 through the 1950s witnessed the construction of some six hundred synagogues and temples. In their imposing size and sumptuous architectural design, they reflected their preeminent place in the suburban landscape as the accepted presence of a Jewish community. At the same time, the secular ideologies and particularistic interests that had existed in the urban neighborhoods faded away or were absorbed by the synagogue-centers or by the broad-based federations of philanthropies.

This blurring of differences during the early postwar years enabled the national coordinating agencies of American Jewry to flourish, particularly those agencies that guided fund-raising campaigns and the policy-making implicit in allocating the funds. The local communities channeled vast sums of money and political influence to these bodies through their federations. They, in turn, dispersed overseas relief, aid to Israel, support for the community relations organizations and help for the national denominational and cultural institutions. There is a striking correlation between the enormous increase in the sums raised to aid Jewish displaced persons in Europe and their resettlement in Israel, which peaked between 1946 and 1948, and the decline in such revenue in the 1950s when the overseas crises seemed to have abated and synagogue-building and domestic concerns were high on the community's agenda. Nevertheless, American Jewry was sufficiently affluent and committed enough to Israel to give more aid to the young state than to any other nonlocal cause.[5]

Two compelling experiences during the first few years following the end of the Second World War gave coherence to these developments and provided the basis for the collective behavior of American Jews that has persisted ever since. The first, the establishment of Israel, has defined the one arena of greatest concern to the Jews. The second, the emergence of an aggressive liberalism, has directed the political energies of the Jewish community into the general American domain. This parity of interests and commitments, which has been at the heart of the Jewish communal consensus for nearly half a century, was firmly in place by the mid-1950s.

In the first instance, at the war's end, American Jews confronted the enormity of the destruction of European Jewry and the urgent need to resettle and rehabilitate the one-third that had survived. This task merged almost immediately with the struggle for Jewish sovereignty in Palestine. Linking the solution of the problem of the survivors with the attainment of statehood created a unity of purpose on a scale unprecedented in the modern history of the Jews.

The American Jewish community mobilized its communal, financial and political resources in a massive outpouring of support. One gauge of this response was the dramatic rise in the contributions to the central communal campaigns. These soared from $57.3 million in 1945 to $131.7 million in 1946 and to $205 million in 1948, when 80 percent of the monies raised went for settling immigrants in Israel. There were other indications of momentous change. Eminent Jews who had taken little part in Jewish affairs now assumed crucial leadership roles, while others who until then had rejected all affirmations of Jewish nationalism rallied their organizations to the common endeavor. Henry Morgenthau, Jr.'s acceptance of the general chairmanship of the United Jewish Appeal in 1946 is one striking case; the collaboration of Joseph Proskauer, president of the American Jewish Committee, with the Jewish Agency in the final diplomatic push for statehood is another. Political figures and presidential advisers such as Herbert Lehman, Felix Frankfurter, David Niles, Samuel Rosenman and Bernard Baruch overtly or covertly aided the Zionist cause, which they now considered to be the sole means of saving Jews.[6]

The three years between the surrender of the German armies and the declaration of Israel's independence also saw many rank-and-file American Jews take part in European rescue work at considerable personal risk. Soldiers, chaplains and merchant mariners participated in the clandestine operations directed by the Jewish Agency and the Yishuv to transport refugees from the Allied-occupied zones in Germany to Mediterranean ports and from there in ships (purchased in the United States) to Palestine. Arms, too, were acquired surreptitiously in the United States with funds given by wealthy American Jews and shipped illegally to the Jewish underground in Palestine. At the same time, Jewish war veterans were recruited for the fledgling Israeli army.[7]

Pockets of animosity or indifference remained. The small but vocal American Council for Judaism opposed the widespread support for a Jewish state with singular passion. Denouncing Jewish nationalism as an aberration of Judaism and support of a Jewish state as a violation of American loyalty, the council was soon swept to the fringes of the community. Some left-wing circles remained outside the consensus. Pro-Soviet, Jewish radicals, except for the brief period when the Soviet Union supported the partitioning of Palestine, opposed the Jewish state; and a number of ex-socialist writers, the children of Jewish immigrants who were beginning to make their mark in intellectual circles, simply took no notice. However, mainstream Jewish America from the very beginning accepted the state of Israel as haven and protector of the Jews. Sovereignty was recognized as the guarantee of security for the dispossessed.[8]

The alacrity with which statehood was embraced was in fact quite extraordinary. The specter of charges of divided loyalties, and the fear of providing grist for the mills of antisemites, had long haunted the Zionist movement in America. Even after the Biltmore Conference in May 1942 declared a Jewish commonwealth to be the immediate postwar goal of Zionism, the American Jewish leadership (including some Zionists) viewed the demand for a sovereign state as being at best an opening gambit for later bargaining and compromise, or at worst an unrealistic if not perilous political program. Yet four years later, nearly the entire American Jewish community joined in the political battle for a Jewish state. To take one symbolic act, in May 1947, in the absence of David Ben-Gurion, Rabbi Abba Hillel Silver of Cleveland, representing the Jewish Agency (then the shadow government of the state-to-be), presented the case for a Jewish state before the United Nations General Assembly.[9]

Today it is a truism that the security and welfare of Israel have literally become articles of faith in the belief system of American Jews. Nurtured by the writings of publicists and theologians, encapsulated in the slogans of communal leaders and celebrated in commemorative and fund-raising events, Israel, as nearly every observer of Jewish life has suggested, has become "*the* religion for American Jews." One must stress, however, that *the conjunction of circumstances*—the crying need, on the one hand, to resettle the surviving remnant somewhere, and the growing recognition, on the other hand, that establishment of a Jewish state in Palestine was the only feasible means of saving the remnant—was the nexus at the heart of the overwhelming support for statehood between 1945 and 1948.[10]

This coupling of circumstances molded the sentiments and attitudes of American Jews. At its birth, Israel's survival became inextricably bound to that other primal remembrance of our times, the destruction of European Jewry. Later events, such as the alarm for Israel's survival in the weeks preceding the Six-Day War in 1967, demonstrated the depth of American Jewry's concern. True, in the 1950s and early 1960s, other concerns appeared to diminish the emotional identity with Israel that marked the years 1945 to 1948 and the years following 1967. Nevertheless, the transcendent place of the "destruction and renewal" theme in the group consciousness of American Jews was actually set in the formative decade beginning in 1945.

At the same time, American Jews were deepening and intensifying their identity as Americans. America's role in the defeat of Nazism and its emergence as leader of the free world—the one effective force blocking Soviet expansion—induced American Jews not only to participate in the civic and political life of postwar America but to do so with unprecedented vigor and effectiveness. The high percentage of

Jewish participation in elections compared with the voting public as a whole, the prominence of Jewish contributors as financial backers for political candidates and the increase in the number of Jewish elected officials are some of the outward indications. No less notable is the ease with which political figures of Jewish background began to move out from Jewish organizational life into the larger political world and then, with their enhanced stature, back again to the Jewish. Philip Klutznik is perhaps the most striking example. His Jewish leadership track took him through the ranks of B'nai B'rith to the presidency of the organization in 1953. In a parallel career in government, Klutznik moved from commissioner of Federal Public Housing under Franklin D. Roosevelt and Harry Truman to U.S. representative to the United Nations at various times during the Eisenhower, Kennedy and Johnson administrations and then to a cabinet post during Jimmy Carter's presidency.[11]

Most significant of all was the new departure of Jewish communal institutions in assuming an active role in American civic affairs. Community relations agencies, formerly almost exclusively concerned with discrimination against Jews, now entered the realm of social action in its broadest sense. They lobbied for legislation directed against racial discrimination, in favor of social welfare programs, against weakening trade unionism and for a foreign policy that stressed internationalism, aid to democratic governments and a tempering of superpower confrontations. So, too, they joined in litigation against racial discrimination and for the strict interpretation of the constitutional principle of separation of church and state. In 1945, the American Jewish Congress created its Commission on Law and Social Action and committed itself to "working for a better world . . . whether or not the individual issues touch directly upon so-called Jewish interests." Soon after, the American Jewish Committee, in a more circumspect manner, moved beyond its original purpose (as expressed in its charter) "to prevent the infringement of the civil and religious rights of Jews and to alleviate the consequences of persecution." It now declared its intention to "join with other groups in the protection of the civil rights of the members of all groups irrespective of race, religion, color or national origin."[12]

The religious wings of Judaism followed suit. By the end of the Second World War, both the Reform and Conservative rabbinic associations had longstanding commitments to pursue the goals of social justice, and the Orthodox Rabbinical Council of America began taking a similar stand. In the 1930s, for example, Reform's Central Conference of American Rabbis had declared that the "individualistic, profit-oriented economy is in direct conflict with the ideals of religion." At the same time, the Conservative Rabbinical Assembly of America announced a program for world peace, declared for a thirty-hour workweek and proclaimed a goal of "a social order . . . based on human cooperation rather than competition inspired by greed." These resolutions, which undoubtedly reflected the social sensibilities of the rabbis, did not go beyond the ritual of affirmation by the annual conferences. But beginning in the mid-1940s, the Reform and Conservative movements as a whole, and not merely the rabbinate, placed both specific domestic issues and international policy matters on their lay agendas. They established commissions, organized local action groups, and collaborated with parallel Protestant and Catholic agencies on behalf of social justice issues. (In contrast, although the Orthodox Rabbinical Council began adopting annual resolutions on a number of welfare state issues such as price and rent controls and continuation of federal housing programs, social activism did not become an integral part of the Orthodox lay associations.) Thus, the militancy demonstrated by rabbinic leaders and Jewish organizations during the 1960s over civil rights, school integration and the Vietnam War stemmed from the Jewish community's active stand on political issues that began in the 1940s.[13]

In a broad sense, American Jewry's two public commitments—assuring Israel's security and striving for a liberal America (and, by extension, a liberal world order)—have constituted the basis for a "functional consensus" ever since the linkage between the two was forged in the aftermath of the defeat of Nazism and the establishment of the Jewish state. On the whole, the two elements have meshed well, and in fact have reinforced each other. American Jewish leaders have presented Israel as both a haven for the persecuted and a doughty democracy surrounded and threatened with destruction by totalitarian Arab regimes allied, until recently, with an expansive Soviet Union. This has been a theme repeated often when U.S. presidents address American Jews and when party platforms are formulated. As a consequence, the dual identity of American Jews has resulted in less anxiety than some would have anticipated. The fear that vigorous support of Israel would give rise to charges of divided allegiance and fan the fires of antisemitism has not been borne out. The patriotic fulminations of right-wing extremists, bearers of a fundamentalist antisemitism, and the revolutionary rhetoric of the radical Left that has equated Zionism with racism have of course been causes for concern, but they have not infected mainstream America. This is not to say that a latent disquiet has never been present, rising on occasion to the surface. For example, Jacob Blaustein, president of the American Jewish Committee, intervened with the government of Israel on a number of occasions until he obtained formal assurances from Prime Minister David Ben-Gurion in 1950 that the Jewish state held no claim on the political loyalties of American Jews, whose sole allegiance, it was stressed, was to the United States.[14]

Nevertheless, American Jews intuitively sensed that the functional consensus based on supporting Israel and defending a liberal America was not sufficient. What was needed was a doctrinal or ideological core that, while identifying the group, would also justify the operative elements of the consensus. During the first postwar decade, American Jews almost unanimously viewed religion as that doctrinal core. It was the way Jews identified themselves. Sociologists studying the new Jewish communities documented its currency. They also noted the paradox of Jews defining themselves overwhelmingly by religion while at the same time showing indifference and apathy for actual religious practice. Contemporary observers explained this incongruity as a form of adjustment to an American society that recognized religious activity alone as justifying self-segregation. These were the years when Jewish communal leaders found so congenial the notion that a trifaith America—Protestant, Catholic and Jewish, "the religions of democracy"—formed the underpinning of the "American Way of Life." This interpretation of American society placed Judaism and its bearers in the mainstream of the nation's cultural and spiritual tradition.[15]

Since Judaism as interpreted by the American rabbi taught its followers to seek social justice, being Jewish in America meant fighting for open housing and fair employment practices, for social welfare and prounion legislation—in short, for the New Deal, the Fair Deal and their successors. Judaism also demanded fulfillment of the religious commandment that "all Israel are responsible for one another," hence the duty to rescue Jews and strengthen the Jewish state. As individuals, Jews identified themselves as belonging to a religious community. As a group, they acted like an ethnic minority.

It is important to remember that, for American Jews, Judaism and Jewishness became identical only during the decade beginning in 1945. Although such a religious self-definition long preceded the postwar years (it was the cornerstone of American Reform Judaism), the East European immigrants had earlier created an ethnic and secular reality that overran without obliterating the purely religious formulation of Jewishness of the older, established community. One need merely mention the variegated Jewish associational life the immigrants created and the flowering of Yiddish literature—the most impressive cultural creation in a foreign language by an American immigrant group—to indicate the range and depth of this Jewish ethnic world. In acculturated form, significant elements of this world carried over into the second generation. Obviously, Zionism and an aggressively secular Jewish radical tradition stand out. Yet the considerable numbers who were brought up in this milieu in the urban neighborhoods of the years before 1945 failed to seriously challenge or to qualify the religious identification of American Jewry that so quickly became so universal in the post-1945 decade. Surely, the prevailing drive for conformity, which was in part a by-product of the Cold War and the accompanying fear of Communist influence at home, saw religion (*any* religion, to paraphrase Eisenhower) as the cornerstone of democratic society and an antitoxin against the Communist heresy. And quite possibly the political and financial aid being so prominently extended to the Jewish state was best explained to the nation as religiously motivated. Separation for religious purposes did conform, after all, with patriotic norms. In part, these factors hastened the trends toward consensus within the Jewish community.

On occasion Jewish secular thinkers gave explicit and anguished expression to this change. In 1951, the Labor Zionist Organization published an essay by C. Bezalel Sherman, "Israel and the American Jewish Community." The Labor Zionist movement, an amalgamation of socialist Zionist parties transplanted to the United States with the mass migration, was staunchly secularist. It had favored the formation of democratically elected Jewish communal polities and bilingual education in a manner similar to its European sister parties. Sherman himself was an ideologue of the organization's left wing. Nevertheless, in reappraising the future of the American Jewish community in the new era ushered in by the establishment of the Jewish state, he abandoned the position that American Jews should strive for the status of nationality. Now he wrote, "America, insensible to the existence of a Jewish nation, insisted on classing them [American Jews] with the religious communities," the only type of ethnic group recognized by "American constitutional life." Sherman continued:

> Jews thus have no other alternative but to constitute themselves as a community operating in a religious framework. . . . The irreligious Jew . . . will have to accept a religious designation for the group of which he wishes to be a member without sharing the tenets of its faith. This is the price a secularist Jew will have to pay for his voluntary sharing in a minority status.[16]

Ten years later, in his study *The Jew Within American Society*, Sherman used this redefinition of Jewish identity to explain Jewish group survival in America. It was the key to understanding Jewish "ethnic individuality." On a note evoking Mordecai Kaplan's analysis of Jewish identity, Sherman concluded: "American Jews can no more conceive of the Jewish faith severed from the framework of Jewish peoplehood than they can conceive of a Jewish community removed from its religious base." Since Jewish peoplehood embraced Jews everywhere, concern for persecuted brethren abroad and the well-being of the state of Israel had increased the sense of "belongingness" among American Jews. "For this reason, they may be expected to continue as a distinct ethnic group—on the level of spiritual uniqueness, religious separateness, ethnic consolidation and communal solidarity, but not in a political sense."[17]

In terms of the Jewish establishment (the synagogue movements, federations, defense agencies and the Zionist organizations), American Jews had created by the early 1950s a consensus and a degree of equanimity they had not known before. They were meeting their dual responsibilities as Americans and Jews admirably. On domestic issues, they aligned with the liberal-centrist position and upheld America's role as defender of the free world. Within the Jewish community, the divisive issues of the interwar years—class differences, the intergenerational tensions between immigrant and native-born, conflicting notions of Jewish identity, the assimilationist-radical deprecation of Jewish life and the strident polemics over Zionism—were vanishing or were gone altogether. Not surprisingly, then, the tercentenary planners proposed stressing not only communal harmony and achievement but also the beliefs and values Jews held in common with all Americans.

In December 1951, Ralph E. Samuel, the vice-president of the American Jewish Committee, announced the formation of a committee to plan the three-hundredth anniversary of the establishment of the first permanent Jewish community in North America. Samuel emphasized the opportunity such celebrations would provide to pay homage to the "American heritage of religious and civil liberty." American Jews had built a "flourishing American Judaism," he declared, and at the same time they had taken part "in building the American democratic civilization that we have today." In his single reference to contemporary affairs, Samuel concluded his remarks with the note that the tercentenary celebration would demonstrate to the world "the strength of the American people's commitment to the principles of democracy in our struggle against communism and other forms of totalitarianism of our day."[18]

This collective undertaking to popularize an American Jewish ideology proved to be an extraordinary enterprise in itself. It also raised a number of questions. Who indeed did the tercentenary organizers represent? How meaningful and tenable could a least-common-denominator ideology be? What were the constraints the planners faced in relating to the American-political and Jewish-political context? Were the provisional tenets Samuel set forth adequate for setting a course for postwar American Jewry?

In January 1952, when the committee on organization met to launch the tercentenary project, Samuel stressed that the American Jewish Committee saw its role as initiator rather than sponsor of the enterprise. In fact, it had been the American Jewish Historical Society that had first proposed the tercentenary celebration. Eager for the broadest communal participation, it had turned to the American Jewish Committee for organizational assistance; the success of the project depended on leaders whose eminence and integrity assured the nonpartisanship of the endeavor.

In addition to Samuel, who was chosen general chairman, two eminent members of the American Jewish Committee were appointed to key committees. Simon Rifkind, who had distinguished himself as a federal judge and special adviser on Jewish affairs to General Dwight D. Eisenhower in 1945 and 1946, headed the "Committee of 300," the policy-making body of the organization. Samuel Rosenman, also a judge, who had served as a principal adviser to Presidents Franklin D. Roosevelt and Harry Truman, chaired the program committee. Another important committee, that of research and publication, was headed by Salo W. Baron, professor of Jewish history at Columbia University.

The composition of the committee reflected nearly the entire spectrum of Jewish religious and communal life. Among the members of the steering committee were Samuel Belkin, president of Yeshiva University; Louis Finkelstein, president of the Jewish Theological Seminary; Israel Goldstein, president of the American Jewish Congress; Samuel Niger, the Yiddish journalist and critic, and Jacob S. Potofsky, president of the Amalgamated Clothing Workers Union.

In April 1953, after nearly a year of deliberations, the program committee, which, in addition to Rosenman, included Benjamin V. Cohen, Adolph Held, William S. Paley and David Sarnoff, submitted its report on the "meaning of the anniversary" to a national meeting of the Committee of 300. Obviously the presence of Paley, the head of CBS, and Sarnoff, the head of NBC, indicated the direction and scale of the celebrations. The proposed theme of the celebration— "Man's Opportunities and Responsibilities Under Freedom"—was in fact suggested by Sarnoff and was approved at this meeting.[19]

The major opening event, the National Tercentenary Dinner with President Eisenhower as guest of honor and keynote speaker, took place on October 20, 1954, at the Hotel Astor in New York. It was preceded and followed by forums, exhibitions, pageants, musical festivals and public dinners organized by local committees in at least four hundred cities and towns. New York, for instance, was the venue of a coast-to-coast radio broadcast of the reconsecration of Congregation Shearith Israel (founded by the original settlers of New Amsterdam) in the presence of representatives of the Jewish and Christian congregations that had either aided or functioned alongside it in the eighteenth century. A special national committee supervised the preparation of a national historical exhibit on the theme "Under Freedom," which was shown at the Jewish Museum in New York and the Smithsonian Institution in Washington, D.C. The Chicago committee commissioned Ernst Toch to compose a symphonic suite for the occasion, while the national committee commissioned David Diamond to compose the tercentenary symphony *Ahavah*, which was given its premiere by the National Symphony on November 17, 1954, in Washington. (The other works on the program were Ernest Bloch's *Israel Symphony* and Leonard Bernstein's *The Age of Anxiety*, a thematically balanced program by Jewish composers.) In Atlanta, Georgia, the local committee presented the city with a portrait of Judah P. Benjamin, secretary of state of the Confederacy.[20]

Television played a major role. The main events, such as Eisenhower's address, received national coverage. Leading commercial programs offered commemoration salutes. CBS broadcast a four-part teledrama, "A Precious Heritage," while NBC followed suit with a four-part series entitled "Frontiers of Faith." The tercentenary also generated a plethora of educational material—filmstrips, curricula and guidebooks on American Jewish history—for use in schools and adult education circles that were sponsored and published by the national organizations. B'nai B'rith organized a nationwide search for historical source materials and provided programs and speakers for its lodges and Hillel foundations. The American Jewish Committee commissioned a series of studies that it published in the *American Jewish Year Book* and an *Inventory of American Jewish History* to further historical research. A volume of studies subsidized by the Workmen's Circle and other Jewish labor organizations gave special attention to the era of the East European Jewish migration.[21]

This history-mindedness anteceded the tercentenary "revival." It was one expression of a self-assertiveness that stemmed from the new position of centrality that had been thrust upon the American Jewish community. And it paralleled the notion of the "American Century," the conviction that became popular during the war years that America had at last taken its "rightful" place as the leader of the free world and the guardian of world order. This national temper stimulated a reexamination of the American past. Historians and political scientists elaborated the idea of an "American exceptionalism." Typical of their writing was Daniel Boorstein's book *The Genius of American Politics*. "I argue, in a word," Boorstein wrote, "that American democracy is unique. It possesses a 'genius' all of its own."[22]

The new era that began in 1945 was, in a sense, also perceived as "the American Jewish Century." The conviction that American Jews were at last "making history" required recovering a "usable past" showing that Jews had indeed been "making history" for some time. One important expression of this sentiment was the Hebrew Union College's announcement, in the fall of 1947, of the establishment of the American Jewish Archives to document the historical record of American Jewry. The need for such an institution was explained in these words:

> American Jewry has become the "center" of world Jewish spiritual life. When the Jewish historian of the next generation reaches the year 1939, he will begin a new chapter in the history of his people, a chapter which must be called, "The American Jewish Center." This Jewish community has now become the pivotal and controlling

factor in that historic development which began in the thirteenth pre-Christian century in Palestine.²³

There were more manifestations of a search for "American Jewish exceptionalism." In 1953, the Jewish Theological Seminary established the American Jewish History Center. Soon after, the center commissioned a series of communal studies and organized regional conferences to generate interest in the projects. The tercentenary accelerated this newfound interest in an American Jewish past. Jewish communities—Buffalo, Rochester, Milwaukee, Cleveland and Los Angeles—allocated money for writing their communal histories. In September 1954, a revitalized American Jewish Historical Society convened the most impressive conference of historians ever held on the writing of American Jewish history. Thus the new self-consciousness American Jewry displayed after the conclusion of the war swelled under the impetus of the tercentenary. Pride and awareness of its preeminence in the Jewish world reverberated in the public and institutional interest in recording and interpreting the Jewish experience in America.²⁴

One interpretive history of Jewish life in America that appeared during the tercentenary year captured the tercentenary ideology faithfully. Oscar Handlin's *Adventure in Freedom* (1954) stressed the process of Jewish integration into a society that was distinguished by its "diversity, voluntarism, equality, freedom, and democracy." Handlin, who taught American social history at Harvard and who had won a Pulitzer Prize for his 1951 study on immigration in American life, *The Uprooted*, was perhaps the most influential writer on the American pluralist tradition. Handlin insisted that American Jews be viewed as one ethnic group among many in a pluralist America that neither impeded nor encouraged ethnic group maintenance. This was the open-ended, wholesome "adventure in freedom." Yet Handlin also struck an ominous note. Although the Jews of America were celebrating the year 1654, they could not forget "the stark facts of our present situation." Jews had not recovered "from the shock of the six million victims of the European catastrophe;" at the same time they shared in the "enormous burden upon American society," which was "locked in unremitting struggle" with "the forces of totalitarianism."²⁵

It was the tercentenary theme, "Man's Opportunities and Responsibilities Under Freedom," that required explication. When the program committee presented its recommendations after months of deliberations and after soliciting the opinions of scores of leaders from all fields and walks of life, it explained the criteria it had used in these words:

> The theme should express the outstanding fact of the past 300 years of our participation in America; that it should describe the significance of the present day for American Jews, and that it should express the hopes and aspirations and objectives of the future for ourselves and for all Americans—indeed, for all human beings throughout the world.

When the recommendations were published as a brochure—thirty thousand copies were distributed—no explicit reference was made to the Jewish community itself, or to the American Jew's "responsibility under freedom" to help other Jews, although the members of the committees in their other communal capacities were deeply involved in Jewish affairs. In a section entitled "All-Embracing Nature of

Celebration," the committee warned that the tercentenary should not be made "a vehicle for propagation of any particular ideology in American Jewish life. . . . It should be neither Zionist, non-Zionist, nor anti-Zionist. It should not try to formulate or advance any particular definition of Jewishness."[26]

The tercentenary committee defined the principal goal of the observance as a celebration of America's democratic ideals. Thus the American Jewish experience was significant in that it bore witness to the success of this free society. No less important was the emphasis placed on the congruence between Judaism and American democratic ideals. Indeed, the authors of the report declared, "The teachings of the Hebrew prophets have vitally affected the growth of freedom and the development of human dignity in America and throughout the world." In a summing-up statement at the conclusion of the year of festivities, David Bernstein, the tercentenary committee's executive director, justified the choice of the theme in these words:

> At a time when the Jewish community and its leaders felt that they were on display before the world, they chose to speak, first, in religious terms and, next, in terms of such political ideas as civic responsibility, strengthening democracy, protecting individual liberty, and expanding civil rights.[27]

Was there perhaps, in the midst of the deserved self-congratulations, also a measure of anxiety and insecurity? What seemed implicit in Bernstein's statement and had been alluded to in Samuel's first announcement of a tercentennial committee four years earlier was stated explicitly in Handlin's measured words. Praising democracy and liberty at a time when the nation was locked in what it perceived to be a global struggle with an aggressive and ruthless totalitarianism was understandable enough. The "golden decade" for American Jews was also the decade of the Cold War, McCarthyism, and fear of Communist subversion.

Abroad, postwar America confronted an expansive Communist power that now possessed nuclear weapons. Not only had an "iron curtain descended across the continent," in Winston Churchill's words in his March 1946 address, but it was followed by the fall of China to the Communists and the invasion of South Korea by the North in 1950. At home, an alarmed government responded with drastic measures to curb and root out real and perceived instances of Communist infiltration. It began in 1947, when Harry Truman put into effect his loyalty program, and it ended, at least symbolically, in December 1954 when the United States Senate censured its member Joseph McCarthy—a time span nearly identical with the first years in the new American Jewish postwar era. Thus the years of optimism were also the years of the "Attorney General's list" of subversive organizations, the Alger Hiss case, the loyalty oaths and security clearances, the high-handed investigations of Senator Joseph McCarthy and the congressional committees who went hunting for Communists and who blacklisted those they termed "Fifth Amendment Communists."

Here was the snake in the garden: the agony and trepidation caused by the conspicuous presence of Jews among those accused of disloyalty and even espionage, and the presence of a marginal but vocal radical Left within the organized Jewish community. Thus the arrest in 1950 of Julius and Ethel Rosenberg for handing atomic secrets to the Soviet Union, and their trial, conviction and execution in 1953, jarred the self-confidence of American Jews. (The trial judge, prosecuting attorney, defense attorneys and the principle witnesses who turned state's evidence were all Jewish.) Arnold Forster, general counsel of the Anti-Defamation League (ADL), recalled the period as a time when American Jewish leaders "came to fear the establishment of a link between being a Jew and being a 'communist traitor' in the popular mind." A bitter fight ensued within the Jewish community over aiding Jewish victims of the anti-Communist crusade. The most prominent instance was the campaign for clemency for the Rosenbergs in which Communist and left-wing groups were active.

The American Jewish Committee created a special committee to combat the "Jewish/Communist stereotype." It launched an educational program exposing the techniques and strategies used by the Communists to infiltrate Jewish organizations and called on the community to expel Jewish "Communist-front" organizations. During the height of the hysteria, the American Jewish Committee was less than forthright in its commitment to civil liberties. On this last score, in contrast, both the ADL and the American Jewish Congress maintained their aggressive stand in defense of civil liberties. In 1952, at the height of McCarthy's influence, the ADL chose to honor Senator Herbert Lehman at its annual convention because of his opposition to McCarthy. The American Jewish Congress, for its own part, waged an incessant battle against congressional and state legislation that required loyalty oaths, providing legal aid in appealing cases where there appeared to have been infringements of constitutional rights. To a considerable degree, the Red Scare hastened the political integration of American Jews. It greatly weakened Jewish radicalism, fortified the liberalism of "the vital center" and drew American Jews, as never before, into a whirl of "American" issues. In dealing with these issues, both civil libertarians and anti-Communist activists operated through Jewish agencies.[28]

The official tercentenary ideology, orchestrated by a group of conservative and cautious leaders, aroused a spirited debate over the direction of American Jewish life. Jewish journals of opinion provided the platforms for a more reflective consideration of the issues. Robert Gordis, editor of *Judaism,* devoted an entire issue to the tercentenary in which contributors evaluated Jewish philosophy, culture and communal life in America. Eugene Kohn gathered a dozen articles from *The Reconstructionist* on the communal and cultural life of American Jews and published them in a volume commemorating the tercentenary. The score of mass-circulation house organs published by B'nai B'rith, Hadassah, the American Jewish Congress and others devoted whole issues to critical essays that examined American Jewish life. For the most part, the conclusions were laudatory and the prognosis for the future optimistic. Typical was Gordis's introduction to the tercentenary issue of *Judaism.* American Jewry, Gordis wrote, had not been "altogether without influence or creativity within the confines of Judaism." It had been innovative in the fields of religion, philanthropy, education and group defense. Indeed, "the instruments for a renaissance of Judaism, in the days to come, are at hand."[29]

There were also dissenting voices. Horace Kallen, the philosopher and ideologue of cultural pluralism, published a blistering piece in the *Congress Weekly* entitled "The Tercentenary, Yomtov or Yahrzeit." He accused the organizers of violating the essence of the "American Idea," that is, of his well-known notion of cultural pluralism. Kallen had interpreted American freedom as granting the right to any ethnic, religious or racial group to preserve and diversify its communal culture. Nothing in the rhetoric of the tercentenary encouraged American Jews to do this, he argued; even the tercentenary emblem was assimilationist. Not a Hebrew word was on it, and above the menorah that dominated the face of the emblem was a star—but it was a five-pointed, American star rather than the six-pointed Magen David. For Kallen, the challenge of American freedom for the American Jewish community meant creating, first of all, a democratic communal polity. A community so organized would then be able to nurture—and here Kallen employed his famous metaphor of the orchestra—the specifically Jewish part in the total orchestrated production that was the pluralistic culture of the American people.[30]

Mordecai Kaplan, the philosopher of Reconstructionism, criticized the planners for failing to confront one of the crucial questions in American Jewish life. "Why is no reference made in all the literature, speeches and lectures concerning the tercentenary to what it means from the standpoint of our survival as a people in dispersion? . . . This is the first time in the history of the Jewish people that it is jubilant over its sojourn in any land outside of Eretz Yisrael." What was the Jewish context of the celebration? What signposts for the future course of American Jewry had the tercentenary offered? The establishment of the state of Israel had raised the question of "the ultimate destiny of the Jewish People." Was Eretz Israel to be the ingathering of the exiles or merely the creative nucleus of the Jewish people? Building on his formulation of living in two civilizations (American and Jewish), Kaplan emphasized the permanence of diaspora and rejected the Israel-Zionist claim that American Jews were in *galut* (exile). For Kaplan, the influence of the American democratic tradition on the Jews *and* "the inexhaustible reservoir of Jewish creativity in Israel" promised a creative future for "the American sector of the Jewish people [that had] at last found a resting place for its feet." But these matters had to be debated, clarified and decided upon.[31]

Ben Halpern, the secularist Zionist thinker, began his study of the American Jewish community, *The American Jew, A Zionist Analysis,* by considering the conviction underlying the tercentenery that "America is different." Indeed it was different, Halpern agreed. In the shadow of Hitler's destruction of Europe's Jews and in the presence of Soviet totalitarianism and Stalin's antisemitism, Jews had special reasons for celebrating America's democratic tradition. However, American Jews had missed one crucial way in which America was different *for them.* As a historic entity, American Jews constituted one of the youngest Jewish centers of the diaspora. In terms of "real history"—of grappling with the specific problems of their existence as a group—American Jewish history began at most with the rise of the first, authentic American Jewish creation, Reform Judaism, and the formation of native American Jewish institutions. Unlike European Jewry, Halpern argued, American Jews had never had to wrestle with the question of emancipation and self-emancipation; American Jewish history began long after the questions of equality and political rights were resolved. His analysis led him to conclude that the indigenous ideologies of American Jews, as programs intended to foster a creative Jewish group life, were failing. Neither the secular ideologies such as cultural pluralism and neo-Zionism nor an innovative religious movement such as Reconstructionism could prevent the erosion of Jewish life. Assimilation? Survival? Was America different than Europe? His answer was: "In Europe, the stick; in America, the carrot." Indeed, Halpern, the fundamentalist Zionist, was utterly pessimistic about American Jewish group survival.[32]

Surely by the final years of the 1950s one could confidently point to a baseline that demarcated American Jewry from what had existed prior to 1945 and that would hold, for the most part, during the decades ahead. The searing recollections of the poverty of immigrant parents or the crushing collapse into destitution of the Great Depression years had been replaced with an affluence that opened new social opportunities. This affluence enabled the postwar generation to devote some of its time and wealth to societal needs. Establishing entirely new communities in the suburbs demanded an enormous collaborative effort. Building communities, expanding the institutions and agencies serving American Jewry as a whole and meeting the needs of world Jewry also required politically sophisticated leaders, trained professionals and efficient organization. An organizational ideology developed "of acts and tasks, of belonging and conforming," of *na'aseh venishma'*. "To be a Jew," one perceptive observer wrote, "is to belong to an organization. To manifest Jewish culture is to carry out . . . the program of an organization."[33] Support for Israel as refuge and home—which more than it swept aside its opponents, co-opted them—became the overarching endeavor, the one that transcended the local and the particular. Hence it came to define the active community.

Purely *Jewish* concerns could also be linked to liberal politics through the argument that to support American liberal causes was in the "Jewish interest," or else group interests could be denied in favor of appealing to the universal teachings of Judaism. Whatever the justification, Jewish *communal* participation in American politics in the decade beginning in 1945 became widespread and was found acceptable. For postwar America commended communal ties that encouraged spiritual self-preservation and self-fulfillment. In the state of fluid pluralism then prevailing—of changing self-images and expectations of religious, ethnic and racial groupings—any number of ways were possible for identifying oneself. Understandably, the Jews, eager to take their place in the more tolerant postwar society, defined their group identity to fit the reigning mood. Judaism as ethnic religion and Judaism as "peoplehood," as "religious civilization" and as one of the three "religions of democracy" were some of the terms that came into use. In the case of the tercentenary platform, Judaism became American democracy, reflecting a strand of insecurity that was present during the golden decade.

A number of ideologues were distressed by the assimilationist thrust of this formulation. They called on American Jews to instead confront the complexity of their dual identity, indeed to view it as the source of an American Jewish distinctiveness. Rabbis and theologians challenged the cult of organization and the emptiness of "religion as the American way." Yet ideologues and rabbis were also committed to a pluralist America. They collaborated in ways that were inconceivable during the prewar years, not only accepting but applauding the internal pluralism of Jewish group life. Precisely the give-and-take of contending movements and ideas within a communal consensus indicated a commitment to group survival. One could understand, for example, the much-criticized slogan, "Man's Opportunities and Responsibilities Under Freedom," as a shrewd strategy to maintain the community. (Rabbis used the phrase as the text for their sermons on the need for better Jewish education, support for Israel and a richer synagogal life.)[34] Unmistakably, whatever ideological issues were placed on the Jewish public agenda during the decade beginning in 1945—which have remained there to this day—no longer called into question the worth or desirability of Jewish survival. The issue henceforth would be the quality and character of Jewish group survival.

Notes

I would like to thank William B. Goldfarb of Goldfarb, Levy, Giniger, and Company, Tel-Aviv, for his close reading of the manuscript and his insightful suggestions. All unpublished letters, reports and minutes are in the tercentennial files of the American Jewish Committee Papers on deposit in the YIVO Institute, New York. I also want to thank Oscar Handlin for allowing me use of his files of the tercentennial committee.

1. Lucy Dawidowicz, *On Equal Terms: Jews in America, 1881–1981* (New York: 1982). Murray Friedman in his *The Utopian Dilemma: New Political Directions for American Jews* (Washington, D.C.: 1985) entitles one of his chapters "The Golden Age of American Jewry (1945–1965)."

2. Charles Liebman, *The Ambivalent American Jew: Politics, Religion and Family in American Jewish Life* (Philadelphia: 1973), vii.

3. In order of their appearance, some of the key studies of the suburbanization of American Jews are Herbert J. Gans, "Park Forest: Birth of a Jewish Community," *Commentary* 11, no. 4 (April 1951), 330–339; idem, "Progress of a Suburban Jewish Community, Park Forest Revisited," *Commentary* 23, no. 2 (Feb. 1957), 113–122; Marshall Sklare and Marc Vosk, *The Riverton Study: How Jews Look at Themselves and Their Neighbors* (New York: 1957); Judith Kramer and Seymour Leventman, *Children of the Gilded Ghetto: Conflict Resolution of Three Generations of American Jews* (New Haven: 1961); Marshall Sklare and Joseph Greenbaum, *Jewish Identity on the Suburban Frontier: A Study of Group Survival in an Open Society* (New York: 1967).

4. Deborah Dash Moore, *At Home in America: Second Generation New York Jews* (New York: 1981), 19-149, 201–242.

5. Marc Lee Raphael, *Profiles in Judaism: The Reform, Conservative, Orthodox and Reconstructionist Traditions in Historical Perspective* (New York: 1984), 119; idem, *A History of the United Jewish Appeal, 1939–1982* (New York: 1982), 136–137.

6. Daniel Elazar, *Community and Polity: The Organizational Dynamics of American Jewry* (Philadelphia: 1976), 297; Melvin I. Urofsky, *We Are One: American Jewry and Israel* (Garden City, N.Y.: 1978), 144–145; Peter Grosse, *Israel in the Mind of America* (New York: 1982), 265–268.

7. Alex Grobman, "The American Jewish Chaplains and the Remnants of European Jewry: 1944–1948" (Ph.D. diss., The Hebrew University, 1981), 100–111, 233–244, 270–280, 308–334; Yehuda Bauer, *Flight and Rescue: Bricha* (New York: 1970), 241–255; Leonard Slater, *The Pledge* (New York: 1970), 92–97, 120–124, 209–218; Doron Almog, *Harekhesh bearzot-haberit* (Tel-Aviv: 1987), 31–34, 43–52.

8. Elmer Berger, *Judaism or Jewish Nationalism: The Alternative to Zionism* (New York: 1957), 15–44; 92–107; Thomas H. Kolsky, "Jews Against Zionism: The American Council for Judaism, 1942–1948" (Ph.D. diss., George Washington University, 1986), 405–479; Arthur Liebman, *Jews on the Left* (New York: 1979), 511–515; Sidney Hook, *Out of Step: An Unquiet Life in the 20th Century* (New York: 1987), 5, 33; Nathan Glazer, "Jewish Intellectuals," *Partisan Review* 51 (1984), 674–679.

9. Emanuel Neumann, *In the Arena: An Autobiographical Memoir* (New York: 1976), 243–245, 349–355; see also Aaron Berman, *Nazism, the Jews and American Zionism* (Detroit: 1990), 178–179.

10. Marshall Sklare, *America's Jews* (New York: 1971), 211–222; Nathan Glazer, "*American Judaism* Thirty Years Later," *American Jewish History* 77 (1987), 284; Jacob Neusner, *Stranger at Home: The "Holocaust," Zionism, and American Judaism* (Chicago: 1981), 66–67; Chaim Waxman, *America's Jews in Transition* (Philadelphia: 1983), 114–115, 119–123.

11. Lawrence H. Fuchs, *The Political Behavior of American Jews* (Glencoe, Ill.: 1956), 79–120, 171–177; Liebman, *Ambivalent American Jew*, 136–139, 148–159; Deborah Dash Moore, *B'nai B'rith and the Challenge of Ethnic Leadership* (Albany, N.Y.: 1981), 213–221; Waxman, *America's Jews in Transition*, 98–103.

12. For this and the following paragraph, see Friedman, *Utopian Dilemma*, 1–35; Naomi W. Cohen, *Not Free to Desist* (Philadelphia: 1972), 384–404. For a political scientist's highly suggestive analysis of these developments, see Peter Y. Medding, "Segmented Ethnicity and the New Jewish Politics," in *Studies in Contemporary Jewry*, vol. 3, *Jews and Other Ethnic Groups in a Multi-Ethnic World*, ed. Ezra Mendelsohn (New York: 1987), 26–48.

13. Albert Vorspan and Eugene J. Lipman, *Justice and Judaism: The Work of Social Action* (New York: 1956), passim.

14. For the exchange of statements between Jacob Blaustein and David Ben-Gurion, see *American Jewish Year Book* 53 (New York: 1952), 564–565. See also Charles S. Liebman's discussion in *Pressure Without Sanctions: The Influence of World Jewry on Israel Policy* (Rutherford, N.J.: 1977), 118–131. For a more recent indication of a continued sensitivity to the question of dual loyalties, see Arthur J. Goldberg, "The Canard of Dual Loyalty," *Hadassah Magazine* (March 1983), 16–17.

15. Will Herberg, *Protestant-Catholic-Jew: An Essay in American Religious Sociology* (Garden City, N.Y.: 1955); for a review of the literature on religious identification, see Waxman, *America's Jews in Transition*, 81–95.

16. C. Bezalel Sherman, *Israel and the American Jewish Community* (New York: 1951), 12. This caveat appeared on the inside of the title page of the pamphlet: "The particular views expressed by the author do not necessarily constitute the official policy of the Labor Zionist Organization of America."

17. C. Bezalel Sherman, *The Jew Within American Society: A Study in Ethnic Individuality* (Detroit: 1961), 223, 226. For an early statement of this thesis, see idem, "Secularism in a Religious Framework," *Judaism* 1, no. 1 (Jan. 1952), 36–43.

18. Quoted by Nina Warnke, "The American Jewish Tercentenary" (unpublished ms.), 1. I am grateful to the author for allowing me to examine this illuminating paper on the ideological meaning of the tercentenary.

19. *American Jewish Tercentenary: 1654–1954, Scope and Theme* (report of the Steering Committee to the Tercentenary Committee of 300, National Planning Conference, 12 April 1953); Minutes, Committee on Organization, Tercentenary Celebration of Jewish Settlement in the United States, 15 January and 24 March 1952; Minutes, Steering Committee, American Jewish Tercentenary Committee, 3 June and 18 November 1952; Minutes, National Planning Conference, American Jewish Committee, 12 April 1953; Ralph E. Samuel to the Tercentenary Committee of 300, final report, 14 July 1955.

20. See David Bernstein, "The American Jewish Tercentenary," *American Jewish Year Book* 57 (New York: 1956), 101–118; see also n. 19.

21. *National Jewish Monthly* 69 (Sept. 1954), 8–12. Beginning with the October issue, the *Monthly* ran feature stories depicting episodes in American Jewish history. Nathan Glazer, Oscar and Mary F. Handlin, and Joseph C. Blau in *American Jewish Year Book* 56 (New York: 1955), 3–170; Moses Rischin, *An Inventory of American Jewish History* (Cambridge, Mass.: 1954); *The Jewish People: Past and Present, 300 Years of Jewish Life in the United States* (New York: 1955) (no ed. named).

22. Daniel Bell, "The End of American Exceptionalism," *The Public Interest*, no. 41 (Fall 1975), 203–205; Daniel Boorstein, *The Genius of American Politics* (Chicago: 1953), 1.

23. *American Jewish Archives* 1, no. 1 (June 1948), 2-3.

24. Moshe Davis and Isidor S. Meyer (eds.), *The Writing of American Jewish History* (New York: 1957); American Jewish History Center *Newsletter*, no. 1 (Spring 1961).

25. Oscar Handlin, *Adventure in Freedom: Three Hundred Years of Jewish Life in America* (New York: 1954), vii-viii, 260.

26. Memorandum, Judge Samuel I. Rosenman to David Bernstein, 7 October 1952; "American Jewish Tercentenary, Scope and Theme (for Steering Committee use only)," n.d.

27. *American Jewish Year Book* 56: 103, 107.

28. Deborah Dash Moore, "Reconsidering the Rosenbergs: Symbol and Substance in Second Generation American Jewish Consciousness," *Journal of American Ethnic History* 8, no. 1 (Fall 1988), 21-37; *idem, B'nai B'rith and the Challenge of Ethnic Leadership*, 226-229; Arnold Forster, *Square One: A Memoir* (New York: 1988), 126-129; *Congress Weekly*, 12 March 1951, 1-3, *ibid.*, 16 Nov. 1953, 3-10, and 23 Nov. 1953, 10-12.

29. Robert Gordis, "American Jewry Faces Its Fourth Century," *Judaism* 3, no. 4 (Fall 1954), 298.

30. Horace Kallen, "The Tercentenary: Yomtov or Yahrzeit?" *Congress Weekly*, 22 Nov. 1954, 8-11; "The Tercentenary Symbol and Slogan: An Exchange of Letters," *ibid.*, 20 Dec. 1954, 14-15.

31. Mordecai M. Kaplan, "The Meaning of the Tercentenary for Diaspora Judaism," *The Reconstructionist* 20, no. 12 (15 Oct. 1954), 10, 16-18.

32. Ben Halpern, *The American Jew: A Zionist Analysis* (New York: 1956), 11-14.

33. Harold Weisberg, "Ideologies of American Jews," in *The American Jews: A Reappraisal*, ed. Oscar I. Janowsky (Philadelphia: 1964), 347-356.

34. See, for example, Israel Goldstein, *American Jewry Comes of Age: Tercentenary Addresses* (New York: 1955). In an address entitled "Facing the Fourth Century," he notes that interpretations of the tercentennial theme "can be as varied as the viewpoints of those who interpret it. The theme itself is more Jewish than would appear" (p. 120).

Jewish Migration in Postwar America: The Case of Miami and Los Angeles

Deborah Dash Moore
(VASSAR COLLEGE)

The Second World War and its aftermath ushered in a period of enormous changes for American Jews. The destruction of European Jewry shattered the familiar contours of the Jewish world and transformed American Jews into the largest, wealthiest, most stable and secure Jewish community in the diaspora. American Jews' extensive participation in the war effort at home and abroad lifted them out of their urban neighborhoods into the mainstream of American life.[1] In the postwar decades, internal migration carried Jews to new and distant parts of the United States. Occurring within the radically new parameters of the postwar world—the extermination of European Jewry, the establishment of the state of Israel and the United States' achievement of unrivaled prominence on the world political scene—Jewish migration nonetheless represented a response to domestic pressures. These migrations gradually changed American Jews, influencing the character of their culture, the structure of their organizations, their pattern of kinship relations, the style and substance of their politics.

This essay offers a historical perspective on the migration process that created new American Jewish communities. It indicates some of the dimensions of internal Jewish migration, its sources, motivations and consequences. By focusing on the extraordinary growth of two Jewish urban populations, the essay suggests some categories for analyzing the communal dynamic of postwar American Jewry. It also explores a number of parallels between immigration and the establishment of indigenous American Jewish communities. Given the historic dependence of the United States upon immigration for its social formation and the critical role of immigration in the growth of the American Jewish community, study of internal migration provides a useful framework to assess certain postwar changes.[2] Specifically, *it encourages an emphasis upon the creation rather than the transformation of communities.*[3] Observing the postwar migrations, Oscar Handlin, the eminent historian of immigration, noted that immigrants differed only in degree from native-born Americans who migrated within the United States. Where the newcomer came from was less important than that the migrant had turned his back upon home and family, abandoned the way he had earned a living, and deserted his community.[4]

Originally published in *Studies in Contemporary Jewry* 8 (1992). Reprinted by permission of Oxford University Press.

Handlin's trenchant reflections not only linked immigration with internal migration, seeing them as a continuum, but made the problem of community central to both.

The mobilization of the war years drew young Jewish men out of the insular urban neighborhoods of their childhood and sent them to distant bases scattered throughout the South and West. Most of the Jewish servicemen, like their gentile peers, had not strayed far from their home towns during the difficult years of the Great Depression.[5] Now, en route to the Pacific war theater, they discovered the West. Thousands of them passed through Los Angeles and were amazed by the apparently prosperous and easy way of life that they saw. Others who joined the Army Air Corps often found themselves stationed in one of the Miami Beach hotels requisitioned for the war. When their wives came down to visit, they, too, took in the beauty of the resort city.[6] Smaller numbers went to bases near such Texas towns as Houston and Dallas. Even a small city such as Tucson, Arizona, attracted Jews who discovered it because of its base for training bombardiers and pilots.[7] Often the opportunities these cities offered excited them. "You betcha, I loved it!" Leon Rabin recalled. "I wrote to my friends in Philadelphia and said there's no way for me to tell you what's going on down here and anything I'd tell you wouldn't make you come down here. But now that I'm here there's no way that I'll ever come back."[8] Rabin was true to his word. He married a native Dallas Jew and spent the rest of his life building a Jewish community that reflected some of the values he had learned growing up in Philadelphia. He also understood how limited was the vision of most East Coast Jews and how reluctant they were to venture beyond the suburbs of their cities until propelled by the war. Once word spread of the opportunities available, however, especially in a large city such as Los Angeles, which had a substantial Jewish population even in 1940, the numbers of Jews who migrated quickly reached substantial proportions.

Jewish migration to these southern and western cities—ones that would subsequently be counted as part of an emerging Sunbelt—reflected a response shared by millions of other Americans to federal initiatives and policies. Not only did the war years lead the government to funnel enormous sums for economic development into southern and western states—California alone received 10 percent of all federal war monies—but these funds often went to provide the capitalization for defense-related industries.[9] From airplane construction in Los Angeles to aluminum manufacturing in Miami to medical and communications research in Houston, entire industrial and postindustrial infrastructures were established. The subsequent eruption of the Cold War sustained the economic growth of these cities.[10] The postwar socioeconomic changes produced regional convergence, with the outlying regions of the South and West growing more rapidly than the developed sections of the country. This rapid social change brought the South and West's economies, social patterns and cultural styles closer to national norms.[11] Federal postwar policies, especially the GI bill, with its low-cost mortgage provisions and college loans, also encouraged a generation to seek its fortunes far from home and family. These portable benefits loosened the ties that bound individuals to networks of kin and friends. No longer needing to rely upon relatives and neighbors to find work, to finance an education or even to buy a house, Jews and other Americans were free to pursue their dreams of the good life. For many Jews particularly, the attractions of the apparently affluent and relaxed style of living of the Sunbelt cities proved irresistible.[12]

The term *Sunbelt* is designed to link fundamentally different parts of the United States that share the characteristics of rapid social change and regional convergence. Nicholas Lemann, executive editor of *Texas Monthly,* argues persuasively that journalists invented the Sunbelt concept in order to speak about new political and economic trends. When the word first acquired popular usage in the mid-1970s, "millions of people were living in the Sunbelt without one of them realizing it," wrote Lemann. "They thought of themselves as Southerners or Texans or Los Angelenos."[13] Of course, the particularisms Lemann mentions, the sense of identity derived from being rooted in a city, state or region, had salience largely for old-timers, not for migrants. They just as often thought of themselves as ex-New Yorkers or former Philadelphians. "I am a refugee from Chicago of several years standing," announced Leonard Sperry, a wealthy migrant to Los Angeles.[14] Sperry's self-definition after close to a decade of living in the City of Angels suggests the extent to which a migrant's identity derived from the home of his childhood. Similarly, the death notices of longtime Miami residents that announced burial in Detroit, or Chicago, or Rochester, appear symptomatic of the unwillingness of Jews to identify Miami as "home."[15] By linking a wide variety of locales, the notion of a Sunbelt helped to smooth away these differences in self-identification between the newcomers and the old-timers.

As the United States became a "nation of strangers," in the words of a popular journalist's account of one out of five Americans' propensity to move every year,[16] Jews developed an ethnic variation on the American theme of internal migration. Federal policies drew Jews out of their old homes, but ethnic networks guided them to new ones. Not only did Jews come disproportionately from large cities where they previously had concentrated, most also settled in only a handful of southern and western cities. Ninety-six percent of Jews lived in urban places in 1957, compared with 64 percent of the total U.S. population—and 87 percent of American Jews lived in cities of 250,000 or more inhabitants. In other words, Jews not only lived in cities, they lived in big cities. Although Jews constituted only 3.5 percent of the American population, they made up 8 percent of the nation's urban residents. The high concentration in the New York City area, which held approximately 40 percent of American Jewry, contributed to the distinctive Jewish demographic profile.[17] Aggregate data reveal the shift away from the Northeast and Midwest to the South and West, yet Jewish patterns of migration remained highly distinctive.[18] Despite significant postwar migration, 75 percent of America's Jews lived in only five states in 1960, as they had prior to the Second World War. When these data are disaggregated, the particularities of Jewish migration appear. Enticed by the vision of easy living under perpetually sunny skies, Jews favored certain Sunbelt cities over others. In these cities the rate of Jewish population growth often exceeded that of the general white population.[19] Above all, Jews went to two coastal cities: Miami in the East and Los Angeles in the West. These cities account for 80 percent and 70 percent, respectively, of the total postwar Jewish migration to the South and West.[20] Thus they provide the best case study of the impact of the postwar Sunbelt migrations on American Jewish ethnic culture.

Miami and Los Angeles: Magnet Cities

The postwar Jewish migration put Los Angeles and Miami on the Jewish map of the United States. Miami and Los Angeles received new settlers in record numbers after the war. Both cities had grown during the war, but neither anticipated the postwar influx. In 1946, observers estimated that each month 16,000 newcomers were arriving in Los Angeles. Of these, slightly more than 2,000 were Jews.[21] The new arrivals more than doubled the substantial Jewish population estimated at 100,000 before the war. By 1950, there were almost 300,000 Jews in the City of Angels. Seventh largest in Jewish population in 1940, Los Angeles displaced Chicago a decade later to rank second behind New York City. The number of Jews in Los Angeles continued to grow throughout the 1950s at an impressive rate of just under 50 percent. The rate of growth of the Jewish population exceeded that of the general population, such that the percentage of Jews in Los Angeles rose steadily. By the end of the decade, there were close to 400,000 Jews living in the City of Angels, roughly 18 percent of the total population. So many newcomers had arrived within such a short time period that only 8 percent of adult Jews living in the city in 1950 were native Angelenos and only 16 percent could be considered old-timers who had settled there before the Second World War. Continued migration in the 1960s and 1970s increased the city's Jewish population to more than half a million Jews, a Jewish city of enormous proportions.[22]

Nowhere near Los Angeles initially in the size of its general or Jewish population, Miami grew at an even more rapid rate. Although the number of Jews doubled from 1940 to 1945, from a mere 8,000 to 16,000, the population increased more than threefold to 55,000 by 1950. This astonishing rate of increase far outstripped the 57 percent growth in the general Miami population. Five years later, the Jewish population doubled yet again to reach 100,000. Thus, within a decade after the war, Miami had zoomed from a small and insignificant concentration of 16,000 Jews to a major urban Jewish center of 100,000 Jews. Thereafter, the rate of growth slowed, but Jewish migration to Miami continued to outstrip general migration until the Jewish proportion of the population had increased to 15 percent. By 1970, Miami contained approximately the same number of Jews as Chicago's greater metropolitan area, roughly 250,000. Miami now ranked among the top five American cities in terms of its Jewish population. Even more than Los Angeles, it was a city of newcomers. A mere 4 percent of the Jewish population had been born in the city; virtually everyone had come from someplace else.[23]

Those who chose to move to these cities charted a different path from the majority who made the more modest and popular move to the suburbs. "They came for several reasons," Bernard Goldstein explained,

> but all of them add up to economics. You had young people who were stationed in the army camps here. And they realized the opportunities—this was an open economic frontier. And as soon as the war was over, if they were single they just stayed here and if they had families they went back to New York or Chicago or wherever, packed their bags and came right back.[24]

A move to the suburbs rarely involved the pursuit of economic opportunity, although it often reflected increased affluence and the pursuit of status. For Jews, moving to the suburbs meant choosing a residence within the city's expanding boundaries. For some, however, the suburbs were a "dress rehearsal" for the big move.[25] "When you grow up in New York City—all the world is Jewish," explained Nathan Perlmutter. "When all the world is Jewish, nobody is Jewish, really." Perlmutter moved to Miami from New York City in 1956 to head the office of the Anti-Defamation League. "You've got to leave major metropolitan areas to fully understand what I mean about a sense of a Jewish community—of a 'we' and a 'they'—in New York, it's all 'we'."[26] Miami and Los Angeles represented alternatives to suburbanization.

The growth of Jewish suburban areas stemmed from a different but related set of federal postwar policies that had promoted internal migration within the United States. The scarcity of adequate housing in the cities, the rapid building of modestly priced single-family houses, the extensive program of highway construction and the easy availability of mortgages all encouraged young families to seek homes on the expanding peripheries of the nation's cities.[27] Although energized by these policies, suburbanization represented a postwar continuation and extension of the movement out of older and poorer city neighborhoods into new and more affluent ones that had started as early as the First World War.[28] Jews who moved to the suburbs did not lose touch with the city, its institutions and culture.[29] Many returned daily to work and more visited on occasion. Nor did suburbanization disrupt the family network; it simply extended the reach of the intergenerational family. Similarly, although suburban Jews organized Jewish life anew, they also imported Jewish institutions.[30] Synagogues frequently followed their more wealthy congregants to the suburbs.[31] Such decisions provided suburban Jews with a significant measure of continuity and reaffirmed deference to established leaders. No changing of the guard took place, in contrast with internal migration, which shattered patterns of deference and disrupted structures of collective continuity.

Alongside the mass internal migration to Sunbelt cities of Jews seeking economic opportunity, one should also note a smaller but steady stream of migrants who moved specifically for occupational reasons.[32] This pattern did not radically change the distribution of the Jewish population, although it did contribute a significant number of newcomers to many established Jewish communities. For example, in Toledo, Ohio, the expansion of the university and the centering of several large national retail chains in the city drew many aspiring Jewish academics and managers there. Toledo, however, experienced no overall growth in Jewish population because 45 to 60 percent of the young Jews raised there abandoned the city after college, seeking opportunity elsewhere.[33] Similarly, Kansas City's relatively static Jewish population since the 1950s disguised both a substantial in-migration of Jewish professionals and managers—approximately 37 percent of Jewish household heads in 1976—and a sizable out-migration of adult children of Kansas City Jewish household heads. In the 1970s, fully half of those sons and daughters who grew up in Kansas City no longer lived there.[34] The data on Omaha, Nebraska, reveal a similar pattern.[35] Sidney Goldstein argues that migration of these young, ambitious Jewish professionals and managers indicates the strength of economic motives over the salience of kinship ties. It points to the predominance of the nuclear family among American Jews. It suggests that the residential clustering so characteristic of eastern and midwestern cities no longer appeals to these Jewish migrants, who have discarded an earlier preference for areas of high Jewish concentration. It reveals the extent to which Jews have come to resemble other Americans in social and cultural behavior, even as their distinctive occupational concentration propels them across the continent in search of jobs.[36]

Given the urban choices, especially the rapid growth of such southwestern cities as Houston and such southern cities as Atlanta, it is worthwhile asking why so many more Jews migrated to Miami and Los Angeles.[37] A different dynamic appears to be at work in the rapid emergence of these two cities in comparison with other patterns of migration, either to the suburbs or for occupational mobility. These two cities attracted Jewish newcomers not only through their climate and leisure style of life and their promise of economic abundance, but also through the substantial and visible Jewish presence in a major city industry. Although it would be unfair to compare the Los Angeles–based motion picture industry's enormous assets and glamour with the much smaller Miami Beach tourist trade, Jewish hoteliers in the latter city compensated in part by catering to Jews, advertising for their patronage and encouraging them not only to visit but to settle in Miami.[38] Such encouragement required Jewish efforts to change southern mores—specifically, to eliminate visible signs of antisemitic bias in Miami.

In 1945, as part of an effort by the Anti-Defamation League to remove discriminatory signs on the beach, seventeen ex-servicemen "paid quiet calls on managers of hotels and apartment houses displaying or advertising 'gentiles only' policies," according to the historian Gladys Rosen. "The tactics and its timing proved effective," she concluded, because more than half of the signs disappeared.[39] Jewish residents of Miami Beach, eager to attract Jewish visitors, then urged the local city council to outlaw antisemitic advertising. Although the Florida courts invalidated the council's 1947 law on the grounds that the municipality lacked jurisdiction, by 1949 the state legislature had enacted enabling legislation that granted the city council the power to prohibit discriminatory advertising. The Miami Beach council then forbade "any advertisement, notice or sign which is discriminatory against persons of any religion, sect, creed, race or denomination in the enjoyment of privileges and facilities of places of public accommodation, amusement or resort."[40] Given the widespread acceptance of legal segregation in Florida—as in the rest of the South—the modest action of the Miami Beach City Council reverberated as a loud rejection of discrimination. By passing the law, the council hung out a welcome sign for Jews, at least on Miami Beach. The law did not eliminate antisemitic discrimination and did not affect resorts outside of the council's jurisdiction, but it made Miami Beach's public milieu more accommodating to Jews and set an important precedent.[41]

Despite their comparable attractions for Jewish migrants, Miami and Los Angeles appealed to slightly different Jews. Once they decided to move, Jewish migrants often allowed ethnic networks to influence their choices. These networks channeled postwar internal migration and sorted Jews.[42] Miami drew a more geographically representative sample, including a sizable number of southern Jews, than did Los Angeles. In 1959, approximately 43 percent of Miami Jews came from New York

City, a proportion that slightly exceeded the percentage of American Jews living in New York after the war.[43] By contrast, only 24 percent of the migrants to Los Angeles in 1950 had left New York City. Los Angeles attracted a disproportionate number of Jews from the cities of the Midwest, especially Chicago. An estimated 17 percent of the newcomers hailed from Chicago (45 percent of all midwestern migrants to Los Angeles came from Chicago), although its Jewish population constituted less than 10 percent of American Jewry. Far more Jewish northeasterners moved to Los Angeles, however, than was true among the general white migrant population, which consisted largely of people arriving from states west of the Mississippi.[44]

If Los Angeles attracted Jews disproportionately from the cities of the Midwest, it drew a representative selection of migrants in terms of age. Most Jewish newcomers were young people seeking work, although some came to the city for health reasons or to retire. Miami initially appealed to a similar age spectrum, but by the mid-1950s an ever-growing percentage of elderly retirees had settled in the city.[45] The mass migration of elderly Jews to Miami Beach, which accelerated in the 1960s, received an impetus from the steady decay of the inner cities, accompanied by the rising rate of crime, the high cost of housing and the arrival of new, poor immigrants. The portability of federal social security benefits and union pensions encouraged mobility among retirees in the way that the GI bill had aided a migration of young men after the Second World War. By 1959, the median age of Jews in Miami had risen to 46 from 33 years, while in Los Angeles it had dropped from 37 to 33 years.

The large number of elderly Jews migrating to Miami contributed to a third difference between the two cities. Most Jews moving to Los Angeles settled down and confined any subsequent moves to different sections of the city. Jews migrating to Miami, however, included in their ranks a sizable contingent of "snowbirds." These restless settlers resided in the city anywhere from one to eight months in the course of a year, spending the rest of their time back "home." Many eventually stayed year-round in Miami. Often the difference between an eight-month "snowbird" and a new resident was more a state of mind than a reflection of behavior.

Jewish migrants to Los Angeles and Miami also adopted different residential strategies. The large contingent of New Yorkers in Miami replicated the familiar pattern of dispersed concentration. The newcomers settled initially in two sections: in the South Beach section of Miami Beach and in the Shenandoah and Westchester areas of the city of Miami. By 1955, these two districts held 75 percent of the Jewish population. As more migrants continued to arrive, they drifted northward to North Miami and North Miami Beach.[46] These patterns of concentration reflected in part a response to the restrictive housing covenants in several of the incorporated cities of Dade County that were part of metropolitan Miami. Jewish entrepreneurs in real estate and the hotel and building industry also influenced Miami Jewish residential patterns. The number of apartment houses constructed soared during the 1950s and on into the 1960s. Miami boosters noted that a new house or apartment was completed in Miami "every seven minutes of the working day for an annual average of more than 16,000 units."[47] The migrants' decision to concentrate in certain sections of the city pointed as well to their immigrant and second-generation origins. The move to Miami represented less a decision to leave the familiar urban world of their past than an attempt to radically extend its boundaries. Jews dubbed Miami "the southern borscht belt" and joked that it had become a suburb of New York City.[48] Their humor underscored the sense of connectedness that the newcomers felt with their old homes, which denied the radical character of their relocation.

In contrast, Jews moving to Los Angeles knew that they had left the old neighborhood behind; few sought to replicate the residential strategies of Chicago or New York. When the newcomers arrived in Los Angeles they settled in newly developing sections of the city, especially on the west side and in the San Fernando Valley. Although significant concentrations of Jews appeared in the Wilshire-Fairfax, Beverly-Fairfax, Beverly Hills and Westwood districts, these sections, with the possible exception of Fairfax, did not resemble eastern and midwestern urban neighborhoods.[49] The intensity of public urban life characteristic of eastern and midwestern cities faded under the California sunshine. Yet an awareness of ethnicity persisted. Growing up in Beverly Hills, one knew that it wasn't 100 percent Jewish, "but it felt like it was," a resident recalled. The big ethnic distinctions were culinary. "All of my Jewish friends ate rye bread with mustard and there was one non-Jewish boy in the group that I went around with and he . . . used mayonnaise on white bread, and we used to call him 'mayo.' "[50] The urban character of Los Angeles also muted distinctions between city and suburb, though residents recognized a difference in cultural style between city Jews and valley Jews.[51] One resident who grew up in Los Angeles during the 1950s never understood what a suburb was until she traveled east to settle in Minneapolis.[52] The migrants reversed the perception, thinking that all of Los Angeles was one big suburb.

A Community of Strangers

Despite their differences in age, motivation for leaving the familiar and their diverse residential strategies, the migrants turned to peer group organization to forge the rudimentary bonds of community. Like the immigrants, they broke intergenerational family ties to reconstitute a voluntary community of peers. The new migrants similarly relied upon shared memories of the past or common values to unite them. Unlike the immigrants, the newcomers to Los Angeles and Miami did not convert their impulse to peer group solidarity into social welfare and mutual aid. The new *landsmanshaftn* remained essentially centers of secular ethnic sociability, anchoring their members in unfamiliar urban territory through nostalgic evocations of the well-known world that had been abandoned. By 1950, several dozen of these social clubs organized around city of origin flourished in Los Angeles, as did a smaller number in Miami.[53] They held monthly meetings and hosted annual picnics. A few engaged in charitable endeavors. In 1947, the five hundred members of the Omaha Friendship Club of Los Angeles decided to raise money for a memorial to Henry Monsky, the recently deceased head of B'nai B'rith, who had lived in Omaha.[54] But the clubs' main purpose was social. Most of the Los Angeles clubs limited membership to adults aged twenty-one to thirty-five. Those who didn't join could use the services of the many introduction clubs that sprang up, but often it was preferable to touch base with fellow *landslayt* whose identity with "home" was linked to the neighborhood of their youth. New York City Jews, for example, founded high school alumni associations in Miami and Los Angeles that encouraged contact between former classmates of the Thomas Jefferson or Abraham Lincoln high schools in Brooklyn, or of the DeWitt Clinton or Morris high schools in the Bronx.

The migrants also swelled the ranks of the handful of established American Jewish organizations. By the early 1950s, the one B'nai B'rith group of 1945 in Miami had multiplied into twenty other lodges with a membership exceeding twenty-five hundred.[55] Labor Zionists, General Zionists, Hadassah and the American Jewish Congress rapidly founded local chapters. Often, "even before a new apartment building is fully occupied," observed a Jewish communal worker, "there is already formed (with officers) a Men's Club, B'nai B'rith Lodge, Hadassah Chapter, etc."[56] The newcomers' visible presence encouraged national organizations to refocus their activities. In 1952, the American Jewish Committee established a chapter in Miami and moved its southern headquarters from Atlanta to the new branch.[57] Miami was rapidly becoming the Jews' new headquarters of the South.[58] In Los Angeles, a similar process of recruitment added thousands to the membership rolls of national organizations already established in the city.

The burst of communal activity also affected religious life. In Miami, migrants joined the half-dozen established congregations—which offered special monthly or even weekly memberships to accommodate the "snowbirds"[59]—while those who found the synagogues inconvenient, undesirable or inaccessible initiated new congregations. By 1947, there were twenty-four congregations in Miami, nineteen of them with rabbis. Given the still modest size of the Jewish population, these figures represent significant communal ferment.[60] Los Angeles, with ten times the Jewish population, supported only seventy-three synagogues, or three times the number in Miami.[61] The newcomers found few precedents impeding their efforts to introduce a wide array of communal activities and organizations. Rabbis could, and did, build congregations that became personal fiefdoms unconstrained by an entrenched laity.[62] These communities, a true frontier, were open to individual and collective entrepreneurship; both also contained significant numbers of exceptionally wealthy Jews.

The "snowbird" phenomenon, however, had a significant influence on Miami's communal development. Although it soon overshadowed Atlanta as the major Jewish city of the South, Miami attracted far fewer colonizers from New York than did Los Angeles. When local leaders tried to interest New York institutions in setting up branches in Miami, they more often encountered resistance. Irving Lehrman, rabbi of the Miami Beach Jewish Center (later Temple Emanu-El), grasped the high visibility potential of his synagogue for visitors and made arrangements to establish a branch of the Jewish Museum in the Center as early as 1950. "It will not only bring prestige to, and raise the cultural level of the community, but will afford an opportunity to the thousands of residents, as well as visitors, to see the vast storehouse of Jewish artifacts and learn more about our cultural heritage," he explained.[63] But Lehrman's vision was rarely shared by eastern leaders. Instead, Miami Beach became the campaign capital for national Jewish fund-raising.[64]

Despite its size and diversity, the Los Angeles Jewish community lacked entrenched interests and thus held enormous potential, especially for an elite of ideologically committed easterners. They came to the Southland after the war to establish branches of their institutions and solicit support among Hollywood's moguls. In a brief five-year period after the war, these committed individuals transplanted an institutional range of ideological diversity that had developed in the East. When the American Jewish Committee sent its field-worker for the West to Los Angeles to start a branch in 1945, he emphasized the unique Committee ideology to overcome the reluctance of older residents to join the organization.[65] Four years later, a young communal worker arrived in Los Angeles and dreamed "the vision of establishing a '92nd Street Y of the West' " in the new Westside Jewish Community Center.[66] In 1946, Moshe Davis, a young professor of American Jewish history at the Jewish Theological Seminary, arrived in Los Angeles to recruit supporters for a new branch of the Seminary, the University of Judaism.[67] As Simon Greenberg, the university's first president, recalled, "We had to overcome the feeling on the West Coast that here was a new community. Why did it have to import the divisions (Orthodox, Conservative, Reform) of the East Coast? Why can't we have one school for the Jews of the West Coast?"[68] Eastern leaders' ability to colonize Los Angeles Jews successfully obviated the need to answer such questions. Of course, not all efforts to transplant ideological institutions succeeded.[69] Los Angeles provided a receptive environment largely to a middle range of organizations in the immediate postwar decade. Their success established the foundation for subsequent colonizing efforts.[70]

In the new urban milieu, Jewish self-perceptions gradually changed. "Jews are now free to be Jewish in a new way as an act of personal choice rather than imposition," writes the sociologist Neil Sandberg.[71] The self-selection that lay behind migration reinforced the principle of personal choice of identity. As the Los Angeles lawyer and communal leader Howard Friedman explained, Jews felt able to innovate, experiment, indulge, in short, "to cultivate ourselves . . . in a context of complete freedom."[72] However, according to Moses Rischin, a historian of Jewish immigrants in New York City, the Jewish way of life in Los Angeles was problematic. "Post-Judaic" and "post-secular," he wrote, the life-style was "remote even from an earlier sub-culture of Jewishness" and sustained neither by traditional religious patterns nor by a vigorous secular ethnicity.[73] Others rejoiced in the absence of traditions. According to Charles Brown, the head of the Jewish Community Council in 1952, "here [in Los Angeles] there are no vested interests, here there are no sacred cows, here there is no cold hand of the past. There is an opportunity to develop new forms of Jewish communal living geared in a realistic fashion to the actual needs of the Jewish community."[74] These new forms included such eclectic institutions as the Brandeis Camp Institute, pioneered by Shlomo Bardin. Constrained neither by traditions nor by vested interests, Bardin orchestrated moments of Jewish solidarity designed especially to appeal to a community of strangers, recruiting both old-timers and newcomers for weekend celebrations/explorations of the Sabbath that often inspired the participants to incorporate elements of Jewish study and observance in their lives. The heart of Bardin's program, however, was a month-long innovative leadership training program that raised the Jewish consciousness of the college youth who attended.[75]

Outsiders to the dominant Protestant communities of Los Angeles and Miami, Jewish newcomers introduced additional ethnic diversity to their new homes. Rabbi Edgar Magnin, a fixture of the Los Angeles Jewish scene for decades as the leader of the Wilshire Boulevard Temple, the most prestigious Reform congregation in the city, deplored the new ethnicity introduced by the newcomers in an interview conducted in 1978. "This is a different ballgame today—you've got another Brooklyn here. When I came here, it was Los Angeles. Now it's a Brooklyn."[76] Magnin exaggerated, of course, but other native-born Californian Jews also expressed unease at the changes introduced (mainly in the 1950s) by the newcomers.[77] Often identifying themselves as white ethnics, despite the absence of other such comparable groups as Italians, some migrants used religious symbols to define their collective identity. Foremost among these symbols was Israel: Zion, homeland, state. The migrants' support for the establishment of the state and their subsequent identification with Israel as the vehicle of Jewish idealism helped to make sentimental Zionism the collective glue uniting American Jews.[78] Their numbers overwhelmed the pockets of anti-Zionist commitment among the old-timers, while the attacks on Communists inspired by McCarthy undermined the organizational viability of the internationalist radicals.

Jewish migrants selected themselves to move to Sunbelt cities—to take advantage of the economic opportunities, to bask in the balmy weather and to escape from the constraining intergenerational intimacies of parents and kinfolk. In the process they elevated the principle of self-selection that initially had guided them as migrants into the grounds for collective action. Thus they influenced the character of American Jewish life by creating new patterns of Jewish communal life that upheld the centrality of the consenting individual. Long before converts to Judaism adopted the label "Jews by choice," newcomers to the Sunbelt cities had transformed Jewishness into a matter of one's choosing. The migrants posited a Jewishness rooted in the future, in peer group sociability, in common values and in personal choice, all linked to powerful but distant surrogates—the old home that had disappeared and the Jewish state of Israel that rose like a phoenix on the ashes of the Holocaust. The newcomers created a loosely knit community that supported these possibilities, that allowed for eclectic Jewish styles and symbols of ethnicity, that provided fertile ground for individual entrepreneurship.

"In the past, Jewishness was absorbed by young people as they grew up in Jewish community and family environments," argues Sandberg. "No parental decision was involved in the creation of a sense of Jewish identification in the young person's growing identity and self-image. They were immersed in a culture where Jewish language, behavior, and symbolism developed as automatic responses. . . . Today," he concludes, referring specifically to Los Angeles, "most Jews have grown up without the support of such a community."[79] Under the bright sunshine of Miami and Los Angeles, Jewishness gradually lost its ineluctability. If Jewishness was "not a matter of natural inheritance," then an individual Jew had to develop a number of interlocking networks to sustain a Jewish identity that meant more than self-definition. In Los Angeles, such networks emerged primarily within occupations and politics. In the postwar period, a majority of Los Angeles Jews shared their workplace largely with other Jews. Political lobbying for Israel also served to define the ethnic identity of Miami and Los Angeles Jews. Ironically, work and politics—the two public arenas that originally generated most intra-Jewish conflict—now provided a sense of shared Jewishness for the migrants. For decades Jewish workers had fought Jewish bosses over the conditions of the workplace, and the scars of the past's bitter political battles among Jews had only begun to heal. Yet in the new golden land, work and politics became sources of ethnic continuity helping to define the collective parameters of Jewishness.

In many ways, the Jewish worlds of Los Angeles and Miami and other Sunbelt cities can be seen as the offspring of the large urban Jewish settlements of New York, Chicago, Philadelphia and Boston, and of the more modest communities of such cities as Omaha, Milwaukee, Cleveland and Detroit. As Jewish New York, Chicago and Philadelphia represent continuity with a European past because they were created by immigrants from the cities and towns of Eastern Europe, so Jewish Miami and Los Angeles are creations of the midwestern and northeastern cities, representing continuity with an American past. American Jews produced in the postwar era a second generation of cities, offspring of the first generation. It was, perhaps, a very American thing to send off the sons and daughters—and even the grandfathers and grandmothers—to colonize the new golden land, to build cities, to plant congregations, to forge symbolic bonds of ethnic identity. Borrowing from America's Puritan past, one might see these internal migrations as American Jews' own errand into the wilderness.

Notes

I am grateful to the National Endowment for the Humanities for a research grant, to Cindy Sweet for help conducting interviews, to Gladys Rosen for generously sharing materials collected on Miami Jews, and to Arthur A. Goren and Paula Hyman for criticism of an earlier draft of this essay.

1. There have been few studies of the impact of wartime participation on American Jews. A pioneering early study is Moses Kligsberg, "American Jewish Soldiers on Jews and Judaism," *YIVO Annual of Jewish Social Science* 5 (1950), 256–265.

2. John Bodnar, *The Transplanted: A History of Immigrants in Urban America* (Bloomington: 1985), is a valuable study of the relationship between immigration and social formation in the United States. Lloyd P. Gartner, "The History of North American Jewish Communities: A Field for the Jewish Historian," *The Jewish Journal of Sociology* 9 (June 1965), 22–29, offers a thoughtful analysis of the relationship between Jewish immigration and secondary migration.

3. For a focus on transformation, see Calvin Goldscheider, *Jewish Continuity and Change: Emerging Patterns in America* (Bloomington: 1985), and Steven M. Cohen, *American Modernity, Jewish Identity* (New York: 1983).

4. Oscar Handlin, "Immigration in American Life: A Reappraisal," in *Immigration and American History: Essays in Honor of Theodore C. Blegen*, ed. Henry Steele Commager (Minneapolis: 1961), 8–25.

5. For comparative mobility statistics by state, see "Series C 25-73," *The Statistical History of the United States from Colonial Times to the Present* (Stamford: 1965), 44–47.

6. Interview with Rabbi Murray Alstet, June 1966; interview with Rabbi Joseph Narot, n.d.

7. Leonard Dinnerstein, "From Desert Oasis to the Desert Caucus: The Jews of Tucson," Moses Rischin and John Livingston, eds., *Jews of the American West* (Detroit: 1991).

8. Interview with Leon Rabin by Cindy Sweet, 19 September 1986.

9. Gerald Nash, *The American West Transformed: The Impact of the Second World War* (Bloomington: 1985), 14, 35–36.

10. Ann Markusen, *Regions: The Economics and Politics of Territory* (New York: 1987), and *idem, The Rise of the Gunbelt* (New York: 1990).

11. Otis L. Graham, Jr., "From Snowbelt to Sunbelt: The Impact of Migration," *Dialogue* 59 (1983), 11–14.

12. Interviews with "the Mavens," Jewish migrants to Los Angeles from New York City, Los Angeles, 14 July 1989.

13. Nicholas Lemann, "Covering the Sunbelt," *Harper's Magazine* (February 1982), rpt. in *Dialogue* 59 (1983), 24.

14. Leonard Sperry, "The Development of Programs in the Los Angeles Chapter." Papers presented at Chapter Leaders Workshop, 16 April 1959, American Jewish Committee MSS (California/Los Angeles Chapter, 52–62), YIVO.

15. Memo from Arthur Rosichan, 2 March 1967, with covering memo probably from Robert Forman, Greater Miami Jewish Federation.

16. Vance Packard, *A Nation of Strangers* (New York: 1972), 7–8.

17. Sidney Goldstein, "American Jewry, 1970: A Demographic Profile," *American Jewish Year Book* 72 (New York: 1971), 37–38.

18. Both the prewar (1937) and postwar (1960) distribution of Jews by state and region produce a consistent rank of 4 on an index of dissimilarity. Figures from *ibid*.

19. Ira M. Sheskin, "The Migration of Jews to Sunbelt Cities" (unpublished paper in author's possession), 9–11, 26–27.

20. The Jewish population in the South rose from 330,000 in 1937 to 486,000 in 1960; Miami's growth accounted for 132,000 of the increase. Similarly, Los Angeles accounted for 300,000 of the increase of Jews in the West, from 219,000 in 1937 to 598,000 in 1960. In the following decade, Los Angeles accounted for 64 percent of the western regional increase, while Miami accounted for only 29 percent of the southern regional increase. Computed from Tables 1, 3 and 5 in Sheskin, "The Migration of Jews to Sunbelt Cities."

21. Max Vorspan and Lloyd Gartner, *History of the Jews of Los Angeles* (Philadelphia: 1970), 225. See 225–237 for a good, concise treatment of Jewish migration to Los Angeles—its sources, motivations and impact.

22. Bruce Philips, "Los Angeles Jewry: A Demographic Portrait," *American Jewish Year Book* 86 (New York: 1986), 141, 160; Fred Massarik, "A Report on the Jewish Population of Los Angeles," Jewish Federation-Council of Greater Los Angeles (1959), 18–19.

23. Ira M. Sheskin, *Demographic Study of the Greater Miami Jewish Community: Summary Report* (Miami: 1984), 4–7.

24. Interview with Bernard Goldstein by Cindy Sweet, 20 September 1986.

25. Interview with Michael Wiener, 14 July 1989; comment by Selma Berrol at Columbia University Urban History Seminar, March 1987.

26. Nathan Perlmutter, Oral History Memoir, 15, Oral History of the American Jewish Committee, William E. Wiener Oral History Library.

27. Robert Fishman, *Bourgeois Utopias: The Rise and Fall of Suburbia* (New York: 1987), 174–179; Kenneth T. Jackson, *Crabgrass Frontier: The Suburbanization of the United States* (New York: 1985), 196–217.

28. Erich Rosenthal, "This Was North Lawndale: The Transplantation of a Jewish Community," *Jewish Social Studies* 22 (April 1960), 67–82.

29. Marshall Sklare, *Jewish Identity on the Suburban Frontier* (New York: 1967). Also see Sidney Goldstein and Calvin Goldscheider, *Jewish Americans: Three Generations in a Jewish Community* (Englewood Cliffs, N.J.: 1968), who indicate continuities as well as changes.

30. Herbert Gans, "Park Forest: Birth of a Jewish Community," *Commentary* 11 (April

1951), 330–339; idem, "Progress of a Suburban Jewish Community," *Commentary* 23 (February 1957), 113–122.

31. Paula Hyman, "From City to Suburb: Temple Mishkan Tefila of Boston," in *A History of the American Synagogue*, ed. Jack Wertheimer (Cambridge, Mass.: 1987).

32. Interviews with "the Mavens" (14 July 1989) reveal a fairly consistent pattern of job changes that occurred upon arrival in Los Angeles. Very few moved for occupational reasons; most had to hunt for jobs when they arrived. Many often entered completely different lines of work from their training or previous experience.

33. Goldstein, "American Jewry, 1970," 50.

34. Avron C. Heligman, "The Demographic Perspective," in *Mid-America's Promise: A Profile of Kansas City Jewry*, ed. Joseph P. Schultz (1982), 389–391.

35. Murray Frost, "Analysis of a Jewish Community's Outmigration," *Jewish Social Studies* 44 (1982), passim.

36. Goldstein, "American Jewry, 1970," 37, 44, 51.

37. Jews did migrate after the Second World War to both Houston and Atlanta, but not at a rate that exceeded the growth of the general population. On Houston, see Elaine H. Mass, *The Jews of Houston: An Ethnographic Study* (Ph.D. diss., Rice University, 1973), 66, 79, 82; and Sam Schulman, David Gottlieb and Sheila Sheinberg, *A Social and Demographic Survey of the Jewish Community of Houston, Texas* (Houston: 1976), 7–9, 13. On Atlanta, see *Metropolitan Atlanta Jewish Population Study: Summary of Major Findings* (Atlanta: 1985), 2–4, 16. The Jewish population of Atlanta grew at a more rapid rate than did the general population in the 1980s.

38. In 1939, there were more movie theaters (15,115) than banks (14,952). Box office receipts totaled $673,045,000. More than fifty million Americans went to the movies each week every year. Movies were the nation's fourteenth-biggest business in terms of volume ($406,855,000) and eleventh-biggest in terms of assets ($529,950,000). Hollywood was bigger than office machines and supermarket chains. See Otto Friedrich, *City of Nets* (New York: 1986), 14. Statistics on Miami Beach's tourist industry are impressive but do not approach the motion pictures; see Miami Beach Chamber of Commerce, Statistical Review, 1955.

39. Gladys Rosen, "Community Relations: 1945–1960 Post-War Period" (unpublished paper in author's possession), 2.

40. *Jewish Floridian*, 24 June 1949; Polly Redford, *Billion Dollar Sandbar: A Biography of Miami Beach* (New York: 1970), 222.

41. The neighboring town of Surfside passed a similar ordinance in 1951. *Jewish Floridian*, 29 June 1951. Enforcement was another problem. Signs remained on the Beach through the 1950s, as noted in the Survey of Resort Discrimination by the Anti-Defamation League, reported in the *Jewish Floridian*, 29 April 1960. In 1953, 20 percent of the Miami Beach hotels barred Jews; by 1957 this figure had declined to only two percent.

42. Interviews with "the Mavens," 14 July 1989.

43. Manheim Shapiro, "The Bayville Survey," American Jewish Committee, Greater Miami Chapter (1961), summary statement, n.p.

44. Fred Massarik, *A Report on the Jewish Population of Los Angeles* (Los Angeles: 1953), 22; idem, "The Jewish Population of Los Angeles: A Panorama of Change," *The Reconstructionist* 18 (28 November 1952), 13.

45. Many of the elderly settled in Miami Beach. The median age of Miami Beach rose from 43 years in 1950 to 54 years in 1960, when there were more than 17,000 people aged 65 and over. By 1965, there were more than 28,000 people in this age category, a very rapid increase of 11,000 in only five years. The elderly made up 28 percent of the Beach population in 1960 and 38 percent in 1965. Jews were estimated to constitute close to 80 percent of the Beach population. Memo from Arthur Rosichan, Greater Miami Jewish Federation, 2 March 1967, 2–3.

46. Letter from Arthur Rosichan to Gladys Rosen, Greater Miami Jewish Federation, 23 May 1968.

47. "Key to Growth: Metropolitan Miami" (brochure of Dade County Development Department), 5.
48. A significant number of Catskill hotel owners purchased or built hotels in Miami Beach, starting with the Grossinger family, which purchased the formerly restricted Pancoast in 1945. Grossinger's Pancoast not only changed the hotel guest policy but installed a kosher kitchen.
49. Philips, "Los Angeles Jewry," 133-137.
50. Dena Kaye, American Jewish Committee Annual Meeting (14 May 1977), Oral History Library Panel Session, 6, William E. Wiener Oral History Library.
51. Interview with Judith Kantor, Robin Hudson and David Hudson, 20 July 1989.
52. Remarks of Riv-Ellen Prell, YIVO Annual Conference, 1988.
53. Vorspan and Gartner, *History of the Jews of Los Angeles*, 228; Irving Lehrman and Joseph Rappaport, *The Jewish Community of Miami Beach* (New York: n.d.), 24.
54. *California Jewish Voice*, 19 December 1947.
55. Harry Simonoff, *Under Strange Skies* (New York: 1953), 313.
56. Memo, probably of Robert Forman, 2 March 1967, Greater Miami Jewish Federation.
57. Background material for Miami chapter, American Jewish Committee, n.d., n.p.
58. Daniel Elazar, *Community and Polity: The Organizational Dynamics of American Jews* (Philadelphia: 1976), 140.
59. Gladys Rosen, "The Rabbi in Miami: A Case History," in *Turn to the South: Essays on Southern Jewry*, ed. Nathan M. Kaganoff and Melvin I. Urofsky (Charlottesville: 1979), 35-37.
60. Memo to Morris Klass from M. C. Gettinger, 16 January 1951; Greater Miami Federation; Census of Greater Miami file (1950-1960), 1.
61. Los Angeles Jewish Community Council, *1950 Jewish Community Directory of Greater Los Angeles*, American Jewish Archives, Nearprint Box, Geography, 1-13.
62. For example, consider the careers of Rabbis Irving Lehrman, Leon Kronish and Joseph Narot in Miami, and Edgar Magnin, Aaron Wise, Isaiah Zeldin and Jacob Pressman in Los Angeles.
63. *Jewish Floridian*, 29 December 1950.
64. Elazar, *Community and Polity*, 244.
65. See correspondence between John Slawson and Maurice Karpf, 19 June and 18 July 1945, American Jewish Archives, Maurice J. Karpf MSS 196, Box 1.
66. Letter from Nathan Hurvitz to Charles Mesnick, 1 October 1956, American Jewish Archives, Nathan Hurvitz MSS, Box 100/4, Jewish Centers Association, 1955-1957.
67. Moshe Davis, conversation with Arthur Hoffnung, June 1985, 3-12, Oral History Interview, University of Judaism.
68. Simon Greenberg, "Some Reflections," *Women's League for Conservative Judaism* 58 (Summer 1988), 22.
69. Both the Reconstructionists and YIVO initially failed to establish viable branches of their movement, although Yiddish was subsequently introduced as a regular language at UCLA and the Reconstructionists did build a number of impressive congregations, e.g., Abraham Winokur's in Pacific Palisades. See letter from Sol Liptzin (recipient's identity unknown), 6 July 1947, YIVO, Max Weinreich MSS, Box 263; Samuel Dinin, "Reconstructionism and the Future of Jewish Life in Los Angeles," *The Reconstructionist* 18 (28 November 1952), 15-16.
70. For example, the University of Judaism and the College of Jewish Studies (later the California School of Hebrew Union College-Jewish Institute of Religion) established the precedent followed by Yeshiva University when it started its branch.
71. Neil Sandberg, *Jewish Life in Los Angeles: A Window to Tomorrow* (Lanham, Md.: 1986), 19.
72. Howard I. Friedman, Oral History Memoir, 58-59; Oral History of the American Jewish Committee, William E. Wiener Oral History Library.
73. Moses Rischin, "Foreword," in *The Jews of Los Angeles, 1849-1945: An Annotated Bibliography*, ed. Sara G. Cogan (Berkeley: 1980), viii.

74. Quoted in Vorspan and Gartner, *History of the Jews of Los Angeles,* 267.
75. Bardin regularly solicited testimonies; there were also unsolicited reflections on the effects of Brandeis Camp Institute. See, for example, Walter Hilborn, "Reflections on Legal Practice and Jewish Community Leadership: New York and Los Angeles, 1907–1975," Oral History Interview, Bancroft Library, University of California, Berkeley, 217–219; and interview with Shlomo Bardin by Jack Diamond, pts. 3–5, Library of Brandeis–Bardin Institute.
76. Quoted in "The Jews of Los Angeles: Pursuing the American Dream," *Los Angeles Times,* 29 Jan. 1978.
77. For example, see interview with Rabbi Paul Dubin, American Jewish Historical Society, Interview Folder, Los Angeles, *I-75, Box 24.
78. Sandberg, *Jewish Life in Los Angeles,* 64, 86; Gladys Rosen, "The Zionist Movement" (unpublished draft essay in author's possession), 2–8.
79. Sandberg, *Jewish Life in Los Angeles,* 131.

The German-Jewish Community of Washington Heights

BY STEVEN M. LOWENSTEIN

The German-Jewish community of Washington Heights in New York City was by far the largest settlement of refugees from Nazi Germany in the United States. Only in that section of Upper Manhattan could one find a neighbourhood with a German-Jewish character, a well-developed immigrant culture and a network of immigrant institutions. A person in search of German refugee life "on the streets" would have to direct their attention to Washington Heights. Yet Washington Heights was not really representative of the refugee wave of immigration as a whole. It represented one pole of a heterogeneous and complex German-Jewish immigrant spectrum. The other pole of that spectrum, one about which a great deal has been written, was made up of the distinguished intellectual émigrés who fled Nazi Germany and had much influence on American intellectual life.[1] Neither this relatively small group of luminaries, nor the much more numerous residents of Washington Heights, were typical; yet each of the two poles represented a self-selection of certain elements within German Jewry. An analysis of the community least like the elite intellectuals will help highlight the range of the German-Jewish immigration.

The very existence of a German-Jewish immigrant neighbourhood made Washington Heights atypical. Studies of the refugees of the 1930s in general (admittedly not free of an apologetic note) emphasise the rapid integration of the group into the American mainstream in contrast to other immigrant groups who created their own enclaves and resisted assimilation.[2] Those German Jews

---

[1]The following are only a few of the best known works on the refugee intellectuals. Note the characteristic titles of many of them:
Donald Peterson Kent, *The Refugee Intellectual. The Americanization of the Immigrants of 1933–1941*, New York 1953; Laura Fermi, *Illustrious Immigrants. The Intellectual Migration from Europe 1930–1941*, Chicago [1968]; Donald Fleming and Bernard Bailyn (eds.), *The Intellectual Migration, Europe and America 1930–1960*, Cambridge, Massachusetts 1969; Jarrell C. Jackman & Carla M. Borden (eds.), *The Muses Flee Hitler. Cultural Transfer and Adaptation 1930–1945*, Washington, D.C. 1983; Anthony Heilbut, *Exiled in Paradise*, New York 1983. By comparison relatively little has been written about the "non-intellectuals". Most thorough of these is Maurice Davie *et. al.*, *Refugees in America*, New York–London 1947. The best article on the Washington Heights community is still Ernest Stock's evocative 'Washington Heights' "Fourth Reich"', *Commentary* (June 1951), pp. 581–588. A first attempt to come to grips with the sociology of the non-elite refugees is Herbert Strauss, 'Zur sozialen und organisatorischen Akkulturation deutsch-jüdischer Einwanderer der NS-Zeit in den USA', in, Wolfgang Frühwald and Wolfgang Schieder (eds.), *Leben in Exil. Probleme der Integration deutscher Flüchtlinge im Ausland 1933–1945*, Hamburg 1981, pp. 235–251.
[2]See, for example, Davie, *op. cit.*, pp. 45–46, 156–170, 189–203 *et passim*; Gerhart L. Saenger, *Today's Refugee, Tomorrow's Citizen*, New York–London 1941.

Originally published in *Leo Baeck Institute Yearbook* (1985). Reprinted by permission of the Leo Baeck Institute.

who moved to Washington Heights, however, were more like other immigrant groups than these studies would imply. Yet even they retained certain bourgeois traits which made them different from most immigrants, especially from those who came to America in the period of mass immigration between 1880 and 1924. They also shared with other members of the German refugee wave a composite culture and identity made up of both Jewish and German elements, though with the Jewish elements stronger than elsewhere.

In the 1930s Washington Heights was a typical area of second settlement with a middle-class character. Its ethnic make-up was mixed, with Jews (both native and foreign-born) being the largest group, though not a majority. There were also many Irish-Americans and some Greeks and Armenians. The refugees began arriving in substantial numbers in the mid and late 1930s with the largest number coming to Washington Heights between 1938 and 1940. Large numbers of vacant apartments and pleasant middle-class surroundings, including many parks overlooking the rivers which surrounded the neighbourhood were an attraction but so, undoubtedly, was the pre-existing Jewish community. The Nazi experience had shattered relations with ethnic Germans. Whereas before the 1930s quite a few German Jews settled in Yorkville, the refugees, even if they did not move to Washington Heights, chose such Jewish neighbourhoods as New York's Jackson Heights, Forest Hills, Kew Gardens, Upper West Side and West Bronx, or their equivalents elsewhere. With the exception of a few intellectuals, the refugees felt much closer to Jews than to Germans. Of the 150,000 or so refugees from Nazi Germany who came to the United States, about one-half settled in New York City and at least 20,000 moved to Washington Heights where they made up over 10% of the population.[3]

Such traits of the ex-refugee community today as choice of residence, relative attitudes towards Israel and Germany, affiliation with synagogues and self-description leave little doubt of their self-conception as part of the Jewish community. Nevertheless, the refugee community created its own sub-group which remained socially and institutionally separate from the bulk of American Jews. Though the German Jews tended to concentrate in the same parts of Washington Heights as other Jews, they created their own network of institutions. Only a minority of German Jews joined native congregations for instance; instead a dozen large German synagogues were founded in Washington Heights between 1935 and 1949.[4] In the pre-war and war years Washington

---

[3]The United States Census of April 1940 counts about 22,400 persons born in Germany in Washington Heights and Inwood (then including all of Manhattan north of 159th Street as well as the area west of Amsterdam Avenue between 135th and 159th Streets). In 1950 the number of natives of Germany was slightly higher. A survey of over 2,000 families resident in Washington Heights undertaken by Columbia-Presbyterian Medical Center in 1965 showed 86% of those interviewees born in Germany or Austria to be of the Jewish religion. Besides the Germans there were some 5,000 Austrians and 1,000 Czechs in 1950, many of whom were also refugees of the 1930s.

[4]Synagogues in Washington Heights founded by refugees from Germany included: Shaare Hatikvah, Emes Wozedek, Ahavath Torah, Tikwoh Chadoschoh, K'hall Adath Jeshurun, Beth Hillel, Agudas Jeshorim, Ohav Sholaum, Nodah Biyehudo, Kehillath Yaakov, Sichraun Kedauschim and Beth Israel. All but Nodah Biyehudo followed the German rite. In addition there

Heights had its own German-Jewish cabarets, social and athletic clubs and even an active association of Jewish veterans of the German army (with over 400 members).[5] German Jews in Washington Heights opened their own kosher and non-kosher butchers' shops, created their own kosher supervision networks, and their own charity and self-help groups. In their social life most stuck to their own circle. Feelings of distance and even hostility between them and native Jews were often mutual, and expressed themselves in numerous ways. One particularly striking issue involved the question of language. Most refugees who came to the United States as adults continued to speak German, often in public as well as in private. Even synagogue sermons were held in German well into the 1960s. The newcomers divorced their often hostile feelings towards Germany from their feelings towards their native language which was so interwoven with their personalities. American Jews resented this tie to German for two reasons. On the one hand, the presence of these conspicuous non-English speakers seemed to jeopardise the American status of the native Jews. On the other, the inability of the Germans to speak Yiddish (indeed their ill-disguised contempt for the language) seemed to many American Jews to show how un-Jewish the refugees were. Some even questioned whether the newcomers were really Jews at all.

Relations with German Jews outside Washington Heights were almost as complex as relations with American Jews. Many German-Jewish organisations were city- or even nation-wide and residents of Washington Heights frequently met their compatriots from elsewhere in the city there. Because Washington Heights was a residential area with few facilities for large scale activities, even organisations based in the neighbourhood had to hold social functions in large midtown hotels. Above all the *Aufbau*, largest press organ of the refugees, helped unite the newcomers and announced their weddings, newborn children and deaths to German Jews all over the world. Even in the press there were signs of tension between the Washington Heights community and the bulk of the émigrés. The *Aufbau* rarely referred to Washington Heights in its news columns; its few references sometimes included snide remarks about small-town habits which hurt the position of the new immigrants.[6] However important Washing-

---

were several short-lived German congregations (e.g. Adath Israel) and at least three congregations founded by "native Jews" which had a majority of German members (Hebrew Tabernacle, Washington Heights Congregation and Fort Tryon Jewish Center).

[5]The most ambitious cabaret was Lublo's Palm Garden at 158th Street and Broadway. Social and athletic clubs include the Prospect Unity Club, Maccabi and an uptown branch of the New World Club. The veterans of the German army of the First World War (most of whom presumably had belonged to the *Reichsbund jüdischer Frontsoldaten* in Germany), formed the Immigrant Jewish War Veterans (later known as the Jewish Veterans Association). Of the over 800 members which the JVA had in New York City more than half were in the Washington Heights branch. The papers of the Jewish Veterans Association are in the Leo Baeck Institute Archives in New York.

[6]Such comments were especially common in the early days of the settlement. Characteristic is the following answer to a letter from "157th Street and Broadway" printed in the *Briefkasten* column of *Aufbau* on 15th July 1939: "Sie haben völlig recht. Diese kleinstädtische Angewohnheit vieler unserer Landsleute, die in Plaudergruppen vor Cafeterien und an Ecken herumstehen, ist eine schreckliche Angewohnheit. Der Amerikaner sieht so etwas erst mit Erstaunen dann aber mit Abneigung und den Schaden trägt die Gesamtheit." A later letter to *Aufbau* (3rd May 1940), this

ton Heights was as a refugee population centre many refugees looked down on it as provincial. Retaliation was also not unheard of. The *Jewish Way*, a smaller, less successful competitor to the *Aufbau*, based in Washington Heights, attacked the *Aufbau* as representing Berlin decadence in contrast to its own deep Jewish feeling.[7]

The German-Jewish population of Washington Heights differed from the bulk of refugees in several ways. Whereas the refugees as a whole were noted for their high percentage of professionals, those in Washington Heights had a low percentage (lower than that of native Jews in the neighbourhood).[8] In origin they also differed. Two-thirds of those in Washington Heights came from Southern and Western Germany (as against three-eighths of a general refugee sample). Jews from Berlin who dominated twentieth-century German Jewry made up 22% of the overall refugees but only 8·8% of those in Washington Heights. Whereas small-town Jews played little role in German Jewry in the twentieth century, three-eighths of those in Washington Heights came from towns with 10,000 or fewer inhabitants and only a minority from cities of over 100,000.[9] Besides their heavier rural and Southern component, those in Washington Heights were also more traditionally religious than the refugees as a whole. The arrival of the German Jews strengthened the traditional elements in Washington Heights Jewry. The newcomers showed a high rate of synagogue affiliation (over 5,000 families in Washington Heights refugee congregations alone) and of synagogue attendance (over one-fourth reported weekly attendance in 1960 and almost three-fifths attended at least monthly.)[10] (By contrast only 14% of New York Jewry today attends weekly and 23% monthly).[11] Most of the synagogues founded by refugees in Washington Heights were Orthodox with the rest being traditionally-orientated Conservative. Self-definition was

---

time in English, again criticises immigrants in Washington Heights for congregating in front of stores.

There were some occasions when *Aufbau* did give Washington Heights more extensive and better coverage. One such example is its extensive treatment in various issues in October 1948 of the congressional campaign between Jacob Javits and Paul O'Dwyer under the rubric 'Der Kampf um Washington Heights'.

[7] In an advertisement on 20th August 1944 *The Jewish Way* referred to itself as "die einzige in deutscher Sprache erscheinende ausschliesslich jüdische Zeitung Amerikas" (the only exclusively Jewish newspaper in the German language in America). It goes on to describe its programme in the following terms: "nicht billige Zerstreuung und Sensation, sondern dem zielbewussten Kampf für den jüdischen Glauben, die jüdische Ehre, die jüdischen Rechte, und für die jüdische Zukunft. ... Nicht seichte Erinnerungen an europäische Grosstadt-Dekadenz, sondern die ewigen unsterblichen Kulturwerte des Judentums."

[8] The 1965 survey by Columbia-Presbyterian Medical Center showed only 12·3% of employed male Jews born in Germany or Austria in professional or technical fields as against 15·4% of employed male Jews born in Eastern Europe and 36% of those employed male Jews born in the United States.

[9] These figures are based on a tabulation of all obituaries in the *Aufbau* in 1960. Most such obituaries included both the former hometown of the deceased (e.g. früher Giessen) and the address of the mourners.

[10] *Community Factbook for Washington Heights, New York City*, 1960–1961, Table 6.5 (based on a 1960 survey by Columbia-Presbyterian Medical Center).

[11] 1981 Jewish Population Survey of New York City. This information was graciously made available to me by Professor Paul Ritterband.

less overwhelmingly Orthodox, with the Orthodox being only about one in four, the Conservatives 40%, the Reform 25% and about one in eight unaffiliated,[12] but this still is a far higher proportion of Orthodox and Conservative Jews than the average for Jews in New York.

Though Washington Heights residents were more traditionally Jewish and more petit-bourgeois than the bulk of the 1930s refugees, they shared with their fellow émigrés certain characteristics which distinguished them from other immigrants. They truly were refugees rather than ordinary immigrants because they left their homeland only because of persecution, not mainly to better their economic situation. In fact, like many other refugee groups, they had to accept greatly reduced status, income and living conditions as the price of freedom and safety. With few exceptions the German Jews (even those in Washington Heights) had lived comfortable bourgeois lives in Europe. The new arrivals did everything they could to retain their former status even in their new poverty. Many brought good clothes and furniture even though they arrived penniless. They moved to respectable areas like Washington Heights; the newly-founded immigrant groups helped the newly declassed retain a feeling of what they had been "formerly" – a favourite word in refugee circles.

The native Americans – both Jews and non-Jews – bitterly resented the fact that the refugees were proud of their former status and that they saw some aspects of their former culture as superior to America's. The widespread view of the German refugees as arrogant stems in part from this resentment against criticism by newcomers. Though the refugees were true refugees who might never have left Germany had there been no Hitler, they were not mere exiles like such refugee intellectuals as Bertolt Brecht or Thomas Mann. It quickly became clear to the vast majority of the Jewish refugees that they would never return to Germany. Virtually all quickly acquired American citizenship and identified their political destiny with America. The United States became "die neue Heimat" (the new homeland).

The first ten years of the new colony were marked by great economic hardships and difficulties of adjustment. Finding work was difficult in the last years of the Depression. The patriarchal German family was strained by the increased economic role of women and especially by the financial independence of children. Those who did work often put in long hours at menial jobs, in many cases violating the Jewish Sabbath for the first time.

In addition to these problems typical of many immigrant groups, the refugees (at least in the period up to the establishment of Israel) were obsessed by international developments. Before Pearl Harbor the main agenda was helping relatives to escape from German-occupied Europe and to procure entry to the United States or to other countries. When the United States entered the war the

---

[12] The 1965 Columbia-Presbyterian Medical Center survey shows the following "denominational breakdown" for Jews born in Germany or Austria:

Orthodox	23%
Conservative	41%
Reform	23%
None of the above	12%

community turned to fervent American patriotism, war bond drives, army service and civilian volunteer work. In this wave of patriotism there were both ironic echoes from the German patriotism of the First World War and the need to prove that German Jews were not the "enemy aliens" that many Americans felt them to be. The concern for the fate of relatives mixed with "win the war" sentiment. Then in 1945 the *Aufbau* was filled with obituaries as the dreadful fate of those who had not been able to get out was revealed. In the immediate post-war years concern for the survivors and interest in the "Palestine situation" filled the German-Jewish press.

After 1948 with a Jewish state established, the Washington Heights community could afford to turn inward. Most of the German-Jewish institutions were founded before 1942, but their nature changed drastically after the war as the community entered an era of growing prosperity. Gradually the synagogues emerged as the dominant institutions of the immigrant community, replacing the social and athletic clubs, cafés and places of entertainment which had been more important previously. There are several reasons for the change. First, the young adult generation married and settled down after the war. The frequent dances, soccer games and lectures were no longer so necessary nor did the young couples have much time for them. Clubs and cafés closed or became less active. Meanwhile the congregations which had begun in loft buildings, storefronts or the basements of existing synagogues, acquired enough funds to buy or build their own edifices. Between 1948 and 1960 most German synagogues moved into modern facilities with social halls and classrooms. Functions which were formerly held in neighbourhood halls or clubs could now be held in congregational halls. Social life and entertainment took place to a large extent within the confines of the congregations. The American model of the synagogue as a community centre had both a conscious and unconscious influence in this area.

Economic conditions markedly improved during and after the war. Most families with apartments were able to dispense with taking in boarders to help pay the rent. Most men could give up menial positions and turn to white-collar work, unionised blue-collar jobs or to opening their own businesses. Many, though not all, women were able to give up working outside the home. After initial difficulties most physicians were able to return to practise. Most of the numerous immigrant businesses operating from home were transferred to proper shops.[13] The German-Jewish population began to decrease in the less socially desirable sections of Washington Heights and increase in the wealthier parts. Families could afford to take vacations in the Catskills or at the beach.[14] This slow re-establishment of a decent, if still modest, economic position was aided by two factors – the refugees' strong "German" tradition of thrift and the

---

[13]Much of the refugee press and bulletins of synagogues and organisations before 1945 were filled with advertisements for products and services (including even barbering) available in the "entrepreneur's" apartment. After 1945 these are far outnumbered by businesses in proper rented shops.

[14]The many advertisements in the *Aufbau* for Catskill resorts in the post-war period are characteristic of the amount of refugee clientele for such places. Certain Catskill towns like Fleischmanns were visited predominantly by German Jews.

beginning of reparations and pension payments by the West German government in the late 1950s.

The disappearance of the outside pressures of economic survival and the need to save European relatives enabled the community to turn its attention to the problem of cultural continuity and generational relations. At first virtually all children of the émigrés attended public schools and many had notable success. Later two Jewish day schools founded in 1937 and 1944 began to gain a large following among the more Orthodox of the German Jews.[15] For most families, however, the main formal vehicle for transmission of the parents' heritage was the supplemental Hebrew school complemented by youth groups and youth worship services. All these youth activities were directed to inculcating Judaism with virtually nothing German about them. Except for the large numbers of young people studying German as a foreign language in school, there was almost no formal attempt to cultivate Germanness. Germanness was transmitted mainly by example: manners, foods, attitudes towards music and books, formality and thrift, which the young were expected to emulate though no one ever expressed this explicitly.

Two generations of young people reacted in different ways to the culture of their parents. Those who were born in Germany but educated in the United States broke away from the community in large numbers. Many consciously avoided the clubs, associations and immigrant habits of the community and tried to become "real" Americans. Whereas most of those who came to the United States aged between eighteen to thirty-five married other German Jews and settled in Washington Heights, a large number of those born in the 1920s and 1930s moved out of the neighbourhood at the first opportunity leaving a permanent demographic gap.[16] In contrast to those born in the twenties and thirties were those born after the Second World War. Washington Heights experienced a post-war baby boom similar to that prevalent throughout the United States. Because of a pattern of very late marriage, these children were often thirty-five or even forty-five years younger than their parents. By the 1960s there was a missing generation in the Washington Heights community consisting of those born between the two world wars. This demographic gap

---

[15]Yeshiva Rabbi Moses Soloveitchik was founded in 1937 by Jews of East European origin. By 1958 it had 550 pupils, many of them the children of German-born Jews. Yeshiva Rabbi Samson Raphael Hirsch was founded by the Breuer community in 1944. In 1953 it had only 125 pupils, but by 1969 the Breuer yeshiva system had 950 students, most of them of German-Jewish background.

[16]In 1965 only 14·3% of Jews born in Germany or Austria living in Washington Heights were between the ages of twenty-five and forty-five. The group born in the 1930s was especially small (2·9%). In K'hal Adath Jeshurun, the congregation with the smallest loss of the younger generation, the percentage of heads of household born between 1933 and 1942 (9·8%) was only about one-half of what would have been expected from a comparable United States urban population, while the 21·8% of heads of household born after 1942 was much closer to what would have been expected. (Adolph D. Oppenheim, *Membership Survey on Preferences regarding Relocation, Branch Development, and Preservation of the Washington Heights Area* – presented to the board of directors of K'hal Adath Jeshurun on 26th July 1977. It should be noted that these figures represent percentages of respondents to the survey rather than percentages of the entire membership. Over 52% of members resident in Washington Heights responded to the questionnaire.)

was accentuated by the famous American "generation gap" of the 1960s. In Washington Heights there was only a pale reflection of the intense conflict between politically radical youth and conservative elders so typical of the period, but there was considerable cultural estrangement. The degree and form of this estrangement differed in various sectors of the Washington Heights community. Within some of the Orthodox congregations, the generational conflict took a particularly striking form. While the fall-off in religious practice and outright rejection of the community was less prevalent in such congregations in the 1960s than it had been in the 1940s, there were often direct and heated confrontations about such matters as liturgical style. Many of the young people desired a type of Jewish life more similar to the informal, enthusiastic styles of American Jews of East European origin, while their elders preferred the formalism of German-Jewish traditions. These young people desired to make the community less German (a process already under way as English rapidly replaced German as the official language of the congregations in the 1960s), but they wished to transform the community, not reject it. In the end all but the most Orthodox of those born after 1945 moved out of Washington Heights, but this was probably caused more by economic and social factors and the decline in the social status of the neighbourhood than by a conscious rejection of the Washington Heights community.

In the 1970s the generational conflict receded into the background as the German-Jewish community was faced with the challenge of rapid demographic change. Even as early as the 1950s, Washington Heights was beginning to lose its status as a comfortable middle-class area.[17] In the 1960s a large influx of Hispanic immigrants led to an out-migration of white ethnic groups including Jews from the southern and eastern portions of Washington Heights. In the 1970s this population shift had so intensified that by 1980 Hispanics made up a majority of the Washington Heights population, while German Jews, now numbering only some 10,000, lived mainly in an enclave of middle-class housing near Fort Tryon Park.[18] The "white flight" in Washington Heights was, however, a relatively slow process and German Jews were among the most stable elements in the white population. The slowness of German Jews to move away was partly a function of their high average age (well above sixty-five), the difficulty of finding apartments as cheap as their rent-controlled ones, and the fact that only in Washington Heights could they continue to live in their own cultural milieu.

The Jewish community of Washington Heights which had previously been split on ethnic (German versus American) and religious (Orthodox versus non-Orthodox, anti-Zionist Orthodox versus pro-Zionist Orthodox) lines, now mobilised, using both German traditions of efficient administration and

---

[17]In 1951 Stock already referred to Washington Heights in terms of "at the moment somewhat shabby – gentility" (p. 583) and a 1954 study by the Protestant Council of the City of New York (*Upper Manhattan – A Communal Study of Washington Heights*) refers to the neighbourhood as a "downhill residential area" (p. 2).

[18]See the census figures for 1960, 1970 and 1980. In 1980 all but some 53,000 of the 176,000 residents of Manhattan north of 158th Street were either Blacks or Hispanics.

American traditions of political mobilisation and social service. Spearheaded by the fifteen hundred member, extremely Orthodox, Breuer congregation,[19] the Jews of Washington Heights formed a community council, set up a car patrol, organised a referral system for social needs, helped settle Soviet Jewish immigrants in the neighbourhood, and purchased and rehabilitated apartment buildings. Representatives of the community sat on the local planning board; despite the fact that by the 1970s there were few Jewish children in local public schools, the synagogues mobilised Jewish voters to choose a Jewish voting list for the local school board, a list whose influence has remained decisive.[20] All of these efforts were intended to keep whatever Jewish influence remained in the area. Despite the fact that the main commercial streets now have an overwhelmingly Hispanic imprint, a considerable Jewish population remains.

In the course of time the traditionalist nature of the German-Jewish community of Washington Heights has been accentuated. Today the Orthodox element, especially the Breuer community, plays a predominant role even though its members are far from the majority. If Washington Heights' German Jews were more traditionally Jewish than other refugees from the start, this contrast has become more striking in recent years.

The concerns of German Jews in Washington Heights today are very much the same as those of other white ethnic groups, especially Jews, in the United States. The tie to and concern with Germany and with the long history of Jews in Germany is very much attenuated. The American-born descendents of the German Jews are rapidly merging into American Jewry and there is little reason to believe that German Jews will preserve a cultural subgroup similar to that of Sephardic Jews.[21]

A look at the Washington Heights community can help give perspectives both on the nature of German Jewry and on the nature of the American

---

[19]The Breuer congregation (K'hal Adath Jeshurun) is the direct descendant of the separatist Orthodox congregation founded in Frankfurt a. Main in the nineteenth century. The dominant rabbinic figure of the Frankfurt congregation in the nineteenth century was Samson Raphael Hirsch, the leading theorist of separatist "Neo-Orthodoxy". His grandson, Joseph Breuer, was the founding rabbi and spiritual leader of K'hal Adath Jeshurun in Washington Heights from 1939 until his death (at the age of ninety-eight) in 1980. For a good thumbnail sketch on the Breuer community see Charles Liebman's article, 'Orthodoxy in American Jewish Life', in the 1965 *American Jewish Yearbook*.

[20]Concerning the struggles over the local school board and the mobilisation of Washington Heights Jews to keep a strong influence see Ira Katznelson, *City Trenches, Urban Politics and the Patterning of Class in the United States*, New York 1981, pp. 154–176.

Activities of the community council are well-illustrated by a beautifully printed 29-page brochure put out by the Jewish Community Council – Preservation and Restoration Corporation – Washington Heights – Inwood, entitled *Directory of Programs and Services* which dates to the early 1980s. On the car patrol see, Yehuda Schorscher, 'The Kehilla – a community stabilizer', *Jewish Observer*, vol. 8, No. 7 (September 1972), pp. 19–21.

[21]Among the older generation there are two different models of the kind of German-Jewish culture they would like to pass on to their children. If one speaks to one group, one hears references to love of literature, music and general culture; if one talks to the other, one hears of Jewish liturgical customs specific to Germany ("our *minhagim*") and to a style of celebrating the Jewish holidays. Each model represents a different picture of German-Jewish culture. Outside Washington Heights the first model predominates; in Washington Heights the two models are more evenly balanced, with the second gaining in influence.

immigrant experience. First, the Washington Heights case forces a re-evaluation of the traditional stereotype of German Jews as assimilated and more German than Jewish. The German Jews of Washington Heights were certainly as Jewish-minded as American Jews, though their Jewishness might be expressed in a different way. Second we see that even a group which prided itself on its modernity and on its cultural (though not religious) identification with the host nation, could, in the American context, act very much like other ethnic groups. Despite certain advantages given by their previous experience in an advanced Western culture, German Jews in America were still "outlandish" and "in need of Americanisation". Earlier arrival in America, from no matter what cultural background, was still more prestigious than foreignness no matter what its former status. German Jews in America had an adaptation process somewhat different from that of most immigrants, since it involved not only adapting to America but also to American Jewry specifically. Finally Washington Heights shows us that an immigrant neighbourhood is by nature the home of the most "ethnic" of the newcomers and may not be typical of the immigrant group as a whole. Even in other ethnic groups where a larger percentage lived in ethnic enclaves, those outside them may have been quite different. A look at those both inside and outside the enclave is needed to assess the immigrant group as a whole. In the German-Jewish case we can see how a look at the main German-Jewish neighbourhood provides an important corrective to a one-sided picture gained by exclusive concentration on an impressive but equally unrepresentative elite.

The Impact of Holocaust Survivors on American Society: A Socio-Cultural Portrait

WILLIAM B. HELMREICH

Introduction

> Their battered suitcases, rolled-up blankets, and other personal belongings, which they held on to during frightful years of captivity or semi-slavery, tell endlesss stories of human suffering ... Reporters aboard the SS Marine Flasher tell us how these passengers, instead of breaking down as a result of their past tribulations, were very active and cheerful throughout the journey. Many volunteered to do odd jobs; a group of orphaned youths helped the short-handed kitchen staff. A barber clipped the hair of the officers.[1]

THUS BEGINS ONE OF THE FIRST ACCOUNTS of the 176,500 Holocaust survivors who came to the United States and Canada in the years 1945 to 1953.[2] There is an almost bouyant quality to some of these early descriptions. Indeed, the immigrants are sometimes described by proponents of immigration eager to garner sympathy for the refugees as "pioneers", emulating America's earlier arrivals. On the other hand, the social work journals tell a somewhat different story. They write of immigrants who had difficulty adapting to the relatives and friends who welcomed them into their homes, and the struggle to find adequate housing and decent jobs.[3] Similarly, the psychiatric

---

1. Alfred Werner, "The New Refugees," *Jewish Frontier*, (July 1946):23.
2. *Kurt Grossman Mss.*, Box 55, Folder 9, "Third Annual Report: New York Association for New Americans Inc." (New York: Leo Baeck Institute); *Council of Jewish Federation and Welfare Funds Papers: Agency Files*, Box 148, "USNA Correspondence Misc., 1944-1955, Budget Reports" (Waltham, Mass.: American Jewish Historical Society); Joseph Kage, "Canadian Immigrants ... Facts, Figures and Trends," *Rescue*, (Fall 1953):5. The number of immigrants to the United States was about 140,000, while the number who entered Canada was approximately 36,500, including 2,000 who came in 1953.
3. See, for example, Beatrice Frankel and Ruth Michaels, "A Changing Focus in Work With Young, Unattached DPs," *Journal of Jewish Communal Service*, 27 (March 1951):321-331; Fred Berl, "The Immigrant Situation as Focus of the Helping Process," *Jewish Social Service Quarterly* 26 (March 1950):377-392; Sidney S. Eisenberg, "Phases in the Resettlement Process and Their Significance for Casework With New Americans," *Jewish Social Service Quarterly* 27 (September 1950):86-96.

WILLIAM B. HELMREICH *is Professor of sociology and Jewish studies at City College of New York and at CUNY Graduate Center.*

Originally published in *Judaism* (Winter 1990). Reprinted by permission of the American Jewish Committee.

literature presents cases of individuals who experienced anxiety, depression and paranoia, often lumping their diagnosis under the now common term, "concentration camp survivor syndrome."[4]

What, in fact, really happened to the survivors in the last forty years? How did they fare in their efforts to start over? How did they do economically? What about their family lives and, in particular, their children? Did those who came in their youth begin new careers or attend universities in any appreciable numbers? What were the contributions of these refugees to American life and to the Jewish communities in which they settled?

There has been very little written about these questions because, until now, the emphasis has been on the pathology of the survivors, their psychological problems and, to a lesser but still considerable extent, their physical ailments.[5] This is due largely to the fact that it is those with the most serious problems who, so far, have come to the attention of psychiatrists, psychologists and social workers. The successful or unsuccessful treatment of these individuals was then written up and published in journals.

Unfortunately, we do not know how representative these cases are of the average survivors who did not request therapy, and those constitute the vast majority of survivors. No doubt there were many survivors who needed treatment and never received it, many who suffered nightmares for years and accepted them as part of the survivor's burden. Nevertheless, we cannot establish patterns from which generalizations can be drawn until we have truly random samples made up of non-clinical groups of survivors. In short, we need a "sociology of the survivor community" that will complement the already significant contributions made by the therapists. Only in this way will we be able to understand the survivors as a whole.[6] What follows in these pages is

---

4. See, for instance, William G. Niederland, "Clinical Observations on the Survivor Syndrome," *International Journal of Psychoanalysis*, 49 (1968):313-315; M.A. Berezin, "The Aging Survivor of the Holocaust. Introduction," *Journal of Geriatric Psychiatry* 14, No. 2 (1981):131-133; G. Bychowski, Permanent Character Changes as an Aftereffect of Persecution," in H. Krystal, ed., *Massive Psychic Trauma* (New York: International Universities Press, 1968), pp.75-86; Bruno Bettelheim, *Surviving and Other Essays* (New York: Knopf, 1979).

5. See P. Chodoff, "Effects of Extreme Coercive and Oppressive Forces: Brainwashing and Concentration Camps" in S. Arieti, ed., *American Handbook of Psychiatry* (New York: Basic books, 1959), pp. 384-405; T. S.Nathan, L. Eitinger, and H. Z. Winnnik, "A Psychiatric Study of Survivors of the Nazi Holocaust; A Study of Hospitalized Patients," *Israel Annual of Psychiatry and Related Disciplines* 2, No. 1 (1964):47-80; Shamai Davidson, "The Clinical Effects of Massive Psychic Trauma in Families of Holocaust Survivors," *Journal of Marriage and Family Therapy* 6, No. 1 (1980): 11-21; V.M. Morosow, "Late Sequelae in Former Deportees and Concentration Camp Survivors," *Journal of Neuropathology and Psychiatry* 58, No. 3 (1958):373-380; H. Krystal, ed., *Massive Psychic Trauma*.

6. An exception is Morton Weinfeld, John J. Sigal, William W. Eaton, "Long Term Effects of the Holocaust on Selected Social Attitudes and Behaviors of Survivors: A Cautionary

a beginning effort to answer the sociological question of what the survivors achieved as a group in the United States.

Arrival in America

In the years between 1945 and 1952, hundreds of ships carrying thousands of refugees traversed the route between Europe, usually Bremerhaven, Germany, and various American ports, most often New York and Boston. Specifically, between October 30, 1948 and July 21, 1952, 308 ships (as well as 284 planes) arrived, bringing almost 400,000 Jews and Gentiles to the U.S.[7] The passengers' fare was often advanced by either the Hebrew Immigrant Aid Society (HIAS) or the United Service for New Americans (USNA). The boats, like the Uruguay, Marine Perch, Marine Jumper, New Hellas, General McRae, General Muir, and the Marine Marlin, were actually U.S. Army transport ships that had been pressed into service after extensive duty during the war.

The accommodations were scarcely luxurious. As Willie Herskovits, a passenger on the Ernie Pyle, who is currently living in Brooklyn, N.Y., described it:

> The boat left from Bremerhaven. But for three months there was a strike. It took us thirteen days and cost $225.00 each for me and my wife. There were maybe 1,000 people on the boat and they were, I think, all Jewish. There were about 200 people to a room and three beds, one on top of the others.[8]

There were no planned activities for the passengers. The small library was usually used as a meeting place where people discussed what they would do once they arrived in America, the occupations that they would enter, and the friends and relatives who would assist them. The majority suffered from seasickness, and many recall spending a good portion of the trip lying in bed. Nevertheless, their discomfort was soon forgotten once the trip ended. Luba Bat, the niece of American labor leader Sidney Hillman, was one of those passengers. Looking out from the deck of the SS Uruguay in 1946 as it steamed into New York's harbor, she observed: "The sight of the grandiose skyscrapers fascinated me; in Poland we called them 'cloud scratchers.'" Her aunt, Bessie Hillman, asked Luba to smile for the photographers as she alighted from the ship. "Why smile?" she asked. "Don't ask *kashes* (questions)," retorted Hillman. "Just smile; this is America."[9]

In most cases, the immigrants were met by representatives of HIAS,

---

Note," *Social Forces* 60 (1981): 1-19. See also, Jack Nusan Porter, "Is There a Survivor Syndrome?: Psychological and Sociological Implications," *Journal of Psychology and Judaism*, No. 1 (1981):33-52.

7. *Memo to America. The DP Story: The Final Report of the U.S. Displaced Persons Commission* (Washington D.C.: U. S. Government Printing Office, 1952).
8. Interview, December 30, 1987.
9. Luba Bat, *Phoenix* (Yad Vashem Archives, n.d.), mimeograph, n.p.

who guided them through customs. These individuals were generally fluent in several languages, including Yiddish, and were trained to deal with a variety of problems that could, and did, come up after the passengers disembarked. Among them might be having an ambulance at the dock for anyone who required hospitalization because of illness that had developed during the trip, serving as interpreter to immigration officials, cutting through red tape so that an immigrant could get on the train bound for St. Louis where he would be met by anxious relatives, and the like. [10]

Resettlement of the Immigrants

The majority of immigrants remained in the New York area, but sizeable numbers of refugees took up residence elsewhere. By the end of July, 1949, arrivals under the 1948 Displaced Persons (DP) Act had been settled in 334 communities in 43 states. HIAS had offices in Boston, Philadelphia, Washington D.C., Chicago, San Francisco, Seattle, and Baltimore. According to the Council of Jewish Federations, family agencies in Newark, St. Louis, Kansas City, Milwaukee, Minneapolis, Oakland, Portland, Oregon, and St. Paul, reported that, in 1948, one-half or more of their caseloads were immigrants.[11]

These figures are important in terms of understanding the contributions of the survivors. What they mean is that the survivors came into contact with a broad cross-section of the American population. They did not settle only in Jewish ghettos. Moreover, those who went elsewhere were forced to interact with others who knew little about their culture and experiences. Indeed, survivors who settled outside of the major Jewish population centers often prided themselves on having become more Americanized than those who did not. One such individual, a resident of Minneapolis, recounted how, after 40 years, she had little in common with survivors who had remained in New York and still thought like "greeners."[12]

In many, perhaps the majority, of instances, refugees settled outside of the New York area at the urging of HIAS, which frequently made the arrangements with their new communities while the refugees were still in the DP camps. In part, this was motivated by a desire to dispel the stereotype that Jews were capable of dwelling only in urban ghettos. There was also the feeling that the immigrants would assimilate faster in places with small Jewish populations.[13]

---

10. Jack Shafer, "HIAS Pier Representatives Welcome Immigrants Here," *Rescue*, (January 1947):4-5.
11. Morris Zelditch, "Immigrant Aid," *American Jewish Yearbook, 1950*, vol.51 (Philadelphia: Jewish Publication Society, 1950), pp. 195,198.
12. Interview, Hinda Kibort, February 25, 1988.
13. Leonard Dinnerstein, *America and the Survivors of the Holocaust* (New York: Columbia University Press, 1982), p. 203.

18 : *Judaism*

Quite a few (how many is not known) immigrants eventually drifted back to major Jewish communities because the adjustment was too difficult in outlying locales. Some, however, found that life in the hinterlands could be appealing. One couple decided that they would stay only one month in the small Texas community of McAllen, to which they had been sent by the resettlement agency, but, much to their surprise, they fell in love with the town and remained: "McAllen had, in short, captivated [the wife] . . . drawn her deeply into its small-town life and ways. The kindness of the people! The warmth they had shown so unstintingly."[14] Another immigrant explained her decision to move to Kansas City as follows:

> I believe they were overcrowded, those states, so we just picked Kansas City. We took the map and we looked at it and we said, the President of the United States (Truman) comes from Missouri. From Independence, but that is close to Kansas City. We took the heart of America and came here.[15]

Among the arrivals were more than 1,000 survivors who became farmers and settled in places like Vineland, New Jersey, Petaluma, California and Danielson, Connecticut. In many cases, the farmers were helped by the Jewish Colonization Association. For example, the Association placed nineteen families of immigrants in the Niagara Peninsula of Ontario, where they established fruit and dairy farms.[16] The Jewish Agricultural Society, which also assisted the immigrants, organized educational and cultural activities to aid the recent arrivals, with talks on purchasing and marketing, poultry medicine, and related topics.[17] These were necessary since many of the refugees had had no experience in farming but had chosen this way of life because they wanted an environment away from the city, with clean air and quiet. In fact, an occupational survey of Jews in European DP assembly centers found that only 2.8% could be classified as being in farm-related activities.[18]

Other survivors were sent to American universities, where, under the sponsorship of the B'nai B'rith Hillel Foundation, many of them made good use of their educational opportunities and became successful professionals. Typical was Eugene Schoenfeld, who studied at Washington University in St. Louis and later became Chairman of the So-

---
14. Dorothy Rabinowitz, *New Lives: Survivors of the Holocaust Living in America* (New York: Avon, 1976), p. 125.
15. Helen Epstein, *A Study in American Pluralism Through Oral Histories of Holocaust Survivors* (New York: William E. Weiner Oral History Library of the American Jewish Committee, 1975) (report).
16. Theodore Norman, *An Outstretched Hand: A History of the Jewish Colonization Association* (London: Routledge & Kegan Paul, 1985), p. 246.
17. Joseph Brandes, *Immigrants to Freedom: Jewish Communities in Rural New Jersey Since 1982* (Philadelphia: Jewish Publication Society, 1971), p. 329.
18. Dinnerstein, *America and the Survivors*, p. 278.

ciology Department at Georgia State University. Another survivor studied at the University of Washington in Seattle and became a successful painter.[19]

Working in America

Knowing the type of work engaged in by the immigrants is of value in assessing the contributions that they ultimately made. We can say, at the onset, that they were handicapped in several ways. First, in most cases, their experiences during the war had tremendously weakened them, and the majority were still recovering, both physically and psychologically, when they arrived in the United States. Second, they spoke little or no English, and were unfamiliar with American culture and ways. How unfamiliar can be discerned from the vignette of a survivor who tells how he arrived in Boston and was told to travel by train to Philadelphia where arrangements had been made for him to work and live. He protested to the agency official in charge that he had relatives in New York City. When told that he could visit them on weekends, he asked how this could be arranged if he had no pass or special privilege allowing him to travel from Philadelphia to New York! He was both amazed and relieved when informed that, in America, no such permission was required.[20]

Most of the immigrants who came here were between the ages of fifteen and thirty-five and were the ones who were most likely to have survived the rigors and hardships of the war. Many of them had been compelled to interrupt their education and training and, thus, were at a disadvantage when it came to starting over in a new land. In addition, the occupations for which they had been trained were not always in demand here. In some professions, such as law, their training was not considered valid or relevant. Added to these problems were the normal ones of adjustment that face all immigrants.

The evidence that we have suggests that the refugees made strenuous, often heroic, efforts to overcome these deficiencies. The resilience and survival skills that they had demonstrated during the war were often transferred to the American scene. Typical of such efforts was the case of Edward Goodman, a resident of St. Paul, Minnesota:

> When I came here I tried to get a job in international trade — like what I was doing in Czechoslovakia. And so I went to all the big companies ... who had an international department. Went to Minnesota Mining, to Cargill, General Mills, Pillsbury, Honeywell. Everybody was very nice ... It's wonderful. Wonderful experience. We'll hire you ... I worked with an agency downtown and they told me, "Ed, there isn't a single Jew working in these companies," and they say "You'll never get a job

---
19. Sylvia Rothchild, ed., *Voices from the Holocaust* (New York: Meridian, 1982), pp. 314-321.
20. Interview, Willie Lieberman, January 6, 1988.

there. You might as well forget it." That was the end of my looking for an affluent career in the United States.[21]

But it was by no means the end for Goodman. It was only the beginning, for, as he recalls: "I was hungry and we had nothing to live on. And I looked for a job high and low. That was in 1948 and there was big unemployment in the United States." Finally, the Jewish Family Service found a job for him — making sandwiches during the graveyard shift in a restaurant called Hasty Tasty. We see here not only the difficulties, but the perseverance that was required, perseverance that did not, as the following account indicates, always pay off:

> They asked me if I am a cook. In fact the only thing I knew how to cook is hot water. But I was making sandwiches and hamburgers and they promoted me the third night to make waffles, and that was my downfall. Was a very busy Friday night, and I forgot to take the waffle out — smoked up the place, lost their customers. They picked me up and they kicked me out so fast they say I should never come back.[22]

In her book, *New Lives,* Dorothy Rabinowitz asserts that "survivors in considerable numbers involved themselves in building and construction careers — immensely successful ones, as it turned out, for some of them."[23] As an example she mentions the Shapell brothers, who survived Auschwitz and who, in this country, became leading manufacturers of prefabricated houses. Although more empirical research is needed, there seems to have been a trend among the survivors to enter occupations where they could be independent. One could speculate that their experiences had made them reluctant to put themselves in a position where others could determine their fate. The initiative required of them, and the risks that they took, were also rooted in their experiences. They were people who had often literally returned from the dead and, therefore, felt that they had little to lose.

In an effort to determine these and other behavioral patterns, 236 oral histories on deposit at Yad Vashem were analyzed. The tapes had been made by survivors who attended the 1981 World Gathering of Holocaust Survivors held in Jerusalem.[24] From them, it would appear that the survivors preferred to operate independently, irrespective of their income level. Here are some instances:

---

21. Minnesota Oral History Archives, Jewish Community Relations Council, Minneapolis.
22. Ibid.
23. Rabinowitz, *New Lives,* p. 19. This is actually the only book-length treatment of post-Holocaust survivors that does not focus exclusively on pathology. Well written and insightful as it is, it is, nonetheless, based on a small, non-random group of survivors. It makes no claim to scientific validity but is, instead, written from a journalistic perspective.
24. For more on the attitudes of these people, see William B. Helmreich, "Research Report: Postwar Adaptation of Holocaust Survivors in the U.S.A.," *Holocaust and Genocide Studies* 2, No. 2:307-315.

So we went to Hartford and there was a *landsman* who owned a fruit store that I met. And he was a son of a bitch; he used me up ... He paid me $42.00 a week. I worked seven weeks. He was a very bad guy ... Then I went to work for myself as a roofer and four years later I got a house that I built for myself.[25]

So we came to Cleveland ... where my sponsor lived. I got a job raking and cleaning on a golf course ... Then, when the golf season ended I got a job as a plasterer. Then I worked as a cabinetmaker. Twelve years ago I went out on my own in draperies.[26]

When I came to America in Richmond in 1947 I decided to open up a service station. Since I saw America as a land on wheels I decided the future for service station is good. Then I went into the auto parts business. Now I have two stores and 28 people working for me.[27]

In 1981 the Federation of Jewish Philanthropies/United Jewish Appeal, under the direction of the sociologists Paul Ritterband and Steven M. Cohen, conducted the largest survey, so far, of Diaspora Jewry. Included in the sample are 112 Holocaust survivors plus about 100 respondents whose spouses were survivors, making it one of the only truly random, nonclinical samples of such individuals.

One question that is of interest is the income level of survivors. A popular stereotype about survivors, among both Jews and Gentiles, is that they have done very well financially when compared to other Jews. Statistics show that this is not the case. However, when one considers the disadvantages which so many survivors had to overcome, their income level assumes even greater significance.

Giving in America

A comparison of contributions to charity, irrespective of its Jewish or non-Jewish nature, between survivors and non-survivors, revealed no significant differences among those who contribute less than $2000 a year. However, among those who donated more than $2,000 annually, survivors outnumbered non-survivors by better than two to one. The differences between the two groups are even more interesting when one examines specific charities. Survivors are more likely to contribute to the Red Cross than are non-survivors, but less likely to give to other medical causes. Why this is so is a matter of speculation. Survivors are less likely than non-survivors to support the arts and other cultural activities. Perhaps this is because the survivors are less assimilated and, hence, less apt to give to non-Jewish activities. There is some support for this hypothesis when we evaluate their contributions to Jewish causes. Both groups contribute equally to the United Jewish Appeal, but their patterns of giving diverge sharply when other Jewish causes

---

25. Abraham Jacubowski, *Yad Vashem Archives* (YV), 26a.
26. Jacob Hennenberg, YV, 195a.
27. Israel Ipson, YV, 371.

are considered. Survivors are considerably more likely to give money to other, Israel-related causes than are non-survivors. They are also more than twice as likely to contribute to local Jewish schools. In part, this may be due to their overrepresentation among the Orthodox segment of the Jewish population. Still, this cannot be the only reason, since the survivors give substantially more than do non-survivors to Jewish causes of all types.[28]

The qualitative research on this question supports the figures given here. The oral histories on file at the American Jewish Committee [29] and the Yad Vashem tapes contain many statements about the pride felt by the survivors regarding their financial support of Jewish causes and, in particular, Israel. Writing about the work of the immigrant organization in Vineland, New Jersey, known as the Jewish Poultry Farmer's Association (JPFA), one observer noted:

> Who would think of a UJA Drive or a JNF Drive without participation of the JPFA. They not only contributed their proportionate share of money in these drives, but banded manpower, leg work and officers to further the projects.[30]

Involvement in Communal Life

In an article that appeared in *Commentary* in 1955, Nathan Glazer discussed at length the Jewish revival in America. The Holocaust and Zionism were, in his view, unimportant factors in this revival, especially when compared to Jewish migration to the suburbs.[31] There is evidence, however, that, even in the 1950s, Holocaust survivors were involved in Jewish affairs, especially with respect to Israel and the Holocaust. Their involvement in fund-raising for Jewish charities in Baltimore was widely praised by community leaders there who cited it as "an exemplary display of their integration into the community ... They have done honor unto Baltimore and honor unto themselves."[32]

The farming communities in which the survivors settled, because they were insular and cohesive, enable us to assess more fully the contributions of the immigrants. In some of the South Jersey locales, like Vineland, the Jews had already been there for some time. In others, like Danielson, Connecticut, they founded new communities. In both instances, the survivors brought with them a desire to preserve Jewish culture and in so doing they raised the level of Jewish consciousness

---

28. A full assessment of the extent of survivors' contributions in relation to their income is currently under way.
29. Wiener Oral History Collection.
30. I. Harry Levin, "Vineland — A Haven for Refugees," *The Jewish Poultry Farmers Association of South Jersey, 10th Anniversary Journal,* 1962:5.
31. Nathan Glazer, "The Jewish Revival in America: I," *Commentary* 20 No. 6 (December 1955):493-499.
32. "Baltimore Newcomers Group Participates in Campaign," *Rescue,* (April-May 1951):5.

to new heights. In some cases, the influx of refugees prevented these communities from dying out entirely, especially in California.[33]

> Here was a real Yiddish life transplanted from Eastern Europe to our shores. Many of our so-called "Native American Jews" had almost forgotten what a Yiddish word was, a Jewish play, a Yiddish concert. The group activities from the very beginning created actually a new Yiddish culture era in Vineland Jewish history ... Some are actively engaged in the work of the Poale Zion, the General Zionist group, Mizrachi, and Hadassah ... Their cultural activities in celebrating our Jewish holidays are something to talk about. It brings back that nostalgic feeling ..., the real side of Jewish life.[34]

There is a perception that interest in commemorating the Holocaust really began to grow after the Eichmann trial. Perhaps; but it is equally clear that the survivors themselves were memorializing the Holocaust almost from the time they arrived in the United States. In an article that appeared in *Der Yiddishe Farmer*, the writer speaks about guilt feelings resulting from leading a happy, contented life while others are dead. Readers are reminded that the Holocaust martyrs had exhorted their fellow Jews: "Don't forget us! Tell the world! Take revenge."[35]

The activities of these communities have been preserved through journals and books written about them, but more research needs to be done on the survivor communities elsewhere. Still, there is no reason to believe that survivors living in New York and in other parts of the country were any less vigilant in remembering the past. Interviews now being done suggest that it was through the *landsmannschaften* that the Holocaust experiences were shared and recalled. All of the major cities in the United States with substantial survivor populations had "Newcomer" organizations, in addition to the *landsmannschaften*, and these served as bridges between the old culture and the new.[36] In 1955, for example, over 300 persons attended a Warsaw Ghetto memorial service at the YMHA Club in Newark, New Jersey. That city was home to an organization founded May 21, 1955 and known as the Association of European Refugees of New Jersey. Its goals included support for Israel, Jewish education, recreational activities, and charitable causes.

---

33. For more information on this process, see Jacob M. Maze, "Petaluma — Oldest Jewish Farm Settlement in California," *The Jewish Farmer*, (September 1957):121; Benjamin Miller, "Jewish Farmers in Connecticut," *The Jewish Farmer*, (May 1958):77-81; Shlomo Zecktser, "*Der Neier Yiddisher Yishuv in Danielson, Connecticut*" (The New Jewish Settlement in Danielson, Connecticut), *Der Yiddisher Farmer*, (May 1958):96 (Yiddish); Shaul Yurista, "*Erste Shritt*" (First Steps), *The Jewish Poultry Farmers Association of South Jersey, 10th Anniversary Journal*, 1962:47 (Yiddish).
34. Levin, *Vineland*, 1962.
35. Breina Goldman, "*Zum 14ter Yizkor Tog Nuch Unzere Kedoishim*" (On the 14th Remembrance Day of Our Martyrs), *Der Yiddisher Farmer*, (June 1957):90 (Yiddish).
36. Interview with Willie Herskovits, December 30, 1987; also, correspondence with Professor Hannah Kliger who is conducting research on *landsmannschaften* in the United States.

It also organized trips to the Farband Unser Camp in Highland Mills, New York, where boating and swimming were available. Kosher food was served and theatrical performances were presented.[37] All of this suggests a rich cultural life that undoubtedly had a profound effect on other members of the larger Jewish communities in which they lived.

Strong support for Israel is another characteristic that distinguishes the survivor community and this must be seen in the context of general Jewish support for Israel among American Jews. Fifty percent of American Jews do not contribute money to Israel, and at least three in five Jews have never visited Israel.[38] Statistics demonstrate conclusively that, even in New York, where Jewish support for Israel has traditionally been quite strong, the involvement of survivors is greater than that of the average New York Jewish resident. Survivors are also far more likely to have visited Israel than non-survivors, but one visit is not especially significant, it can be argued, because, for the most part, it does not represent a real commitment. People may go to celebrate a child's *bar* or *bat mizvah;* they may travel to Israel as part of an organization-sponsored activity. True commitment can more readily be judged when people visit the country more than once. Survivors are *more than three times as likely* as non-survivors to have visited Israel at least twice. This suggests a continuing and deeply felt involvement with the State. It can be safely assumed that such individuals are also likely to be more involved with Israel-related activities in the United States and that they make contributions in varying ways toward enriching Jewish life. Although the analysis is still incomplete, available data seem to indicate that survivors are considerably more apt to belong to Jewish organizations of all sorts than are non-survivors.[39] If so, this would further substantiate the argument that survivors have had a major impact on Jewish life in America.

The Children of Survivors

A community is often measured by what happens to its children. Do they identify with the culture? How successful are they in their own lives? As in the case of survivor studies, much of the literature has focused on pathology.[40] The validity of these studies in terms of

37. Josef Butterman, *Jewish Displaced Persons in Germany and in the United States of America, 1945-1960: A Report* (New York, 1960), available at Yad Vashem.
38. William B. Helmreich, "Misguided Optimism," *Midstream,* (January 1988):31.
39. Based on preliminary results made available through the North American Jewish Data Bank, City University of New York.
40. S. Rustin, *Guilt, Hostility and Jewish Identification Among Adolescent Children of Concentration Camp Survivors,* Unpublished PhD. Dissertation (New York University, 1971); Judith Kestenberg, "Psychoanalytic Contributions to the Problem of Children of Survivors from Nazi Persecution," *Israel Annals of Psychiatry and Related Disciplines,* 10, No. 4

generalizations can be challenged on the grounds that the samples are small, are not random, and are drawn from clinical populations, namely, those who have sought help. In any event, these researchers have rarely dealt with the question of achievement among children of survivors.

One exception to this pattern is the work of Helen Epstein, who, in a report prepared for the American Jewish Committee, notes that 85 percent of the survivors who were interviewed were married, more than half of their children were students, and 23 percent of their children had entered the professions.[41] She estimates that there are about 500,000 children of survivors alive today, and she describes them as largely middle-class and college-educated.[42]

Until more systematic research is conducted it will be impossible to evaluate fully the contributions of the survivors' children, but it can be stated that, simply by having children, the survivors contributed to the continuity of the Jewish community. They did not take the position that the world was too horrible a place in which to raise children. Commenting on this, Steven Riskin, a rabbi currently living in Israel, said: "What makes Jews remarkable is not that they believe in God after Auschwitz, but that they have children after Auschwitz; that they affirm life and the future."[43] Generally speaking, when survivors are asked what achievement they take the greatest pride in, they reply: "My children [and grandchildren]."

The psychological literature discusses at great length the various problems that can, and do, afflict children of survivors. Included in these are anxiety, depression, hostility, and shame. Some children learn to cope with these feelings better than others, but the experiences of the parents affect almost all children in one way or another. In a recent novel, Barbara Finkelstein discusses the problem with great insight. She notes that there exists a paradox in that the survivors are frequently seen by their children as all-powerful, even indestructible, people who "made it through hell," notwithstanding the nightmares and paranoia from which they subsequently suffered. What is important is that *they made it.* On the other hand, in their ill-fitting clothes, short physical stature, foreign accents, and discomfort as immigrants to a new culture, they seem frail and weak. "How did these *schleppers* ever make it?," wonders the child of such a family. "Were they once strong and self-confident?"[44] For a child searching for a role model, these are difficult matters to sort out. And, yet, it is precisely because children of survivors

---

(1972):311-325; Hillel Klein. "Families of Survivors in the Kibbutz: Psychological Studies," in H. Krystal and W. Niederland, eds. *Psychic Traumatization* (Boston: Little Brown, 1971).
41. Epstein, *Study in American Pluralism*, pp. 11-12.
42. Helen Epstein, *Children of the Holocaust* (New York: Bantam, 1980), pp. 178-179.
43. Address at *Israel Center,* Jerusalem, April 25, 1987.
44. Barbara Finkelstein, *Summer Long-a-Coming* (New York: Harper & Row, 1987), p. 247.

must carry such burdens with them that they have the opportunity, through heightened sensitivity and awareness, to make others understand such issues. Future studies will more properly evaluate the processes and dynamics that are involved here. In the meantime, it is possible to comment on the effect that the survivors themselves have had on making the larger society aware of their own unique experiences.

A Moral Legacy

Until now we have been speaking of the effect of the survivor on the Jewish community, but, with respect to the issue of morality and values, the survivors' impact extends to the Christian community also. Every time that survivors speak to classes of students or participate in a community forum, they contribute to an awareness of the meaning of the Holocaust. No one has as yet counted the number of such events, but there have surely been thousands of them. Every such encounter, every life touched, represents a contribution made by the survivors towards ensuring that a Holocaust will not happen again. It is both their self-imposed duty and their opportunity to serve as the world's conscience as long as they are alive and, to the degree that they succeed in this endeavor, they affect the course of history.

Inasmuch as the survivors tend to see everything through the prism of their unique background, they influence society's thinking in other ways, too. The analysis of the Yad Vashem tapes reveals a heightened concern for the rights of *all* minorities among the survivors. One says:

> We live in a small world. We cannot afford to let anyone suffer. When the air is destroyed we all breathe it ... if the Jewish people or any other people are treated badly, we are all in for a bad time. If anything happens to one group of people, all the other minorities should stand up for them.[45]

Whether this feeling is true of survivors in general awaits further study. Still, wherever and whenever such views are expressed, they demonstrate an ability to extrapolate from personal experiences in a way that enhances the general good.

Other ways of thinking predicated on Holocaust experiences also emerge in the Yad Vashem tapes. One woman expressed her sympathy for both the hostages in Iran and the returning Vietnam War veterans in this way: "I feel a lot for the Vietnam soldiers. When I came back from the war, nobody cared if I lived or died."[46] Along with several others, she expressed the deep fears that the Watergate trials aroused:

> I watched Watergate. It's almost identical to Germany. Haldeman and Erlichman. They were of German descent. It's all loyalty. They say you have to lie. And the hush money. That was always going on in Germany.

---
45. Sam Harris, YV, 10; Rabinowitz, *New Lives*, p. 108.
46. Rose Murra, YV, 317.

I didn't eat; I didn't sleep. I was sitting at the TV. And I used to sit and cry. Nixon brought back all the Germans to me.[47]

No studies have yet been done on political participation among survivors, though currently there is one Congressman who is a survivor, Tom Lantos of California, while Sam Gejdenson of Connecticut is a child of a survivor. What is clear, however, is that the survivors have a highly favorable attitude toward America. The respondent cited above asserted that, despite her apprehensions, the fact that the Watergate burglars had been held accountable proved that America was a good country. Other researchers and writers have similarly commented on the appreciation that survivors have for the United States as a land that accepted them into its midst. [48] Interviews done so far by this researcher suggest that the majority of them vote in elections and that they do so because of an acute awareness of what is means to have such rights denied and abrogated.

****

In sum, it is apparent that survivors have made contributions in a number of areas. By settling in many different communities they have made certain that their influence will be felt throughout the country. They have entered a wide variety of occupations and professions and, despite the disadvantages of their circumstances, have managed to do quite well. A large proportion of them seem to have been self-employed. The survivors have also shown themselves to be quite generous in terms of charity, especially for Jewish causes, and their involvement with the State of Israel and other Jewish concerns has been uniformly high. Their children have also done well, although more research needs to be done on this question. Finally, the survivors have contributed in a tangible way to raising the level of moral consciousness in this country and, one can assume, everywhere else, too.

How many of them have actually spoken about their experiences to others is not so important. What is significant is that, because of what they represent when they do good, they can have an enormous effect on others that is totally out of proportion to their numbers. To the extent that they have succeeded in doing so, it can be said that theirs is a message of hope and renewal, a message that, even after one has experienced terrible trauma and suffering, it is still possible to remain human — and humane.

---

47. Ibid.
48. See Doris Kirschmann and Sylvia Savin, "Refugee Adjustment — Five Years Later," *Jewish Social Service Quarterly*, 30 (Winter 1953):200; Rabinowitz, *New Lives*, p. 139; Epstein, *Study in American Pluralism*, p.3; G. R. Leon, *et al*, "Survivors of the Holocaust and Their Children: Current Status and Adjustment," *Journal of Personality and Social Psychology* 41 (1981):503-516.

The Sephardim of the United States: An Exploratory Study

by MARC D. ANGEL

WESTERN AND LEVANTINE SEPHARDIM • EARLY AMERICAN SETTLEMENT • DEVELOPMENT OF AMERICAN COMMUNITY • IMMIGRATION FROM LEVANT • JUDEO-SPANISH COMMUNITY • JUDEO-GREEK COMMUNITY • JUDEO-ARABIC COMMUNITY • SURVEY OF AMERICAN SEPHARDIM • BIRTHRATE • ECONOMIC STATUS • SECULAR AND RELIGIOUS EDUCATION • HISPANIC CHARACTER • SEPHARDI-ASHKENAZI INTERMARRIAGE • COMPARISON OF FOUR COMMUNITIES

INTRODUCTION

IN ITS MOST LITERAL SENSE the term Sephardi refers to Jews of Iberian origin. *Sepharad* is the Hebrew word for Spain. However, the term has generally come to include almost any Jew who is not Ashkenazi, who does not have a German- or Yiddish-language background.[1] Although there are wide cultural divergences within the

---

Note: It was necessary to consult many unpublished sources for this pioneering study. I am especially grateful to the Trustees of Congregation Shearith Israel, the Spanish and Portuguese Synagogue in New York City, for permitting me to use minutes of meetings, letters, and other unpublished materials. I am also indebted to the Synagogue's Sisterhood for making available its minutes.

I wish to express my profound appreciation to Professor Nathan Goldberg of Yeshiva University for his guidance throughout every phase of this study. My special thanks go also to Messrs. Edgar J. Nathan 3rd, Joseph Papo, and Victor Tarry for reading the historical part of this essay and offering valuable suggestions and corrections, and to my wife for her excellent cooperation and assistance.

[1] See Cecil Roth, "On Sephardi Jewry," *Kol Sepharad*, September-October 1966, pp. 2–6; Solomon Sassoon, "The Spiritual Heritage of the Sephardim," in Richard Barnett, ed., *The Sephardi Heritage* (New York, 1971), pp. 1f; Abraham Levy, *The Sephardim: A Problem of Survival* (London, 1972), pp. 9f; José Faur, "The Sephardim: Yesterday, Today and Tomorrow," *The Sephardic World*, Summer 1972, pp. 5–6.

Originally published in *American Jewish Year Book* (1973). Reprinted by permission of the *American Jewish Year Book*.

Sephardi world, common liturgy and religious customs constitute underlying factors of unity. Thus, whether a Jew traces his background to Africa, Asia, or the Sephardi communities of Europe, he may still feel part of Sephardi Jewry.

Jews also may be classified as Sephardim if they have been culturally assimilated into the Sephardi fold and consider themselves to be Sephardim. To define the group only on the basis of genetics or lands of origin is inadequate; it is essential to broaden the definition to include cultural behavior and identity.

Sephardim of all backgrounds live in the United States. The majority are of Turkish and Balkan origins; their mother-tongue was Judeo-Spanish. There is also a large group of Syrian Jews of Arabic-speaking background. Other segments of the Sephardi population have come to the United States from various parts of Africa, Asia, and Western Europe.

Because Sephardi communities in different lands developed under differing cultural and historical conditions, it would be more proper to speak of Sephardi cultures than of one monolithic Sephardi culture. Each group has had unique experiences and has made contributions to Jewish and general civilization. Each group deserves to have its own historians and researchers. However, for the sake of clarity, it may be helpful to delineate certain general cultural characteristics of several major Sephardi groups in the United States. In his book, *Hispanic Culture and Character of the Sephardic Jews*, Professor Maír José Benardete describes two strains of Sephardim: the Western Sephardim and the Levantine Sephardim.

Western Sephardim

The Western Sephardim are descendants of ex-Marranos who returned to Judaism and established communities throughout Western Europe—in such places as Amsterdam, Bayonne, Bordeaux, Hamburg, London, Paris. Their communities were characterized by pride, wealth, culture, and grandeur. Benardete draws on the description by Ezra Stiles, then president of Yale University, of the colonial American Sephardi merchant Aaron Lopez to indicate the general qualities of these Sephardim. According to Stiles, Lopez "did business with the greatest ease and clearness, always carried about a sweetness of behaviour, a calm urbanity, an agreeable and unaffected politeness of manners."[2]

The Western Sephardim formed an aristocracy within the Jewish world. Eminent not only for their social graces but also for scholarship and cultural contributions, they were the envy of many non-Sephardi Jews. One striking example of the attempt of Ashkenazim to emulate Sephardim is found, oddly enough, in tombstone inscriptions in Leghorn. The ex-Marranos carried their hidalguism to their cemeteries, adorning their tombstones with lavishly engraved artwork, as well as with poetry written in Spanish. Ashkenazi Jews who tried to imitate their Sephardi brethren in life also tried to imitate them in death, and a number of their tombstones bear Spanish inscriptions.

Western Sephardim migrated to the New World in the hope of finding and cultivating opportunities for economic advancement. They settled in such places as Curaçao, Surinam, St. Thomas, Jamaica, and Recife. In 1654, as we shall see later, they began to settle in North America. For various reasons the Western Sephardim have dwindled in number and influence, so that today very few congregations of this tradition still enjoy a vibrant existence.[3]

Levantine Sephardim

In the course of the century beginning with the persecutions of 1391 and closing with the expulsion of 1492, Spanish Jews who refused to convert to Catholicism left their homes and settled in more tolerant lands. They migrated to Turkey, North Africa, as well as points in Europe, where they established significant communities and produced extraordinary literatures in Judeo-Spanish and Hebrew. The Jewish world has not really been fully aware of the importance of their cultural contributions. Scholarly research into their history has begun only recently.

The Judeo-Spanish Sephardi communities in the Levant suffered a gradual cultural erosion, which began in the latter part of the 17th century. The Shabbetai Zevi debacle, Turkey's economic decline, and

---

[2]Maír José Benardete, *Hispanic Culture and Character of the Sephardic Jews* (New York, 1952), pp. 44–45.

[3]*Ibid.*, p. 43; see also bibliography at the end of this article for works dealing with Western Sephardim.

low cultural standards of the general population, all contributed to the disintegration of Sephardi life. To be sure, Levantine Sephardim have made significant contributions to Jewish life up to our own day; but the masses drifted into relative ignorance. Thus the cultural influences most instrumental in shaping modern Levantine Sephardim have been folk qualities. The Sephardi's sense of poetry, music, and aesthetics has been shaped by his rich Judeo-Spanish heritage. His view of the harmony between religion and secularism and his love of the joys of life have been inherited from his Levantine Sephardi ancestors.

The Sephardim who lived in Arabic lands and who spoke Judeo-Arabic were influenced by their cultural milieu. They established well-organized, tightly-knit communities and produced rabbis, poets, and thinkers. Many of these Jews developed a keen sense of business, trade, and barter.

The Sephardim of Asia and Africa were strongly affected by the French-language schools of the Alliance Israélite Universelle, which brought Western education to thousands of their young and imbued them with the desire to advance academically. Although some Sephardi Hispanicists have objected to the Alliance's stress on French, the fact remains that its schools served a valuable and needed purpose. Many Sephardim who have advanced in American society owe much of their success to their early training in Alliance schools. The most notable individual who came from the Alliance to work with the Sephardim in the United States was Nissim Behar (1848–1931).[4]

DEVELOPMENT OF AMERICAN COMMUNITY

Early Settlements

The history of the Jewish community of North America actually begins with the founding of Congregation Shearith Israel in New Amsterdam in September 1654. Most of the twenty-three refugees

---

[4]See David N. Barocas, *Albert Matarasso and His Ladino* (New York: Foundation for the Advancement of Sephardic Studies and Culture, Inc., 1969), p. 56; Benardete, *op. cit.*, pp. 169–70; *La America*, February 13, 1914, p. 2; October 13, 1916, p. 3; *Jewish Charities*, June 1914, p. 28; Z. Szajkowski, "The Alliance Israélite Universelle in the United States, 1860–1949," *Publications of the American Jewish Historical Society*, Vol. 39, June 1950, pp. 406–43.

from Recife, Brazil, who founded the congregation were of Spanish and Portuguese descent, and they were the ones who set the communal organization patterns and synagogue customs. Other communities developed later in Newport, Philadelphia, Savannah, Charleston, and Montreal. All were Spanish and Portuguese, stemming from the ex-Marrano or Western Sephardi tradition.

It is a widespread myth that Jewish immigration to the American colonies was overwhelmingly Sephardi. The fact is that relatively many Ashkenazim also came during this period, working with the Sephardim to build Jewish life on American soil. In New York, for example, the Ashkenazim outnumbered the Sephardim by 1730, the year the first synagogue building was completed on Mill Street. While the synagogue was under construction, the Sephardi Moses Gomez presided over the community in the first half of 1729, and the Ashkenazi Jacob Franks in the second half.[5] The often-repeated claim that the Sephardim looked down on the Ashkenazim is not borne out by the facts. On the contrary, the two groups got on surprisingly well together in spite of original cultural differences. They cooperated in every area of Jewish life. Marriages between Sephardim and Ashkenazim were extremely common.[6]

Students of the Spanish and Portuguese settlements in North America often have underplayed the profound Sephardi cultural influence on the Ashkenazim. It has been stated that because of widespread Sephardi-Ashkenazi intermarriages, "the resultant mixture, often miscalled Portuguese, was really more Ashkenazic than Sephardic."[7] The final determination of what makes a community Sephardi or Ashkenazi is based on culture rather than genetics. So long as the Spanish and Portuguese culture predominated in the community

---

[5]David de Sola Pool, *The Mill Street Synagogue* (New York, 1930), p. 50.

[6]See Samuel Kohs, "The Jewish Community," in Louis Finkelstein, ed., *The Jews: Their History, Culture and Religion* (New York, 1955), Vol. 2, p. 1275, who claims that German Jewish immigrants "were not too cheerful about the welcome they were receiving." Yet Ashkenazim served as officers in the various Sephardi synagogues, and from available evidence it seems that the two groups cooperated reasonably well. Hyman Grinstein, *The Rise of the Jewish Community of New York* (Philadelphia, 1947), p. 166, states that the "so-called Portuguese Jews . . . felt superior to and disliked the Ashkenazim," but notes on the very next page that Sephardi-Ashkenazi intermarriages were so common that, after a short time, "there were virtually no real Portuguese left."

[7]Grinstein, *ibid.*, p. 167.

it could be accurately described as Sephardi, even if all its members were of Ashkenazi origin.

The dominant role of Sephardi culture in Colonial America, therefore, justifies calling the early communities Spanish and Portuguese, even those where Ashkenazim actually outnumbered Sephardim. The Sephardim had pride in themselves as well as in their ancestry. They had ability in commerce. They had the traditional Western Sephardi savoir faire and social flexibility. At their best, they could adapt admirably to American life and still retain their distinctive Sephardi Jewish tradition. As happened in other communities where Western Sephardim met Ashkenazim, the Sephardim in America prevailed in the cultural sphere. Since Ashkenazim admired the cosmopolitan and enlightened Sephardim, they attempted to become Sephardim—and very often succeeded.

That Sephardi culture more than descent determined the Sephardi character of the early communities is well demonstrated by the history of Congregation Shearith Israel, the Spanish and Portuguese Synagogue of Montreal. In the 1760s Jewish settlers began to arrive in that Canadian city. Of those whose names we find in the synagogue's early records, nearly all were of non-Sephardi origin. The earliest minutes of the congregation, dated 1778, established the structure of the community according to Spanish and Portuguese custom. A *parnas, gabay,* and a *junto* of three elders served as leaders. Yet not one of the seven men who signed the minutes had a Spanish or Portuguese name. The same was true of the thirteen men who signed the congregation's by-laws in 1778.[8] Thus it is obvious that what influenced these men to establish a Spanish and Portuguese synagogue was not their own descent, which was either completely or partly non-Sephardi, but their cultural attachment to the Sephardi ways.

The strong influence exerted by the Sephardim on the Ashkenazi settlers accounts for the survival of the three remaining Spanish and Portuguese synagogues in North America: Shearith Israel in New York City, Mikveh Israel in Philadelphia, and Shearith Israel in Montreal, each of which has long had a high percentage of non-Sephardi members. They could never have survived unless Ashkenazim were attracted to Sephardi culture. Ashkenazim *wanted* to be part of the

---

[8]Solomon Frank, *Two Centuries in the Life of a Synagogue* (Montreal, 1968), pp. 28, 32.

Sephardi community. And this would explain why, between 1654 and 1825, Shearith Israel in New York was the only Jewish congregation, a fact that has troubled some historians.[9]

Being Sephardi in outlook, the communities were quick to adapt to their new society. Western Sephardim were receptive to the forces of secularism; they did not isolate themselves in self-imposed religious ghettos. Thus Gershom Mendes Seixas, the famous minister of Shearith Israel in New York (1768–1816), not only showed enthusiasm for science but was known also to quote from the New Testament. Because of his receptivity to matters not strictly religious or Jewish, some students today wonder about Seixas' "Orthodoxy."[10] Indeed, Jacob Rader Marcus likens Seixas to Israel Jacobson, founder of Reform Judaism. Marcus makes a point of Seixas' "insistence on Western dress, decorum, dignity, and an increasing use of the vernacular."[11] And yet, all these characteristics were common to Western Sephardi religious leaders long before Seixas was born. Certainly he was influenced by his American milieu; but his Sephardi roots must not be forgotten.

Though they made many significant contributions to Jewish and American life,[12] the Spanish and Portuguese communities gradually diminished in influence. Assimilation and intermarriage cost them some losses. The comparatively large immigration of Ashkenazi Jews in the early 19th century engulfed the old Sephardi communities. Ashkenazim founded synagogues and institutions of their own. To be sure, they borrowed ideas from their Spanish and Portuguese predecessors, but there could be no doubt that the Sephardi influence decreased with each new shipload of Ashkenazim. As the Ashkenazi immigration began to skyrocket, there was not time for the Sephardi

---

[9]Grinstein, *op. cit.*, p. 40.

[10]J.R. Marcus, *Handsome Young Priest in the Black Gown* (Cincinnati, 1970); reprinted from *HUC Annual*, Vol. 40–41, 1969–70), pp. 43, 49.

[11]*Ibid.*, p. 67.

[12]The Spanish and Portuguese Synagogue in New York, for example, founded, or helped found, such institutions as Mt. Sinai and Montefiore hospitals, the traditionalist Jewish Theological Seminary, and the Union of Orthodox Jewish Congregations of America. Members of the community were among the founders of the New York Stock Exchange. The Hendricks family developed the copper industry in America. For more information, see David and Tamar de Sola Pool, *An Old Faith in the New World* (New York, 1955); Maxwell Whiteman, *Copper for America* (New Brunswick, 1971).

synagogues to absorb the newcomers. There simply were too many arrivals for the Spanish and Portuguese communities to cope with; the immigrants needed their own communal organizations.

At the same time, there was so little Sephardi immigration that the few remaining Spanish and Portuguese congregations must have felt that they were being overrun. They tenaciously clung to their synagogal customs and rituals, fearful that without such rigor the entire *minhag* would collapse.

When Sephardi Jews from the Levant began to come to the United States in the early 20th century, the old Sephardi institutions felt new hope. The *Shearith Israel Bulletin* (New York) of February 1912 recorded: "The great increase in the number of Sephardic Jews in America is a happy guarantee of the survival and spread in the United States of the ancient *minhag* of our Congregation." Now, for the first time in a century, Sephardi culture in America had the opportunity to grow and spread. But these Levantine immigrants, though authentic bearers of the Sephardi tradition, were mostly poor and uneducated, and the question was how they would adjust to conditions in America.

Levantine Jewish Immigration

In the course of the 19th century, the Sephardi communities of the Levant began to absorb Western ideas. The Alliance Israélite Universelle established a network of schools throughout the Oriental Sephardi dispersion so that modern French education was reaching an increasing number of young people. The result was a slowly developing undercurrent of discontent with the established modes of life. In particular, the have-nots began to seek new opportunities for economic and social advancement; the old mode of life offered nothing but a future of hard work and poverty.

As Western education spread, and as Levantine businessmen on their travels became aware of modern ideas and attitudes, a subtle change in thinking occurred in the Sephardi communities. More and more of the Sephardim became imbued with the modern spirit of progress and were ready to seek out opportunities in other lands. To be sure, the majority remained in the Old World, but their attitudes too were undergoing transformation. They realized that their long-standing cultural isolation was coming to an end, that their communities were going to face demographic as well as ideological changes. A new era had begun.

The progressive among the Sephardim urged the youth to study in Western schools and to advance academically. Since the economic and intellectual opportunities in the existing communities were usually limited, ambitious Sephardim set their visions on new worlds. They would migrate. They would become wealthy. They would send money back to the Old Country, or perhaps they would even return some day to their hometowns to live in luxury. Though some Sephardim migrated to various places in Europe, Africa, and South America, by far the greatest number was attracted to the promise of the United States.

In the history of Sephardi migration many incidents revealed the transition from the traditional to the modern milieu. One anecdote serves to illustrate the tragicomic element in Levantine Jewish life at the turn of the century.[13] On the Island of Rhodes, an ancient and illustrious Sephardi community of about 6,000 persons, lived a man named Jacob Aroghetti. He avidly campaigned for emigration to America, claiming that only in this way could the people progress. He made plans for himself and a group of followers to settle in Seattle, Washington, where a small group of Sephardim was already established. But when he bought the tickets he asked for passage to Washington, not bothering to specify the city, Seattle. As a result, he and his group landed in Washington, D.C. After a hopeless search for his Seattle Sephardi friends in Washington, D.C., Aroghetti finally realized his mistake. He was discouraged from traveling across the country, and settled in New York City where he became a leading figure in the Sephardi immigrant community.

The Sephardim were not the first people from the Levant to come to America. Hundreds of non-Jewish Greeks and Slavs had preceded them by a generation. When the earlier immigrants sent news of America back to the Levant, the Jews probably learned of the opportunities the new land offered. Also, some Sephardi merchants had visited the United States to attend various expositions.[14] Young Sephardi bachelors were most apt to believe the glittering reports about America. Those who ventured to the New World sent letters back home, often enclosing money. The fame of America loomed larger and larger.

---

[13]In personal conversation with Dr. Maurice Amateau, who was born in Rhodes and presently lives in New York.

[14]Benardete, *op. cit.*, p. 139.

The changes in the *Zeitgeist* which led to an increased interest in migration among the Levantine Jews brought a steady stream of immigrants to the United States. The total number was not large. According to figures derived from the records of the United States Commissioner General of Immigration, 2,738 Levantine Sephardim came to the United States between 1890 and 1907.[15] The figure reported by the Hebrew Immigrant Shelter and Aid Society (HISAS, later known as HIAS) was somewhat higher.[16] Soon, however, events militated for a rise in Levantine Sephardi immigration.

In Turkey, the 1908 revolt of the Young Turks, which aimed at securing constitutional government, created hardships for many Jews. The institution of compulsory military service, for the first time also for Jews in the Levant, made it more difficult for the men to support their families and interfered with religious observance. The disruptions of life in a country torn by revolution, the Turko-Italian war, as well as natural disasters such as a fire and earthquake, contributed to the insecurity of the country's Jews.[17] During the 1912-13 Balkan war against Turkey, the Sephardi communities in the belligerent countries were ravaged. When defeated Turkey ceded territory to the Balkan allies, the latter began to battle among themselves for the distribution of the newly-won territories. In July all-out war involved Rumania, Greece, Serbia and Bulgaria. A treaty at Bucharest ended the war in August 1913.

When peace came, the tragically worsened conditions of Levantine Jewry became apparent. Poverty was rampant. Constantinople and Salonika were crowded with refugees from the war zone. Besides, the allies imposed economic measures which proved injurious to the Jews. Major cities of Sephardi settlement, such as Monastir, Janina, Castoria, Kavala, and Andrianople, were severely hit by the wars. The Jews of Bulgaria were forced to appeal to European and American

---

[15]Louis M. Hacker, "The Communal Life of the Sephardic Jews in New York City," *Jewish Social Service Quarterly*, Vol. 3, December 1926, p. 34.

[16]David de Sola Pool, "The Immigration of Levantine Jews Into the United States," *Jewish Charities*, June 1914, p. 20.

[17]David de Sola Pool, "The Levantine Jews in the United States," AMERICAN JEWISH YEAR BOOK, Vol. 15 (1913–14), pp. 209–10; Benardete, *op. cit.*, p. 139.

Jewry for help. It was estimated that 200,000 Jews in European Turkey were poverty-stricken.[18]

The troubles for the Jews in the Levant were not to subside with the end of the Balkan wars. It was not long before World War I engulfed them. Jacques Magid, HIAS representative in Constantinople, reported in February 1920 that there were hundreds of persons in and around Constantinople who had relatives in America and who were in dire need of aid. A second HIAS report supported his statement.[19] Magid was asked to prepare a list of the needy so that "a reasonable amount of money" might be spent to relieve their condition.

It was to be expected that many Levantine Sephardim decided to leave their homelands. According to United States government figures, 10,033 of them entered the United States between 1908 and 1914. Immigration lessened during World War I, but between 1920 and 1924 another 9,877 came. In 1925 the figure was drastically reduced to 137 persons as a result of new quota restrictions. But Levantine immigration had begun to slacken considerably earlier, after the adoption of a temporary measure in 1921.[20]

Distribution of Population

According to government figures, a total of 25,591 Levantine Sephardim entered the United States between 1899 and 1925.[21] The actual figure was somewhat higher because a number of Sephardim no doubt were counted as non-Jewish Turks, Greeks, Syrians, and others. Various estimates of the number of Sephardim in the country and of their concentration in New York City are as follows:

---

[18]"The Balkan Wars and the Jews," AMERICAN JEWISH YEAR BOOK, Vol. 15 (1913–14), pp. 186–206. See especially, pp. 189–95.

[19]*Minutes of the Hebrew Immigrant Aid Society*, February 10, 1920, p. 91. See also minutes for July 28, 1920, p. 128. Microfilms available at Yivo Institute, New York City.

[20]Hacker, *op. cit.*, p. 34. The increased immigration was due not merely to the Balkan wars, but as said before, also to a growing desire for economic and social betterment. See AMERICAN JEWISH YEAR BOOK, Vol. 15 (1913–14), p. 431; HIAS Minutes, *op. cit.*, December 13, 1921, p. 249, note a drop in Levantine immigration.

[21]Hacker, *ibid.*

Year	U.S. Total	New York City
1913	9,000[a]	80 to 90 per cent [b]
1916	32,000[c]	vast majority
1926	50-60,000[d]	at least 40,000
1930		45,000 (Spanish-speaking)[e]
1941		25,000 (Spanish-speaking)[f]
1946	55,000[g]	40,000
current	100,000[h]	

[a] *Jewish Charities*, March 29, 1913, p.11.

[b] Pool, "The Levantine Jews in the United States," *op.cit.*, p. 212; the *American Hebrew* (December 12, 1913, p.190) figure of 15,000 seems to be exaggerated.

[c] In an unpublished talk to the Sisterhood of the Spanish and Portuguese Synagogue, New York, November 1916, Cyrus Adler estimated some 30,000 Levantine Jews, most of them Ladino-speaking, had immigrated since 1907.

[d] Hacker, *op.cit.*, p. 34.

[e] Max Luria, "Judeo-Spanish Dialects in New York City," in J. Fitzgerald and P. Taylor, eds., *Todd Memorial Volumes* (New York, 1930), Vol. 2, p. 7. If Greek- and Arabic-speaking Jews were to be included, the New York figure would be 50,000-60,000, and the U.S. figure some 80,000-90,000, or more.

[f] Barocas, *op.cit.*, p. 64; Matarasso's estimate appears to deal only with Spanish-speaking Sephardim.

[g] Joseph Papo, "The Sephardic Community in America," *Reconstructionist*, Vol. 12, October 20, 1946, p. 13.

[h] This figure appears in brochures published by the Yeshiva University Sephardic Studies Program. There may be many more if children of Sephardi-Ashkenazi marriages were included.

Although there are some serious discrepancies, all estimates agree that by far the largest group of Sephardi immigrants settled in New York City. Estimates for 1913, 1916, and 1926 seem more reliable than later figures, mainly because the bulk of the Sephardim at that time were immigrants, and immigration figures, though not completely accurate, were available. Therefore the Sephardi population could be reasonably accurately established without having to guess at rates of natural increase. In later years, with the increase of American-born Sephardim, estimates were less likely to be accurate. The present estimate of 100,000 is no more than a guess; it may be much larger, but probably is not smaller.

The Sephardi immigrants can be classified into three major groups having distinct cultural characteristics and mother tongues. The great majority spoke Judeo-Spanish and came from Turkey and the Balkan countries. Of the two smaller groups one was Greek-speaking and the other, largely from Syria, Judeo-Arabic-speaking. There was also a trickle of Levantine Ashkenazi immigration. Thus even within the ranks of Levantine immigrants there was diversity of language and culture.

By Western standards most Sephardi newcomers were uneducated and unskilled, and poorly prepared to meet the challenges of America. They encountered their first problem on Ellis Island, even before entering the United States. A lead article in the national Judeo-Spanish weekly *La America*, June 9, 1911, complained that Jews from Turkey were having real difficulty with American immigration officials. These Jews were not familiar with American immigration laws and did not know how to answer the questions put to them. Thus some poor frightened immigrants were detained for weeks before setting foot in this country. Others were actually sent back to Turkey. In an effort to help, *La America* printed American immigration regulations in Judeo-Spanish.

Many Sephardi immigrants were saved from deportation by American Jews. In the fall of 1916 some recent arrivals from the ports of Salonika and Kavala were in serious difficulty because they had diseases which, according to the provisions of immigration laws, barred them from entering the United States. Because deportation to their war-torn homes endangered the lives of these Jews, HIAS persuaded Beth Israel and Montefiore hospitals to admit them as patients.[22]

When the Sephardi Jews finally were admitted, they found themselves in complete isolation. Of course, all immigrants needed a period of adjustment; but Sephardim were more severely handicapped than Ashkenazim because the American Jewish community did not quite know what to do with them. All its immigrant facilities were geared to Yiddish-speaking Jews. What was to be done with several thousand Spanish-, Greek-, and Arabic-speaking people? Who could even understand them?

The burden of responsibility naturally fell on the one existing Sephardi congregation in New York, the ancient Spanish and Portuguese Synagogue Shearith Israel. HIAS helped by establishing an Oriental Bureau, and other individuals and groups also became

---

[22]HIAS Minutes, *op. cit.*, October 10, 1916, p. 113.

involved. But, as we shall see later, attempts at assisting the Sephardim were less than successful.

In the early stages of Sephardi immigration—and of Ashkenazi as well—attempts were made to settle the newcomers outside New York City. The theory was that they would develop better in less unwieldy groups than those in New York. The scatter program would also ease the burden of New York Jewry. Thus, in 1907, the Industrial Removal Office, a Jewish organization begun as part of the Jewish Agricultural and Industrial Aid Society, sent a number of Levantine Sephardim to Seattle, Gary, Cincinnati, Toledo, Columbus, and Cleveland. The New York *Kehillah*, the communal organization of the New York City Jews, established Sephardi colonies in Glenham, N.Y., and Raritan, N.J.[23]

Yet despite all these attempts, perhaps as many as 90 per cent of the Sephardim settled in New York, on the Lower East Side and later also in Harlem. In 1914 other Sephardi communities were in Seattle (about 600), San Francisco (100), Atlanta (100), Rochester (90), and Portland, Ore. (80). Smaller communities were found in Chicago, Los Angeles, Indianapolis, and Montgomery.[24]

Since most of the Sephardi immigrants spoke Judeo-Spanish, it was believed that they would more easily adjust in Spanish-speaking countries, and that they therefore should be encouraged to settle in Latin America. Dr. David de Sola Pool of Congregation Shearith Israel, who was also chairman of the Oriental Committee of its Sisterhood, considered such proposals. The Oriental Committee of Congregation Mikveh Israel, the Spanish and Portuguese synagogue of Philadelphia, apparently also considered this possibility. HIAS explored living conditions in Cuba. Some Sephardim were indeed sent to Latin American countries; but the overwhelming majority settled in the United States.[25]

The adoption of the 1924 Immigration Act, which embodied the national origins quota system, led to the sharp curtailment of the main

---

[23]Pool, "The Levantine Jews in the United States," *op. cit.*, p. 212.

[24]*Ibid.*

[25]*Minutes of the Oriental Committee of the Sisterhood of the Spanish and Portuguese Synagogue*, October 13, 1914, pp. 43–44; December 11, 1916, p. 95. See also, Mark Wischnitzer, *Visas to Freedom* (New York, 1956), p. 68; Arthur Goren, *New York Jews and the Quest for Community*, (New York, 1970), p. 69.

sources of Jewish immigration. The Levantine immigration in particular was almost completely choked off.[26] *La America,* October 17, 1924, published "A New Chapter of Sephardi History in America," by its editor M.S. Gadol, who reported that many Sephardim were going to Cuba in the expectation of being permitted to enter the United States a year or so later. This, Gadol stated, would not be possible in view of the strict quota law. He felt that Sephardim in the United States, whose numbers would no longer be replenished by new waves of immigrants, now had to rely on their own resources to create viable communities.

New York City Community

In the midst of the many thousand Yiddish-speaking immigrants on the Lower East Side, a relatively small community of Sephardim led an insular life. In the early days, the language barrier cut them off almost entirely from the Ashkenazim. And within the Sephardi community, those speaking Spanish, Greek, and Arabic were separated from each other as well. Even in matters of religion the Sephardim and Ashkenazim formed distinct tribes. Variations in ritual, synagogue liturgy, and pronunciation of Hebrew enlarged the gulf separating them. The Sephardim really had no choice but to form their own community; they were far too uncomfortable in an Ashkenazi setting.

The story goes that the first Sephardi settlers simply were thought not to be really Jewish by the city's Ashkenazim, for their names, language, appearance, and mannerisms were strange. In light of such cultural differences, Sephardim naturally tended to develop separate communities.

Some New York Ashkenazim at first thought that the Sephardim could be integrated into the general Jewish community, but this idea was immediately rejected as impossible. It would have been not only impossible; it would have been a mistake to try to strip the Sephardim of their identity. Dr. Pool argued that the Sephardim would advance

---

[26]*Minutes of the Trustees of Congregation Shearith Israel, The Spanish and Portuguese Synagogue in the City of New York,* Vol. 9, March 4, 1924, p. 267, records their resolutions against proposed immigration quotas, which were submitted to Congressmen serving on the House Immigration Committee.

more readily if allowed to have their own synagogues and schools, and to function in a milieu that was comfortable and natural for them; that, in time, they would become Americanized socially while maintaining their own distinctive Sephardi ritual, a development that was to be desired.[27] Some twelve years later, Hacker, too, discussed the isolation of the New York Sephardim which, he said, was caused by religious, linguistic, and psychological distinctiveness.[28] As a result they established their own institutions: not only synagogues and Talmudé Torah, but also grocery stores, restaurants, and cafés catering to Sephardi taste and eating habits.

As a matter of fact, the coffee houses became a source of contention between the Sephardi immigrants and the American Jewish establishment. Only the male Sephardim frequented them while the women remained at home with the children. After the day's work the men would go to the café, their only outlet for recreation and social intercourse, and their one escape from the bleak tedium of daily life. They would sip Turkish coffee, tell jokes, gossip, complain, discuss politics, read the Judeo-Spanish papers, laugh, cry, and dream. The coffee house, a regular feature of the communities in the Levant, had always been popular with the working people and always unpopular with the rabbis.[29] The Sephardi cafés in New York were no exception to this rule.

As a Sephardi rabbi, Dr. Pool felt keen responsibility for the welfare of the new group of Sephardim. He considered the coffee house a bad influence, condemning it as the enemy of progress, a place of idleness, gambling, and other undesirable activities. However, his words had little influence on reducing patronage of the cafés. Indeed, lay leaders among the Levantine Jews avidly defended them.[30]

Like all Sephardim, the Levantine Jews had a strong sense of pride. They were particularly proud of their ancestry, of their historic Sephardi names. They therefore did not like to feel that they were a "problem." Neither did they consider themselves to be part of the

---

[27]Pool, "The Immigration of Levantine Jews Into the United States," *op. cit.*, p. 24.

[28]Hacker, *op. cit.*, pp. 32–33.

[29]See for example, M. J. Israel, *Shenoth Yamin* (Smyrna, 1867), pp. 10b, 56a.

[30]Pool, "The Immigration of Levantine Jews Into the United States," *op. cit.*, p. 16; "The Levantine Jews in the United States," *op. cit.*, p. 218. See Joseph Gedelecia's defense of the coffee houses in *Jewish Charities*, June 1914, p. 29.

lower classes, although they were poor. This pride—which sometimes bordered on stubbornness—made them even more of a problem than they otherwise would have been. Traditional methods of aiding immigrants were seldom effective with them. They resented charity and violently opposed any person or group attempting to help them in a conspicuous manner.

Maurice Hexter, conducting a study of the Cincinnati Sephardi colony in 1913, asked the assistance of Maír José Benardete, who later became a recognized Sephardi scholar. Recalling his work with Hexter, Benardete, commented: "It was not a very comfortable feeling to have, as the thought dawned upon my boyish mentality, that the small tribe in the cheapest section of the sooty city by the muddy Ohio River, was presenting difficulties to the charitable agencies of the Ashkenazic Jews who were by comparison numerous and prosperous."[31] But it was a fact. How could aid be given to Levantine Jews if they hindered those who wanted to help?

Again and again Levantine spokesmen insisted on their self-dependence. Again and again they asked their would-be benefactors to treat them with respect. They were not beggars. They quickly gained the reputation of being people who would not appeal to local charities except in the most urgent cases, and they rarely appealed a second time.[32] As Dr. Cyrus Adler summed it up: "The Oriental Jews unless they be decrepit, blind or maimed ask and take no charity, and to maintain themselves no work is too hard."[33] According to Hacker, the Sephardim "consider themselves a people apart; they are 'Spanish Jews' with a distinct historical consciousness and, often, an inordinate pride."[34]

No doubt the Levantine immigrants created a serious problem for American Jewish agencies. Delegates from two Sephardi organizations, the Ahavath Shalom Society of Monastir and the Union and Peace Society, who attended a meeting of the New York *Kehillah* in February 1911, told the gathering in no uncertain terms that not even

---

[31] Benardete, *op. cit.*, p. 140.

[32] Pool, "The Immigration of Levantine Jews Into the United States," *op. cit.*, p. 19.

[33] Address to the Sisterhood of the Spanish and Portuguese Synagogue, New York, November 27, 1916, as recorded in its Minutes. See also Pool, "The Immigration of Levantine Jews Into the United States," *op. cit.*, p. 15.

[34] Hacker, *op. cit.*, p. 33.

one member of their societies would need communal assistance during the coming year; that they themselves could handle any problems that might come up.[35] The Sephardi community approved of this stand. At a conference of Jewish social work leaders, Joseph Gedelecia, a Levantine Jew of Ashkenazi origin, admitted that the immigrants were a problem to the American Jewish establishment, but he added that the latter did not know how to cope with the situation properly. Defiantly he exclaimed: "But it is a problem you do not understand. When the Yiddish Jews go to Turkey, they, too, are a serious problem there."[36]

In view of the barrier existing between the Jewish social service agencies and the Sephardi Jews, Dr. Pool advised local federations and charities not to assist the Levantine Jews unless asked to do so. He also suggested that, whenever possible, aid should be given to the Sephardim through their own organizations.[37]

Although in the early days of the Sephardi settlement misery and poverty prevailed, the future held promise. The overwhelming majority of the Sephardim were unskilled, struggling, and working long hours as candy peddlers, bootblacks, cloakroom attendants, waiters, and the like. Many sold fruits and vegetables. But it was not long before they began to rise economically. They were careful to save money and, in time, bootblacks became owners of shoe-repair shops; fruit vendors opened grocery stores; candy salesmen bought candy concessions in movie theaters, and some went on to buy the theaters as well.

Sephardi children went to public schools; some went on to college. On June 8, 1917, *La America* reported that Jack David Hananiah, who had come from Smyrna, received a dentist's diploma; he was the first of New York's new Sephardi colony to enter that profession. Soon there there were also Sephardi doctors and lawyers. As early as 1914, Joseph Gedelecia boasted that New York's Sephardi community had eighteen doctors, three lawyers, sixty teachers, four professors, and various civil engineers and manufacturers. Several of the Sephardim amassed large fortunes, as, for example, the Schenazy brothers who were cigar manufacturers. Although Gedelecia's statements may have

---

[35]*La America*, February 17, 1911, p. 1.

[36]*Jewish Charities*, June 1914, p. 29.

[37]Pool, "The Immigration of Levantine Jews Into the United States," *op. cit.*, pp. 25-26.

been somewhat exaggerated, they were nevertheless indicative of the upward mobility of the community.[38] The economic progress continued with each succeeding generation, so that today the Sephardi community is relatively comfortable.

A serious problem of New York's Sephardim since their arrival early this century has been disunity. They formed societies, and even social clubs, based for the most part on geographical origin. Thus there were two clubs of Syrian Jews, one for those from Damascus and the other for people from Aleppo. Greek-speaking Jews formed Ahavah veAkhvah Janina and Tikvah Torah. The Spanish-speaking community had, for example, the following organizations: Ahavath Shalom for Monastir Jews; Hesed veEmet for those from Castoria; Mekor Hayyim for those from the Dardanelles; Yeshu'a veRahamim for Rhodes Jews; Hayyim veHesed for those from Gallipoli; Etz Hayyim for those from Smyrna, and Ezrath Ahim for those from Rodosto, Silivria, and Tchorlu. A progressive group of Turkish and Moroccan Jews formed the Union and Peace Society whose official language was English. The Progressive Oriental Society was composed mostly of Ashkenazim from Turkey. And as the Sephardi population increased, the number of these groups multiplied.

In 1912 twelve congregations of Judeo-Spanish-speaking Jews held High Holy Day services. Most of them had originated as benevolent and self-help societies.[39] In 1926, Hacker reported, the Sephardim had a number of small, struggling synagogues: eight on the Lower East Side, three in Harlem, and three in Brooklyn. They also had some thirty-six burial and mutual-aid societies.[40]

In the intervening years, there had been several major attempts, as well as a host of minor ones, to achieve unity among the New York Sephardim.

---

[38] *Jewish Charities*, June 1914, p. 29. For statements of the poor conditions in the early days see *La America*, November 25, 1910, p. 2; David de Sola Pool, "A New Communal Need," *Jewish Charities*, March 29, 1913, p. 11; David N. Barocas, *Broome and Allen Boys*, (New York: Foundation for the Advancement of Sephardic Studies and Culture, Inc., n.d.), p. 6. For statements of early progress, see *La America*, January 21, 1916, p. 2; Hacker, *op. cit.*, p. 38.

[39] *La America*, January 5, 1912, p. 2; Pool, "The Levantine Jews in the United States," *op. cit.*, p. 217.

[40] Hacker, *op. cit.*, p. 35.

FEDERATION OF ORIENTAL JEWS

Since none of the Sephardi societies was large enough to support adequate schools and synagogues or to provide enough social and cultural services to serve the many needs of the entire community, Sephardi leaders urged the groups to unite into a central authoritative organization.[41]

Early in 1912 it seemed as though unity was about to be achieved. *La America* of March 22, 1912, carried a front-page article by Gadol announcing the consolidation of different societies into the Oriental Jewish Federation of America. The Federation of Oriental Jews, as it came to be known, did not really solidify itself until December 1913. At a Federation-sponsored mass meeting held on December 7, the Sephardi leadership announced their intention to found a "self-supporting Ladino community where all the emigrated Jews from the Orient may find themselves 'at home.' "

Funds for community institutions would come from an annual fee of $12.00 to be paid by each Federation member for the support of religious schools, a social house, an employment bureau, and a "spiritual adviser." The meeting unanimously adopted a resolution which underscored the desire for financial independence: "Be it hereby resolved, that it is the sense of this meeting, that in the future, any organization or individual applying for funds for Oriental Jews, are doing so against the expressed wishes of our people and against the principle that, henceforth, we intend to carry on our own work without outside assistance."[42]

This resolution irked the non-Oriental individuals and groups who had taken up the cause of these newcomers. The Oriental Committee of the Sisterhood of the Spanish and Portuguese Synagogue of New York felt insulted and outraged. It left the Federation, and stated in its letter of resignation that it intended to take full control of the Uptown Talmud Torah in Harlem, thus severing all official cooperative ventures with the Federation of Oriental Jews.[43]

---

[41]*La America's* editor, M.S. Gadol, often called for such unity; see for example the issue of January 12, 1912, p. 2.

[42]*American Hebrew*, December 12, 1913, p. 190. See also issue of December 19, 1913, p. 220.

[43]Sisterhood Minutes, December 17, 1913, pp. 9–11.

For all its grand plans, however, the Federation did not succeed. It was little more than a loosely connected union of various small, independent societies, made powerless by each group's insistence on autonomy. If any member-society disapproved of a project, the Federation could proceed only at the risk of resignations.

Recognizing the impotence of the Federation as then constituted, Gadol ultimately turned against it. He argued that the Sephardim needed a central community organization with a community house. He reported some progress toward this end in 1916.[44] *La America* announced, in its issue of July 6, 1917, the election of a provisional committee to establish a democratic Sephardi community. A month later (August 3), the paper outlined the functions and scope of the community. On October 12 *La America* invited everyone to a meeting two days later, at which the "Sephardi Community" was to be officially founded. This attempt, too, was abortive.

During the years of these early struggles for unity, the question of appointing a *haham* (chief rabbi) for the Sephardi community was often discussed. As already mentioned, the Federation of Oriental Jews advocated such a move. *La America* dealt with the issue as early as January 25, 1913. Dr. Pool discussed the matter with Dr. Judah L. Magnes, the head of the New York *Kehillah*, and it was agreed that Shearith Israel would be given charge of the finances in order to employ a chief rabbi[45] who, it was hoped, would achieve unity in the community.

When the Federation learned that non-Oriental groups were interested in a *kolel*—a community with a chief rabbi and a governing body of responsible lay leaders—it refused to go along with the idea.[46] A letter from Magnes to Gadol, published in *La America*, June 9, 1916, expressing the *Kehillah's* frustrations, said in part: "I regret to

---

[44]*La America*, March 17, p. 2; March 31, p. 4; July 28, p. 2; August 25, p. 2; December 8, 1916, p. 2.

[45]Sisterhood Minutes, November 24, 1913, p. 2; December 11, 1913, p. 6.

[46]Trustees Minutes, Vol. 8, January 24, 1914, p. 455; Sisterhood Minutes, May 19, 1914, p. 37. A letter dated May 20, 1914, from Mr. Mayer Swaab, Jr. of Shearith Israel to Dr. Magnes of the *Kehillah* complains that though Shearith Israel had agreed to pay $500 to start a *kolel* under the auspices of the *Kehillah*, the Federation of Oriental Jews refused to cooperate. Swaab attacked the leaders of the Orientals as being destructive to the welfare of their community. See also David de Sola Pool, "Report of the Committee on a Progressive Policy in the Congregation," April 22, 1927, p. 7 (in possession of New York Congregation Shearith Israel).

say that it is not possible for me to keep up with the difficulties and controversies that seem to disturb the Oriental or Sephardi Jewish community. I do sincerely hope that some way may be found of bringing about greater harmony and more united activity on behalf of the Jewish cause." The community was to remain without a chief rabbi until 1941.[47]

SEPHARDI JEWISH COMMUNITY OF NEW YORK, INC.

In 1924 another major effort was made by New York's Sephardim to establish a central communal institution, this time the Sephardi Jewish Community of New York, Inc. This organization had little success, as Louis Hacker reported. It, too, was based on the local societies, not on the community as a whole. In 1926 it had approximately $6,000 in its treasury, but no definite program for which to spend the money.[48] Still, Dr. Pool called it "a stable and responsible organization."[49] It purchased a community house on 115th Street and seemed to be heading in the right direction. But in time, this organization, too, disintegrated; it lacked vigorous leadership and broad vision. And, as the Sephardi population moved from Harlem, the Community collapsed.

UNION OF SEPHARDIC CONGREGATIONS

The problem of Sephardi unity was not confined to New York City. Numerous small colonies of Sephardim were scattered throughout the United States, each existing as an island. The Sephardim in America had no focal point, no recognized organization which could spur their activities and development.

The need for guidance in religious matters was particularly acute. Each synagogue had its own prayer book, so that there was no uniform Sephardi liturgy. Jewish education was sorely inadequate. Sephardim

---

[47] *The Universal Jewish Encyclopedia* (New York, 1942), Vol. 8, p. 586, states that, until 1941, Dr. Pool was "the sole spokesman for Sephardic Jewry in the U.S. representing both the newer arrivals from the Levantine countries and the Sephardim who had lived for many generations in the English-speaking lands." However, he never officially held the post of chief rabbi.

[48] Hacker, *op. cit.*, p. 36.

[49] Pool, "Report. . . ," *loc. cit; also Shearith Israel Bulletin*, February, 1927, p. 7.

were not producing religious leaders and teachers. Dr. Pool envisioned the establishment of the Union of Sephardic Congregations to deal with the many problems of Sephardi synagogues. In 1928 committees of Shearith Israel in New York met with representatives of Mikveh Israel of Philadelphia and Shearith Israel of Montreal, and these three ancient congregations took the lead in founding the Union. Sephardi congregations throughout the country responded to the call and the Union was born.[50]

The Union's main accomplishment was the publication of Sephardi prayer books, translated and edited by Dr. Pool. It also held a number of conventions, but these seldom spurred constructive actions. (At the May 1949 convention held at Shearith Israel Dr. Pool deplored the failure of so many New York congregations to send delegates.) It asked that promising young men be sought for Sephardi rabbinic training; that Jewish education receive top priority; that Sephardi synagogues adopt a uniform *minhag*.[51] But the Sephardi Jews, as a whole, had no interest in such matters. In the course of time, the Union of Sephardic Congregations has become relatively inactive.

CENTRAL SEPHARDIC JEWISH COMMUNITY OF AMERICA, INC.

The last attempt at unity was made by Rabbi Nissim J. Ovadia, born in Turkey and recognized as a scholar and leader by the Sephardim in Europe. Shortly after his arrival in the United States in 1941, he succeeded in his effort to establish the Central Sephardic Jewish Community of America, Inc., at a meeting in May of Sephardim of all language backgrounds. Although the organization was concerned mainly with New York City, its membership included Sephardim of other cities as well. Rabbi Ovadia served as chief rabbi until his death in August 1942, at the age of 52.[52] Rabbi David Jessurun Cardozo, then assistant minister of Shearith Israel, began to work with the community; he helped organize its women's division, together with

---

[50]Trustees Minutes, Vol. 9, January 5, 1928, p. 411; April 3, 1928, p. 430; November 12, 1928, p. 462; May 7, 1929, p. 487; Pool, "Report. . . ," *op. cit.*, p. 9; *Shearith Israel Bulletin*, May 2, 1929, p. 2; May 25, 1930, p. 3.

[51]Annual report of Union of Sephardic Congregations, 1948; report of Union's convention, May 21-22, 1949.

[52]See *Kol Sepharad*, Vol. 4, July-August 1967, p. 22; *The Sephardi*, September 30, 1943, pp. 1-3; May-June 1945, pp. 3-4; March-April 1952, pp. 3, 9-10.

Mrs. Mazal Ovadia and Mrs. Acher Touriel. Rabbi Isaac Alcalay became the community's chief rabbi, a position he continues to hold today.

The Central Sephardic Jewish Community of America set itself important goals. It worked to maintain Sephardi tradition in worship; to give religious education to the young; to deal with immigration problems; to Americanize Sephardi immigrants as quickly as possible; to find employment for Sephardim; to provide social welfare; to create a Sephardi *Bet Din,* an authoritative rabbinical court. It also sponsored cultural and social programs.

The Central Sephardic Jewish Community seemed to have a real chance of succeeding. In September 1943 it launched a bulletin, *The Sephardi,* whose purpose, its first issue stated, was "to awaken the Sephardi masses to the necessity of a united Sephardi community throughout the Western Hemisphere." It appeared intermittently until 1957, when it ceased publication.

In December 1944 Joseph M. Papo, a trained social worker, was appointed the Community's executive director.[53] This was a felicitous move; for, if the organization was to succeed, it needed trained, able professionals. John Karpeles was hired as director of youth activites. In 1946 the community's Youth League[54] had four chapters: in the Bronx, on Lower East Side, in New Lots, and in Sheepshead Bay. Papo initiated a census of New York's Sephardim to determine the condition of Sephardi life, but this was never completed. The Community's post-war activities aiding Jewish survivors of World War II depleted its financial resources.[55]

However, despite its initial structural strength, today the Community does not receive the support it needs. Its Women's Division does much constructive work, but it has had difficulty recruiting younger members. Perhaps the main reason for the Community's weakness is that the younger generation is not vitally interested in its survival. The young Sephardim did not have a good religious and Sephardi education and, as they married and moved into new neighborhoods which often

---

[53]Joseph Papo, "The Sephardic Community of America," *Reconstructionist,* Vol. 12, 1946, pp. 13–14; *The Sephardi,* March 1945, p. 1.

[54]See *The Sephardi,* March 1946, p. 6; June 1946, p. 7.

[55]*The Sephardi,* March 1945, p. 7; May–June 1945, p. 7.

had no Sephardi synagogues, they lost their interest in the Sephardi community.

RELATIONS BETWEEN NEW AND OLD SEPHARDIM

The old Sephardi congregations, most of their members being of Ashkenazi or mixed Sephardi descent, were relatively affluent and certainly quite Americanized. The Spanish and Portuguese Synagogue in New York occupied a grand building on the corner of Central Park West and Seventieth Street. It saw the influx of poor, unskilled, seemingly uncouth Levantine immigrants as a significant challenge, especially since the two groups shared little except a common past in Spain centuries ago. Still, considering their many differences, there was relatively little conflict between them. Many of the Levantine immigrants attached themselves to Shearith Israel with singular devotion, and there has been truly remarkable harmony between them and the old Sephardi families.

To be sure, relations between the affluent and the poor were not always completely cordial, and there were misunderstandings. Some of the old-line Sephardim apparently felt uneasy because the new immigrants called themselves Sephardim. They were afraid the term would fall into disrepute, and they urged that the newcomers be called "Orientals." HIAS acceded to a request that it change the name of its Sephardi Committee to Committee on Oriental Jews.[56]

The immigrants at first accepted the new designation, but later came to resent it deeply as a slur against them. The impression had been created that the Sephardim were noble and rich, while the Orientals were ignorant and poor. As one Ashkenazi leader once said to M.S. Gadol, the Sephardim were those who belonged to the Spanish and Portuguese Synagogue, while the immigrants were nothing but "Orientals" and "Ladinos."[57] The irony was that many of the immigrants who were pure-blooded Spanish-speaking Sephardim were called Orientals, while Shearith Israel members who were Ashkenazi and of mixed blood were considered the true Sephardim. Realizing that

---

[56]Sisterhood Minutes, January 28, 1914, p. 16, and March 9, 1914, pp. 26–27; HIAS Minutes, February 10, 1914, p. 3; February 15, 1914, p. 2.

[57]*La America*, October 13, 1916, p. 3; see also issues of October 29, 1915, p. 2; November 3, 10, 17, and 24, 1916, all p. 2; July 5, 1918, p. 4.

the immigrants resented being called Oriental and Levantine, the Spanish and Portuguese establishment eventually abandoned these designations.

Shearith Israel felt a moral obligation to help the newcomers, but its outstanding efforts were not always recognized or appreciated. The Sisterhood established an Oriental Employment Bureau. And, maintaining that the "Oriental brethren, proud though poor, ask of us only an opportunity for honest employment," *Shearith Israel Bulletin* in March and April 1912 appealed to members to help them find jobs, especially the kind that would not involve the violation of the Sabbath.

Dr. Pool made every effort to make the immigrants feel at home. Thus, at a meeting in February 1912 to which the leaders of Shearith Israel invited some fifty of them, he stressed that they and the members of the congregation shared the same Sephardi customs. But one of Shearith Israel's ladies made a speech which, though well-intentioned, hopelessly missed the essential needs of the newcomers. Among other things, she said she would see to it that Sephardi girls learned to play the piano and to speak pure Castilian Spanish instead of their Judeo-Spanish—skills that were far removed from the practical needs of the immigrants. Gadol therefore felt that Shearith Israel's promises were empty; rather the newcomers needed a first-rate Talmud Torah. If Shearith Israel could help establish one, this would be a real service. The congregation rose to this challenge and later announced plans for such a school.[58]

The old Spanish and Portuguese group soon became deeply involved in every phase of the immigrants' welfare. Shearith Israel often was asked, and very rarely refused, to give financial aid and to lend religious articles to new Sephardi synagogues.[59]

---

[58]*La America*, February 16, 1912, p. 3; February 23, 1912, p. 1; March 1, 1912, p. 1. For a general picture of Shearith Israel's relations with the Sephardi immigrants, see David and Tamar de Sola Pool, *An Old Faith in the New World* (New York, 1955), pp. 43f.

[59]For some dealings involving Shearith Israel and the Sephardim, see Trustees Minutes, Vol. 8, May 1, 1906, p. 294; December 6, 1910, p. 384; October 19, 1914, p. 474; November 5, 1914, p. 475; January 5, 1915, p. 479; February 2, 1915, p. 481; Vol. 9, October 5, 1915, p. 6; November 15, 1915, p. 8; April 4, 1916, p. 16; May 22, 1916, p. 20; October 16, 1916, pp. 26–27; April 1, 1919, p. 99; May 6, 1919, p. 101; June 13, 1922, p. 207. See also Sisterhood Minutes, December 6, 1913, p. 384; December 17, 1913, p. 8; May 19, 1914, pp. 38–39. *La America*, on January 30, 1914 reported one of many cases of death among the immigrants in which Shearith Israel conducted burials at no cost. The earliest cases are recorded in Trustees Minutes, November 9, 1908, p. 343; April 8, 1909, p. 349; May 3, 1910, p. 373.

Since 1909 Shearith Israel had been conducting free Holy Day services in its auditorium for the needy, most of whom were Oriental Jews. Gadol, who attended such "overflow services" in 1913, found that 90 per cent of the worshipers were middle-class Turkish Jews, and he argued that they should have been permitted to occupy empty seats in the main synagogue. Gadol felt that the congregation was degrading the immigrants by asking them to go to the services in the auditorium downstairs, and he urged Turkish Jews to stay away from the "overflow services" and attend their own synagogues.[60]

Gadol's charges clearly illustrate Shearith Israel's frustrations, for no matter what it did for the newcomers, it was attacked in the Judeo-Spanish press. What did Gadol and his sympathizers actually want? But if Gadol was fanatical and more than unfair in his charges, his attitude made some sense: he did not want immigrant Sephardim to become accustomed to taking charity. If they relied on the "overflow services," they would never make an attempt to build their own synagogues, to stand on their own feet. While Shearith Israel was giving temporary help, it was not, thought Gadol, teaching the Sephardim to become independent, to plan for stable synagogues of their own.

However, Shearith Israel continued its free services until 1924, when the trustees decided to stop the practice. In a letter to Mortimer Menken, then president of the congregation, Dr. Pool argued against the move which, he thought, would undermine the gradually improving relations between Shearith Israel and the Oriental community. It would give rise to mistrust and antagonism among the Oriental Jews and "representative and influential members of the Oriental Jewish Community, such as Mr. [Jack] Barkey, Mr. [Victor] LaHana, Mr. John H. Levy and Mr. [Edward] Valensi, [who] have joined our Congregation." The free High Holy Day services were reinstituted in 1927.[61]

Shearith Israel invited members of the Sephardi colony to attend other services and programs it conducted. This, too, led to controversy at times. A particularly unfortunate incident occurred on Sukkot of

---

[60]*La America*, October 17, 1913, p. 2.

[61]Pool, "Report. . . ," *loc. cit.* Excerpts of Dr. Pool's unpublished letter to Mr. Menken, dated November 25, 1924, are printed with the permission of Mrs. David de Sola Pool. Interestingly, *La America* criticized Shearith Israel for canceling its free services—after a long history of agitating against them.

1924, when visitors, some of them new Sephardim, were barred from the synagogue's overcrowded *succah*. Again, Dr. Pool pacified Mortimer Menken, who was close to losing patience with the immigrants, by writing: "We should be prepared to forego much for the sake of harmony and peace, for the sake of the broader interests of our own Congregation, for the sake of the welfare of the Oriental Sephardi community, and more especially for the sake of their American-born children who can so easily be lost without our friendship and solicitude."[62] Had this not been Shearith Israel's general approach, relations between the old and new Sephardi communities would have been disastrous. The congregation ultimately won the friendship and admiration of most of the Oriental Sephardim, who now are counted among its most active and generous leaders.

SETTLEMENT HOUSE

The Sisterhood of Shearith Israel, in particular, dedicated itself to helping the newcomers. In the early days of immigration it operated a Neighborhood Settlement House on the Lower East Side which emphasized the need of the Sephardim to become Americanized. The Sisterhood gave parties, put on plays, and arranged all kinds of celebrations. Independence Day in 1912 saw a gathering of some 500 guests; music was supplied by the Fourth of July Committee of the City of New York. The Sisterhood distributed to each guest the text of the Declaration of Independence and an especially prepared Judeo-Spanish translation of it (perhaps the first in American history).[63]

The Neighborhood House also had its own synagogue, Berith Shalom. In return for regularly attending services at that synagogue, worshipers and their families were offered, in March 1914, associate membership in Shearith Israel at a charge of fifty cents per month. This

---

[62]*La America*, October 17, 1924, p. 7; Trustees Minutes, Vol. 9, October 23, 1924, p. 289; Minutes of joint meeting of Trustees of Shearith Israel, the Sisterhood, and Berith Shalom, December 2, 1924, pp. 2-3.

[63]See *Shearith Israel Bulletin*, September 1912, p. 15. The Sisterhood often sponsored Purim celebrations, serving free dinners to all guests. Unfortunately, Gadol's bitterness led him to condemn the Sisterhood even for such generous parties. See *La America*, March 20, 1914, p. 2; April 3, 1914, p. 2. Other information dealing with various celebrations may be found in *Shearith Israel Bulletin*, March 1912, pp. 6-7; *La America*, March 8, 1912, p. 2; June 28, 1912, p. 1; March 8, 1918, p. 3.

entitled them to all services granted or performed by the synagogue, including the use of a section in its Long Island cemetery. Membership privileges, however, were limited to eleven months a year (excluding the High Holy Day season) and were withdrawn for boys after their eighteenth birthday. The plan was warmly received by many downtown Sephardim.[64]

By 1912 the Neighborhood House dedicated itself exclusively to the needs of the Sephardi immigrants. The difficult task of giving leadership to the Berith Shalom worshipers and of maintaining harmony between Shearith Israel and the synagogue was successfully performed by Reverend Joseph de A. Benyunes. He was a humble and good man, a member of the old Spanish and Portuguese community. Social workers, club directors, Talmud Torah teachers, and other trained personnel were engaged to direct other activities.

NEED FOR JEWISH EDUCATION

Responsible individuals and groups within the Sephardi colony continued to advocate Americanization. English classes were held, and immigrants were strongly urged to study and apply for American citizenship. Indeed, the desire to Americanize was so strong among the younger Sephardim that there was fear the new generation would be lost to Judaism.[65] The Sephardim now desperately needed high-quality Jewish educational programs to maintain the young people's interest in their heritage. But no such schools existed, and the resultant loss to the religious sensibilities of both the Sephardi and general Jewish communities is immeasurable. The Sephardim were busy establishing themselves and had neither time, resources, nor the will to establish good schools. And now, several generations later, neither time, resources, nor will can fully compensate for what has been lost forever.

Reverend Benyunes did all he could to preserve the Sephardi heritage by working with the Sisterhood's downtown and uptown

---

[64]For a record of these events, see Trustees Minutes Vol. 8, March 8, 1914, p. 459; March 16, 1914, p. 461; April 7, 1914, p. 461; May 25, 1914, p. 465; July 1, 1914, p. 469. At a meeting on October 23, 1916 the Trustees abolished the special associate membership.

[65]*La America*, November 25, 1910, p. 2; August 4, 1911, p. 1; December 29, 1911, p. 1; July 21, 1916, p. 2. See also Sisterhood Minutes, December 22, 1913, p. 14.

religious schools. But the problems with these and other Sephardi Hebrew schools were manifold: inadequate staffing, lack of discipline and organization; erratic attendance of students; antiquated curricula.[66]

SEPHARDI CLUBS

The Sisterhood's Neighborhood House, for its part, sponsored clubs to keep the young involved in Jewish life. The Jewish Friendship Circle, founded in January 1914, was the first organization of this kind for Sephardi children. The members had parties, put on dramatic performances, played games and had other activities. Arrangements were made for children to attend camps during the summer months.[67] Benyunes worked with this group as well as with the Society of Helpful Women, which was also designed to strengthen religious observance among the Sephardim.[68]

As the programs expanded, the old Neighborhood House became inadequate and facilities were twice moved to larger quarters: to Orchard Street in 1913 and to Eldridge Street in 1916.[69]

The boys who had outgrown the services of the Settlement House founded their own clubs, such as the Alba and the Sephardic Progressive. In 1918 young Sephardi men in Harlem founded the Filo Center Club, which is still in existence. Other clubs for the Judeo-Spanish were the Zenith, Sunray, and much later, the Abravanel Square Club. The Greek-speaking Jews met at the Athenian Club. The Broome and Allen Boys, one of the Judeo-Spanish groups still

---

[66]Sisterhood Minutes, November 24, 1913, p. 2; December 11, 1913, p. 5; January 28, 1914, p. 18; March 9, 1914, p. 29; November 16, 1914, p. 49; December 21, 1914, p. 53; January 26, 1915, p. 57; October 6, 1915, p. 69; January 24, 1916, pp. 79f; February 8, 1916, p. 82; April 11, 1916, pp. 86–88; December 26, 1916, p. 98. See also *Shearith Israel Bulletin*, January 31, 1924, p. 2.

[67]*La America*, February 13, 1914, p. 2. Trustees Minutes, Vol. 9, December 12 (p. 188) and 25, 1921, p. 190; October 17, 1922, p. 220. Barocas, *op. cit.*, p. 10. Sisterhood Minutes, *op. cit.*, January 28, 1914, p. 19; March 9, 1914, p. 27; March 15, 1915, p. 61, all deal with the problem of rowdyism at the Neighborhood House clubs.

[68]Sisterhood Minutes, January 28, 1914, pp. 18–19; December 21, 1914, pp. 52–53.

[69]Trustees Minutes, November 14, 1910; Sisterhood Minutes, *op. cit.*, November 24, 1913, pp. 2–3; *La America*, December 5, 1913, p. 2; *Shearith Israel Bulletin*, March 15, 1914, p. 45; Barocas, *The Broome and Allen Boys, op. cit.*, pp. 8–9.

functioning,[70] undertook as its permanent task to provide needy children with summer camp vacations. This they did in recognition of the help they received from the Sisterhood when they were boys.

COMMUNITY IN TRANSITION

Relations between Shearith Israel and Berith Shalom showed signs of improvement in 1923, largely due to the efforts of Henry S. Hendricks, Berith Shalom's president and an outstanding leader of Shearith Israel. In March Berith Shalom added to its name "of Shearith Israel." The *entente cordial* lasted until the spring of 1925, when Berith Shalom dropped its formal association with its mother congregation.[71] By this time, the community was largely self-sufficient. Many of the Sephardim had been in America for a decade or more, so that the initial problems they had faced as immigrants were rapidly disappearing. There no longer was a valid reason for remaining under the wings of the Spanish and Portuguese Synagogue.

In his famous report of 1926,[72] Louis Hacker spoke of the changing character of the Sephardi community. He pointed out that the Sisterhood's Neighborhood Settlement House was steadily losing influence as Sephardim were moving away from from the Lower East Side. No new immigrants requiring its services were arriving. But while the Sephardim no longer needed welfare, they continued to need spiritual and cultural guidance; for this they lacked proper leadership.

Indeed, the last years of the decade and the early 1930s were a period of transition for the Sephardim of New York City, as well as for the other communities in the United States. The first American-born generation was old enough to marry. The old clubs were breaking up. Neighborhoods were changing. This was the beginning of a new era in Sephardi history in the United States.[73]

---

[70]Barocas, *ibid.*, pp. 1, 12–15.

[71]*Shearith Israel Bulletin*, February 2, 1923, p. 2; Trustees Minutes, Vol. 9, November 17, 1924, p. 291; November 25, 1924, p. 296; December 2, 1924, p. 297. A letter dated November 20, 1924 from N. Yohai of Berith Shalom to I. Phillips Cohen, clerk of Shearith Israel, deals with the problems between the two organizations. For the formal break, see Trustees Minutes, Vol. 9, June 3, 1925, p. 310. For later attempts to improve relations, see Pool, "Report. . . ," *op. cit.*, pp. 6f.

[72]Hacker, *op. cit.*, pp. 36–37.

[73]Barocas, *op. cit.*, p. 14.

Sephardi Communities Outside New York City

The small Sephardi communities scattered throughout the country shared a common development. The problems of one could, with changes of names and places, serve as a fairly accurate description of the problems of all. The difficulties plaguing the New York Sephardim were those of the Sephardim in Seattle, Atlanta, Los Angeles, Rochester, Indianapolis, and elsewhere.

In his 1913 study of the Sephardi colony in Cincinnati,[74] Maurice Hexter counted 219 immigrants with 27 American-born children and three Russian-Jewish wives. Most of the families came from the Dardanelles, a minority from Salonika. Their language and culture isolated them from the rest of the community. Attempts at Americanization had not yet been successful, and Hexter urged that the Sephardim be encouraged to become citizens. They were at the bottom of the economic ladder, working as peddlers, petty salesmen, unskilled workers, shoemakers, tailors, waiters. Of the fifty families in Cincinnati, forty-three lived in tenements. Many took in boarders or lodgers to supplement their meager incomes. Hexter noted that here, too, "their social centers are two pernicious poolrooms and coffee houses." As in New York, little progress was made in Jewish education.

Just as the New York Sephardim were fragmented into groups based on geographic origins, so were several other, much smaller, communities. Thus Jews from the Island of Rhodes, always eager to maintain their own synagogues and benevolent societies, established separate organizations in Seattle, Los Angeles, and Atlanta. The Atlanta community split into two factions in 1912, but reunited two years later. Seattle, with only some forty Sephardi families in 1910, had two distinct religious groups and three mutual-aid societies. To this day, it has two Sephardi synagogues; one for those originating on the Island of Rhodes, and the other for those from the Turkish mainland, particularly from the Marmara littoral. The Rhodes Jews also maintain their own synagogue in Los Angeles.

Sephardi communities with sizable groups of different geographic

---

[74]Maurice Hexter, "The Dawn of a Problem," *Jewish Charities*, December 1913, pp. 2–5.

origins usually had to struggle for unity. But, as in New York, they seldom achieved more than moderately peaceful coexistence. They organized no cultural or educational institutions of their own, except synagogues and mediocre Hebrew schools. Even fairly united communities, which usually were small in size, did not properly plan for cultural and spiritual survival.[75]

It is difficult to estimate the number of Sephardi congregations in the United States. Some are too small and others too new to be known. The *Diary and World-Wide Directory of Sephardic Congregations,* published annually by Shearith Israel in New York, lists a total of thirty-six. Though this listing is not complete, it is doubtful whether there are more than fifty or sixty. A few of them are growing and expanding, but many are stagnant and some are on the verge of dying. While, at present, nostalgia still ties the Sephardim to their past, this will no longer be true in a generation or two.

Sephardi Cultural Endeavors

One of the bright spots in the intellectual history of the Sephardim in the United States is the Judeo-Spanish press. *La America* began publication in 1910 as a national weekly. It closed down in 1923. Besides Sephardi news, it printed provocative editorials, historical essays, poetry, and fiction. Reading *La America* is an exciting experience even today; one is stirred by the vigorous and perceptive intellect of its editor, M.S. Gadol.

Other national Judeo-Spanish publications were published later: *La Boz del Pueblo, El Luzero Sephardi, La Luz, El Progresso, El Emigrante,* and *La Vara. La Vara,* which appeared from 1922 until February 1948, was by far the most important and popular. Its circulation rose from 9,000 in 1926 to 16,500 in 1928.[76] In a 1924 series of articles, *La Vara's* editor, Albert Levy, called for the publication of a daily Sephardi newspaper,[77] pointing to the need for such a cultural organ. The idea never became reality. On December

---

[75]Helen Shirazi, "The Communal Pluralism of Sephardi Jewry in the United St..es," *Le Judaisme Sephardi,* January 1966, p. 25.

[76]Harry Linfield, *Communal Organization of the Jews in the United States,* 1927 (New York, 1930), p. 175.

[77]*La Vara,* August 29, 1924, p. 4.

14, 1923, *La Vara* announced the establishment of the Sephardi Publishing Company on Rivington Street. It was not possible to determine the extent of its activities. When *La Vara* ceased publication, the Judeo-Spanish press in America came to an end.

Various Sephardi societies also issued publications, some written in Judeo-Spanish but most in English. Among them were *The Sephardic Bulletin*, an English-language Zionist paper of the late 1930s;[78] *The Progress*, the newspaper of Seattle's Sephardim, 1934-35;[79] *El Ermanado*, an annual published by the Sephardic Brotherhood of America.

The Sephardic Home News, a monthly newsletter with a national circulation of about 10,000, is published currently under the editorship of Dr. Joseph Dalven. (It is the organ of the Sephardic Home for the Aged in Brooklyn, established by Sephardim of Judeo-Spanish and Greek backgrounds. The Home, founded in August 1951, is the only institution of its type created by and for Sephardim. It has an impressive record of growth and expansion.)

Every Sephardi community put on biblical and historical plays like *Joseph, the Righteous, and his Brothers* and *Dreifus*, written in, or translated into, Judeo-Spanish by Sephardi playwrights for local showing. In Seattle, for example, Leon Behar excelled as both producer and playwright. But this kind of theater no longer exists in the United States.[80]

Within the past decade there has been some creative activity in the American Sephardi communities. In 1964 Yeshiva University established a Sephardic Studies Program. Originally conceived by the Sephardi Chief Rabbi of the British Commonwealth, *Haham* Solomon Gaon, and Dr. Samuel Belkin, president of Yeshiva University, the program includes not only academic courses and cultural events but also community service activities. In this area, Rabbi Herbert C. Dobrinsky of Yeshiva has done much to promote unity among the Sephardim. The Sephardic Studies Program also publishes *The American Sephardi*, an annual scholarly journal which circulates in

---

[78]Levantine Sephardim were Zionists ever since their earliest settlement in the United States. Gadol was a devoted Zionist.

[79]See Marc D. Angel, "'Progress'—Seattle's Sephardic Monthly, 1934-35," *American Sephardi*, Vol. 5, Autumn 1971, pp. 90-95.

[80]See Marc D. Angel, "The Judeo-Spanish Theater of Seattle's Sephardim," scheduled to appear in *American Jewish Archives*, November 1973.

every Sephardi community of North America and is on file in many university Judaica libraries.

In 1969 the Foundation for the Advancement of Sephardic Studies and Culture was incorporated, mainly through the efforts of Professor and Mrs. M. J. Benardete, David Barocas, and Louis N. Levy. It publishes tracts on various phases of Sephardi history and culture. Though the Foundation's impact has been limited because of inadequate staff and financial support, it has created some cultural waves, especially among Sephardim of Judeo-Spanish origin.

Most recently, an organization calling itself the World Sephardi Institute has begun publishing a newsletter, *Sephardic World*. While major support of this group seems to come from Sephardim of Arabic background, the newsletter attempts to reach all Sephardim. On another front, there also has been an attempt to strengthen the American branch of the World Sephardi Federation through the encouragement of the Jewish Agency.

Mention should be made of the interest in Sephardi studies by the Spanish government whose Supreme Council for Scientific Studies established the Instituto Arias Montana de Estudios Hebraicos in Madrid in 1939. The Institute's quarterly journal, *Sefarad*, deals with all phases of Jewish history and culture, but focuses on the Sephardi past. The 1960s also witnessed a revival of the study of general and Hispanic Jewish culture in Spain. The universities of Madrid, Barcelona, and Granada established chairs of Hebrew language, Jewish history, and Jewish literature. An institute of Sephardi studies was established in Madrid. In 1964 a Sephardi center was created in Toledo by decree of the head of state.

The Instituto Ibn Tibbón of the University of Granada, directed by Professor David Gonzalo Maeso, has initiated the publication of *Biblioteca Universal Sefardi* in collaboration with *Editorial Gredos*. So far they have produced several volumes of the *Me'am Lo'ez*, the great Judeo-Spanish Bible commentary, with introduction and notes. The books are printed in Latin letters, not in the Rashi script of the original.[81]

---

[81]The first volume in this series was the *Proleqómenos* to the *Me'am Lo'ez* (Madrid, 1964). See also Iacob Hassan, T. Rubiato, and E. Romero, eds., *Actas del primer simposio de estudios sefardies* ("Proceedings of the First Symposium of Sephardi Studies; Madrid, 1970), 789 p., for the record of a historic symposium in Spain, held in 1964.

Syrian Sephardi Community

In a recent survey of American Sephardim, Hayyim Cohen of the Hebrew University found that, while Jews of Judeo-Spanish origin are scattered throughout the United States, almost all Sephardim of Syrian origin are concentrated in one neighborhood in Brooklyn (there are also small communities in Bradley Beach and Deal, N. J., and in Myrtle Beach, S. C.);[82] that Egyptian Jews, most of whom actually are of Syrian origin, live in the same neighborhood, as do several hundred Lebanese Jews; that Iraqi Jews are found in Queens, Manhattan, and Long Island.[83]

Cohen estimates that some 5,000 Syrian Jews are living in Brooklyn;[84] Syrian leaders, however, put the number at some 20,000,[85] a more realistic estimate. The Syrian Jews maintain a number of synagogues, all of them very well attended.

The Syrian community has risen to relative affluence during its several generations in America. Many of its members are proprietors of retail stores. The number of professionals is rising, though not to the degree found among Judeo-Spanish Sephardim. This is because Syrian Jews are more business-oriented, and fewer attend college.[86]

Of all the Sephardi communities in the United States, the Syrian community of Brooklyn is doubtless the strongest and most viable. Syrians have kept their neighborhood intact. When the young marry, they often choose to settle within the community. Syrians also tend to

---

[82]See also Victor D. Sanua, "A Study of Adjustment of Sephardi Jews in the New York Metropolitan Area," *Jewish Journal of Sociology*, June 1967, Vol. 9, pp. 25–33; Ben Frank, *American Examiner-Jewish Week*, October 14, 1971, p. 10; *Ma'ariv*, December 27, 1968, p. 16; Helen Shirazi, *op. cit.*, p. 25.

[83]Hayyim Cohen, "Sephardi Jews in the U.S., Marriage with Ashkenazim and Non-Jews," *Dispersion and Unity* (Jerusalem), Vol. 13–14, 1971–72, pp. 152–53. See also, Ben Frank, "Lebanese, Syrian, Egyptian Jews Settle in Brooklyn," *Southern Israelite*, Vol. 47, July 7, 1972, p. 1.

[84]*Ibid.*, p. 159.

[85]*Jewish Life*, May–June, 1971, p. 55.

[86]For some indications of the cultural characteristics of Syrian Jews in Brooklyn, see Morris Gross, *Learning Readiness in Two Jewish Groups* (New York: Center for Urban Education, 1967).

marry within their own group to a far greater extent than other Sephardim. Intermarriage with non-Jews is extremely rare.[87]

The Syrian Jews are the only Sephardim who have developed an educational system of their own. They support several day schools attended by an estimated 85 to 90 per cent of all school-age children. The Syrians also have several *yeshivot* for advanced Jewish learning, the largest and most important of which is the Sephardic Institute directed by Rabbi Mosheh Shamah. The Institute is attended by over fifty young men, many of whom are also studying for degrees in colleges or graduate schools. The Syrian community can boast of dozens of rabbis and talmudic scholars who attended its own or Ashkenazi *yeshivot*.

North African Sephardim

Sephardim of North African origin have settled throughout North America. In the United States, they are represented in small numbers in nearly all Sephardi communities. They generally have enjoyed a steady upward mobility educationally, economically, and socially. In Washington, D.C., a group of 250 Moroccan Jews has established its own congregation.[88]

A far greater number of North African Jews settled in Canada, notably in Montreal and Toronto. In June 1967 Professor Jean Boulakia[89] of Montreal estimated that of some 9,000 Sephardim (about 8 per cent of the total Jewish population) living in Montreal, some 7,000 were of Moroccan origin. The rest of the Sephardim came from Tunisia, Iraq, Iran, Egypt, Algeria, Italy, Greece, and elsewhere.

Most Sephardim in Canada are French-speaking and are thus separated linguistically from the English-speaking Ashkenazi majority. The Montreal and Toronto communities[90] are plagued by poverty and associated social ills. The new immigrants are having adjustment

---

[87]Cohen, *op. cit.*, pp. 153f.

[88]See article in *Potomac Magazine* of *Washington Post*, July 26, 1970, pp. 12f.

[89]"Profil d'une communauté," *American Sephardi*, Vol. 1, June 1967, pp. 48–51.

[90]Ben Kayfetz, "The Development of the Toronto Jewish Community," *Tradition*, Vol. 13, Summer 1972, pp. 16–17, briefly discusses the influx of North African Jews to Toronto.

114 / AMERICAN JEWISH YEAR BOOK, 1973

problems similar to those of the Sephardi immigrants in the United States earlier in this century. They too suffer from lack of unity and internal leadership, but the situation seems to be improving.

SURVEY OF AMERICAN SEPHARDIM[91]

Under the sponsorship of the Union of Sephardic Congregations this writer conducted a study of American-born Sephardim of Judeo-Spanish background. Between January and March 1972, a total of 941 questionnaires were mailed. We received a total of 251 acceptable responses from Atlanta, Denver, Detroit, Highland Park (N. J.), Indianapolis, Los Angeles, Montgomery, Portland (Ore.), Rochester, Sacramento, Seattle, and from all parts of Metropolitan New York. (Since all respondents did not answer each question, the totals in the discussion below do not always add up to 251.) It must be remembered that this study does not deal with other Sephardi communities, as, for example, the Syrian.

The survey was essentially exploratory, since there was no way of selecting a truly random sample of American Sephardim. Mailing lists were made available by Sephardi synagogues and organizations, usually with American-born members designated. Questionnaires were sent to every qualified person on these lists, but that excluded many Sephardim who had completely dropped out of the Sephardi fold. At the same time, over 24 per cent (61) of the respondents were not affiliated with Sephardi synagogues and therefore only nominally connected with the community.

Because the questionnaire was sent almost exclusively to Sephardim who were still somewhat tied to the community, the study may be more important than it otherwise would have been. Data on the perpetuation of culture, for example, will have been drawn from Sephardim who were in some way involved in their community. If a

---

[91]For helping me obtain lists of American-born Sephardim, I would like to thank Rabbi Michel Albagli, L. Bill Angel, Rabbi Benjamin Aronson, Dr. Irving Benveniste, Rabbi Murray Berger, David Chicorel, Rabbi Solomon Cohen, Rabbi David Glicksman, Rabbi William Greenberg, Rabbi Eli Greenwald, Rabbi S. Robert Ichay, Rabbi Solomon Maimon, Rabbi Arnold Marans, Joseph Papo, Rabbi Myron Rakowitz, and Victor Tarry. I would also like to thank all survey participants for their cooperation.

cultural decline occurred among these, it can be safely assumed that the decline was even greater among those entirely separated from the Sephardi world.

This study takes into account that the survival of Sephardim in the United States involves a two-fold survival—as Jews and as Sephardim having particular cultural characteristics. Sephardim who drift from Jewish life will be lost to the Jewish community altogether. Those who live a Jewish life but adopt non-Sephardi characteristics in place of their own will be lost to the Sephardi community. The continuity of Sephardi life demands then that Sephardim exist as a small minority within a small minority—an awesome task.

At the outset, we must recognize that the social characteristics of Sephardim strongly resemble those of the Ashkenazim. Living in the same open society, both groups have been exposed to similar social forces. Except for groups having maintained closely-knit communities, most middle-class, American-born Jews share a host of characteristics.

Birthrate

The low birthrate among Jews is a well-known phenomenon. But it usually is not known that the Sephardi birthrate, too, is quite low. To be sure, the families of Syrian Jews have been larger than the average American Jewish family.[92] Among Sephardim of Judeo-Spanish origin, however, the birthrate has dropped sharply over the past several generations, a decline reflecting changing ideas and attitudes among Levantine Sephardim under the influence of secular society. Table 1 shows birthrate trends, as derived from the survey data. For the sake of clarity, respondents have been divided into three categories: 1) the 40-years-of-age or older, generally raised in tight Sephardi neighborhoods; 2) the under-40-years-of-age, but still of the second generation, generally raised under more open and prosperous conditions and more strongly influenced by Americanization forces; 3) the third generation, generally raised in middle-class, Americanized families. The birthrate of each of these three groups is compared with that of their parent groups.

---

[92]Barocas, *op. cit.*, pp. 67–68.

TABLE 1. BIRTHRATES OF AMERICAN-BORN SEPHARDIM AND THEIR PARENTS

Category	Number of Families	Number of Children	Average Family Size
Over 40	137	393	2.9
Parents	137	625	4.6
Under 40 (2nd generation)	36	96	2.7
Parents	36	207	5.8
Under 40 (3rd generation)	28	65	2.3
Parents	28	89	3.1

In view of the drop in birthrates, it is doubtful whether Sephardi communities in the United States can depend on natural increase to compensate for cultural defections in order to assure survival. Neither can they depend on an increase by immigration, which is practically nonexistent.

Sephardim have become quite Americanized and more affluent, and it is ever more difficult to hold the new generation in the community. The Sephardi neighborhoods—where one lived within walking distance of most relatives; constantly heard Judeo-Spanish chatter; looked to the synagogue as the center of life, and learned and observed Sephardi customs in the course of living—have almost completely disintegrated. People are moving to the more fashionable suburbs. The young are encouraged to attend college and learn a profession. Broadening interests and mobility have sharply decreased the need for neighborhood activities. And, as neighborhoods cease to be the once strong cultural force, the influence of non-Sephardi social patterns naturally becomes stronger. The result is that some Sephardim completely lose their sense of group belonging.

Economic Status

The survey data indicated that most of the respondents were fairly well-to-do (Table 2). Nearly all who listed incomes of between $5,000–10,000 were either retired or young people just starting jobs. Of the 214 respondents who listed their occupations only four were unskilled laborers, all being over 40 years old. For employed

Sephardim under the age of forty, the occupational pattern is particularly revealing: businessmen, 53 per cent; professionals, 39 per cent; artists, 5 per cent; skilled laborers, 3 per cent. By contrast the first generation of Sephardi immigrants for the most part had been unskilled laborers.

Table 2. ANNUAL INCOMES OF HOUSEHOLDS

Income	Number of Respondents	Per Cent
$50,000 or more	21	11.4
30,000–49,999	26	14.1
20,000–29,999	29	15.8
15,000–19,999	45	24.5
10,000–14,999	40	21.7
5,000–9,999	23	12.5
Under 5,000	0	0.0
Total	184	100.0

Secular Education

Implicit in these figures is the fact that the level of education among the Sephardim is higher than it was in their parents' generation. Indeed, the Sephardim consider college education almost an essential for their children's future. In response to the question, "Did, do, or will your children attend college?", 203 Sephardim answered yes and only three answered no.

On the other hand, when asked to list their fathers' educational backgrounds, the responses of 139 American-born Sephardim aged 40 and over were as follows: 120 said that their fathers had received less than a high school education; 15 said they graduated high school; 3 that they attended a college, and only one that his father was a college graduate.

The older, second-generation American Sephardim often were poor. Although many attended college, a large percentage dropped out of school to help support their families. For second-generation Sephardim under the age of 40 and for third-generation Sephardim, who generally enjoyed a higher economic status, college was more readily available (Table 3).

TABLE 3. EDUCATION OF AMERICAN SEPHARDIM

Level of Education	Aged 40 and Over				Under Age 40			
	Men	Per Cent	Women	Per Cent	Men	Per Cent	Women	Per Cent
Less than high school	5	5.1	1	2.9	0	0.0	0	0.0
High school graduation	42	42.8	24	68.5	1	1.5	10	50.0
Some college	19	19.4	8	22.9	8	12.5	4	20.0
College graduation	19	19.4	2	5.7	33	51.6	5	25.0
Higher degrees	13	13.3	0	0.0	22	34.4	1	5.0
Total	98	100.0	35	100.0	64	100.0	20	100.0

With college education so prevalent, young Sephardim inevitably are being strongly influenced by the egalitarian spirit on the campus. Because the Sephardi students constitute a small number, they find it hard to maintain themselves as a particular group and therefore mingle freely with fellow students of all backgrounds. Thus, an examination of some of the major sociological features shared by Sephardim and Ashkenazim with the American middle class indicates that many of the Sephardi characteristics have been lost in the course of three generations. The birthrate, neighborhoods, economic condition, and educational background of the modern Sephardi differ radically from those of the immigrant generation. Although signifying material progress, these changes also constitute a serious challenge to the continuity of Sephardi life in the United States.

Jewish and Sephardi Education

As stated earlier, Sephardi survival depends on the strength of the group both as Jews and as Sephardim. Sephardi literature, folklore, customs, language, law, and cuisine are inextricably linked to Jewish sources. Sephardism separated from Judaism is a gross mutation. Because this is so, the survey sought to elicit information that would give a general idea of the state of Jewish education, observance, and belief among Sephardim. The results showed a definite correlation between attachment to Judaism and attachment to Sephardi culture.

A culture can be transmitted only through the process of education. While some immigrant Sephardim had attended good Jewish schools in the old country, many had received no formal Jewish education. But this was compensated by the fact that all lived in an intensely Jewish environment where religion and culture were absorbed in daily living. However, in the United States, formal Jewish education soon became crucial. Children no longer could readily learn religious values and teachings from the people around them. Things had changed. Social and economic pressures in America pulled Sephardim from their old ways.

When the Sephardim came to this country, they found no Sephardi schools for their children. Because they were poor, stubborn, and without adequate leadership, they set up a host of small afternoon Talmudé Torah which, as already noted, were almost always poorly run, poorly staffed, poorly attended. But it was in these schools, which certainly did not equip them to perpetuate Jewish and Sephardi values, that most second-generation American Sephardim received their Jewish education.

With the rise of the Jewish day school, some Sephardim have chosen its more intensive training for their children, especially in Seattle and, to lesser degrees, in Atlanta and New York. The Sephardim also have access to synagogue schools which, with time, have become better organized and staffed. Still, a growing number of their children either receive no formal Jewish education at all or only go to Sunday school. Among the American-born Sephardim aged 40 and over, about 10 per cent received only Sunday school education or less, while the rest had more intensive schooling. The percentage increased to 15 for those under the age of 40. For the third- and fourth-generation Sephardim, it jumped to nearly 30 per cent, thus indicating a definite rise in the number of Sephardi youths who receive practically no Jewish education.

Even Sephardim who had a good Jewish education did not know enough about their Sephardi heritage. For example, they seldom studied the history of their ancestors in the Levant. They seldom were told of the significant rabbinic and poetic literatures created by the Sephardim of the past four centuries. They were not given a real awareness of their cultural roots, and therefore did not really understand Sephardism.[93] Table 4 indicates a general decline in Sephardi education.

Religious Observance

Although the vast majority of Sephardi immigrants had been observant Jews, the conditions of American life soon brought a relaxation of religious observances. Sabbath observance was often the first to be discarded, since poverty drove immigrants to work on that day. *Kashrut*, too, sometimes was compromised as a result of economic or social pressures. But if the first generation struggled to adhere to ritual, their children were less inclined to do so. This was, of course, also the experience of the Ashkenazim.

Of 219 respondents, 68 per cent (150) reported their homes were

---

[93]See Marc D. Angel, "Ruminations on Sephardic Identity," *Midstream*, March 1972, pp. 64–67.

TABLE 4. SEPHARDI ORIENTATION OF RELIGIOUS EDUCATION

	Respondents Age 40 and Over		Under 40	
Extent	Number	Per Cent	Number	Per Cent
Completely	81	58.3	27	29.6
Somewhat	33	23.7	35	38.5
Not at all	25	18.0	29	31.9
Total	139	100.0	91	100.0
Children of Respondents				
Completely	19	14.1	8	18.2
Somewhat	54	40.0	18	40.9
Not at all	62	45.9	18	40.9
Total	135	100.0	44	100.0
Respondents' View of Emphasis on History of Levant				
Great deal	7	4.8	2	2.3
Moderate amount	36	25.2	18	20.3
Very little	52	36.4	38	43.2
None at all	48	33.6	30	34.2
Total	143	100.0	88	100.0

less observant than those of their parents. Eighty per cent of the immigrant generation had kept kosher homes, as compared with only 28 per cent of their children; 95 per cent of the immigrants had at least some special Sabbath observances, as compared to a reported 63 per cent of their children.

Since the synagogue is the only Jewish cultural institution in most Sephardi communities, an attempt was made to establish trends in terms of synagogue attendance (Table 5).

The apparently paradoxical finding that the percentage of men under 40 attending services weekly is higher than of those over 40 can be explained by the fact that 11 of the 17 younger men live in Seattle and are members of observant families. In other cities the rate of weekly attendance is far lower. Also, Table 5 indicates that 17.9 per cent of men under 40 attend only on High Holy Days or not at all, while this is true of only 7.3 per cent of men over 40. The figures also reflect the diminishing stress on synagogue attendance by women in the Sephardi community. A general pattern of less frequent synagogue attendance

TABLE 5. SYNAGOGUE ATTENDANCE

Frequency	Men 40 and Over Number	Per Cent	Women 40 and Over Number	Per Cent
At least weekly	20	18.4	4	11.1
At least monthly	33	30.3	11	30.6
Only on holidays, special occasions	48	44.0	17	47.2
Only on High Holy Days	7	6.4	3	8.3
Not at all	1	.9	1	2.8
Total	109	100.0	36	100.0

	Men Under 40 Number	Per Cent	Women Under 40 Number	Per Cent
At least weekly	17	25.4	0	0.0
At least monthly	8	11.9	5	22.7
Only on holidays, special occasions	30	44.8	12	54.6
Only on High Holy Days	8	11.9	2	9.1
Not at all	4	6.0	3	13.6
Total	67	100.0	22	100.0

can hardly be denied. And this means that the only institution on which Sephardi survival now rests is gradually losing its influence.

That Sephardi synagogues are in difficulty is also indicated by data on affiliation (Table 6). The third-generation figures were derived from answers of third-generation respondents (who were also included in the under 40 category) and from the second-generation respondents who listed the affiliations of their adult children. Aside from indicating serious movement away from Sephardi synagogues, the findings imply a sharp decline in synagogue affiliation generally.

The decline in religious observance and affiliation is indicative of the secularization of American Sephardim. While nearly all the immigrants were Orthodox, the American-born generations drifted from Orthodoxy. Of the 47 respondents who are members of Ashkenazi synagogues, 5 (10.6 per cent) belong to Orthodox, 23 (48.9 per cent) to Conservative, and 19 (40.4 per cent) to Reform congregations. Although some chose a particular synagogue for convenience and physical proximity, the majority no longer claim to hold Orthodox beliefs. This is true also of members of traditional Sephardi synagogues. Table 7 analyzes responses to the question,

TABLE 6. SYNAGOGUE AFFILIATION

Type	40 and Over Number	40 and Over Per Cent	Under 40 Number	Under 40 Per Cent	3rd Generation Number	3rd Generation Per Cent
Sephardi	123	77.4	67	72.8	49	44.6
Ashkenazi	33	20.8	14	15.2	32	29.0
None	33	1.8	11	12.0	29	26.4
Total	159	100.0	92	100.0	110	100.0

TABLE 7. RELIGIOUS BELIEFS

Belief	40 and Over Number	40 and Over Per Cent	Under 40 Number	Under 40 Per Cent
Orthodox	32	21.8	18	20.7
Conservative	87	59.2	46	52.9
Reform	22	15.0	17	19.5
Other	6	4.0	6	6.9
Total	147	100.0	87	100.0

"Are your religious beliefs most in harmony with Orthodox, Conservative, or Reform Judaism, or something else?" The data shows that, although there has been movement away from Orthodoxy, most of the Sephardim have not gone all the way to Reform. For the time being at least, reverence for tradition remains a strong force in shaping religious attitudes.

Hispanic Character

A distinguishing characteristic of Levantine Sephardim throughout the past four and a half centuries has been their language. They spoke a tongue known variously as Judeo-Spanish, Judezmo, Ladino, Spaniolit. They thought, spoke, wrote, and sang in this sonorous language. But when they came to America, it was bound to undergo change and decline.

First-generation Sephardim spoke their language regularly because they lived in closely knit communities. They even Hispanicized some English words and used them in conversation. Thus "parkear" meant to park, "drivear" to drive. One of the most peculiar words to enter the language was "abetchar," meaning to bet, which derived from the

English slang phrase "I betcha." But when their children began to go to public school, English became the dominant language. For the third and fourth generations it has become, for all practical purposes, the only language. Responses from third- and fourth-generation Sephardim indicated that 73.6 per cent could not speak Judeo-Spanish at all. Roughly half of the second-generation respondents thought the disappearance of Judeo-Spanish as a spoken language would be a cultural tragedy; the other half felt that its disappearance was inevitable. About 9 per cent did not care whether or not the language survived.

The third generation of American Sephardim marks a transition in Sephardi history. Many still have nostalgic memories of their Judeo-Spanish heritage. But while most can remember hearing parents, grandparents, and older relatives chattering, singing, and cursing in Judeo-Spanish, they hardly speak it well enough—if at all—to transmit the language to the next generation.

One element of the Hispanic character of Sephardim is their feeling toward Spain. It is often stated that they have a strong emotional attachment to that country for historic and linguistic reasons. The Spanish scholar Federico Castro, romanticizing the Sephardim's love for Spain, wrote that they still reminisce about the old cities of their forefathers with love and emotion, with tears in their eyes.[94] There is no doubt that some Sephardim do feel deeply attached to Spain; but our study indicates that this should not be generalized or exaggerated (Table 8).

TABLE 8. FEELING OF AMERICAN SEPHARDIM FOR SPAIN

Degree	Over Age 40 Number	Over Age 40 Percent	Under Age 40 Number	Under Age 40 Percent
Deep respect and love	6	4.7	2	2.3
More attraction for Spain than other countries	35	27.3	17	19.8
Little or no feeling	82	64.2	63	73.3
Other	5	3.8	4	4.6
Total	128	100.0	86	100.0

[94]Federico Perez Castro, "España y los judios españoles," in Richard Barnett, ed., *The Sephardi Heritage* (New York, 1971), p. 311.

Customs and Foods

Since many customs are tied to religious precepts, their observance has declined among American Sephardim along with religiousness. About 73 per cent of the 40-and-over respondents indicated they observe Sephardi customs, as compared with 61 per cent of those under 40. The most commonly practiced customs today are related to the Seder and the Rosh Ha-shanah evening meals, and are often observed for nostalgic rather than purely religious reasons.

One of the ancient Sephardi customs has been to name children after living grandparents, often to the dismay of observing Ashkenazim. It has been the cause of many disagreements between the spouses in Sephardi-Ashkenazi "mixed" marriages, but the Sephardi partner usually has prevailed. Of the Sephardi respondents married to Ashkenazim, 79 per cent (89) stated they named or will name children after living grandparents. The percentage is about the same for men and women.

This custom is widely observed today, but often with modifications. For example, if a grandparent has a Spanish or Turkish name, the grandchild will be given an English equivalent. A growing trend is to give the child an English name of one's choice (perhaps with the first letter identical to the first letter of the grandparent's name), while giving him the grandparent's Hebrew name for religious purposes. This type of modification is also common among Ashkenazim.

A major aspect of the folk culture of a people is its cuisine. The so-called "Jewish" foods, such as gefilte fish, tzimmes, or kreplach, were completely unknown to the immigrant Sephardim. "Jewish" food meant something quite different to them. On the Sabbath, for example, Sephardim would eat *huevos haminados* (hardboiled eggs, cooked in water, oil, and onion skin so that they become brown in color); *bolemas* (a turnover filled with spinach or eggplant, and cheese); *borekas* (a pastry filled with eggplant or potato, and cheese).

In the course of time the Sephardi cuisine has been greatly modified and now includes many other dishes, some typically Ashkenazi. Yet, of 234 respondents only 5 stated they never eat Sephardi foods; 124 said they eat them regularly. The others eat Sephardi foods only on holidays or special occasions. Although the under-40 group scored less than those 40 and over, only slightly more than 3 per cent of the younger group claimed never to eat Sephardi foods. Within the past several years, a number of Sephardi women's groups published Sephardi cookbooks, in Seattle, Los Angeles, and Atlanta. Evidently, cuisine is a strong factor in group identity and pride.

Group Consciousness

As Sephardim mingle with the Ashkenazi majority and with non-Jewish Americans, their group identity is severely challenged. They feel less and less the need to remain within their own group or to perpetuate their group's values and culture. Yet they continue to feel a sense of kinship with other Sephardim. Responding to a query about their feelings when meeting another Sephardi for the first time, 88 per cent of the 40-and-over survey sample and 82 per cent of the under-40 said they felt a special kinship.

Respondents also were asked two highly subjective questions aimed at discovering what Sephardim thought of themselves and their heritage (Tables 9 and 10). The replies to both questions show a somewhat lower degree of group chauvinism in the under-40 group. Negatively expressed, this means that fewer of the younger Sephardim feel that non-Sephardi Jews discriminate against them (Table 11).

In sum, it can be said that, while Sephardi group consciousness has shown a slight decline among the younger generation, most Sephardim—regardless of how much or how little they are steeped in Sephardi culture—feel a special relationship to others in their group. They do indeed take pride in their Sephardi identity.

Sephardi-Ashkenazi Intermarriage

Almost all Sephardi immigrants of the early 20th century had Sephardi spouses, assuring the perpetuation of Sephardi values and customs in their homes. American-born Sephardim, on the other hand, often chose Ashkenazi mates. Stories of prejudice on the part of both Sephardi and Ashkenazi families against the other, though certainly rooted in fact, tend to be exaggerated. Ashkenazi parents had to be convinced that their children were actually marrying Jews. After all, the Sephardim did not speak Yiddish, did not have "Jewish" names,

TABLE 9. "Do you think Sephardim generally have more self-pride than Ashkenazim?"

Reply	40 and Over Number	40 and Over Per Cent	Under 40 Number	Under 40 Per Cent
More	76	52.8	45	52.3
Same	47	32.6	24	27.9
Less	7	4.9	3	3.5
Don't know	14	9.7	14	16.3
Total	144	100.0	86	100.0

TABLE 10. "Do you feel that the Sephardi heritage is generally superior to the Ashkenazi?"

Reply	40 and Over Number	40 and Over Per Cent	Under 40 Number	Under 40 Per Cent
Superior	71	50.7	39	47.6
About the same	54	38.6	35	42.7
Inferior	1	.7	0	0.0
Don't know	14	10.0	8	9.7
Total	140	100.0	82	100.0

TABLE 11. "Do you feel discriminated against in your contacts with non-Sephardi Jews?"

Frequency	40 and Over Number	40 and Over Per Cent	Under 40 Number	Under 40 Per Cent
Nearly always	3	2.0	1	1.2
Sometimes	51	33.8	25	28.7
Not at all	97	64.2	61	70.1
Total	151	100.0	87	100.0

and never ate gefilte fish. Sephardi parents, too, were reluctant to give their children in marriage to non-Sephardim. Despite cultural barriers, however, American-born Sephardim and Ashkenazim found that they had much more in common than not. Third-generation marriages of

Sephardim to Ashkenazim are quite common; one might say that they have become the rule, rather than the exception (Table 12).

TABLE 12. BACKGROUND OF WIVES OF SECOND-GENERATION AMERICAN SEPHARDIM*

Background	40 and Over Number	Per Cent	Under 40 Number	Per Cent
Sephardi	61	58.1	8	15.7
Ashkenazi	40	38.1	35	68.7
Christian	2	1.9	4	7.8
Other	2	1.9	4	7.8
Total	105	100.0	51	100.0

*The response of women regarding their husbands' background was too small to be meaningful.

The figures for third-generation Sephardim are even more dramatic. They are based on replies of third-generation as well as second-generation Sephardim who listed the spouses of their children (Table 13).

TABLE 13. BACKGROUND OF SPOUSES OF THIRD-GENERATION AMERICAN SEPHARDIM

Background	Number	Per Cent
Sephardi	12	12.8
Ashkenazi	70	74.5
Christian	11	11.6
Other	1	1.1
Total	94	100.0

The figures for the spouses of children of Sephardi-Ashkenazi marriages, though too small to be conclusive, may indicate a pattern. Of the 21 respondents, only 1 was married to a Sephardi, 17 were married to Ashkenazim, and three to non-Jews.[95]

The high rate of Sephardi-Askenazi marriages makes it inevitable that Sephardi culture has been, and will continue to be, subject to changes. All such marriages require compromises by both sides, even

---

[95]See Hayyim Cohen, op. cit., pp. 154–55.

by the dominant partner. For the Sephardi community this means a decline in Sephardi culture, at least in such obvious manifestations as food, custom, and language. To what extent, then, has Sephardi-Ashkenazi marriage influenced Sephardi life in America?

The findings of the study indicate that Sephardim married to Ashkenazim are more likely to drop out of Sephardi synagogues than are Sephardim married within their group. This is especially true of Sephardi women who marry Ashkenazi men.

There was a total of 61 responses from Sephardim who are not affiliated with Sephardi congregations: three are single; 40 are married to Ashkenazim; 18 are married to other Sephardim. Expressed in percentages, 35.4 per cent of all Sephardim with Ashkenazi spouses, men and women, left the Sephardi synagogue, as compared with 22 per cent of those who married other Sephardim. Of the Sephardim who are married to Ashkenazim but belong to Sephardi synagogues, 20.5 per cent are also members of Ashkenazi synagogues. Dual synagogue membership is held by 6.3 per cent of Sephardim married to other Sephardim. Since the rate of Sephardi-Ashkenazi intermarriage is presently about 75 per cent (see Table 13), Sephardi synagogues are very likely to lose more members. Supportive evidence is the synagogue affiliation of the adult children of Sephardi-Ashkenazi marriages: of 47 respondents, 13 (27.7 per cent) belong to Sephardi synagogues; 18 (38.3 per cent) to Ashkenazi; 16 (34 per cent) to none.

Sephardi synagogues have in fact kept the majority of "mixed" marriages within the fold. A concerted effort to make the Sephardi synagogue meaningful to Ashkenazim, especially to those married to Sephardim, will most probably assure its continued existence. The Sephardi congregation with only Sephardi members is rapidly becoming a thing of the past. Sephardi leaders must recognize changes in their community and adjust synagogue planning accordingly. This does not mean adopting non-Sephardi innovations in their services. It is hoped that the beauty and nobility of the Sephardi synagogue tradition will attract many non-Sephardi members, if they are made to feel welcome. Sephardi synagogues will have to make cultural converts: people who will want to be Sephardim though they have little or no Sephardi blood.

Sephardim married to Ashkenazim reported slightly less observance of Sephardi customs, use of Judeo-Spanish, and consumption of Sephardi foods than did Sephardim married to other Sephardim. This was to be expected. Moreover, there was little difference between the two categories in identification with the Sephardi group. For example, 85.3 per cent of the intermarried claimed to feel a special kinship for a Sephardi in a first meeting; 55.1 per cent believed Sephardim had more self-pride than Ashkenazim; 45.4 per cent thought the Sephardi heritage was superior to the Ashkenazi. As for feeling discriminated against by non-Sephardi Jews, 32.1 per cent stated they did. This surprisingly high figure may be explained as a reaction to the attitudes of Ashkenazi in-laws. One Sephardi respondent commented typically: "My Ashkenazi in-laws don't exactly discriminate against me. But they still have no idea where Salonika is, and they don't think I'm really Jewish."

In the matter of providing Sephardi education for their children, Sephardim married to Ashkenazim fare somewhat worse than those married to Sephardim. But in both cases the level of education is too low.

TABLE 14. SEPHARDI ORIENTATION OF RELIGIOUS EDUCATION OF CHILDREN OF SEPHARDIM MARRIED TO ASKENAZIM AND OF THOSE MARRIED TO SEPHARDIM

Degree	Sephardi-Ashkenazi Number	Per Cent	Sephardi-Sephardi Number	Per Cent
Completely	13	12.4	14	18.9
Somewhat	44	41.9	28	37.8
Not at all	48	45.7	32	43.3
Total	105	100.0	74	100.0

Of course, the categories of degree are somewhat vague. Different Sephardim will have different definitions of "complete" or "somewhat." If children study in an Ashkenazi school where they learn Ivrit, some parents may evaluate the orientation as being "somewhat" Sephardi, others may feel it is "not at all" so. Still others think that as long as their children attend a Sephardi Talmud Torah, even though the teachers may not be Sephardim and may know nothing about Sephardi history and tradition, their education is "completely" Sephardi-oriented. However, even with these possible differences in interpretation, the figures fairly accurately reflect the true situation.

Four American Communities

The data considered above reflect general tendencies on a national scale. However, it is also valuable to focus attention on several specific Sephardi communities to detect local deviations from national trends. The communities selected were Metropolitan New York, Atlanta, Seattle, and Portland, Ore. New York has the largest number of Sephardim. Atlanta and Seattle have the most viable Sephardi communities. Portland's small community appears to be on the verge of collapse. The respondents of Atlanta, Portland, and Seattle were almost equally divided between the 40-and-over and the under-40 age groups. In the New York area two-thirds of the respondents were over 40, a fact that must be taken into account in analyzing the data.

ROLE OF SYNAGOGUE

A comparison of synagogue affiliation and attendance in these four cities reveals some specific characteristics of each community (Tables 15 and 16).

Atlanta shows the largest percentage of Sephardim belonging to a Sephardi synagogue; it also has the best general attendance record. Although Seattle has more Sephardim who attend weekly, Atlanta has a much higher percentage of those who attend at least once a month (63.9 per cent, as against 47.9 per cent in Seattle). To be sure, the Seattle community has a hard core of faithful synagogue goers; but the majority of the Sephardim attend only on holidays. The community is polarized between observant and nonobservant, much more so than in Atlanta.

The Sephardim in the New York area attend synagogue and are affiliated with Sephardi synagogues much less frequently than those in Atlanta and Seattle. Here the size of the city is an important factor; in smaller communities there is more communal pressure and more need for formal affiliation. In the smaller communities, too, many of the Sephardim are related to each other or originate from the same cities in the Levant. They are, therefore, more apt to join synagogues and feel part of the community.

The Portland Sephardim are not strongly attached to their

TABLE 15. SYNAGOGUE AFFILIATION

Type	Atlanta	Per Cent	NewYork	Per Cent	Portland	Per Cent	Seattle	Per Cent
Sephardi	43	89.6	41	66.1	7	50.0	41	83.7
Ashkenazi	4	8.3	13	21.0	7	50.0	7	14.3
None	1	2.1	8	12.9	0	0.0	1	2.0
Total	48	100.0	62	100.0	14	100.0	49	100.0

TABLE 16. SYNAGOGUE ATTENDANCE

Frequency	Atlanta	Per Cent	NewYork	Per Cent	Portland	Per Cent	Seattle	Per Cent
Weekly	9	19.2	6	9.8	2	14.3	16	33.3
Monthly	21	44.7	7	11.5	5	35.7	7	14.6
Holidays, special occasions	13	27.7	37	60.7	6	42.9	23	47.9
High Holy Days	3	6.4	6	9.8	1	7.1	2	4.2
Not at all	1	2.0	5	8.2	0	0.0	0	0.0
Total	47	100.0	61	100.0	14	100.0	48	100.0

synagogue, and some who do belong are also members in Ashkenazi synagogues.

The same pattern emerged for the adult children of the respondents (Table 17).

TABLE 17. SYNAGOGUE AFFILIATION OF ADULT CHILDREN OF RESPONDENTS

Affiliation	Atlanta	Per Cent	NewYork	Per Cent	Portland	Per Cent	Seattle	Per Cent
Sephardi	13	65.0	9	25.7	4	44.4	10	58.8
Ashkenazi	4	20.0	8	22.9	4	44.4	5	29.4
None	3	15.0	18	51.4	1	11.2	2	11.8
Total	20	100.0	35	100.0	9	100.0	17	100.0

Again, the Atlanta Sephardi community is the most successful in holding its young. The New York Sephardim show the least ability to keep their children in Sephardi synagogues and, indeed, to keep them in any synagogue.

RELIGIOUS ORIENTATION

A consideration of the religious beliefs of the Sephardim in each of the four communities will do much to explain the difference in religious observance and affiliation. Portland shows an almost even spread in religious belief. New York has a large percentage of Conservatives, but also a fairly sizable percentage of Orthodox. Atlanta is overwhelmingly Conservative. Seattle is more polarized than the other communities, with by far the largest and strongest Orthodox group, but (except for Portland, where the numbers are quite small) also the largest and strongest Reform group. In Seattle, 7 of the 7 respondents who are not members of a Sephardi synagogue belong to a Reform temple. In Atlanta, the ratio is 1 of 4; in New York, 3 of 13; in Portland, 2 of 7.

TABLE 18. RELIGIOUS BELIEFS

Type	Atlanta	Per Cent	New York	Per Cent	Portland	Per Cent	Seattle	Per Cent
Orthodox	5	10.4	11	18.6	4	30.8	21	42.9
Conservative	37	77.1	38	64.4	5	38.4	15	30.6
Reform	4	8.3	7	11.9	4	30.8	10	20.4
Other	2	4.2	3	5.1	0	0.0	3	6.1
Total	48	100.0	59	100.0	13	100.0	49	100.0

When asked whether their homes are more observant than their parents', Sephardim responded as follows (Table 19):

TABLE 19. "Is your home more observant than that of your parents?"

Degree	Atlanta	Per Cent	New York	Per Cent	Portland	Per Cent	Seattle	Per Cent
More	4	9.1	4	7.0	1	7.2	6	13.6
Same	18	40.9	12	21.1	3	21.4	8	18.2
Less	22	50.0	41	71.9	10	71.4	30	68.2
Total	44	100.0	57	100.0	14	100.0	44	100.0

These figures only reflect possible trends, not actual levels of religious observance. Homes considered to be more observant than parents' homes may still be quite nonobservant. Conversely, homes may be less observant than parents' homes, and be quite observant.

Whereas half of Atlanta's respondents said they were at least as observant as their parents, this was not true of the Sephardim in the other cities. Again, Seattle has a higher rate of increased observance than Atlanta; but it also has a more dramatic increase in Sephardim who are less observing than their parents.

ADHERING TO SEPHARDI TRADITION

The four communities more or less resemble each other in Hispanic character, with Seattle showing a higher rate of adherence to Sephardi customs than the others.

The Seattle Sephardim had the highest proportion of in-group marriages, about 51 per cent. This compares with 30 per cent for Atlanta, 45 per cent for New York, and 38 per cent for Portland. However, in all cities these are for the most part in the 40-and-over age group.

The Sephardim in the four communities have a strong feeling of kinship with other Sephardim, and a high degree of group identity. Ninety per cent of Atlanta respondents feel a special kinship at the very first meeting with other Sephardim. This is true of 85 per cent of the Sephardim in New York; 86 per cent in Portland; 81 per cent in Seattle.

Tables 20 and 21 indicate patterns of Sephardi chauvinism in the four communities. The data show greater group pride among Sephardim in Atlanta and New York than in Portland and Seattle. There seems to be some correlation between this characteristic of Sephardim and Ashkenazi discrimination against them: where discrimination has been more pronounced, Sephardim have been more inclined to think less of themselves.

As for the religious education of Sephardi children in the four communities, Seattle has the largest percentage (25) in day schools, but Atlanta has the largest percentage (92) attending Talmud Torah at least several times a week. In New York the percentage receiving no Jewish education at all is highest (25). Portland's children generally attend only Sunday school (64 per cent).

TABLE 20. "Do you feel that the Sephardi heritage is generally superior to the Ashkenazi?"

Degree	Atlanta	Per Cent	New York	Per Cent	Portland	Per Cent	Seattle	Per Cent
Superior	25	54.4	31	53.5	7	50.0	16	34.8
About the same	19	41.3	23	39.6	6	42.9	22	47.8
Inferior	0	0.0	0	0.0	0	0.0	1	2.2
Don't know	2	4.3	4	6.9	1	7.1	7	15.2
Total	46	100.0	58	100.0	14	100.0	46	100.0

TABLE 21. "Do you think Sephardim generally have more self-pride than Ashkenazim?"

Degree	Atlanta	Per Cent	New York	Per Cent	Portland	Per Cent	Seattle	Per Cent
More	29	60.4	38	64.4	5	35.7	19	39.6
About the same	12	25.0	13	22.0	6	42.9	18	37.5
Less	1	2.1	2	3.4	2	14.3	3	6.3
Don't know	6	12.5	6	10.2	1	7.1	8	16.6
Total	48	100.0	59	100.0	14	100.0	48	100.0

TABLE 22. "Do you feel discriminated against in your contacts with non-Sephardi Jews?"

Degree	Atlanta	Per Cent	New York	Per Cent	Portland	Per Cent	Seattle	Per Cent
Nearly always	0	0.0	2	3.3	0	0.0	1	2.0
Sometimes	15	31.3	13	21.3	5	35.7	21	42.9
Not at all	33	68.7	46	75.4	9	64.3	27	55.1
Total	48	100.0	61	100.0	14	100.0	49	100.0

Of all the Sephardi communities in the United States, Seattle has produced by far the largest number of rabbis and religiously-educated laymen. Almost every year a few Sephardi students leave for other cities to continue their studies at *yeshivot*. Six have been ordained in the past few years, and three of them are rabbis in Sephardi synagogues.

Students who want advanced Jewish educations must leave Seattle because the city has no *yeshivah* high school or theological seminary. And since some of the *yeshivah* students choose to go into the rabbinate or Jewish-education fields, they seldom return to their native city for lack of positions, as well as for other considerations. Despite this drain of talent, the Seattle Sephardi community has the strongest core of religiously educated and committed Jews of any other in the country.

Conclusion

If there is no reversal in the trends indicated by our data, no viable Sephardi communities may be left in the United States in two or three generations from now. Clearly, synagogue buildings alone cannot insure the survival, let alone growth, of Sephardi culture. Sephardim must establish good schools of their own, or insist that existing day schools teach more about the Sephardi past. They must also create meaningful cultural institutions—Sephardi theaters, newspapers, libraries. They must encourage their youth to pursue higher Jewish education and, if necessary, provide financial incentives to promising students. It is to be hoped that these efforts will strengthen religious observance, and wipe out the widespread ignorance of Judaism and Sephardi Jewish tradition. Unless this can be accomplished now, the Sephardi heritage will be lost.

APPENDIX

Readers wishing to study Sephardi history and culture will find it helpful to refer to the following works:

JEWISH LIFE IN SPAIN

BAER, YITZHAK, *A History of the Jews in Christian Spain*, Vol. 1, 1961, Vol. 2, 1971, (Philadelphia).

BARNETT, RICHARD, *The Sephardi Heritage* (New York, 1971).

KATZ, S., *The Jews in the Visigothic and Frankish Kingdoms of Spain and Gaul* (Cambridge, 1937).

NEUMAN, ABRAHAM, *The Jews in Spain* (Philadelphia, 1944).

NETANYAHU, BENZION, *Don Isaac Abravanel* (Philadelphia, 1968).

THE MARRANO AND EX-MARRANO COMMUNITIES

EMMANUEL, ISAAC and EMMANUEL, SUZANNE, *History of the Jews of the Netherlands Antilles* (Cincinnati, 1970).

HYAMSON, ALBERT, *The Sephardim of England* (London, 1951).

ROTH, CECIL, *History of the Marranos* (New York, 1966).

Sephardi Melodies (London, 1931).

YERUSHALMI, Y. H., *From Spanish Court to Italian Ghetto* (New York, 1971).

COLONIAL AMERICAN SEPHARDIM

CHYET, STANLEY, *Lopez of Newport* (Detroit, 1970).

GRINSTEIN, HYMAN, *The Rise of the Jewish Community of New York* (Philadelphia, 1947).

GUTSTEIN, MORRIS, *The Story of the Jews of Newport* (New York, 1936).

MARCUS, JACOB R., *The Colonial American Jew, 1492–1776* (Detroit, 1970).

———, *Early American Jewry* (Philadelphia, 1951–53).

POOL, DAVID and TAMAR DE SOLA, *An Old Faith in the New World* (New York, 1955).

POOL, DAVID DE SOLA, *Portraits Etched in Stone* (New York, 1952).

REZNIKOFF, CHARLES, *The Jews of Charleston* (Philadelphia, 1950).

WOLF, E., and WHITEMAN, M., *The History of the Jews of Philadelphia* (Philadelphia, 1957).

LEVANTINE SEPHARDIM

BENARDETE, MÁIR JOSÉ, *Hispanic Culture and Character of the Sephardic Jews* (New York, 1952).

CHOURAQUI, ANDRÉ, *Between East and West* (Philadelphia, 1968).

EMMANUEL, ISAAC, *Histoire des Israélites de Salonique* (Paris, 1936).

HASSAN, IACOB, RUBIATO, T., and ROMERO, E., eds., *Actas del primer simposio de estudios sefardies* (Madrid, 1970).

MOLHO, MICHAEL, *Literatura Sefardita de Oriente* (Madrid, 1960).

———, *Usos y Costumbres de los Sefardies de Salonica* (Madrid, 1950).

NEHAMA, JOSEPH, *Histoire des Israélites de Salonique* (Salonika, 1935–59).

ROSANES, SOLOMON, *Dibrei Yemei Yisrael beTogarmah*, 6 vols. (published in various places, 1907–45).

See also the voluminous writings of Abraham Galante.

JUDEO-SPANISH FOLK LITERATURE

ALGAZI, LEON, *Chants Sephardis* (London, 1958).

ANGEL, MARC D., "The Pirkei Abot of Reuben Eliyahu Israel," *Tradition*, Spring 1971, pp. 92–98.

ARMISTEAD, S., and SILVERMAN, J., *The Judeo-Spanish Chapbooks of Yacob Abraham Yoná* (Berkeley, 1971).

LEVY, ISAAC, *Chants Judéo-Espagnols* (London, 1959).

LEVANTINE SEPHARDIM IN THE UNITED STATES

ANGEL, MARC D., "'Progress'—Seattle's Sephardic Monthly, 1934–35," *American Sephardi*, Vol. 5, 1971, pp. 90–95.

———, "Ruminations on Sephardi Identity," *Midstream*, March 1972, pp. 64–67.

HACKER, LOUIS, "The Communal Life of the Sephardic Jews in New York City," *Jewish Social Service Quarterly*, Vol. 3, December 1926, pp. 32–40.

HEXTER, MAURICE, "The Dawn of a Problem," *Jewish Charities,* December 1913, pp. 2-5.

PAPO, JOSEPH, "The Sephardic Community of America," *Reconstructionist,* Vol. 12, 1946, pp. 12-18.

POOL, DAVID DE SOLA, "The Immigration of Levantine Jews into the United States," *Jewish Charities,* June 1914, pp. 12-27.

————, "The Levantine Jews in the United States," AMERICAN JEWISH YEAR BOOK, Vol. 15 (1913-14), pp. 207-20.

SANUA, VICTOR, "A Study of Adjustment of Sephardic Jews in the New York Metropolitan Area," *Jewish Journal of Sociology,* Vol. 9, June 1967, pp. 25-33.

SHIRAZI, HELEN, "The Communal Pluralism of Sephardi Jewry in the United States," *Le Judaisme Sephardi,* January 1966, pp. 23-25, 32.

SEPHARDIM AND ASHKENAZIM

COHEN, HAYYIM, "Sephardi Jews in the United States, Marriage with Ashkenazim," *Dispersion and Unity,* Vol. 13-14, 1971-72, pp. 151-60.

GROSS, MORRIS, *Learning Readiness in Two Jewish Groups* (New York, 1967).

ZIMMELS, H. J., *Ashkenazim and Sephardim* (London, 1958).

PUBLICATIONS WITH GENERAL INFORMATION

American Sephardi, journal of the Sephardic Studies Program of Yeshiva University.

Publications of the Foundation for the Advancement of Sephardic Studies and Culture, New York.

Shearith Israel Bulletin, published by the Spanish and Portuguese Synagogue in New York.

OCCUPATIONAL PATTERNS OF AMERICAN JEWS

By Nathan Goldberg

Friends and foes alike not infrequently exaggerate the economic position, importance and power of the American Jews. Isaac Markens, an American Jew, wrote in 1888 that "within half a century the Hebrews of this country will control the balance of trade." [1] Three years later the *New York Sun* wrote on the subject of the Jewish immigrants from Europe that the United States is the land of promise for their race at the present day.

"Nowhere else have they advanced so signally as here. They land on our shores poor, start out oftentimes as peddlers, with their packs on their backs, and yet in a few years the majority of them are well to do in the world, and many of them are competitors in trade feared by their Christian neighbors. Broadway from Fourteenth Street down is lined with the signs of Jewish firms. Wall Street is full of them. They have obtained an immense place in the retail dry goods trade in New York. In the professions of the law and medicine they are numerous and powerful. Very many of the most accomplished musicians are Jews, many of the actors, and many of the caterers for public amusement and refection. In every department of activity where intellectual acuteness and keenness of perception are requisite they are forging ahead." It then added: "Of late years, also, they have become conspicuous for investments in landed property. Some of the most notable of the purchasers at the Real Estate Exchange are Jews." [2]

New York City, according to this newspaper, was not an exception. "Everywhere the Jews are prospering. They push their way with every advance of civilization, and wherever they plant themselves they win in the competition." The *Sun* observed, however, that the Jews "seem to be far more numerous than they are really" and that they were easily discoverable "because of their physiognomy."

Some twenty years later Professor Sombart wrote that New York's Jewish merchants had almost conquered Broadway, that the economic control of the Jews was increasing daily, and that the entire real estate business and the clothing industry were in Jewish hands.[3]

Inimical as such statements are, American Jews are not always in a position to prove that they are exaggerations of fact. Their socio-economic status is to a certain extent part of the realm of the "great unknown," for the reason that the U. S. Census Bureau does not collect any data on the religious or ethnic origin of the population.[*] Statements on the economic position of the American Jews often go unchallenged because of a lack of accurate and authentic data. If, however, we analyze the available facts, then the story is an altogether different one.

These facts show that changes have occurred in the economic structure of the American Jews and that there is a certain degree of interdependence between the occupational trends of the general population and those of the Jews, although there are also considerable differences.

The economic development of the United States since 1900 has been marked by an expansion of the commercial, clerical and professional services. The percentage of those engaged in agriculture, forestry and fishing decreased from 35.9 per 100 gainfully employed in 1900 to 17.9 in 1940. The percentage of persons engaged in manufacturing and in construction dropped from 31.1 to 28.8, although their absolute number increased from approximately 9,055,000 to

---

[*] The Census Bureau publishes data on the mother tongue and country of birth of the inhabitants. The Jews are not classified as Jews except those who state that Yiddish is their mother tongue. The gainfully employed are not classified even according to their mother tongue.

14,235,100. On the other hand, the percentage of those rendering professional and related services increased from 3.9 to 6.9. There was also an upward trend in the demand for transportation, communication, and office workers.[4] Recent technological developments, changes in our standard of living, and certain other factors account for the present occupational pattern of the American people.

Although the occupational changes of the Jews have, to a certain extent, been similar to those of the general population, we must also bear in mind that there is a certain relationship between their occupations, concentration in the largest urban centers, and specific vocational preferences.

Our large cities do not have the same occupational pattern as our small or rural communities. The former are industrial, commercial, financial, and educational centers. Thus we find that 34.8 per cent of the gainfully employed in New York, Chicago and Philadelphia in 1940 were engaged in manufacturing and in construction as compared with 28.8 per cent for the country as a whole; 7.4 per cent of the former and 6.9 per cent of the latter were in the professions; 21.6 per cent of those living in these three cities, but only 16.4 per cent of the total population, were wholesalers or retailers.

Moreover, each city has its own occupational pattern. According to the Census Bureau, 8 per cent of the New Yorkers and only 6.4 per cent of the Chicagoans were rendering professional and related services in 1940; 40.6 per cent of the Philadelphians and only 31.7 per cent of the New Yorkers were engaged in manufacturing and in construction. The economic structure of communities varies with their natural resources, manpower, accessibility to markets, proximity to raw materials as well as with certain historical and psychological factors. And the occupational pattern of cities is changing. The percentage of New Yorkers in the several professions increased from 5.2 in 1900 to 8.0 in 1940 and of those in manufacturing and construction decreased from

36.3 to 31.7. The Census Bureau reports a similar trend for Chicago, Philadelphia and other communities. The rate of change varies, however, from locality to locality. The percentage of Philadelphians in the several professions increased from 4.6 in 1900 to 7.0 in 1940 and that of the Chicagoans from 5.5 to only 6.4.

The economic pursuits of an ethnic group also vary with its geographical location, history, occupational preferences, traditions, values and many other psychological and sociological factors. The Jews are not an exception. We cannot understand their occupational preferences if we overlook the fact that there was a time when they were excluded from certain economic activities, that their social, political and economic status was that of outcasts and that they had to live behind ghetto walls. Their religion was another important factor. The desire to observe the Sabbath led them to seek employment in trades and in shops which would not interfere with their religious customs. There was a demand for Jewish bakers, butchers, and food dealers because of the desire to observe the Jewish dietary laws; there was a demand for Jewish tailors because the Jews wanted their garments to be made in accordance with the Mosaic law. In brief, the religious needs of the Jewish community had an effect on the economic structure of the Jewish people.

The changes which have occurred in the occupational structure of the Jews in America since the beginning of the present century stem from the American environment plus the Jews' own vocational preferences, traditions, and values which, like those of any other ethnic group, are a result of historical development, religious traditions, and the like.

AT THE TURN OF THE CENTURY

Very little is known of the economic position of the American Jews prior to 1900. Most of the available information[5] is based on opinions or impressions rather than on careful observation and study.

Two studies of the economic structure of the Jews prior to 1900 are, however, worthy of mention. Dr. John S. Billings analyzed the economic pursuits of approximately 18,000 gainfully employed Jews in 1889. More than four-fifths of this group were immigrants from German-speaking countries with their American born children. Bankers, brokers, company officials, and wholesale merchants constituted approximately 15 per cent of the informants; retail dealers about 35 per cent; accountants, bookkeepers, clerks and copyists 17 per cent; salesmen, commercial travelers, collectors, agents, and auctioneers about 12 per cent; those employed in professional service almost 5 per cent; the rest were skilled and unskilled workers, farmers, planters, drovers, and stock breeders. It is interesting to note that only 0.9 per cent of this group were hucksters and peddlers, and that not more than 3 per cent were tailors.[6] Whether or not this group was representative of the German Jews in this country, the other Jewish immigrants certainly lived under less favorable economic conditions.

This observation is based in part on the results of a study made in 1890 by the Baron Hirsch Fund. It was found that three-fifths of approximately 22,400 gainfully employed Jews living in three of New York's Jewish districts were needle workers, and fifteen per cent were bakers, carpenters, machinists, etc.; peddlers constituted 11 per cent and retail store proprietors almost 13 per cent; the rest were teachers or musicians.[7]

These figures can, however, hardly be regarded as representative of all Jewish immigrants from Eastern Europe. Although it is a well known fact that the Jewish immigrants from

Russia, Poland, Lithuania, Hungary, Galicia and Rumania lived in those days under less favorable social and economic conditions than their brethren who had settled here prior to 1880, it is, nevertheless, questionable whether three-fifths of them were actually clothing workers and capmakers. In brief, this group was probably no more representative of the Jews who came here in the 1880's than was Dr. Billings' group of the German Jewish immigrants. The most these two studies indicate is a general trend—there can be no doubt that in 1890 the German Jewish group was more prosperous than the Jewish immigrants from Eastern Europe—but the studies fail to present an accurate picture of the socio-economic status of the Jewish immigrants from German and Slavic countries.

More valuable for a knowledge of the economic structure of the American Jews will be our analysis of the occupations of the Russian Jews in the United States at the time of the 12th census in 1900. They and their American-born children now constitute, numerically speaking, a very important element of the Jewish population; they have also played a leading role in the economic, social and cultural evolution of the American Jewish community. For this reason, the analysis of the occupational distribution of these erstwhile immigrants may serve as a basis on which to trace the changes in the economic activities of American Jews in general since the beginning of the present century.

This analysis of the occupational distribution of the Jewish immigrants from the former Russian empire is based on a report, published by the U. S. Census Bureau, which has been hitherto practically overlooked. To be sure, nothing is said in the report under consideration about the economic activities of this particular group. It can be shown, however, that the overwhelming majority of those who were reported in 1900 as Russians were actually Jews from Russia. This is particularly true of those immigrants from Russia who, at the time of the 12th census (1900), lived in cities with 250,000 or more inhabitants.

This assumption is based on the following facts. The U. S. Census Bureau did not classify Finns and Poles, groups which immigrated to the United States in 1880-1899, as Russians and we may, therefore, assume that very few, if any, of them were reported as Russians. Very few immigrants whose mother tongue was Russian, and Lithuanians from Russia were to be found in America before 1900.

77,321 immigrants whose mother tongue was Russian arrived here in the years 1899-1910 and only 40,542 foreign-born Russians were here at the time of the 1910 census; 168,740 Lithuanians from Russia arrived here in 1899-1910 and there were only 137,046 Lithuanians and Latvians from Russia in 1910. Approximately 364,000 immigrants from Russia, not including Finns, Poles and Jews from that country, arrived here in the years 1899-1910 and there were only about 340,400 foreign born from Russia, excluding Poles, Jews and Finns, at the time of the 1910 enumeration.[8] It thus appears that the overwhelming majority of these non-Jews from Russia arrived here after 1900, even if we assume that some of these 364,000 immigrants returned to their country of origin and that a certain percentage of those here died before 1910.

We may, therefore arrive at the conclusion that practically all the Russians in the cities of the United States in 1900 were Jews from Russia. There were, of course, non-Jews from Russia at the time of the 12th census, but their number was exceedingly small and, moreover, very few of them lived in large cities.

An analysis of the geographical distribution of the several ethnic groups from Russia in the United States leads to the same conclusion. The correlation coefficient (degree of association) between the geographical distribution of the Yiddish-speaking immigrants in 1910 and of the Russians in 1900, most of whom, according to our assumption, were Jews, is $+0.984 \pm 0.003$; the correlation coefficient between the geographical distribution of the Russians and of all the

Jews in the country in 1900, as reported in the *American Jewish Year Book,* 1900, is +0.972±0.005. The difference between these coefficients is statistically not significant. * The results are not inconsistent with the hypothesis that those reported as Russians in 1900 had the same geographical distribution as the Yiddish-speaking immigrants and the total Jewish population in the U. S., while the non-Jews from Russia show a different geographical distribution.[9] This would mean that the distribution of those reported in 1900 as Russians was practically the same as of the Yiddish-speaking immigrants but unlike that of the non-Jews from Russia. **

The United States Immigration Commission is of the same opinion. It says in its analysis of the occupations of immigrants in 1900 that "the distinctive features of the occupational classification of those male breadwinners in the United States whose parents were born in Russia doubtless reflect the characteristics of the Russian Jew."[10]

---

* The following formula was used for testing the significance of the difference between two correlation coefficients:

$$\frac{Dz - 0}{\text{Sigma } Dz}$$

** The assumption that a large percentage of the Poles in 1900 were Jews (*Yevereyskaya Entziklapedia,* II, pp. 264-265; Lestchinsky J., "The Social Physiognomy of American Jewry," *Yivo Bleter,* Vol. XVII, No. 3, p. 197 [in Yiddish]) is open to question. The U. S. Census Bureau says very explicitly that "it is probable that the persons reported born in Poland in 1900 and at earlier censuses were mainly Poles by blood, as persons of other nationalities coming from Poland would be likely to report Austria, Germany, or Russia as their birthplace." At any rate, there is a difference between the geographical distribution of the Russians in 1900 and the Poles, and less similarity between the occupational patterns of the Poles and the traditional economic pursuits of the Jews. 0.48 per cent of the gainfully employed Russian males in New York City in 1900 were physicians, surgeons or dentists and only 0.2 per cent of the Poles living there; 5.2 per cent of the former and only 2.9 per cent of the latter were hucksters or peddlers. In the case of Chicago, one of the principal centers of the Poles in the U. S., the dentists, physicians and surgeons constituted only 0.14 per cent of the Russian males; 1.5 per cent of the former and 7.9 per cent of the latter were peddlers or hucksters. There were more bookkeepers and accountants, clerks, typists and salesmen among the second generation Russian males than among the native born children of parents from Poland; the proportion in 1900 was 2.7:1.

At the time of the 12th census there were 15 cities with a population of 250,000 or over—Baltimore, Boston, Buffalo, Chicago, Cincinnati, Cleveland, Detroit, Milwaukee, New Orleans, New York, Philadelphia, Pittsburgh, San Francisco, St. Louis, Washington. About 60 per cent of the total number of Russians and 61 per cent of the gainfully employed Russians lived in these 15 cities in 1900. These Russian Jews probably constituted more than 60 per cent of the total number of Russian Jews in this country, for the reason that they were more concentrated in the largest urban centers than their non-Jewish compatriots.

TABLE 1

OCCUPATIONAL DISTRIBUTION OF RUSSIAN JEWS IN CITIES WITH 250,000 INHABITANTS OR MORE, 1900 [11]

	Number			%		
Occupation	Total	Male	Female	Total	Male	Female
Total	150,694	120,052	30,642	100.0	100.0	100.0
Manufacturing	89,748	68,491	21,257	59.6	57.1	69.4
Trade	31,047	27,971	3,076	20.6	23.3	10.0
Domestic and Personal Service	12,138	8,349	3,789	8.0	7.0	12.4
Clerical	10,016	8,127	1,889	6.7	6.8	6.2
Professions	3,958	3,521	437	2.6	2.9	1.4
Transportation and Communication	2,613	2,467	146	1.7	2.1	0.5
Agriculture, Fishing, Forestry, Mining	698	651	18	0.5	0.5	0.2
Public Service	476	475	1	0.3	0.4	—

Approximately three-fifths of the Russian Jews in the United States living, in 1900, in cities with 250,000 and more inhabitants were engaged in manufacturing and in construction. Manufacturing and trade were the two most important economic activities of the Russian Jews. More than one-third of the gainfully-employed Jews, 35.3 per cent, were engaged in the production of men's and women's clothing, hats, caps and other apparel.[12] No other ethnic group had such a relatively large number of workers in the garment industry as the Jews. Four of every 100 gainfully employed Jews were in the building trades and 3.5 per cent of them were in the tobacco industry. Very few, 2.1 per cent, of those in industry were manufacturers or officials of manufacturing establishments. Most of the Jews in industry were engaged in the production of consumers' goods.

Approximately one-fifth of the Jews were engaged in trade. Almost one-fourth, 24.5 per cent, of those in trade were hucksters or peddlers and nearly one-half, 47.4 per cent, were proprietors of retail stores. 72 of every 100 Jews in trade were hucksters, peddlers or owners of retail stores. Only one per cent of the Jews in trade were in wholesale business.

Almost one-fourth, 24.2 per cent, of the professionals were teachers. About one-eighth of this group, 12.8 per cent, were physicians and surgeons and 2.9 per cent were dentists. 117 of every 1,000 professionals were clergymen and 66 were lawyers. The medical men, lawyers, teachers and clergy constituted, however, only 1.5 per cent of the total gainfully-employed Russian Jews. As a matter of fact, the percentage of Jewish immigrants from Russia who were rendering professional services was smaller than stated, for the reason that some of them were American-born children of parents born in Russia. As we shall see, there was a relatively larger number of professionals among the native born than among their immigrant parents.

Four-tenths of those in clerical occupations were clerks or copyists. Bookkeepers and accountants constituted 15.7 per cent of those rendering clerical services. More than one-third, 36.7 per cent, of the bookkeepers and accountants were women. More than four-fifths, 82.1 per cent, of the

532 typists and stenographers were women. Included in this entire group are second-generation Americans, who, as in the case of the professional group, had a relatively larger representation than their immigrant parents. The percentage of Russian Jews in the clerical occupations was therefore less than stated.

Of the 2,613 in transportation and communication, 50.6 per cent were hackmen, draymen, teamsters and the like. They constituted, however, only 0.9 per cent of the gainfully employed. Almost one-seventh, 14.8 per cent, of the transportation and communication employees worked for railroad and street car companies.

More than two-fifths, 42.3 per cent, of the group "domestic and personal service" were laborers "not specified." Many of them were unskilled laborers willing to accept any job. They constituted 3.4 per cent of the labor force. More than one-fourth, 27 per cent, of this entire group were domestic servants or waiters. Almost seven-eighths, 84.8 per cent, of the servants and waiters were women.

The occupational pattern of the Russian Jews in the United States was significantly different from that of the Jews who lived in Russia in 1897. * The first point to be noted is that only 39.5 per cent of the gainfully employed Russian Jews, in cities with 100,000 and more, excluding those in military service, were engaged in manufacturing, forestry and mining.[13] Three-fifths of the American group and only two-fifths of those in Russia were in industry. It

---

* We must, however, bear in mind that the two groups are not strictly comparable because of differences in the classification of occupations. The Russian census bureau included forestry and the extraction of minerals under the heading "manufacturing;" the manufacture of artificial flowers, shoes and textiles under "clothing;" proprietors of hotels, restaurants and of furnished rooms under "trade;" professions under "public service." Secondly, the Russian group lived in cities with 100,000 and more inhabitants, and the American group in cities with 250,000 and more inhabitants. There were also differences in the political, social and in the educational status of these two groups which undoubtedly had a certain effect on their economic activities.

is questionable whether the observed differences can be attributed entirely to differences in classification. The difference is statistically significant and we may safely assume that a relatively smaller number of the Russian group was engaged in manufacturing than of those who had settled in the United States. We may also assume that a larger percentage of the American group in industry were wage workers than of those in Russia.

Equally significant are the differences in the proportions of those in the apparel industry. 37 per cent of the American group were engaged in the manufacture of men's and women's garments, shoes, caps and hats, but only 17.2 per cent of the Russian group were engaged in the manufacture of these articles as well as in the manufacture of textiles, artificial flowers and similar commodities. The difference is again statistically significant. There was also a relatively larger number of the American than of the Russian group in the tobacco industry, the proportion being 3.5:0.9.

There was a greater concentration of the Russian than of the American group in trade. The percentages were 30.9 and 20.6 respectively. It is interesting to note that 18.6 percent of the gainfully employed Russian Jewesses and only one-tenth of those in the United States were engaged in trade.

The Russian Jews also had a larger percentage of those in domestic and personal service. The percentages were 16.1 and 8.0, respectively. There was, however, almost no difference in the relative number of Russian and American Jewish males who were rendering such services; the percentages were 7.6 and 7.0, respectively. The observed difference (16.1 and 8 per cent) was actually due to the number of women engaged in such occupations. 39 per cent of the gainfully employed Russian Jewesses and only 12.4 per cent of their sisters in America were rendering such services. There is reason to believe that many of the Russian Jewesses who were servants and maids came from small towns where the economic opportunities were limited. The

Jewesses in the United States apparently preferred to work in factories and to be free after work.

As shown in Table 1, the number of Russian Jews in America in the professions was rather small. Professionals and government employees constituted only 2.9 per cent of the labor force. In the case of the Jews living in Russia in cities with 100,000 inhabitants or more, 3.6 were rendering such services in 1897. Because of differences in classifications, it is difficult to ascertain whether there were actually significant differences in the number of Russian and American Jews who were professionals and government employees. It seems, however, that there was a relatively larger number of physicians among the Russian than among the American group: 1.5 per cent of the former were physicians or sanitary workers and only 0.4 per cent of the American group were physicians, surgeons and dentists.

Finally, 26.4 per cent of the gainfully employed Russian Jews and only 20.3 per cent of those in the United States were women. The differences were probably due to differences in age, marital and economic status as well as to differences in the system of enumeration and classification. Let us recall the fact that the homes of some of the Russian Jews in the United States were in 1900, to a certain extent, boarding houses under the care and supervision of their wives, who probably hesitated to report that they were contributing to the support of their families; the same may be said about some married Jewesses who worked at home for a contractor or helped their husbands who were doing work for a contractor or sub-contractor. We may therefore assume that the number of Russian Jewesses in the U. S. who were at that time (1900) actually contributing to the family income and might be regarded as gainfully employed, was actually greater than reported by the Census Bureau.

The preceding analysis has shown that there were significant differences between the occupational pattern of the Russian Jews and that of their brethren and compatriots in the United States. This was due to a variety of causes. Many of the immigrants were poor men and women who, being without any means, went to work in factories and shops. Many of them became garment workers because, among other reasons, some of their compatriots were already in the clothing industry and it was probably easier for them to get a job there than in some other industry. It was probably also easier to learn to use a needle, scissors or an iron than to use more complicated tools. Moreover, immigration is a process of selection. Some of those who were willing to work and to take a chance came to the United States and remained here. Another fact to be remembered is that immigrants are more free to do certain things than others because they are strangers. It is known that some immigrants who had hesitated to work in a factory in their native town, because of their social status or family ties, were glad to become a "hand" in a shop or factory in New York.

If we compare the occupational distribution of the Russian Jews in the United States with that of the general American population, we find significant differences between these two groups. An analysis of the economic pursuits of those who lived in Chicago, New York and in Philadelphia in 1900 shows that 61 per cent of the Russian Jews and only 37.6 per cent of the general population there were engaged in manufacturing and in construction; 2.7 per cent of the former and 5.1 per cent of the latter were rendering professional services; the proportion of those in clerical occupations was 69:117, respectively, and of those in transportation and communication 16:69. The Jews had, however, a larger percentage, 19.1, in trade than the general population, 12.6. It should be noted that the former had a relatively smaller number of bankers and wholesalers and a larger percentage of hucksters, peddlers and proprietors of small stores than the general non-Jewish population.

No less significant is the fact that there were important differences in the economic activities of Russian Jews and

Jewesses in the United States. It will be recalled (Table 1) that 69.4 per cent of the gainfully employed women and only 57.1 per cent of the men were in manufacturing and in construction. The difference is statistically significant, which means that the observed difference is not due to pure chance. The relatively large number of women in industry was due to the fact that the garment industry was demanding such workers and that the Jewish women were willing to work for less than other workers. Whatever the cause, the fact is that 53.6 per cent of the Jewesses and only 30.7 per cent of the gainfully employed Jews from Russia were in the apparel industry; the former constituted 77.3 per cent and the latter only 53.7 per cent of those in manufacturing. There was also a relatively larger number of women than of men in the tobacco industry, the proportion was 53:31, respectively.

Only one-tenth of the gainfully employed women and 23.3 per cent of the men were in trade. Almost two-thirds of the women in trade, 66.2 per cent, were saleswomen; the salesmen constituted only 16.3 per cent of the men in trade. Few women were hucksters or peddlers. The number of women in retail business was also very small.

The proportion of women to men in the several professions was approximately 1:2, respectively. Almost two-fifths, 38.2 per cent, of the professional women were teachers. A larger percentage of women than of men were in the domestic and personal services. Almost three-fourths, 73.4 per cent, of these women were servants or waitresses. Finally, 1,015 of the 1,889 women in the several clerical occupations were stenographers, typists or bookkeepers. The men were rendering other types of clerical services.

The occupational pattern of the Russian Jews in the United States varied from locality to locality. 53.7 per cent of those in Baltimore and only 20.3 per cent of those in Chicago were in the garment industry. The proportion of those in Boston and in New York who were engaged in trade was 286:184, respectively. Only 2.0 per cent of the Philadelphia group and 3.0 per cent of those in Chicago were professionals.

Briefly stated, the present analysis shows that there were statistically significant differences in the economic activities of the Russian Jews who lived in the various types of American cities. The larger cities had relatively more Jews in industry and fewer in trade. 36.7 per cent of those in cities of 250,000—499,999 inhabitants were in trade, 27.4 per cent of those in communities with a population of 500,000—749,999 and only 21.8 per cent in the three largest cities. On the other hand, the percentage of the gainfully employed males in manufacturing was 38.1, 55.0 and 58.6, respectively. The selection of occupations probably varied with the skills and experiences of the immigrants, their ambitions, determination and adaptability, the economic opportunities a community offered, the presence or absence of relatives, friends and compatriots who were willing to give friendly advice and some financial aid and with many other economic, social and psychological factors.

To sum up, our analysis has shown that three-fifths of the Russian Jews in 15 of the largest American cities were engaged in manufacturing. The percentage of the general population living in these cities who were engaged in such activities was significantly smaller. The results are, howevr, only approximations in the sense that they show a general trend at a particular moment in the economic history of the Russian Jews in the United States.

The concentration of Jews from Russia in industry was to a certain extent due to their poverty, type of education, and the training they had received, as well as to their inability to understand or speak English. Moreover, many of them were total strangers in a country radically different from their own. Few of them had relatives or friends here who could give them friendly advice or some financial assistance. In brief, many of the Jewish immigrants at the end of the 19th century became factory workers because they had no other choice. Some of them, for reasons that cannot be dwelt on here, soon succeeded, however, in becoming manufacturers, executives, merchants or professionals.

It was somewhat different with the Jews who came here at the beginning of the present century. Many of them came to their parents, children, brothers, sisters, relatives or friends who were willing and ready to help them. Some of them could, therefore, select the particular occupation which they preferred. Even those who had come on their own initiative and had no one to help them had in those days better opportunities to prepare themselves for the economic activities in which they were interested than their brethren who had preceded them. The working day was already shorter than at the close of the 19th century; and the earnings of the workers were on the increase. The educational opportunities were not bad. American colleges and professional schools had no *numerus clausus* in those days; some of them did not even charge any tuition fee; a considerable number of high schools and colleges were offering evening courses. It was, therefore, to a certain extent easier to become a professional than in the 1890's, when tailors, cloakmakers and others had to work twelve hours and even more a day. Similar opportunities were offered those who were interested in vocational or industrial training or in clerical work.

Whatever the opportunities, the fact is that a smaller percentage of the more recent newcomers went to work in the clothing industry than of those who had come here prior to 1900. The study made by the U. S. Immigration Commission (appointed in 1907) shows that 74.2 per cent of the 1,223 Russian Jews of both sexes in the several branches of industry who had been in the country 10 years or longer, were in the clothing industry, whereas only 64.8 per cent of the 2,548 who had been less than 5 years in the United States, were in this branch of industry.[14] In the case of Jews from other countries, only 69.6 per cent of the 423 less than five years in the country but 79.3 per cent of the 719 Jewish immigrants here ten years and longer were in the clothing industry. The difference is statistically significant. We may, therefore, conclude that a smaller percentage of the more recent immigrants probably became clothing workers than of those who arrived in the 1890's or before. It is true that the report of the Immigration Commission is not based on a sample of the Jewish immigrants in general but of a particular group in certain localities.[15] We may, nevertheless, assume that this has been the trend since the beginning of the present century.[16]

The same study reveals that there were statistically significant differences between the occupational distribution of Jewish immigrants from Russia and those who came from other countries. Of those employed in manufacturing and mechanical industries, sixty-eight per cent of the Russian Jews and seventy-five per cent of those from other countries were in the clothing industry.* Other differences to be noted are: almost 11 per cent of the Russian Jews, but only 3.7 per cent of their co-religionists from other countries were in the shoe industry; there were 8.5 times as many of the latter as of the former in the iron and steel industry. There was a greater concentration of the Russian Jews than of the others in the several branches of the textile industry and a relatively larger number of the latter in the leather and meat industries.

There were other equally important and significant differences between the occupational patterns of Russian and other Jews in the United States at the time of the study made by the Immigration Commission. A relatively smaller percentage of Russian than of other Jews were rendering

---

* It is interesting to note that 22 per cent of the Russian Jews and 27.5 per cent of the other Jews in the clothing industry were engaged in trade before coming to the United States.

domestic and personal service; the ratio was 10:34, respectively. In the case of those rendering professional service, the ratio was 100:165, respectively; the difference is not statistically significant. There was practically no difference between these two groups in the case of trade: 34.9 percent of the Russian and 37.4 per cent of the other Jewish immigrants were in business. As for those in manufacturing and mechanical industries, 57.2 per cent of the Russian Jews in this country at the time of the investigation and only 43.9 per cent of Jewish immigrants from other countries were engaged in such work.[17]

Finally, the occupational pattern of the Jews varied from locality to locality. 61.5 per cent of 364 Jews in Boston and only 42.9 per cent of 240 in Chicago were in manufacturing; almost one-half of 161 Jewish immigrants in Cleveland and approximately one-third of 166 in Philadelphia were engaged in trade.[18] (Although the observed differences are statistically significant, one should, however, bear in mind that the results are based on small samples).

The differences between Jewish and other immigrants were, however, greater * than those between the Russian and other Jews. Of 9,256 non-Jewish male immigrants, 16 years of age and over, in Boston, Buffalo, Chicago, Cleveland, Milwaukee, New York and Philadelphia, only 16.1 per cent were in trade; of the 2,109 Jewish immigrants in the same seven localities, 35.3 per cent were in business. There were five times as many of the non-Jewish group as of the Jewish in domestic and personal service. A larger percentage of the Jewish than of the other immigrants was engaged in manufacturing. The reverse was true in the case of transportation. But a relatively larger number of

---
* 3.2 per cent of approximately 286,400 non-Jewish immigrants and 70 per cent of 7,152 Jews were in the clothing industry. There were 24 times as many of the former as of the latter in the coal-mining industry, approximately 14 times as many in the iron and steel industry and 13 times as many in the cotton goods industry. A larger percentage of the non-Jews than of the Jewish immigrants was engaged in the mining and smelting of copper and in the manufacture of glass, furniture, leather, oil and sugar.

non-Jewish than of Jewish immigrants was engaged in the production of durable or producers' goods; the Jews were primarily engaged in the manufacture of consumers' goods. Finally, 1.8 per cent of the Jews, but only 1.1 per cent of the others were rendering professional services.[19] The observed difference in this particular case is not quite statistically significant.

There were, however, very definite indications at the time when the Immigration Commission was making its study that the number of Jews in the professions would rapidly increase. Of 2,979 foreign-born male students in American colleges and universities, 37.1 per cent were Jews. Moreover, of 6,652 native-born male students of foreign-born parents in such schools, 16.1 per cent were of Jewish descent.[20] In brief, the Jews constituted almost one-fourth, 22.6 per cent, of these two groups of students, a percentage which was several times higher than the proportion of Jews to non-Jews in the general population. Thus a relatively larger number of Jewish immigrants and of native-born Jews of immigrant parentage were preparing themselves for the professions than those of other ethnic groups.

If we compare the results of the study made by the Immigration Commission with those of our analysis of the 1900 census, it appears that there were several significant differences between these two groups. The percentage of Jewish men in trade and in the clerical occupations increased from 30.1 to 34.9; the relative number of those in domestic and personal service was about one-half of the 1900 figure; the percentage of those rendering professional service declined. There was practically no change in the relative number of those engaged in manufacturing and in transportation. The results of these two studies are not, however, strictly comparable for the reason that the findings of the Immigration Commission were based on a small sample and that the 1900 group was not 100 per cent Jewish, but **they may indicate a general trend of the changes occurring among the Jewish immigrant group in America.**

NOTES

1 Markens, Isaac. *The Hebrews in America* (1888), p. 1.

2 "The Progress of the Jews," *The New York Sun*, May 31, 1891.

3 Sombart, Werner. *Die Zukunft der Juden*, (Leipzig 1912), p. 25.

4 U. S. Bureau of the Census, *Occupations*, (1900), pp. 7-9; *Occupations*, (1930), p. 6; *Labor Force*, (1940), III, part 1, Table 74.

5 Markens, I. *op.cit.*; Cohen, M. "The Jews in Business" *American Hebrew*, May 22, 1891; "Will the Jews Own New York?" *New York Journal*, June 14, 1896; Isaacs, A. J., "Jewish Progress in the United States" *American Jewish Annual*, 1889.

6 Billings, John S., "Vital Statistics of the Jews" *United States Census Bulletin*, No. 19, December 30, 1890, pp. 7-8.

Of 47 gainfully employed German Jews who, in 1890, lived in Easton, Pa., 17 per cent were merchants, 4.5 per cent cattle and horse dealers, 8.5 per cent clerks, two were peddlers, one was in the insurance business, two were agents (not specified), four were gentlemen (the term is not defined), 4.3 per cent were tailors and 6.4 per cent clothiers, two tobacconists and 4.3 per cent laborers. (Trachtenberg, J., *Consider the Years* [1944], p. 234).

7 George M. Price's Correspondence in *Nyedyelnaya Khronika Voskhoda,,* November 1891, p. 489; also his *Russkie Yevreii v Amerike*, (St. Petersburg 1893), pp. 26-32.

8 U. S. Immigration Commission, *Reports*, III, pp. 62-63; U. S. Census Bureau, *13th Census, Population*, I, p. 968; E. Tcherikower, ed. *History of the Jewish Labor Movement in the U. S.* (Yiddish) I, pp. 338-340.

9 The correlation coefficient between the geographical distribution of the so-called Russians at the time of the 12th census (1900) and of the Russians, Latvians, and Lithuanians from Russia in 1910 is, however, only $+0.685 \pm 0.05$. The difference between this correlation coefficient and the one between the geographical distribution of the Yiddish-speaking population in 1910 and of the so-called Russians in 1900 ($+0.984$) is statistically significant. The results are not consistent with the hypothesis that the overwhelming majority of those who were reported as Russians in 1900 were not of Jewish origin. Finally, the correlation coefficient between the geographical distribution of the Yiddish-speaking immigrants and of the Russians, Latvians and Lithuanians from Russia in 1910 is only $+0.606$. The difference between this coefficient and the preceding one ($+0.685$) is statistically not significant.

10 U. S. Immigration Commission. *Reports*, XXVIII, p. 189.

11 U. S. Bureau of the Census, 12th *Census, Occupations*.

12 The income of these workers was, according to a recent study ("The Economic Status of the Jewish Clothing Worker in the U. S. 1880-1900, *Yivo-Bleter*, March-April, 1944), lower than of those in some other industries.

13 Brutzkus, B. D., *Professyonalny Sostav Yevreyskavo Naselenya Rossii*, (1908), p. 56.

[14] U. S. Immigration Commission, *Reports*, XX, pp. 81, 97, 110-111.

[15] The report is based on a study of 19,502 garment workers in New York City, Chicago, Baltimore and Rochester, N. Y. We are dealing here with a rather small group. It is therefore questionable whether the Immigration Commission really had an adequate and representative sample. The entire report on immigrants in manufacturing and mining is based on an analysis of 507,256 employees; 7,017 of them were Jewish immigrants. 5,211 of these Jews were from Russia; 5,183 of these Jewish workers were males. (U. S. Immigration Commission, *Reports*, I, p. 305; XX, p. 73).

[16] A more recent study of the initiation dates of 5,720 members of the Amalgamated Clothing Workers shows that nine-tenths of those who joined the union in New York in 1908-1912 were Jews, approximately 54 per cent of those who became members in 1918-1922 and not more than 23.6 per cent of those who joined the union of the men's garment workers in 1933-1937. Although we are dealing here with a small and not strictly representative sample, we know, however, that not many American-born Jewish children become tailors and that the percentage of Jews in the clothing industry is decreasing. (Loft, J., "Jewish Workers in the New York City Men's Clothing Industry," *Jewish Social Studies*, II, p. 64.)

[17] U. S. Immigration Commission, *Reports*, XX, pp. 61-62; XXVI, pp. 130-131.

[18] *Op.cit.*, XXVII, p. 499.

[19] *Op.cit.*, XX, pp. 61-62, 73; XXVI, pp. 130-131.

[20] *Op cit.*, XXIV, pp. 154-155.

OCCUPATIONAL PATTERNS OF AMERICAN JEWS II *

By Nathan Goldberg

Occupational Trends in the 1920's

The American economic, political, social and cultural environment had a definite effect on the evolving economic structure of the Jewish immigrants and their children. Being free to apply their abilities and talents and to settle in any part of the country, they could select any occupation they preferred and could prepare themselves for the economic activities in which they were particularly interested or which were more profitable. Their occupational choices were not the result of any legislative restrictions, but were mostly influenced by the situation of the country.

The changes in the occupational pattern of the American Jews since the beginning of the present century have, generally speaking, resembled those which have occurred in the economic structure of the country as a whole, although not of the same magnitude. The percentage of Jews in manufacturing and mechanical industries continued to decline in the 1920's, while the percentage of those rendering professional and clerical services and those engaged in commerce increased.

This trend comes to the fore in a study of immigrants made on the basis of the results of the 1920 census. N. Car-

* cf. The Jewish Review III, 3 ff.

penter analyzed a sample of immigrants living in Massachusetts, Michigan, Minnesota, New York, Pennsylvania and Wisconsin, comprising an area in which over a half of the Jewish population in America was concentrated. According to this study, about three-fifths of the Jewish immigrants were in commerce. In 1920, 59.7 percent of 22,025 gainfully-employed Jewish male immigrants were salesmen; 26.6 percent were carpenters; 7.6 percent were foremen and overseers in manufacturing establishments and 4.1 percent were physicians and surgeons. In these four occupations were concentrated 98 percent of the Jews included in the survey. There were about twelve times as many salesmen and seven times as many medical men among the Jewish immigrants as among other newcomers. About two-thirds, 67.3 percent, of 17,840 gainfully-employed foreign-born Jewish women worked in 1920 in clothing factories and 22.1 percent were stenographers and typists. These two groups of workers constituted 89.4 percent of the 17,840 gainfully-employed Jewish women; only 24.5 percent of the gainfully-employed foreign-born non-Jewish women were engaged in these two occupations.[21]

Dr. Carpenter thinks that this was the economic structure of the Jews living at that time in Massachusetts, Michigan, Minnesota, New York, Pennsylvania and Wisconsin, the area covered by his study. The validity of this assumption is, however, questionable for his sample may not have been representative. All that can be said is that his sample shows a general trend and that "the precise percentages do not, of course, carry any particular weight, because of the restricted nature of the data from which they have been computed".[22]

Studies made in the 1920's show that the occupational pattern of the Jews was not the same as that of Carpenter's group. A survey made in 1924 of the economic pursuits of Jews in 36 cities[23] showed that only 47.4 percent of 33,194 gainfully-employed were engaged in commerce and that 16.3 percent of them were in manufacturing. Studies made in 1925[24] showed that manufacturing accounted for more than two-fifths, 42.8 percent, and trade for only 30.8 percent.

The results of the survey of 36 cities were reported by the American-Jewish Economic Commission of the Aleph Zadik Aleph (A.Z.A., B'nai B'rith Youth Organization) and were based on a sample. The other studies were prepared at the request of Rabbi Edward L. Israel. According to him, "only in certain indicated instances does the survey claim to be exact, in the other cases it was accepted as a fairly approximate analysis by local people".[25] The two sets of studies are not strictly comparable because of differences in the methods of collecting the data and in the classification of the occupations. But the results of these studies probably show the approximate trend of the occupational distribution of the Jews.

TABLE 2

PERCENTAGE DISTRIBUTION OF GAINFULLY-EMPLOYED JEWS IN 46 CITIES, 1924-1925

Occupations	A.Z.A. Group (36 Cities) Total	Male	Female	Israel Group (10 Cities) Total
Total	100.0	100.0	100.0	100.0
Trade	47.4	51.1	35.4	30.8
Manufacturing	16.3	18.6	8.8	42.8
Professions	10.1	10.7	8.0	9.6
Clerical	16.8	9.5	40.8	8.4
Domestic & Personal	5.0	5.4	4.0	6.7
Transportation and Communication	2.2	2.2	2.1	1.0
Public Service	2.0	2.3	0.9	----
Other	0.2	0.2	----	0.7

It will be noticed that almost 43 percent of 25,351 (Israel group) and only 16.3 percent of 33,194 (A.Z.A. group) gainfully-employed Jews were in manufacturing and mechanical industries. The difference is in this particular case statistically significant. The Israel group had a relatively smaller number of persons in trade, in the several professions, in transportation and communication and in the clerical occupations than the A.Z.A. group, but a larger percentage in domestic and personal service.

These percentages were, of course, not alike in every one of the communities studied. The economic structure of the Jews, as of other groups, varies with prevailing local conditions—climate, natural resources, local demands, market conditions and the density of the Jewish population—as well as with the training and experiences of the individuals and their occupational preferences and economic interests. Some of them settle in certain cities because of the opportunities they offer; others are where they are for no particular reason. This then accounts to a certain extent for the local variations in the occupational pattern of the Jews.

The studies of 1924 reveal that 62 percent of 33,194 gainfully-employed were employees. More significant is the fact that wage earners and salaried persons constituted 72 percent of those in manufacturing, approximately 62 percent of the professional and semi-professional group, 97.9 percent of those engaged in clerical occupations and 50.6 percent of those in trade.

The study of 1925 showed that 9.6 percent of the gainfully-occupied Jews in trade were grocers, one-twelfth were hucksters or peddlers, 4.1 percent had retail clothing stores and 30.7 percent were salesmen. These 4,119 Jews constituted 52.8 percent of the Jews engaged in trade and 16.2 percent of the total gainfully-occupied Jews.

As was to be expected, the men had a different occupational pattern from that of the gainfully-employed women. Almost 41 percent of the women were doing clerical work. Equally significant is the fact that 93.7 percent of the gainfully-employed women were employees and only 52.4 percent of the men. Most of the women in trade, 90.6 percent, were employees: clerks in stores, salesladies and the like, whereas only 42.2 percent of the men engaged in trade were employees. The proportion of men to women employees in manufacturing was 10:14, respectively, and in the professions 10:29, respectively.

The results of these studies lead to the conclusion that most of the Jews are employees and that a relatively large number of them are engaged in the manufacture and distribution of consumers' goods.

Furthermore, these two sets of studies show that the occupational pattern of the Jews in 1924-1925 was not the same as of the Russian Jews in American cities in 1900 (Table 1). The relative number of those in manufacturing decreased during these 25 years. 35.3 percent of the gainfully-employed Jewish immigrants in 1900 were in the clothing industry as compared with only 19.1 percent of the Israel group. The percentage of those in domestic and personal service also dropped. The relative number of those in the professions, clerical occupations and in trade increased.

To be sure, these groups are not strictly comparable. The 1900 group consisted of a large number of recent immigrants from Russia, while the A.Z.A. and Israel groups consisted of a considerable number of American-born Jews and of immigrants from various parts of the world who had arrived here prior to the beginning of World War I in 1914. Secondly, the 1900 group lived in cities with a population of 250,000 and more, and the A.Z.A. and Israel groups lived in various types of communities, most of them in small localities. Inasmuch as the occupational pattern of large cities is not the same as that of smaller communities, it is quite possible that some of the observed differences were not primarily due to changes in the occupational distribution of the Jews. Finally, the 1900 study was based on a census of the entire population and the Israel and A.Z.A. studies were based on samples or on estimates.

Although these groups are not strictly comparable, we may, nevertheless, assume that the A.Z.A. and Israel studies show changes in the occupational distribution of the erstwhile Jewish immigrants from Russia. A large number of the Jews in 1925 were still immigrants and probably three-fifths of the foreign-born Jews were from Russia. Moreover, about 63 percent of the A.Z.A. group lived in cities with a population of 150,000 and more in 1920 and about 83 percent of the Israel group lived in such communities. We may, therefore, conclude that the occupational distribution of the erstwhile Jewish immigrants changed in the years 1900-1925. There was an upward trend in the professions, trade and in the clerical occupations, and a downward trend in manufacturing and in domestic and personal service. The erstwhile Jewish immigrants suffered and struggled; some of them managed, however, to save part of their meager earnings for the purpose of opening a shop or a store; others prepared themselves for some profession or clerical occupation in which some of them finally achieved success; and a certain number were promoted because of their outstanding ability, proficiency or resourcefulness. In brief, some of the former immigrants succeeded in their efforts and endeavors, and they tried to give their children a good start in life. It also happened that the sons and daughters helped their parents to attain economic independence and social security.

Other studies show that the occupational preferences of the Jews are not the same as of other ethnic groups. A study made of 1,536 gainfully-employed Jewish males, 17 years of age and older, in Scranton, Pa., in 1924, showed that 69 percent of them were engaged in trade, 23 percent in manufacturing, and 3.3 percent in the professions; the others were government employees, draymen, waiters, etc. [26]

The percentage distribution of 1,409 gainfully-occupied Denver Jews in 1924 was: 59.5 in trade, 16.3 in manufacturing, 10.6 in domestic and personal service, 6.5 in the professions, 5.2 in clerical occupations; about 2 percent were in agriculture, transportation and in public service. [27] (Some of this group were probably tubercular patients.)

Detroit, Mich., had during these years an upward trend in manufacturing while trade was somewhat on the decline. Studies made there of 424 Jews in 1910 and of 1,570 in 1922-1923 [28] showed that 23.1 percent of the former and 30.6 percent of the latter were in manufacturing; 65.1 and 61.2 percent, respectively, were in trade; and that 4.5 percent of the 1910 group and 5.7 per cent of the other group were professionals. The upward trend in manufacturing was probably due to the opportunities offered by the rapidly growing automobile industry. (This study was based on a small sample and the results are perhaps suggestive but not conclusive).

The trends at the end of the 1920's were generally similar to those noted in the studies of the mid-1920's. The smaller communities had a relatively larger number of Jews in trade than the large American cities where many of the Jews were in the manufacturing and mechanical industries.

M. Langer's study of the so-called Easton community, a town near New York City with a population of 31,275 in 1930, approximately 10 percent of whom were Jews, showed that more than four-fifths, 81.6 percent, of 1669 Jewish heads of families were in 1931 engaged in trade; 12.4 percent were in manufacturing; and only 3.6 percent were rendering professional service. This occupational distribution is more or less typical of Jews in small communities where the economic opportunities are rather limited. The occupational pattern of 136 unmarried children of 200 Jewish families there was, however, not the same as of the older generation. Three-fifths of them were engaged in commerce; 17.8 percent were professionals; approximately one-tenth were doing clerical work; and about one-sixteenth (6.8 percent) were in manufacturing.[29] Although we are dealing here with a small sample, we may, nevertheless, say, assuming that most of the older group were immigrants and most of the unmarried children were American-born, that the economic opportunities and preferences of the immigrants are generally not the same as those of their American-born children.

Surveys made by the Bureau of Jewish Social Research in Omaha, Nebraska, in 1929, and in Pittsfield, Mass., in 1930, show that from five to six-tenths of the gainfully-employed Jews in these cities were in trade. Only 9.2 percent of 1,973 Omaha Jews were in manufacturing and 12.9 percent of 418 Pittsfield Jews were factory workers and 2.9 percent were manufacturers. Approximately one-seventeenth of the Omaha group and one-twelfth of the Pittsfield group were rendering professional services; the observed difference is, however, statistically not significant. About one-fourth of the Pittsfield group and almost 16 percent of the Omaha Jews were clerical workers.[30] This occupational pattern is not, however, typical of Jews living in large cities.

Jaffe, for instance, reports that one-third of 2,643 Chicago Jews, 35-64 years of age, were in manufacturing in 1930; 54 percent were engaged in trade; and approximately one-twentieth were rendering professional services.[31] His findings are, however, suggestive rather than conclusive, because they are based on data of a selected age group.

The several studies referred to above show that the economic structure of the Jews after the first World War was not the same as at the beginning of the present century. The relative number of Jews in trade, clerical occupations and in the professions increased, and the percentage of industrial and other workers decreased. These changes were, in a sense, due to the general development of the country and to the successful adjustment of a considerable number of our erstwhile immigrants to the socio-economic environment of the United States, as well as to the occupational preferences of their American-born children.

DEPRESSION AND RECOVERY

The 1930's were marked by a slump at the beginning of the decade, followed by the New Deal and partial recovery in the last pre-war years.

From a purely economic point of view, the 1930's were a very critical period in the history of the United States. Several attempts were made to reduce the number of unemployed, but with limited success. Almost one-fourth, approximatetly 11,065,000, of the labor force were still unemployed, or only partly employed, in 1937. Those seeking work and on public emergency work constituted, even in 1940, one-seventh, or 14.4 percent, of the total labor force; 7,622,316 persons were at that time without regular employment.[32]

During the first years of the crisis, a "back to the soil" movement, the unemployed taking up abandoned farms or returning to the farms of their parents, was discernible. In the later years of the 1930's this trend lost its impetus and the "normal" tendencies of advanced capitalism, urbanization and an increase in trade and clerical occupations, reappeared. The results of the 1940 census show that during the 1930's, the percentage of those employed in agriculture dropped from 21.4 to 17.7, and that of government employees increased from 1.8 to 3.9. There was also a slight increase in the relative number rendering professional service; physicians and dentists, for instance, constituted in 1930: 0.46 percent of the labor force and 0.52 percent a decade later. Similarly, the percentage of stenographers and typists increased from 1.7 to 2.3. There was also an increase in the number of persons engaged in wholesale and retail trade, banking, insurance and real estate. Generally speaking, there was an increase in the number engaged in the distribution of goods as well as of those rendering professional, clerical and kindred services.

Although the exact effects of the economic depression on the Jews are not known, the following facts merit consideration. The years of the economic depression were also years when Hitler came to power in Germany and when anti-Semitism was on the increase. They were also years of discrimination in employment against Jews. Studies made of help-wanted advertisements show a decided rise in the "Christian only" type of notice.

"Our survey indicates that discriminatory specifications have varied directly with the rise and fall of the business cycle, but that this tendency was true to a greater degree in the depression of 1932 than in that of 1921. We have also found that since the advent of Nazism, the frequency of discriminatory specifications has grown progressively higher, until 1937-1938, these frequencies, especially in the (employment) agency ads, have reached heights far in excess of preceding years." [33]

Another investigator reports that advertisements specifying Christians or Gentiles in the Sunday edition of the *Chicago Tribune* increased from 4 per 1,000 in 1921 to 4.8 in 1927-1931 and to 9.4 in 1937. [34]

It was in those days more difficult for a Jewish white-collar worker or professional to find employment than for a non-Jew. One investigator who had applied for 100 jobs as stenographer, secretary, accountant and auditor was in 91 cases told that a Jew would not be acceptable. A study made of young men and women in New York City in 1935 showed that unemployment was more widespread among Jewish than among Protestant white-collar workers. [35] We may assume that New York was not an exceptional case.

Equally significant for the economic situation of the Jews is the fact that unemployment was more widespread in the largest cities where the majority of the Jews in America are concentrated. There was a relatively larger number of unemployed, 17.1 percent, in New York, Chicago, Philadelphia, Detroit and Los Angeles, where about seven-tenths of the Jews live, in 1940 than in cities with less than a million but with more than 100,000 inhabitants, where only 15.7 percent were unemployed. In brief, only 83.7 percent of those in cities with 100,000 or more inhabitants, in which about nine-tenths

OCCUPATIONAL PATTERNS OF AMERICAN JEWS 171

of the Jews live, were employed in 1940 as compared with 86.5 percent in the rest of the country. Unemployment was also more prevalent in such cities in 1930 and in 1937.[36]

This situation affected the Jews in more than one way. Inasmuch as they are a so-called marginal group, it is generally more difficult for them to find a suitable job, other things being equal, in places with a relatively large number of unemployed than in other localities. Moreover, Jewish storekeepers, whose clients usually are from the middle and poor classes, were somewhat affected because unemployment was more prevalent among these classes than among other groups. In some instances, however, unemployed Jewish workers began to engage in petty trade. Meeting with discriminatory attitudes in non-Jewish enterprises, some turned to Jewish commercial enterprises. Youth, unable to find employment elsewhere, entered the stores of their parents. These tendencies are depicted in the results of inquiries into the economic situation of the Jews made in the 1930's.

We present here a summary of surveys of the economic structure of the Jews in 72 communites. 50 of them were made in 1934, 2 in 1935, 1 in the following year, 8 in 1937, 7 a year later, 1 in 1939, 2 in 1941, and one in 1942. There is reason for the assumption that no very significant changes occurred during the years of 1934-1942 and that the results may, therefore, be combined and treated as a unit.

Approximately 2,817,000 Jews lived in these communities. They constituted about three-fifths of the total Jewish population. More than four-fifths, 84.2 percent, lived in cities with a Jewish population of 50,000 and more; 6.5 percent were in places with 20,000-49,999 Jews; 4.6 percent lived in cities having a Jewish population of 10,000-19,999; 3.2 percent were in communities with 5,000-9,999 Jews; 1.1 percent lived in towns having 1,000-4,999 Jews; only 0.4 percent of the entire group were in communities with a Jewish population less than 1,000 .

Several methods were employed for the collection of the data. Some of the investigators used the method of sampling, others made a survey of the entire population. One organization, however, made 48 of these surveys, which covered approximately 7 percent of the gainfully employed under consideration; one individual made six of these studies; two individuals made two studies each. There was also lack of uniformity in the classification of the occupations. Although these studies are not strictly comparable, they do, nevertheless, show the approximate occupational trend in the 1930's.

TABLE 3

PERCENTAGE DISTRIBUTION OF GAINFULLY-EMPLOYED JEWS

Occupations	61 Communities [38]	5 Communities [39]
Total	100.0	100.0
Manufacturing	12.4	34.8
Trade	47.3	33.3
Professions	11.9	11.3
Clerical	15.7	----
Domestic and Personal	6.8	12.4
Public Service	2.9	2.6
Transportation and Communication	1.9	3.7
Other and Unknown	1.1	1.9

The table summarizes the occupational distribution of 913,276 gainfully-employed Jews. 835,605 of them lived in the 5 communities: New York, Detroit, Stamford, Worcester and New Orleans; almost 800,000 of them were in New York City. The occupational pattern of these five cities as presented in the table is, therefore, in a sense the occupational distribution of the New York Jews, which is based on estimates. Approximately one-eighth of those in the 61 communities and 34.8 percent of the other group were in industry;

47.3 percent of the former and only one-third of those in the 5 communities were engaged in trade.[40]

There were, to be sure, differences in the classification of occupations; the investigators of the five cities did not single out the clerical workers. It is doubtful, however, whether differences in classification account in this particular case for the observed differences in the occupational distribution. Furthermore, although this may be the cause of the difference in the relative number of persons in manufacturing, it does not account at all for the relatively smaller number of persons engaged in trade in the cities where the clerical workers, a large number of whom were working in mercantile establishments and were, therefore, included among those in trade, were not classified separately.

The differences are rather due to the fact that the occupational distribution of Jews living in large cities which are industrial centers, is not the same as of those living in smaller communities. Thus we find that the manufacturers and industrial workers constituted 35.3 percent of the gainfully-employed Jews in New York City, 23.3 percent of those in Detroit and only about one-ninth of those in Dallas in 1939.

These studies also show that the occupational pattern of the Jews, like that of other ethnic groups, varies from locality to locality. 22.5 percent of the gainfully-employed Jews in Passaic in 1937 and only 11.7 percent of those in Trenton in the same year were engaged in manufacturing; 43.2 percent of the former and 53.7 percent of the latter were engaged in commerce. Inasmuch as the same investigator made both these surveys, we may assume that the differences were not in any way due to differences in the classification of occupations. In the case of New London and Norwich, Conn., the percentages of the gainfully-employed Jewish males in manufacturing were 18.5 and 24.5, respectively, and of those rendering professional service 11.2 and 8.2, respectively. The observed differences in this particular case are not, however, statistically significant. In 11 of 47 cities surveyed by the A.Z.A., one-eleventh of the gainfully-employed Jewish population was in industry and in the other 36 cities almost one-eighth; almost three-fifths of the former and only 43.4 percent of those in the 36 cities were in commercial pursuits; in the case of those rendering professional services the percentages were 7.4 and 13.8, respectively. The observed differences are statistically significant. The data at hand suggest that the occupational distribution of the Jews varies to a certain extent, directly or inversely, with the occupational pattern of the general population [41] as well as with the training, opportunities and occupational preferences of the Jews.

This does not, however, mean that the American Jews have no occupational pattern of their own. Although their occupational distribution varies from locality to locality, there is, nevertheless, a certain uniformity in this very diversity. It can even be shown that the occupational distribution of the Jews is nowhere the same as of the general population. A comparison of the percentage distribution of the gainfully-employed Jewish males in 47 communities in 1934 and of the total gainfully-employed males in 41 of these cities in 1930 shows that there were approximately 3.2 times as many of the general as of the Jewish male population in industry and 5 times as many in transportation and communication. The reverse was true in the case of those engaged in commerce and in the professions. The ratio of Jewish to the general gainfully-employed male population engaged in trade was 2.6:1; in the case of those in the professions, the ratio was 2.3:1. The differences were probably somewhat greater, for the reason that, in computing the percentages, the Jews had not been excluded from the general population. [42]

There were also statistically significant differences between the occupational distribution of the gainfully-employed Jewish and other women. Of 14,740 women in 47 cities (A.Z.A. group), only 5.4 percent were engaged in industry; 19.7 percent of the total gainfully-employed women in 41 of these 47 cities were, in 1930, doing similar work. In the case of those engaged in trade, there were 363 Jewish women per 100 gainfully-employed women in the general population; 1.8 times as many of the Jewish women as of those in the general population, were doing clerical work; there was no significant difference between the percentage of professional women among Jews and other groups.

TABLE 4

PERCENTAGE DISTRIBUTION OF GAINFULLY-EMPLOYED MALES
1930 AND 1934

Occupations	Jews, 1934 [4]	General Population, 1930 [4]
Total	100.0	100.0
Manufacturing	13.7	43.6
Trade	51.1	19.6
Professions	13.1	5.7
Clerical	9.3	8.7
Domestic and Personal	6.8	6.7
Transportation and Communication	2.2	11.1
Public Service	3.6	2.7
Other and Unknown	0.2	1.9

The Jews, moreover, are primarily engaged in the manufacture and distribution of consumers' goods. Because of this, the position of the Jews in the American economy is of minor importance: they certainly do not control the ebb and flow of the production and distribution of commodities.

As in the case of the general population, the occupational pattern of the Jewish males was not the same as of the females. Almost one-fifth, 18.6 percent, of 64,638 gainfully-employed males were engaged in manufacturing and only 7.7 percent of 20,201 females: there was also a relatively larger number of the former than of the latter in trade. The reverse was true in the case of those engaged in clerical occupations.

SOCIO-ECONOMIC STATUS

There was a relatively larger number of employees than employers among Jews in the 1930's than in the 1920's. According to the A.Z.A. study, 38 percent of 33,194 gainfully-employed Jews in 36 cities in 1924 were employers and only 35.8 percent of 46,610 in the same cities in 1934. Small as the difference is, it is, nevertheless, statistically significant. The results of this study seem, therefore, to suggest that the relative number of Jewish employees is increasing and the percentage of Jewish employers is decreasing. This is probably due to the fact that our native-born children, who are on the increase among our gainfully-employed, prefer to be employees rather than proprietors of small groceries, candy

TABLE 5

EMPLOYERS AND EMPLOYEES

Industry	Total Number	Percent Employers	Percent Employees
Total	60,360	37.1	62.9
Manufacturing	7,105	36.7	63.3
Transportation & Communication	1,227	27.3	72.7
Domestic & Personal Service	4,394	44.8	55.2
Clerical Occupations	9,652	2.5	97.5
Public Service	2,062	----	100.0
Professions	7,477	60.3	39.7
Trade	28,344	44.6	55.4
Agriculture	99	74.7	25.3

and cigar stores and similar retail establishments. Thus we find that the percentage of employees among those in trade increased from 50.66 in 1924 to 55.9 ten years later. The American-born Jews are interested in commerce; they prefer, however, to be salesmen or buyers rather than proprietors of small retail stores. A recent study of the vocational interests of Jewish high school graduates shows that the majority of them prefer to be salaried workers.[46] The percentage of employees among Jews in large cities is even greater than in the cities studied by the A.Z.A. It is estimated that 91 percent of the New York City Jews in manufacturing and 71 percent of those in trade were in 1937 employees. The corresponding percentages for the non-Jewish employees were 97 and 88.[47]

An analysis of 592,285 gainfully-employed Jews in 55 [48] large and small cities shows that fully 78.2 percent of them were employees in the 1930's. The Jews in the very large cities are essentially employees.

The largest concentration of employers and self-employed was in trade and in the several professions. Of 22,381 employers and self-employed, 56.5 percent were in commerce and 20.1 percent were rendering professional service. This was, to a certain extent, to be expected. Many professionals are self-employed; two-thirds of the professionals under consideration were such persons. A considerable number of those in commerce are usually proprietors of stores or some other mercantile establishments. The Jews have more self-employed among those who are in trade because they have a relatively larger number of small shopkeepers than other ethnic groups.

Practically all of those in the clerical occupations, 97.5 percent, were employees. Almost three-fourths of those in transportation and communication were wage or salary workers. More than three-fifths of those in manufacturing and approximately fifty-five of every hundred in trade were employees.

As stated above, this is the approximate distribution of Jews who do not live in the very large cities. The percentage of employees among those who live in New York City, Chicago and other large cities is much greater.

The socio-economic distribution of the Jews is not the same as that of other ethnic groups. We usually have a relatively larger number of professionals, clerical workers and proprietors. As in the case of the occupational distribution, this also varies from locality to locality. One-seventh of the

Buffalo Jews and approximately one-ninth of the San Francisco group were professionals. Buffalo had three times as many skilled workers as San Francisco. San Francisco had a relatively larger number of proprietors and clerks and three times as many semi-skilled workers as Buffalo. Finally, the San Francisco Jews included a larger percentage of professionals, proprietors and clerical workers but less skilled and unskilled workers than the other ethnic groups there.

TABLE 6
Socio-Economic Status of Jews in 7 Communities [?]

Status	Number	Percent
Total	58,635	100.0
Clerks and Kindred Workers	22,935	39.7
Proprietors, Managers, Officials	15,932	27.6
Professionals	5,678	9.8
Skilled Workers	5,018	8.7
Semi-Skilled Workers	6,236	10.9
Public Service	34	0.1
Laborers	1,510	2.6
Others	371	0.6

Table 6 shows that 4 of every 10 Jews are clerks or kindred workers. This includes those who work in offices as well as salesmen, saleswomen, buyers and the like. Approximately 28 of every 100 are proprietors, managers and officials. One-tenth are professionals and another tenth are semi-skilled workers. The others are skilled workers, government employees, and unskilled workers.

Many Jewish proprietors are owners of small business and manufacturing establishments. We have a relatively smaller number of bankers, brokers and of proprietors of large industrial plants than some other ethnic groups. When comparing the socio-economic status of Jews with that of other groups, it is, therefore, important to bear in mind that there are significant differences between Jewish and other proprietors, managers and officials.

OCCUPATIONAL PATTERNS OF AMERICAN JEWS 179

ROLE OF JEWS IN AMERICAN ECONOMY

A study made of bankers in the United States showed that only 0.6 percent of them were of Jewish descent, although the Jews constituted approximately 3.5 percent of the total population. The ratio of Jews to non-Jews in the population and in banking was, in other words, about 6:1. The New York Jews constituted approximately 28 percent of the total population, but not more than 6 percent of the bankers; Jews constituted 8 or 9 percent of the Chicago population and only 2.8 percent of its bankers. There are many cities which have no Jewish bankers and no Jewish bank officials. Moreover, the Jewish bankers play, as a rule, a minor role in the financial world. One cannot find a Jew among the executives or officials of the largest commercial banks and investment houses.[5"]

Let us also recall, in this connection, the results of the study made in 1935 by the Editors of *Fortune*. They found that only 7.1 percent of the directors of the 19 members of the New York Clearing House in 1933 were Jews. Moreover, the most important Jewish investment house in New York City, had only 2.88 percent of foreign loans outstanding on March 1, 1935, while the poorest non-Jewish investment house there had 4.23 percent of such loans. Approximately 18 percent of the members of the New York Stock Exchange were at that time of Jewish descent; this was much less than the proportion of Jews to non-Jews in the general population. No less important is the fact that the Jewish and half-Jewish firms constituted only 12.4 percent of those listed in the Exchange Directory. There were very few Jews in the insurance business, although about one-half of the New York insurance agents at that time were Jews.

According to the Editors of *Fortune*, there were very few Jews in the important industries. Steel is not a Jewish industry, although Jews control about 90 percent of the scrap iron and steel business. The coal industry is almost entirely non-Jewish; so are the telephone and telegraph, lumber, rubber, automobile, shipping, petroleum, chemical and many other industries. The control by the Jews of the motion picture industry is declining. They do, however, have an appreciable control of some branches of the textile and clothing industries.[51]

Their conclusion is that "the number of Jews who can be thought of as threatening non-Jewish control of U. S. industry is not so large as the *seeming* prevalence of Jews would make it appear. The Jews *seem* to play a disproportionate part for two reasons: the Jews and particularly the Polish Jews with their ghetto background are the most urban, the most city-loving of all peoples, and the favored occupations of Jews in the cities are those occupations which bring them into most direct contact with the great consuming public." (pp. 34-35)

The Jews, in other words, seem to play an important part because a relatively large number of them are proprietors of retail stores, groceries, candy and cigar stores. It is estimated, for instance, that four-fifths of those who were selling apparel in New York City in 1937 were Jews and that they constituted 62 percent of the drug store employees and approximately 47 percent of those working in food stores. The Jews constituted, however, only one-eighth of those in the automotive business in New York City. Similarly, 82 percent of those in the manufacture of fur and fur goods in New York in 1937 were Jews and 55.5 percent of those engaged in the manufacture of clothing, cloth goods and headwear. The Jews constituted, however, only one-fifth of the New Yorkers in the manufacture of rubber and composition goods, 18 percent of those in the metal industry, less than 5 percent of those engaged in the production of transportation equipment and about one of every twenty-five in the machine-shop industry.[52]

Koenig's study shows that the Stamford Jews are also concentrated in the retail rather than in the wholesale business. A relatively large number of those engaged in the distribution of food, wearing apparel, dry goods, furniture, cosmetics and other consumers' goods were Jews. The role the latter played in the financial world of the town was, however, "entirely negligible". The two financial houses controlled by Jews were "quite small, and their place in the economic life of the town" was "of comparatively little importance". As for the Jewish real-estate and insurance agencies, they were "far from holding a leading position in the field." [53]

These studies show that the Jews do not play a dominant role in the economic life of the United States. Very few of them are in agriculture. There is also a smaller percentage of them than of other groups in banking. Although a relatively large number of Jews are engaged in commerce, they are primarily concentrated in the distribution of consumers' goods. Few of them are engaged in the production and distribution of producers' goods. Inasmuch as they deal with the consumer, some people, therefore, think that the Jews are actually playing a dominant role in the economic life of the country; inasmuch as consumers see the Jewish storekeeper, but not the non-Jewish producer and wholesaler, some non-Jews conclude that Jews control the ebb and flow of commodities and prices. Studies made by the Opinion Research Center of Colorado University in 1942 and 1943 show, for instance, that three-fifths of a group of non-Jews thought that Jews had too much economic power; two percent said they had just as much as they were entitled to. [54]

The Jews' share is being exaggerated because, among other things, a relatively large number of them are in retail business. The same applies to the professions. Inasmuch as there is a relatively larger number of Jews in the medical, legal and other self-employed professions than of non-Jews, some assume that they control these professions. The truth of the matter is not so; Jews play a relatively minor role even in those professions in which a relatively large number of them are engaged.

NOTES

The following abbreviations have been used:
JPS—*Jewish Population Studies*, edited by Sophia M. Robison. New York, 1943.
JSS—*Jewish Social Studies*.
JSSQ—*Jewish Social Service Quarterly*.

21 Carpenter, Niles. *Immigrants and Their Children, Census Monograph*, VII, 1927, pp. 286-290.
22 Carpenter, p. 284.
23 The American Jewish Economic Commission of the A.Z.A. (Aleph Zadik Aleph), *The 1937 Annual Report, Statistics of Surveys in 48 Cities*, submitted by Ernest O. Eisenberg, 1937 (typewritten), Table I. The cities are: Akron, O., Aliquippa and Allentown, Pa., Asheville, N.C., Atlanta, Ga., Atlantic City, N.J., Bangor, Me., Bethlehem, Pa., Camden, N.J., Columbus, O., Dallas, Tex., Dayton, O., Donora, Pa., Duluth, Minn., East Liverpool, O., Grand Forks, N.D., Granite City, Ill., Huntington, W.Va., McKeesport, Pa., Memphis, Tenn., Middletown, Conn., Milwaukee, Wis., Minneapolis, Minn., Montclair, N.J., Oakland, Calif., Paterson, N.J., Portland, Ore., Pottsville, Pa., Pueblo, Colo., Reading, Pa., Rock Island, Ill., Toledo, O., Topeka, Kan., Warren, O., Waukegan, Ill., Woonsocket, R.I.
24 Israel, Edward L. "The Occupations of Jews", *Yearbook of the Central Conference of American Rabbis*, XXXVI, pp. 286-291. The cities are: Alexandria, Va., Erie, Pa., Jacksonville, Fla., Los Angeles, Calif., Omaha, Nebr., St. Joseph, Mo., Syracuse, N.Y., Vicksburg, Miss., Wilmington, Del., Worcester, Mass.
25 *Ibid.*, p. 286.
26 *Ibid.*, p. 292.
27 The American Jewish Economic Commission of the A.Z.A. *The 1937 Annual Report*.
28 Meyer, Henry J. "The Economic Structure of the Jewish Community in Detroit", JSS. II, (1940), p. 134. The study was based on the following names appearing in the Detroit city directories: Cohan, Cohen, Cohn, Cohone, Freidman, Friedman, Gold, Goldberg, Goldenberg, Goldman, Goldstein, Levene, Levenson, Levey, Levi, Levin, Levine, Levinson, Levy, Rosen, Rosenbaum, Rosenberg, Rosenblatt, Rosenfield, Rosenthal, Rosenzweig. Most of them were men.
29 Langer, Marion. *A Study of the Jewish Community of Easton*. New York: Graduate School for Jewish Social Work, 1936, (typewritten), pp. 258, 273.
30 Bureau of Jewish Social Research, *Jewish Communal Survey*, Omaha, 1929, p. 44; Pittsfield, 1930, pp. 450-451; quoted from Kinzler, E., *Some Aspects of the Occupational Distribution of Jews in New York City*, New York: Graduate School for Jewish Social Work, 1935, (typewritten), pp. 6-7, 225.
31 Jaffe, A. J. "A Study of Chicago Jewry (1930) Based on Death Certificates", in JPS., p. 142.
32 *Census of Partial Employment, Unemployment and Occupations*, I, p. 1; U. S. Census Bureau, *16th Census*. 1940, *Population*, III. *The Labor Force*, Part I. p. 3.
33 Cohen, Jacob X. *Towards Fair Play for Jewish Workers*, (New York, 1938), p. 9.

34 Severson, A. L. "Nationality and Religious Preferences as Reflected in Newspaper Advertisements," *American Journal of Sociology*, XXXXIV, (1939), p. 541.

35 Cohen, Jacob X. *Jews, Jobs and Discrimination*, (New York, 1937), p. 10; McGill, Nettie Pauline, "Some Characteristics of Jewish Youth in New York City", JSSQ, December, 1937, p. 265; McGill, N. P., "The Religio-Cultural Backgrounds of New York City's Youth", *Better Times*, April 5, 1937, pp. 23-24.

36 U. S. Census Bureau, 16th *Census*: 1940, *Population*, Vol. III, Part I, pp. 58-59; *Census of Partial Employment, Unemployment and Occupations*, Vol. I, p. 3; 15th *Census*: 1930, *Unemployment*, Vol. I, p. 17.

38 The 36 cities enumerated in note 23; also: Augusta, Ga., 1934, Braddock, Pa., 1934, *A.Z.A. Report;* Bridgeport, Conn., Koenig, S., *Yivo Bleter*, XVII, pp. 14-27; Denver, Col., Fargo, N.D., Grand Rapids, Mich., 1934, *A.Z.A. Report;* Hartford, Conn., Koenig, *op cit.;* Hazelton, Pa., Kansas City, Mo., 1934, A.Z.A. Report; New Britain and New London, Conn., Koenig, *op. cit.;* New London and Norwich, Conn., Wessel, in JPS., pp. 65-67, 77-79; Omaha, Nebr., 1934, A.Z.A. Report; Passaic, N.J., Robison, S.M., in JPS., pp. 30-35; Pittsburgh, Pa., JPS., pp. 98-107, Taylor, M., *Jewish Community of Pittsburgh*, Section IV; Sheboygan, Wis., South Bend, Ind., Spokane, Wash., *A.Z.A. Report;* Stamford, Conn., Koenig, *op. cit.;* Staten Island, N.Y., Fleischman, A.A., *Some Aspects of the Jewish Population of Staten Island*, New York: Graduate School for Jewish Social Work, 1937, pp. 49-57; Stockton, Calif., *A.Z.A. Report;* Trenton, N.J., Robison, S.M., in JPS., pp. 13-17; Urbana, Mandelbaum, D.G., "A Study of the Jews of Urbana", JSSQ., December, 1935, pp. 228-229; Waterbury, Conn., Koenig, *op. cit.*

See also: Wolff, Kurt H., "Traditionalists and Assimilationists", in *Studies in Sociology*, IV, nos. 1-2, p. 22, published by the Department of Sociology, Southern Methodist University, Dallas, Tex. His study is based on a sample of the Jewish population in Dallas, Tex. Papo, Joseph M., "A Study of the Jewish Community of Duluth", JSSQ., December, 1941, pp. 222-223. Jewish Welfare Federation of Duluth, *Social, Recreational and Educational Survey of the Jewish Community of Duluth*, 1944, pp. 9-11. A summary of the occupational distribution of the Jews living in Dallas, New London, Norwich, Passaic and Trenton will be found in *Patterns of Jewish Occupational Distribution in the United States and Canada*, issued by the Jewish Occupational Council as Report No. 6, 1940.

39 The cities are:

Detroit, 1935, Meyer, Henry, J., "A Study of Detroit Jewry, 1935", in *JPS.*, pp. 119-123, and his "The Economic Structure of the Jewish Community in Detroit", JSS. *April*, 1940; pp. 129-131, pp. 129-131;

New Orleans, 1938; Feibelman, J. B., *A Social and Economic Study of the New Orleans Jewish Community*, 1941, pp. 39-41, 51-52;

New York City, 1937, Committee on Economic Adjustment Information Service in Cooperation with the Conference on Jewish Relations, *Industrial Classification of Jewish Gainful Workers in New York City*, 1937, typewritten, pp. 9-13;

Stamford, Conn., Koenig, S., "The Socio-Economic Structure of an American Jewish Community", in *Jews in a Gentile World,* edited by I. Graeber and S. H. Britt, (1942), pp. 207-216;

Worcester, Mass., 1942, Mopsik, S., "The Jewish Population of Worcester", JSS., VII, (1945), pp. 57-59;

A summary of three of these studies, New York, Detroit and Stamford, will be found in the report of the Jewish Occupational Council referred to above.

40 The approximate occupational distribution of the 14,832 Jews living in the Avondale district of Cincinnati, Ohio, in 1935, was: one-half in trade, one-fifth in industry, one-ninth were professionals, 4 percent in domestic and personal service and the others were engaged in transportation and communication, public service and in clerical work. (Jeter, H. R., *Leisure Time Needs and Resources of the Jewish Community of Cincinnati,* 1941, typewritten, p. 7).

According to L. Bloom, 7 or 8 percent of the dentists and lawyers in the so-called community of Buna, a city in the Midwest, were Jews, although the 5,000 Jews there in 1939 constituted only 2 percent of the total population. He says that a "disproportionate number of the (Jewish) population (there) is still to be found in the mercantile occupations . . . The bulk of the poorer Jewish population is to be found working as small, independent merchants. There are many hucksters and peddlers and for these subsistence is a precarious matter which may hinge on a minor fluctuation in the price of junk . . . Numerous clerks and stenographers in Buna are Jews, and there are a considerable number in drugstores, dry-cleaning establishments and laundries . . . Jewish manual workers are to be found in fair number, largely in the building trades." (Bloom, Leonard, "The Jews of Buna", in *Jews in a Gentile World,* pp. 192-194.)

The percentage distribution of the gainfully-employed Jews living in Springfield, Mass., in 1941, was: 71 in trade, 14 in industry, 7 in the professions, 7 were doing clerical work, one percent was engaged in other work. (Springfield Study Committee, *Community Study of Springfield, Mass.,* 1943, typewritten, p. 4).

The so-called Yankee City, a town near Boston, Mass., had in the 1930's about 400 Jews, who constituted 2.4 percent of the total local population and 2.45 percent of the gainfully employed. A relatively large number of the Jews were proprietors of retail stores. (Warner, W. Lloyd and Lunt, Paul S., *The Social Life of a Modern Community,* 1941, pp. 257-259.)

41 The correlation coefficient between the percentage of Jews and of the general population in trade in ten cities is —0.5176 ±0.156; in the case of those in the professions and in manufacturing, the correlation coefficient is —0.08 and ±0.044, respectively. The results of this analysis are based on a small number of communities. Further studies along this line are necessary.

42 The percentage distribution of clients known to Jewish family agencies in 1932 and of those studied by the Federal Employment Relief Agency, FERA, among whom there were also Jews was:

OCCUPATIONAL PATTERNS OF AMERICAN JEWS

Occupation	Baltimore Jewish	Baltimore FERA	Boston Jewish	Boston FERA	Cleveland Jewish	Cleveland FERA	Detroit Jewish	Detroit FERA	New York Jewish	New York FERA	St. Louis Jewish	St. Louis FERA
Total	100.0	100.0	100.0	100.0	100.0	100.0	99.9	100.0	100.0	100.0	100.0	100.0
Professional	1.6	1.7	2.4	2.1	1.2	1.9	2.5	1.9	1.8	4.9	0.5	1.3
Clerical	12.7	8.8	13.4	9.8	10.1	8.3	11.9	8.0	10.8	11.4	14.9	7.5
Owners (including Hucksters)	7.7	3.5	8.0	2.0	18.9	5.5	21.0	4.0	11.8	4.6	14.9	4.6
Manual Workers	55.5	73.2	54.9	69.2	42.3	66.3	43.2	72.2	54.8	64.0	41.6	66.7
Trade	18.9	7.9	18.0	7.4	21.0	8.0	14.5	6.1	11.1	6.7	22.5	7.7
Domestic	3.0	2.8	1.6	4.3	3.6	3.6	4.3	2.8	7.7	4.9	2.9	10.3
Servants	0.6	2.1	1.7	5.2	2.9	6.4	2.5	5.0	2.0	3.5	2.7	1.9

(*Notes and News*, June 1, 1935, p. 7).

The differences in the occupational distribution of Jewish and other applicants for relief reflect to a certain extent the prevailing differences between the economic structure of the Jews and others. There were also significant differences among the Jewish clients themselves as well as among those studied by the FERA.

43 A.Z.A. group, except Denver, Colo.

44 A.Z.A. group of cities, except Braddock, Denver, Donora, East Liverpool, Grand Forks, Middletown, Pottsville. The occupations of those living in these 41 cities were reported by the U. S. Bureau of the Census, *Population*, 1930, vol. IV.

45 The cities are: A.Z.A. group, 47 cities, 1934; Norwich and New London, 1938.

46 *Jewish Occupational Bulletin* IV, 1944 No. 3 p. 11.

47 Committee on Economic Adjustment, Information Service in Cooperation with the Conference on Jewish Relations, *Industrial Classification of Jewish Gainful Workers in New York City*, (1937) pp. 10-11.

48 A.Z.A. group, 48 cities, 1934; New London, Norwich, New Orleans and Pittsburgh, 1938, op. cit., Buffalo and San Francisco, 1938, in *JPS.*, pp. 41-43, 170-175, New York City, 1937, op. cit.

49 The cities are: Buffalo, Engelman, U. Z., "*The Jewish Population of Buffalo, 1938*", in *JPS.*, p. 41; Pittsburgh, Taylor, Maurice, *Ibid*, 103; Detroit, Meyer, H. J., *Ibid*, 124; San Francisco, Moment, S., "Study of San Francisco Jewry, 1938", op. cit. 175; New Orleans, Feibelman, op. cit.; Baltimore, Jewish Occupational Council, *Some Characteristics of 408 Baltimore Jews*; Los Angeles, Kohs. S. C., *Survey of Recreational and Cultural Needs of the Jewish Community of Los Angeles*, 1941, typewritten, Section 19, p. 30. "The Jewish Community of Los Angeles" *The Jewish Review II*, 124 ff.

50 Eisenberg, E. O. "93,000 Bankers; 0.6% Are Jews!", *The National Jewish Monthly*, February, 1939, pp. 190-191.

51 Editors of Fortune, *Jews In America*, (1936), Chapters 6-10.

52 Committee on Economic Adjustment Information Service in Cooperation with the Conference on Jewish Relations, *Industrial Classification of Jewish Gainful Workers in New York City*, 1937, pp. 10-11.

53 Graeber, I. and Britt, S. H. *Jews in a Gentile World*, pp. 207, 210-211.

54 Graeber, I. "The Economic Role of the Jews in the United States", *Zukunft*, June, 1945, p. 361 (in Yiddish).

OCCUPATIONAL PATTERNS OF AMERICAN JEWS *

By Nathan Goldberg

Occupational Trends Among American-Born Jews

The changes in the occupational pattern of the American Jews are generally due to one or more of the following causes. The pattern varies with the general technological progress and market conditions; new inventions and an increased or decreased demand for certain commodities invariably leads to changes in the occupational distribution of the general population as well as of the Jews. The desire for a higher standard of living and for more or greater economic security and social prestige is another factor. Add to this the proverbial devotion of Jewish parents to their children; some of them seek better economic opportunities in the hope that their new position or business will eventually enable them to give their children a better start in life. Discrimination in employment leads to changes in the occupational pattern. Finally, the changes are at present also due to an increase in the number of native-born among the gainfully-occupied Jews, for the reason that the vocational preferences, economic interests and social values of American-born Jews are not quite the same as those of their immigrant parents.

According to the above mentioned A.Z.A. studies, there was a relatively smaller number of Jews in manufacturing and commerce and a larger one in public service, professions and in domestic and personal service in 1934 than in 1924. These changes were to a certain extent due to the presence of a relatively larger number of American-born among the gainfully-employed Jews in 1934 than in 1924. Let us recall, in this connection, that the occupational pattern of the immi-

---

* *Concluded.* See *The Jewish Review* III (1945), 161-186.

grants from Russia in 1900, most of whom, as shown above, were Jews, was not the same as that of their American-born children. The males of the latter group had, for instance, 6 times as many lawyers and 7 times as many bookkeepers and accountants and only one-third as many in the garment and headwear industries as the former. Similarly, approximately 46 of every 100 gainfully-employed women from Russia were in the several branches of the apparel and headwear industries and only 25 percent of the native-born whose parents were from Russia. The latter had, however, 3 times as many clerks and copyists, 2.2 times as many saleswomen and 5 times as many stenographers and typists as the former.[55] The occupational preferences of the American-born children were in many instances not the same as those of their foreign-born parents. Many of the latter sent their children, often at a great sacrifice, to college and helped them become professional men or women, office workers or merchants. In brief, the vertical social mobility of the second-generation American Jews was even then, in 1900, a fact.

Recent studies also show that a relatively larger number of our young generation than of those of other ethnic groups and of Jewish immigrants are doing clerical and professional work. According to the New York youth study, which was made in 1935, almost two-thirds, 65 percent, of the Jewish boys and girls 16-24 years of age were doing clerical and kindred work and only 43.3 percent of the non-Jewish youth, which comprised some Negro boys and girls. The difference is statistically significant. The Jewish youth group had 4 times as many bookkeepers, accountants and cashiers and about twice as many stenographers and typists as the other groups of the same age; the ratio of salesmen and saleswomen among Jews and others was 17:10. Moreover, we had only about two-thirds as many semi-skilled workers, almost one-fifth as many unskilled workers and only one-tenth as many service workers as the other youth groups. Finally, 3.8 percent of our youth and 3.2 percent of the non-Jewish youth were rendering professional service.[56] The difference in this particular case is not, however, statistically significant.

The Baltimore study shows that there were differences between the occupational distribution of Jewish parents and their American-born children. This study embraced 408 Jewish boys and girls 16-24 years of age, 96 percent of whom were born in the United States. Of their fathers, about 85 percent were immigrants. Only 4.7 percent of the fathers and 13.4 percent of the children were rendering professional or technical services in 1936. More significant is the fact that almost one-half, 49.2 percent, of the children preferred to do professional or technical work. About one-sixth of the fathers and 53 percent of their children were office workers or salesmen. (It is interesting to note that only 25.6 percent of the children were actually interested in such work.) Only 2.4 percent of the children and almost one-third of the parents were skilled workers. There were, however, more semi-skilled and unskilled workers among the children than among the adults. This is quite natural because some youngsters have to start from the very bottom. Finally, there were less professionals, office workers, semi-skilled, unskilled and service workers, but significantly more proprietors, among the Jewish than among the other adults.[57] The lower percentage of professionals and office workers among the Jews was probably due to the fact that most of them were immigrants.

Of 282 young Jewish men and women in Cincinnati in 1941, most of whom were born in the United States, 54 percent were office workers or salespeople, approximately 21 percent were professionals, and 11.7 percent were proprietors, managers or officials; the others were skilled, semi-skilled and unskilled workers. A relatively larger number of women than of men were professionals, clerical and skilled workers.[58] The occupational pattern of the Cincinnati group differed significantly from those in New York and in Baltimore; the two latter had fewer professionals than those in Cincinnati. The difference was probably due to differences in age; the Cincinnati group comprised the 13-34 years age group.

A recent analysis of the occupations of parents of 921 Jewish college students showed that the American-born parents did not have the same occupational distribution as those who had come from Europe. 41 percent of the American-born parents and only 26 percent of the immigrant group were professionals or were holding managerial positions; the difference is statistically significant. Moreover, the foreign-born group had about three times as many skilled and nine times as many semi-skilled workers as the native group. The percentage of office workers and salespeople was about the same in both cases.[59] The fact that 27 percent of this group of foreign-born parents were skilled, semi-skilled and service workers is very significant. It shows that Jewish parents are trying to give their children a college education. The 27 percent of foreign-born parents under consideration were sending their sons to a private college and were probably intending to send them to a professional school, although they themselves were poor workers.

TABLE 7

PERCENTAGE DISTRIBUTION OF GAINFULLY-EMPLOYED JEWS ACCORDING TO THEIR NATIVITY

Occupations	Total Native	Total Foreign	Male Native	Male Foreign	Female Native	Female Foreign
Total	100.0	100.0	100.0	100.0	100.0	100.0
Manufacturing	10.5	18.0	11.9	19.9	9.6	8.0
Trade	53.0	62.2	54.1	57.9	33.2	63.7
Professions	19.1	6.6	18.0	8.5	20.6	7.5
Clerical	5.4	1.5	6.4	1.7	22.5	6.6
Public Service	1.3	0.5	1.1	0.6	0.8	0.4
Domestic and Personal	4.3	7.2	3.2	7.1	3.9	10.6
Transport. and Communication	2.8	2.5	1.8	2.1	0.6	0.9
Others and Unknown	3.6	1.5	3.5	2.2	8.8	2.3

Table 7 shows the occupational distribution of 2,272 foreign-born and of 2,313 native-born Jews in New London and Stamford, Conn., and in Staten Island, New York City.[60] There were almost twice as many of the first as of the second generation American Jews in industry and approximately three times as many of the native as of the foreign-born Jews in the professions. The difference is in each case statistically significant. Equally important is the fact that some of the native-born Jews do not work in the same industries as the immigrant group. 3.6 times as many of the Americans as of the foreign-born were doing clerical work. A relatively smaller number of the native than of the immigrant group was in trade. The percentage of proprietors of groceries, clothing, cigar and stationery stores was greater among foreign-born than among American-born Jews. There were 2.6 times as many of the native as of the other group in public service. The American-born Jew has better opportunities to obtain a civil service appointment than the immigrant.

COLLEGE STUDENTS AND PROFESSIONALS

The percentage distribution of students preparing themselves for the several professional services can to a certain extent be used for measuring and forecasting trends in certain occupations. The correlation coefficient between the percentage distribution of persons in certain professions in 1930 and of students preparing themselves for the same pursuits in 1934 is +0.955; the correlation coefficient between the percentage distribution of students in professional schools in 1918 and of those rendering certain professional services in 1920 is +0.73. Assuming that this holds true also to a certain extent in the case of Jews, we use the enrollment of Jews in professional schools for an analysis of the trends in professions among them.

There is a relatively larger number of Jews in American colleges and universities than of other ethnic groups. Foreign-born Jews constituted approximately 36 percent of a group of 3,366 foreign-born students in American colleges and universities in 1908/09.* Moreover, 95.2 per cent of the foreign-born students at the College of the City of New York, 35.4 per cent of such students at Columbia University and 29.5 per cent of the students of the same nativity at Harvard were at that time Jewish immigrants. Native-born Jews of foreign parentage constituted 15.5 percent of 8,304 college and university students of the same parentage. American-born Jews of foreign-born parents constituted approximately four-fifths of students of such nativity at the College of the City of New York, 22.6 percent of students of the same parentage at Columbia University and one-fifth of those at Harvard.[61] In brief, these

---

* It should be pointed out, however, that we are dealing here with a sample; the actual proportion of Jews to non-Jews in colleges and professional schools was considerably smaller because many colleges not included in this study had no Jewish students, but it was greater than the proportion of Jews to non-Jews in the general population at that time.

two groups of Jews constituted 21.4 percent of first and second generation Americans enrolled in various colleges and universities in 1908/09.

It is estimated that 2.8 percent of the total number of college and university students in 1915/16 were Jews and that the Jews constituted only 2.5 percent of the total population. According to this study, 15.7 percent of the Columbia University and 15.3 percent of the Johns Hopkins students were Jews. They constituted 7.7 percent of those studying at Harvard, 20.9 percent of the New York University students, 27.5 of those who were studying at the Brooklyn Polytechnic Institute and 28.7 percent of the Hunter (N.Y.C.) students. According to the investigator, the results of this study "cannot be exact". They are an estimate based on "names as might fairly be assumed to be Jewish".[62] It is, therefore, possible that the percentage of Jews in colleges and universities was even higher.

According to another study, 9.7 percent of those enrolled in 1918/19 in 106 colleges and universities in or near large Jewish population centers were Jews. This study, like the previous one, was based on a sample of 106 schools, and on the selection of names "judged Jewish".[63] Inasmuch as these schools were located in or near large Jewish population centers, it is very likely that the percentage of Jews among all college and university students was actually somewhat less than 9.7.

Finally, a study which was based on reports from schools and on estimates for schools not having any data relative to the religious affiliation of their students shows that 9.3 percent of the college and university students in 1934/35 were Jews.[64] At the time of the investigation the Jews constituted about 3.5 percent of the general population. In other words, the relative number of Jewish students was about two and one-half times as high as their share in the general population.

Although we are dealing with estimates and do not therefore know the *exact* number of Jewish college and university students, we may, nevertheless, assume that we have a relatively larger number of such students than the other ethnic groups. It is reported, for instance, that 14 percent of a group of Pittsburgh Jews under 30 years of age who were not attending school in 1938 were college graduates. More than one-fourth, 26.3 percent, of the New Orleans Jews had a college education. More than one-third, 34.7 percent, of a group of American-born Jews living in Dallas, Tex., in 1939 had a college education. One-third of a group of foreign-born Jews were sending their children to college.[65]

There are several reasons for the relatively large number of college graduates among Jews. Most of us live in the largest cities where many of the American colleges and universities are located. The higher I.Q. of Jewish children is another factor. The Jew's traditional respect for education has also to be taken into consideration; and finally, the Jews have a large number of college students because many of them intend to enter a professional school.

TABLE 8

PERCENTAGE DISTRIBUTION OF STUDENTS IN PROFESSIONAL SCHOOLS [66]

School	Jews 1908	Jews 1918	Jews 1934	Non-Jews 1908	Non-Jews 1918	Non-Jews 1934
Total	99.9	100.1	99.9	100.1	100.0	100.0
Pharmacy	15.4	6.1	4.6	7.6	2.0	1.4
Dentistry	3.3	12.0	5.9	5.4	4.7	1.6
Medicine	21.2	18.4	12.8	22.9	11.2	6.6
Law	32.4	14.7	22.6	17.6	6.4	6.6
Commerce & Finance	----	23.2	22.2	----	11.8	10.9
Education	----	5.0	16.3	----	13.5	50.5
Engineering	26.6	16.3	9.2	46.6	30.9	12.9
Agriculture & Forestry	----	1.6	0.8	----	8.1	3.0
Others	----	2.8	5.5	----	11.4	6.5

The trend in professions, as shown in Table 8, has changed. The percentage of Jews studying pharmaceutics dropped from approximately 15 in 1908/09 to 4.6 in 1934/35. The American-born Jew is less interested in pharmacy than the one born abroad. There were, as a matter of fact, 3.6 times as many immigrant as American-born Jews in pharmacy schools in 1908/09. Inasmuch as most of our 1934/35 students were native born, we conclude that this was one of the reasons for the relatively smaller number of Jews now studying pharmaceutics, although a similiar trend is to be observed among non-Jews too.

A drop in the relative number of medical students is observable in both the Jewish and the general groups. In the case of the Jews, however, this was due to the fact that it is becoming increasingly hard for a Jew to enter a medical school.

The Rev. Dr. Alphonse M. Schwitalla of the St. Louis University said in 1929 that the "selection of freshmen in our schools of medicine is based on other factors than scholarship alone." Dr. Richard B. Dillehunt, dean of the University of Oregon Medical School, said: "I have been told that some medical schools have a policy of limiting the percentage of Jewish applicants, but I am not sure that it is true." According to Dr. William A. Pearson, dean of the Hahneman Medical College, Philadelphia, "it is unfair to admit a disproportionate number of Jewish students." Dr. Paul S. McKibben, dean of the University of Southern California Medical School, expressed himself that "it is undesirable that too large a proportion of the prospective physicians should be Jews." The opinion of Dr. H. E. French, dean of the University of North Dakota School of Medicine, is that "there are too many Jewish students seeking admission to medical schools." According to Dr. John Wyckoff, dean of the Bellevue Hospital Medical College, New York City, most of the medical schools "try to have a relationship between the racial group population in the school and the population content of the country." His school, he said, admitted students on the basis of "scholarship, personality and character." [67]

This *numerus clausus* unquestionably accounts for the drop in the number of Jews studying medicine. It is estimated that there were in 1938 almost one-third, 31 percent, less Jewish medical students than in 1933. [68]

According to Frank Kingdon, who recently made a study of discrimination in American medical schools, "the evidence of anti-Jewish discrimination is overwhelming. Although the annual applications for entrance by Jewish Americans has not declined, the number of Jewish students in medical schools has been reduced by roughly 50 percent in the last twenty years. 'The drop' has become precipitate in recent years. The class of 1937 included 794 Jewish students, the class of

1940 only 477—a 40 percent drop in three years." This decline was not in any way due to a decrease in the number of Jewish applicants. The survey shows that three out of every four non-Jewish applicants are given a chance to study medicine, while only one out of every thirteen Jewish applicants is admitted. "These ratios," says Kingdon "do not have the slightest relation to mental equipment, natural aptitudes and other rational, scientific standards of selection." [69] Jewish applicants are not admitted for the reason that they are Jews.

Moreover, it is often hard for Jewish physicians to find a place for interneship, post-graduate studies or for research. In view of this, a subcommittee of the Conference on Jewish Relations advised Jewish hospitals to provide facilities for specialized training. [70] It is stated in the report of this committee that "unless these institutions will take the necessary steps to meet both the technical requirements and the ethical standards which have been evolved, the time is not far off when Jewish physicians will find it extremely difficult to enter certain specialties and at best will find their opportunities very seriously restricted in others."

The Jews have a relatively larger number of those studying dentistry than the other ethnic groups. It is probable that some Jews turn to dentistry because they know that medical schools are restricting the number of Jewish students.

The ratio of Jews to others who were preparing themselves for the legal profession in 1934/35 was 3.4:1. Not all Jews who take such courses practise law. And, on the other hand, the large percentage of Jews in the legal profession does not mean that Jewish lawyers wield any great influence. The large industrial corporations as well as the railroad, insurance, banking and other companies are usually clients of non-Jewish law firms. This situation probably accounts for the fact that the income of Jewish lawyers, according to a study made in New York City, is less than that of their non-Jewish colleagues. [71]

There is a relatively larger number of Jews (and non-Jews) in the teaching profession now than at the beginning of the present century. Jews are turning to teaching because they anticipate less discrimination in this than in some other professions. Some colleges do, however, prefer to have non-Jews on their teaching staffs. Most of the Jewish teachers in the elementary and high schools are women.

The percentage of Jews and non-Jews in the engineering schools has declined. In the case of the Jews, the fact that the large industrial corporations prefer to employ non-Jewish engineers probably contributed to this trend.

As stated above, the enrollment in professional schools varies with the demand for professional services. In the case of Jews, however, we have also to consider the factor of discrimination. Hence we find that the correlation coefficient between the percentage distribution of Jews in professional schools in 1918/19 and 1934/35 is only $+0.6834 \pm 0.1198$ and in the case of the other students $+0.996 \pm 0.0018$. The difference is statistically significant. This was the time when certain professional schools very definitely limited the number of Jewish students. This, in turn, led to changes in the enrollment of Jews in professional schools. It should be pointed out, however, that the correlation coefficient between the distribution of these two groups in the professional schools in 1934/35 is $+0.7128 \pm 0.1106$. The Jews, in other words, are generally preparing themselves for professions for which the others are also preparing themselves.

The percentage distribution of Jewish professionals in Trenton and Passaic in 1937 and in New London, Buffalo and San Francisco in 1938 was:

Dentists	6.3	Teachers	16.5
Physicians	12.9	Pharmacists & Chemists	7.6
Lawyers	18.1	Others	38.7

Their distribution varied from locality to locality. The dentists constituted 10.6 percent of the Jewish professionals in Trenton, but only 6.2 percent of those in Passaic; the former had 2.5 times as many physicians as the latter. Approximately one-fifth, 20.7 percent, of the Jewish professionals in Buffalo and only one-seventh, 14.2 percent, of those in San Francisco were teachers.

The percentage distribution of Jewish professionals in Worcester, Mass., in 1942, was: physicians 16.4, lawyers

17.5, dentists 7.4, accountants 10.6, teachers (excluding those who teach in Jewish schools) 12.7, others 35.4. There was a relatively larger number of physicians, dentists, lawyers and accountants among the native than among the immigrant Jews. The seven rabbis were immigrants but the 24 teachers were born in the U. S. Three-fourths of these teachers were women.[72]

A study made of Jewish professionals in Ohio[73] in 1938 shows that we have a relatively larger number of medical men, lawyers and pharmacists in the smaller than in the larger communities. Jews living in cities with 100,000-500,000 inhabitants had one Jewish physician for every 224 Jews there and those in cities with 10,000-100,000 inhabitants had one for every 168 Jews; the large communities had one Jewish dentist for every 555 Jewish inhabitants and one Jewish lawyer for every 148 Jews, while the other cities had a ratio of 1:215 and 1:117, respectively. Similar differences were reported for teachers, engineers and pharmacists.

The Jews had a relatively larger number of physicians, dentists, lawyers and pharmacists but a smaller percentage of teachers and engineers than the other ethnic groups. The Jews constituted about 7.7 percent of those in Greater Cleveland and almost 21 percent of the physicians there were Jews. There were approximately four times as many Jews among the dentists in Ohio as among the general population. One-eleventh of the lawyers and only 3.3 percent of the total population in cities with 100,000-500,000 inhabitants were Jews. The Jews in Greater Cleveland constituted, however, only 4.7 percent of the teachers and 2.6 percent of the engineers there, although it is estimated that 7.7 percent of the general population were Jews.

It thus appears that there is a greater concentration of Jews in the "self-employed" professions—medicine, dentistry, law, pharmacy—than in the "employee" professions—engineering, teaching, etc. Their preference for the former type of professions is to a certain extent due to the unwillingness of some individuals and firms to employ Jewish professionals.

SUMMARY AND OUTLOOK

The occupational distribution of the present generation American Jews is not quite the same as of the Jewish immigrants in the United States at the beginning of the present century. The change has been in the direction from factory to store and office.

Excluding manufacturers and officials of industrial plants, 57.5 percent of the gainfully-employed Jews from Russia living in the 15 largest American cities in 1900 were factory or shop employees. Next in importance was trade; approximately one-fifth of them were engaged in such occupations. Almost 7 percent of this group were clerical workers and approximately one of every forty was a professional. Approximately three-fifths of those in manufatcuring or 35 percent of the gainfully-employed were in the various branches of the clothing industry.

The relative number of Jews in manufacturing was less and in trade and in the several professions more in the 1930's than in 1900. Approximately one-eighth of 77,671 gainfully-employed Jews in the 1930's living in 61 communities located in various parts of the country were in manufacturing, 47.3 percent were in commerce, 15.7 percent were clerical workers and almost 12 percent were professionals. Surveys of Jews in New York City, Detroit, New Orleans, Worcester and Stamford show, however, that approximately 35 percent of the Jewish labor force are in manufacturing, one-third is engeged in trade and that about one-ninth are professionals. Generally speaking, the large cities have a larger percentage of Jews in manufacturing and mechanical industries.

No less significant is the fact that the proportion of Jewish factory workers to manufacturers has decreased. 96.5

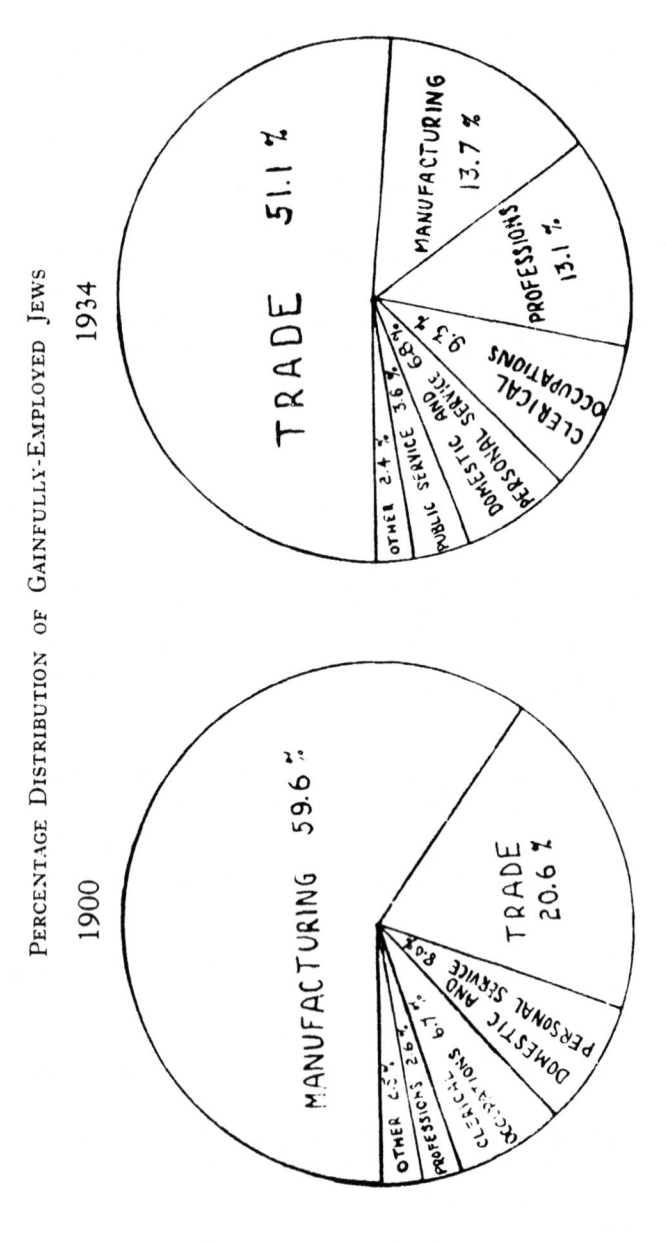

OCCUPATIONAL PATTERNS OF AMERICAN JEWS

Percentage Distribution of Gainfully-Employed Jews

1934

- TRADE 51.1%
- MANUFACTURING 13.7%
- PROFESSIONS 13.1%
- CLERICAL OCCUPATIONS 9.3%
- DOMESTIC AND PERSONAL SERVICE 6.8%
- PUBLIC SERVICE 3.6%
- OTHER 2.4%

1900

- MANUFACTURING 59.6%
- TRADE 20.6%
- DOMESTIC AND PERSONAL SERVICE 8.0%
- CLERICAL OCCUPATIONS 2.6%
- PROFESSIONS 6.1%
- OTHER 2.5%

percent of the Jews from Russia in manufacturing were in 1900 employees and approximately only 63 percent in the 1930's.

The changes in our occupational pattern have to a certain extent coincided with those of the general population. The occupational preferences of the young American are not quite the same as those of his grandfather or even of his father. Recent trends in occupations are correlated with technological changes, cityward movement, growth of large-scale and highly integrated commercial and industrial enterprises and similar factors.

Changes in the occupational distribution of the Jews have also coincided with the acculturation and successful adjustment of some of our erstwhile immigrants. Many of these newcomers were young, ambitious and energetic persons. They learned to read and write English; they studied American life and American methods of production; they also tried to save money. Some of them went to college and prepared themselves for professional services and some of them eventually succeeded.

The gradual increase in the proportion of native to foreign-born Jews is another factor. The occupational preferences and training of the former are not quite the same as of immigrants. There is generally a larger percentage of professionals and clerical workers and a smaller one of factory employees among American than among foreign-born Jews. There is also a greater concentration of foreign-born than of native Jews in commerce. The American-born Jews probably prefer to be salesmen or buyers rather than proprietors of small retail stores.

The occupational pattern of the Jews is not the same as of the other ethnic groups. We have a relatively larger number of professionals, clerical workers and those engaged in trade, and a smaller one in manufacturing than the general population. While this is true, it does not necessarily imply that the Jews play an important role in the economy of the country. Jews are generally engaged in the production and

OCCUPATIONAL PATTERNS OF AMERICAN JEWS 277

distribution of consumers' goods, such as clothing, food, and household wares. There are very few Jews in the metal, coal, automotive, wood, glass, rubber and chemical industries. Jews are also found less frequently than non-Jews, in proportion to their numbers, in banking, transportation and in communication. They may be numerous among those who are engaged in retail trade and among those who practise law, medicine and dentistry, but they wield no influence or power commensurate with their numbers.

In the light of what has been said, we may expect the number of proprietors of retail stores among Jews to decline. Generally speaking, American-born Jews do not want to be grocers or proprietors of candy, cigar or other retail stores.

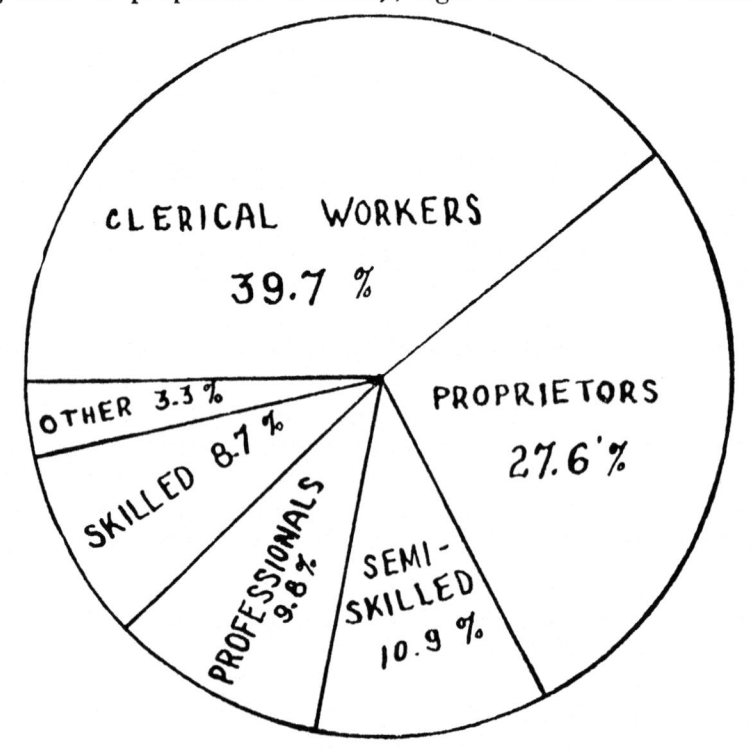

CLERICAL WORKERS 39.7 %
OTHER 3.3 %
SKILLED 8.7 %
PROFESSIONALS 9.8 %
SEMI-SKILLED 10.9 %
PROPRIETORS 27.6 %

SOCIO-ECONOMIC STATUS OF JEWS

If the chain stores continue to expand, then we may expect a further decline in the number of Jews in retail business.

The Jews may further be affected adversely by the relocation of some of our industries. It is quite possible that many of the war plants erected in the South and in other parts of the country, where the number of Jews is rather small, will eventually be converted into factories for the production of consumers' or producers' goods. Cities like New York and Philadelphia, where approximately 50 percent of the American Jews live, may lose some of their domestic or foreign markets. The Jews there will then be affected either directly or indirectly by the emergence of new industrial centers. They will be affected directly if the new plants produce the same or similar goods as they are producing. Even if they do not have to face any direct competition, they may, nevertheless, be affected adversely by the possible movement of some of the population from the Atlantic coast to the new industrial centers.

The economic position of the Jews may also be influenced by the emergence of new industries. The introduction of new products may eventually lead to the disappearance of some industries in which Jews are concentrated. On the other hand, new industries may offer new opportunities for the investment of capital as well as for employment of Jews.

Another factor to be considered is the possible effect the war will have on the economic structure of the American Jews. Some of them worked in defense plants and thus succeeded in acquiring new skills; Jews also moved to the new industrial and commercial centers. Some of the Jews in the armed services learned new technical skills.

Equally important is the fact that many of the Jewish boys in the armed forces could not begin or successfully complete their professional studies. Will they return to the colleges and universities after having spent several years, in some cases, four or five years, in the armed services? The economic reorientation of some of these veterans may have a certain effect upon the occupational pattern of the Jews in the years immediately following the war.

The number of Jews in the several professions and in other occupations will also depend, to a certain extent, upon the attitude of non-Jews toward them. Some of them became government employees in the 1930's because, among other things, of discriminatory practises on the part of certain employers. If discrimination diminishes or becomes non-existent some Jews will turn to other occupations. Given equal opportunities, American Jews will undoubtedly adjust themselves to the post-war economy and to other changes.

EVALUATION OF THE STUDIES

The foregoing analysis is based on a number if different surveys and estimates which give an approximate picture of the existing situation. We do not at present know the exact occupational distribution of the American Jews, for the United States Census Bureau classifies the gainfully-employed only according to race: White, Negro, etc. Privately sponsored studies are at present our only source of information. Some of them are mere estimates; others are studies of samples of the Jewish population within a given locality, while still others are surveys or censuses of Jewish communities. The value of these studies varies with the care and thoroughness with which they were made.

The worth of some of these studies is questionable. The study made of the occupational distribution of the Jews living in New York City in 1937, for instance, was based on statements made by leaders of labor unions and heads of trade associations about the general and Jewish membership of their respective organizations as well as on directories listing names of proprietors.[5f] We are told that the "information in this report is based on estimates". How good were these estimates?

They were, with one exception, far from accurate. According to this report, 670,843 of the gainfully-employed New Yorkers in December, 1937, were engaged in manufacturing; according to the Census Bureau,[74] however, 746,466 of those employed in April, 1940, were engaged in such occupations and 107,788 of those seeking employment wanted to do such work. According to the 1937 study, only 19.9 percent of the labor force in New York was in manufacturing and mechanical industries; the Census Bureau reported, however, that 26.3 percent of the employed were in such industries and 25.9 percent of the employed and of those seeking employment. The 1937 estimate was that 330,728 New Yorkers,

9.8 percent, were in construction and the Census Bureau reported only 191,569, including the unemployed, 5.8 percent, in such occupations. There were, according to the New York survey, only 573,780 persons, 16.9 percent of the labor force, in retail and wholesale trade; the Census Bureau, however, found in trade 621,575 persons or 21.9 percent of the employed. The 1937 report probably overestimated the number of persons in transportation and in other public utilities and in domestic and personal service while underestimating the number of persons in public service, banking, insurance and in real estate business. It is doubtful whether these differences were due to differences in the classification of the gainfully-employed; it is also doubtful whether such increases and decreases actually occurred in the years 1938-1939.

This raises the question of the reliability of the estimated number of Jews in each of the several major occupational groups. If, as we have reason to assume, the 1937 study underestimated the number of persons in manufacturing, commerce and in the several professions, did it not also either underestimate or overestimate the number of Jews engaged in these occupations? Secondly, it is quite possible that the Jews did not constitute approximately 41 percent of those in trade, 31 percent of the professionals or 12 percent of those in banking and in insurance, because the number of non-Jews in these occupations was probably greater than estimated. In brief, the 1937 study gives us only the approximate, certainly not the exact, occupational distribution of the gainfully-employed Jews living in New York City.

The 1937 estimate is also at variance with the one made in 1929.[75] According to the 1937 survey, the Jews constituted 53.8 percent of the workers in the needle industry whereas according to the 1929 estimate they constituted 58.85 percent of those in the needle trade unions. The difference is statistically significant.* The 1937 study reported that only one-

---

* The difference may, however, be a result of changes which occurred in the years 1929-1937 (decline in the number of Jewish needle workers etc.).

fourth of the printers were Jews, but according to the 1929 survey they constituted 37.2 percent. The 1937 estimate was that the Jews constituted only 38.2% of the leather workers and the 1929 estimate was that two-thirds of those in the union of leather workers were Jews. These two estimates are not, to be sure, strictly comparable, for the reason that the one made in 1929 was based on union membership and the other on the total number of employers and employees in these industries. It is, however, doubtful whether this really accounts for the differences. As stated before, the 1937 study was also based on union membership; secretaries of labor unions were asked to state the number of persons belonging to their respective unions as well as the number of Jews among them and among the unorganized workers. Secondly, practically all the clothing factories and printing shops in New York City employ only union members. It thus appears that at least one of these two estimates has to be revised.

Again, the results of the 1937 study are at variance with those of Esther Kinzler's study ** of the occupational distribution of 16,736 gainfully-employed Jews living in Manhattan and Bronx (N.Y.C.) in 1933. The percentage of Jews in manufacturing and construction, excluding the unemployed, was 35.3 according to the 1937 survey and only 30.6 according to her study; Kinzler reported that only 7.4 percent

---

** These two studies are not strictly comparable. Kinzler's study was based on a small sample, 16,736 persons, which constituted approximately two percent of the gainfully-employed Jews. Moreover, her group lived in only two of the five boroughs. She analyzed the occupations of only the Friedmans, Ginsbergs, Goldbergs, Goldsteins and Levys listed in the *New York City Directory* for 1932-1933. Furthermore, there were differences in the classification of the gainfully-employed; the group "clerical workers" does not appear in the 1937 study.

Incidentally, there are statistically significant differences between the occupational distribution of each of Kinzler's five groups of names used. Only 8.4 percent of the Friedmans, but 12.1 percent of the Ginsbergs were professionals. Almost one-fourth, 23.9 percent, of the Levys and only 13.4 percent of the Goldsteins were brokers or salesmen. Finally, 2.1 percent of the Friedmans and 4.8 percent of the Goldbergs were rendering domestic or personal services. In view of this, we cannot be certain that Kinzler had a really representative sample.

were professionals whereas the 1937 estimate was 11.4 percent. The percentage of Jews in domestic and personal service was 5.3 according to Kinzler and 12.6 according to the 1937 survey. According to Kinzler's study, only 30.5 percent of the gainfully-employed Jews were in commerce; the 1937 estimate was that 32.3 percent were engaged in such occupations; again, the difference is statistically significant. The 1937 study reported three times as many Jews in public service as Kinzler.[76]

Whether Kinzler's group was a representative sample of the Jews living in Manhattan and Bronx or not, the Jews living in Staten Island, New York City, had, as far as we know, an altogether different occupational pattern. It was reported that only 13 percent of 752 gainfully-employed Jews in Staten Island in 1936 were in manufacturing, 44.5 percent were engaged in trade and 14.1 percent were professionals.[77] Kinzler reported, however, 30.6, 30.5 and 7.4 percent, respectively.

Again, the results of the Staten Island study referred to above differ to a certain extent from those of another study made there in 1934-1936.[78] According to the 1936 study, 16.7 percent of the gainfully-employed males were in manufacturing and 13.4 percent were professionals; according to the 1934 survey, the percentages were 10.9 and 21.4, respectively. The differences are statistically significant. Both investigators reported approximately the same percentage of Jews in trade—49.8 and 49.5, respectively—and in clerical occupations—10.7 and 10.2, respectively.

The observed differences may to a certain extent be due to differences in the method of selecting the samples. Fleischman's (1936) group consisted of 200 persons who were members of certain organizations; he excluded, however, those organizations comprising older persons or Yiddish-speaking individuals. He also made a house-to-house canvass of every fifth of the remaining 1,000 Jewish families. Fleischman's group consisted of approximately 750 persons. Ryckoff's group consisted of 885 gainfully-employed persons who were members of Jewish organizations. He obtained most of his information on their occupations from the *City Directory*. It is quite possible that the observed differences can be attributed to differences in the age composition of these two groups.

Similarly, the differences observed between the 1936 and 1938 studies of the occupational distribution of the Jews living in New London, Conn., may probably be attributed to differences in the age composition of the two groups. Meyer's study was based on the city directory for 1936, in which only the occupations of those 20 years of age and older were stated; Wessel's group consisted of all the known gainfully-employed Jews 15 years of age and over in 1938. Meyer reported that 15.9 percent of the males were in manufacturing and Wessel found that 18.5 percent were engaged in such occupations. The percentages of those in trade were 59.2 and 58.6, respectively. 10.9 percent of Meyer's group and 11.2 percent of Wessel's were professionals. The percentages of those in domestic and personal service were 6.6 and 6.3, respectively. The observed differences are not statistically significant. Both investigators reported the same percentage of males in clerical occupations.[79]

These seven studies have been selected here to show some of the problems which students of the economic structure of the American Jews are facing. For reasons stated above, privately-sponsored investigations are practically our only source of information. Those who make such studies often have to resort to the method of sampling because it is in many cases difficult to make a survey of the occupational distribution of all the gainfully-employed Jews living in a certain locality, especially of those who live in large Jewish communities, such as New York, Chicago, Philadelphia or Los Angeles. Some persons are inclined, however, to collect data which are easily obtainable; some samples may be adequate but not representative or typical of the group under consideration. Hence it is necessary to examine and to evaluate the methods of selecting samples and of collecting the desired or necessary data.

It is also important to know how each investigator classifies the occupations of his group. Some follow the classification used by the U. S. Census Bureau, while others do not adhere to it. The following are a few illustrations of the lack of uniformity in the classification of occupations. Fleischman, following the Census Bureau classification, included accountants in the group "clerical occupations"; Ryckoff and Koenig included them in the group "professions"; according to Kinzler, they are semi-professionals. Journalists, according to her, are semi-professionals, whereas the Census Bureau includes them among professionals. Kinzler's group "unclassified" includes bank employees, engineers, dental laboratory workers and post office clerks. Are not engineers professionals? Are not bank employees clerks? Ryckoff's group "miscellaneous" includes bankers, musicians, models, notaries and newspaper publishers. The Census Bureau, however, includes musicians among professionals and bankers among those engaged in commerce and finance.[80]

The Stamford Jews, according to Koenig, had no stenographers, typists, bookeepers and cashiers. One looks in vain down his list of occupations for persons doing such work. Is it really possible that there were no stenographers, typists or bookkeepers among the Stamford Jews? Koenig's group "unclassified" consists of 7.2 percent of the gainfully-employed Jews living in Stamford. Is it possible that one-fourteenth of them were engaged in such occupations for which it was impossible to find an appropriate classification? He had previously reported that 22.5 percent of a group of gainfully-employed Jews were engaged in "miscellaneous" occupations.[81] The inclusion of such a relatively large number of persons in the group "unclassified" and "miscellaneous" shows that the investigator's classification was far from adequate.

Other investigators have failed to include certain specifically Jewish occupations. If we are to accept the results of Rabbi Israel's studies of the occupations of Jews,[24] then we have to conclude that the Los Angeles Jewish community, for instance, had no rabbi. Although the Vicksburg, Miss., survey was made by Sol L. Kory, at that time rabbi of the local congregation Anshe Chesed, he was, nevertheless, not included among the gainfully-employed Jews living there. Ten communities, according to Rabbi Israel's report, had no cantors. He reported, however, that Worcester, Mass., had six *Shochtim*. Like improper classifications, such omissions, though quantitatively not very significant, are open to criticism.

Uniformity in the classification of occupations is desirable since otherwise results of the studies are not always strictly comparable. Moreover, lack of uniformity in classification may at times lead to invidious comparisons. The inclusion, for instance, of accountants among Jewish and not among other professionals invariably increases the number of professionals among Jews; the inclusion of Jewish restaurateurs among Jewish merchants and not, as the Census Bureau does, among those who are in domestic and personal service, invariably increases the number of Jews in trade. Such reports may lead, especially in the case of uncritical readers, to incorrect conclusions.

Another point to be considered is who is or is not to be regarded as a member of the Jewish community.

"A Jew was defined", writes M. Taylor, "as one born of Jewish parents or of a mixed marriage. In addition, a gentile married to a Jew or related by marriage to a Jewish person living in the same household and identifying himself with the Jewish group was included in the count. No one, whether born a Jew or not, who was unwilling to be so identified was included. Children of mixed marriages not being brought up as Jews and not so considered by the parent or parents were likewise not counted."

Moment included in his survey of the San Francisco Jewish community only those who "acknowledged that they were Jews." [82] Others define a Jew as a person with a Jewish sounding name.

Is a member of the Episcopal Church a Jew? Consider the following case. *The New York Times* of March 28, 1944, reported that "more than 1,000 friends, relatives and business associates of Jules S. Bache, banker and art patron, who died in his winter home . . . at the age of 82, attended a funeral service yesterday afternoon at St. Thomas Episcopal

Church, Fifth Avenue and Fifty-Third Street", New York City. He appears, nevertheless, in the *Who's Who in American Jewry* and he is included among Jewish bankers.

A precise definition is important and necessary for the reason that intermarriage is on the increase. The San Francisco study referred to above disclosed that "of every 100 Jewish families in San Francisco in 1938, 7 had one or more non-Jewish members. While this does not include the undetermined number of families in which the head or his spouse was born a Jew but no longer considered himself or herself one, perhaps as many as one in ten Jewish families had one or more non-Jewish members in 1938" (p 176). Koenig reported that "in 1938 there were 59 Jewish-Gentile families" in Stamford. He added that "this number of intermarriages is probably an underestimate, particularly in the case of the women, concerning whom data were less easily obtainable." These 59 couples constituted 7.2 percent of the Jewish families there. [83] Are we, then, to include the children and grandchildren of these couples among Jews? Whether they are included or not, the point to be remembered is that uniformity in this matter is highly desirable.

In view of what has been said, the data at hand are merely approximations. We do not know *exactly* the occupational distribution of the American Jews, because the results of many of our surveys are only based upon samples of the Jewish population and because there is a lack of uniformity in the collection, analysis and classification of such data.

There are, however, some ways in which we may supplement our information on Jews and thus make them more reliable. Many, though not all, Jewish parents send their children to various types of Hebrew, Yiddish, religious and Sunday Schools. If the teachers or principals of these schools were to ask their students for data on the regular occupations of their parents, brothers and sisters, the industries in which they work and on their employer-employee status, then we would have very valuable information from an adequate and representative sample of the Jewish population.

The collection of such data annually will serve a very useful purpose. We shall be able, firstly, to ascertain the present occupational distribution of the Jews. Secondly, we shall eventually be able to study and analyze the changes in our economic structure as well as the economic history of certain individuals.

There is, moreover, another source of information concerning the economic activities of some American Jews. The Census Bureau collected data in 1910, 1920, 1930 and 1940, on the occupations of those whose mother tongue was Yiddish. It is quite possible that the Census Bureau will cooperate with those interested in the occupational distribution of the immigrant and native-born whose mother tongue is Yiddish and will facilitate the use of these data.

The centralization and proper utilization of such and similar data presupposes, however, the establishment of a central agency for the collection and analysis of such materials. Such a bureau will also be able to guide and aid individuals interested in such studies; it will be able to give them professional advice and aid, and will in due time introduce a uniformity in methods of collection and classification of occupations. Until such time, however, we must rely upon studies of the type analyzed and summarized here which, although far from exact, probably show general trends.

NOTES

[55] U. S. Immigration Commission, *Reports,* Vol. XXVIII, Table IVa-IVb.
[56] McGill, N. P. "Some Characteristics of Jewish Youth in New York City", *JSSQ.,* December 1937, p. 263.
[57] Jewish Occupational Council. *Some Characteristics of 408 Baltimore Jewish Youth,* 1940, mimeographed, pp. 13-14.
[58] Jeter, H. R. *Leisure Time Needs and Resources of the Jewish Community of Cincinnati,* 1941, mimeographed, pp. 13-14.
[59] Shuey, A. M. "The Intelligence of Jewish College Freshmen as Related to Parental Occupation", *Journal of Applied Psychology,* XXVI, (1942), 663.
[60] Meyer, Lena. *A Study of the Occupational Distribution and Early History of the Jewish Population of New London, Connecticut,* New York: Graduate School for Jewish Social Work, 1938, typewritten, pp. 64, 72; Koenig, S., *op. cit.;* Fleischman, *op. cit.*

The study of the Worcester Jews shows that 8.1 percent of the gainfully-employed native and only 3.6 percent of the immigrant Jews were rendering professional and kindred services; there were 3.4 times as many of the American-born as of the immigrant Jews in government service; 2.5 times as many of the native as of the other Jews were in amusement and recreation enterprises; 9.1 percent of the immigrant and only 3.7 percent of the other Jews were rendering personal service; the immigrants also had a relatively larger number of those in construction, the percentages being 6.5 and 1.5, respectively. Mopsick, S., op. cit.

[61] U. S. Immigration Commission, Report, Vol. XXIX, pp. 154-156.

[62] Feinberg, Charles, K., "A Census of Jewish University Students", The Menorah Journal, 1916, pp. 260-262; 1917, pp. 252-253.

[63] "Professional Tendencies Among Jewish Students in Colleges, Universities and Professional Schools", American Jewish Year Book, XXII, (1920/1921), pp. 383-393.

[64] Levinger, Lee J. The Jewish Student in America, (1937), pp. 8-9, 15-16.

[65] Robison, S. M., ed., Jewish Population Studies, p. 96; Feibelman, op. cit., p. 23; Wolff, K. H., op. cit., p. 23; Hofman, B., ed., 1,000 Years Pinsk, 1941, p. 450 (in Yiddish)

The percentage of the white population 25 years old and over who had in 1940 a college education was: Dallas 6.7, New Orleans 6.1, Pittsburgh 5.9. (U. S. Census Bureau, 16th Census of the U. S., Population, II, Part 3, p. 429, Part 6, pp. 220 and 1,029.)

[66] U. S. Immigration Commission, op. cit.; American Jewish Year Book, vol. XXII; Levinger, op. cit., p. 70. "Other" includes: architecture, journalism, library science, social work, health, physical training, music, fine arts, household economy, optics and military training.

[67] Broun, H. and Britt, G., Christians Only, pp. 141-142; Baumann, Leo, "What About the Jew in Medicine? The Jewish Examiner", January 18, 1935.

[68] Goldberg, J. A., "Jews in the Medical Profession", JSS., I, (1939), 327-336; Otis, D., "Discrimination in Medical Colleges", Opinion, January 25, 1932.

[69] Kingdon, Frank, "Discrimination in Medical Colleges", American Mercury, October, 1945, pp. 291-299.

[70] "Facilities of Jewish Hospitals for Specialized Training", JSS., III, (1941), p. 382.

[71] Fagen, M. M. "The Status of Jewish Lawyers in New York City", JSS., I, pp. 87, 92, 98.

[72] Mopsick, S. op. cit., p. 59.

[73] Levinger, Lee J. "Jews in the Liberal Professions in Ohio", JSS., II, (1940), pp. 401-434.

[74] U. S. Bureau of the Census, Population, 1940, III, Part 4, 460-461.

[75] Linfield, Harry S., The Communal Organization of the Jews in the United States, (1930), p. 129.

[76] Kinzler, E., Some Aspects of the Occupational Distribution of Jews in New York City, Table 113, p. 214. Tables 82-95.

[77] Fleischman, Abraham A., Some Aspects of the Jewish Population of Staten Island, N. Y. p. 57.

[78] Ryckoff, Irving M., *Jewish Organizations and Their Memberships, Staten Island, N. Y.*, New York: Graduate School for Jewish Social work, 1938, typewritten, pp. 82-95.

[79] Meyer, Lena, *A Study of the Occupational Distribution and Early History of the Jewish Population of New London, Conn.*, 1938, typewritten, p. 77.

[80] For the purpose of this study, the several classifications were made uniform, wherever it was possible.

[81] Græber and Britt, *Jews in a Gentile World*, p. 209; Koenig, S., "The Role of Various Ethnic Gruops in the Economic Life of Connecticut, *Yivo Bleter*, XVII, Table 1.

[82] Robison, S. M., *op. cit.*, p. 83, 161.

[83] Graeber and Britt, *op. cit.*, pp. 235, 237.

The Postwar Economy of American Jews

Barry R. Chiswick
(UNIVERSITY OF ILLINOIS, CHICAGO)

Introduction

Jews in the United States are a distinctive population. They are primarily the descendants of turn-of-the-century (1880–1924) immigrants from Eastern Europe and Russia, reinforced after the Second World War by displaced persons. They have ascended from economic deprivation to impressive achievements in cultural and economic matters. These achievements have often been cited and frequently celebrated in articles and books, both fiction and nonfiction, that recount the struggles and achievements of individual Jews in the arts, business, the professions, academia and public service. Even writings that do not focus on the high achievers, such as Ande Manner's *Poor Cousins* (1972) and the turn-of-the-century study by Hutchins Hapgood, *The Spirit of the Ghetto* (1902), are largely anecdotal and celebratory rather than analytical and dispassionate.

This paper presents a picture of the state of the economy of American Jews, using quantitative techniques and the most reliable data available. In so doing, it follows in the tradition established by Arthur Ruppin, Simon Kuznets and Arcadius Kahan in their important research on the immigrant and mid-twentieth-century experience of American Jews.[1]

For a population that has been so thoroughly analyzed in the literary world and anecdotal accounts, there is remarkably little systematic quantitative research on its economic and labor market status.[2] This is surely not due to the scarcity of Jewish social scientists (either sociologists or economists). Jews are well represented in these fields and have been at the forefront of scholarly research on other American minorities, including blacks, Hispanics, immigrants and women. One explanation often advanced is the fear that revealing Jewish economic success would invite anti-Jewish sentiment. Another possible explanation is that the focus of research on minorities is on disadvantaged groups, including groups perceived to suffer current disadvantage because of deprivations in the past. Thus, Jews, Mormons, the descendants of the American Revolution patriots and those of northwest European origin are "less interesting" to study.[3] A more compelling explanation is that Jews are a difficult group to study, not because of any characteristic inherent in the Jews themselves but because of the virtual absence of the key ingredient for such an analysis—the data.

Originally published in *Studies in Contemporary Jewry* 8 (1992). Reprinted by permission of Oxford University Press.

On the whole, Americans are perhaps an "overmeasured" population. Government and private data-collection efforts have produced an inordinate amount of statistics describing various facets of the population. Teasing out data on Jews from the wealth of data, however, is extraordinarily difficult for several reasons. First, the most important data collection agency in the United States, the Bureau of the Census, has not and will not include a question on religion or code a response (such as to an ethnic-ancestry question) that would reveal the respondent's religion. The one exception to this rule provides an important source of data for this study. Second, Jews constitute a small proportion of the population (about 2.5 percent), so that even surveys that include a question on religious preference and retain a separate code for Jews generally have too few identifiable Jews for a meaningful statistical analysis. Third, Jewish communal surveys, which clearly identify Jews, typically ask numerous detailed questions about Jewish religious practice and community involvement; designed for comparisons among Jews, they lack a parallel sample of non-Jews for comparative purposes. As a result, the research to date comparing American Jews with others has relied on a variety of indirect methodologies for identifying Jews (such as a Yiddish mother tongue or Russian ancestry) and on special surveys.

The discussion in this paper relies primarily on three independent sets of data. Although each data set taken separately has either methodological or sample size problems, the fact that they all paint the same picture greatly enhances our confidence in the results. A description of the data sets is followed by analyses of Jewish/non-Jewish differences and trends in educational attainment, labor supply, occupational and self-employment status, and earnings. The summary and conclusion tie together what has been learned from the analysis.

The Data

The Current Population Survey (CPS) has been conducted every month since the late 1940s by the Bureau of the Census for the Bureau of Labor Statistics, U.S. Department of Labor. In March 1957, in addition to the usual questions on demographic and labor market characteristics, the CPS asked for the first and last time the respondent's religion. The sample consisted of about 35,000 households. Jews constituted 3.2 percent of the population aged 14 and over, and were nearly all urban residents (96.1 percent), with few living in the South (7.7 percent). Unfortunately, only two very limited reports were released by the Census Bureau in which a variety of socioeconomic variables were cross-tabulated by religion.[4]

The long questionnaire administered to 15 percent of the population for the 1970 Census of Population affords another, albeit indirect, opportunity to study Jews. A mother-tongue question was asked of the respondent: Was there a language other than or in addition to English spoken in the home when you were a child? With the data limited to second-generation Americans (those born in the United States with at least one foreign-born parent), those reporting Yiddish, Hebrew or Ladino can be identified as Jews, while non-Jews are identified as those raised in a home in which only English or some other language was spoken. The study population is limited to second-generation Americans because non-English mother tongues virtually disappear by the third generation. It has been shown elsewhere that, although this procedure underestimates the number of Jews, it provides a reliable first approximation for the characteristics of second-generation American Jews around 1970.[5]

The third data set is the General Social Survey (GSS). Conducted by the National Opinion Research Center, the GSS is a random probability sample conducted nearly every year since 1972 of about fifteen hundred independently selected individuals. The data file studied here (1972–1987) is centered on 1980. In addition to asking the respondents numerous questions about their own demographic and socioeconomic characteristics, they were asked their religious preference currently and at age 16. This provides a wealth of data on adult Jews and non-Jews in the U.S. labor market for the period around 1980.[6] A major limitation of the GSS, however, is the small sample size for adult Jewish men (about 150 observations). Religion at age 16 is used to identify Jews, as this is less likely than current religion to be influenced by current economic status.

Finally, the GSS also asked the respondents numerous questions regarding the demographic and socioeconomic characteristics of their parents when they, the children, were age 16. Since the sample is centered on 1980 and the average age of the adult respondents was 42, the reports regarding their fathers and mothers refer to the early 1950s. Because the respondents in the GSS include an equal number of males and females, the sample of fathers is about double that of the male respondents (about three hundred observations), as is that of the mothers.

Taken together, these data permit an analysis of the patterns of Jewish economic achievement over the course of the post–Second World War period. Unfortunately, the data are not strictly comparable, as there are subtle and perhaps not-so-subtle differences in methodologies, definitions and the manner in which the data were made available by the survey agency. Yet they can be used to present a picture, not previously available, of the patterns of American Jewish achievement relative to non-Jews over this long interval.

Educational Attainment

Educational attainment is a complex concept involving both the quality of a unit of schooling and the number of units acquired. Quality differences are particularly difficult to measure, as are the differences in characteristics that students bring to the classroom that can greatly influence the extent to which they acquire productive skills in school.[7] For these reasons, this study follows the tradition of using "years of schooling completed" to measure individual and group differences in educational attainment.

In spite of disadvantages associated with immigrant parents or grandparents, and discrimination against Jews in access to higher education and many professions requiring higher education, American Jews had achieved a remarkably high level of educational attainment by the early postwar years.[8] Among adult men in the early postwar years (the GSS fathers), American Jews had an average of 11.6 years of schooling, compared with 9.7 years for white non-Jews (Table 1). This schooling

Table 1. Distribution of Schooling of the Adult Male Population (Jews and Non-Jews)

Schooling (Years)	GSS Fathers[a] Jews	GSS Fathers[a] Non-Jews	1957 CPS[b] Jews	1957 CPS[b] Non-Jews	1970 Census[c] Jews	1970 Census[c] Non-Jews	GSS Respondents[d] Jews	GSS Respondents[d] Non-Jews
0–7	15.0	24.7	10.6	18.6	1.5	7.1	2.0	5.3
8	9.7	20.5	11.2	17.1	3.6	13.3	1.3	5.3
9–11	12.6	12.3	10.6	19.4	12.4	21.5	2.7	13.8
12	30.0	24.0	24.3	26.5	28.5	32.0	12.7	30.9
13–15	8.9	7.9	14.9	8.4	17.5	11.7	16.7	20.2
16	12.1	6.2	28.5	9.9	14.8	7.1	28.0	12.5
Over 16	11.7	4.3			21.6	7.3	36.7	12.0
Total	100.0	100.0	100.0	100.0	100.0	100.0	100.0	100.0
Median	12	10	12.7	11.2	13	12	16	12
Mean	11.6	9.7	NA	NA	13.7	11.5	15.7	12.8

Sources: U.S. Bureau of the Census, "Tabulations of Data on the Social and Economic Characteristics of Major Religious Groups, 1957" mimeo, n.d., Table 12; U.S. Bureau of the Census, 1970 Census of Population, Public Use Sample, 1/100 sample (15 percent questionnaire); and National Opinion Research Center, *General Social Surveys, 1972–1987, Cumulative Data File* (Chicago: 1987).

Notes:
NA = Not available in source.
Figures may not add up to 100 percent because of rounding.
[a] Educational attainment of the fathers of adult (aged 25 to 64) white male and female respondents at age 16. Sample size: 247 Jews and 9,043 non-Jews.
[b] Employed males aged 18 and over for Jews and all (Jews and non-Jews). Sample size: about 35,000 households.
[c] Adult white men not enrolled in school and born in the United States with at least one foreign-born parent. Jews defined as those raised in a home in which Yiddish, Hebrew or Ladino was spoken instead of or in addition to English. Based on a 1/100 sample of the 1970 Census of Population (15 percent questionnaire).
[d] Adult (aged 25 to 64) white male respondents. Sample size: 150 Jews and 5,199 non-Jews.

difference of 1.9 years increased over time to a 2.9-year advantage among the GSS respondents.

Perhaps more telling are the differences in the proportion with at least four years of college education. Among the Jewish men, the proportion increased continuously over the time period, from 24 percent in the early postwar years to 29 percent in 1957, to 36 percent in 1970 and to 65 percent in the 1980 period. By contrast, the proportions for non-Jews increased only from about 10 percent in the early postwar years and 1957 to 14 percent in 1970, and was still only 25 percent in 1980.

The pattern among women is similar. As shown in Table 2, Jewish women have a higher level of education than non-Jewish women, and the difference in educational attainment has increased over time. For example, the Jewish mothers in the GSS had 11.4 years of schooling, and 13 percent had 16 or more years of schooling, in contrast to the 10.2 years and 7 percent, respectively, for non-Jews. By about 1980, the Jewish women averaged 14.4 years of schooling (40 percent with 16 or more years), in contrast to 12.3 years (16 percent with 16 or more years).

Table 2. Distribution of Schooling of the Adult Female Population (Jews and Non-Jews)

Schooling (Years)	GSS Mothers[a] Jews	Non-Jews	1957 CPS[b] Jews	Non-Jews	1970 Census[c] Jews	Non-Jews	GSS Respondents[d] Jews	Non-Jews
0–7	9.1	17.0	6.5	13.0	1.4	6.7	0.0	3.8
8	9.5	18.8	9.2	13.6	4.5	12.8	0.0	4.7
9–11	10.9	14.5	11.3	18.4	11.4	21.1	2.4	16.1
12	45.8	34.4	40.1	36.9	51.3	41.6	28.3	41.7
13–15	11.6	8.8	16.4	9.3	15.5	10.5	29.5	18.0
16	8.4	5.0	} 16.4	} 8.5	8.7	4.4	24.1	9.5
Over 16	4.7	1.6			7.2	2.9	15.7	6.2
Total	100.0	100.0	100.0	100.0	100.0	100.0	100.0	100.0
Median	12	11	12.6	12.1	12	12	14	12
Mean	11.4	10.2	NA	NA	12.5	11.1	14.4	12.3

Sources: U.S. Bureau of the Census, "Tabulations of Data on the Social and Economic Characteristics of Major Religious Groups, 1957" mimeo, n.d., Table 12; U.S. Bureau of the Census, 1970 Census of Population, Public Use Sample, 1/100 sample (15 percent questionnaire); and National Opinion Research Center, *General Social Surveys, 1972–1987, Cumulative Data File* (Chicago: 1987).

Notes:
NA = Not available in source.
Figures may not add up to 100 percent because of rounding.
[a]Educational attainment of the mothers of adult (aged 25 to 64) white male and female respondents at age 16. Sample size: 275 Jews and 10,067 non-Jews.
[b]Employed females aged 18 and over for Jews and all (Jews and non-Jews). Sample size: about 35,000 households.
[c]Adult white women not enrolled in school and born in the United States with at least one foreign-born parent. Jews defined as those raised in a home in which Yiddish, Hebrew or Ladino was spoken instead of or in addition to English. Based on a 1/100 sample of the 1970 Census of Population (15 percent questionnaire).
[d]Adult (aged 25 to 64) white female respondents. Sample size: 166 Jews and 6,358 non-Jews.

It is interesting to note that the gender difference in favor of males is larger for Jews than for non-Jews. In the most recent period, Jewish men had 1.3 years more schooling than Jewish women, an increase over the virtual equality in schooling in the early postwar years. Among non-Jewish men, however, the recent male advantage is only 0.5 years, in contrast to an earlier male disadvantage (comparing GSS mothers and fathers) of 0.5 years. Does this mean that Jewish parents sacrificed the educational attainment of their daughters to enhance that of their sons? Apparently not, as adult Jewish women in the 1980 period had a schooling level that substantially exceeded that of non-Jewish men, with this differential not changing over the four time periods (compare Tables 1 and 2).

A question can be raised, however, as to whether the high level of Jewish educational attainment is attributable to where Jews live (predominantly in the urban areas and states outside of the South), and to their parents' higher level of education.[9] An analysis of the Jewish/non-Jewish difference in educational attainment in the early postwar years indicates that the observed 1.9-year schooling difference declines to a still statistically significant 1.0-year difference when father's residence (when the respondent was age 16) and the respondent's age (a proxy for the father's age) are held constant. Among the GSS respondents (around 1980), controlling for age and residence at age 16 reduces the educational advantage from 2.9 to 2.5 years for men and from 2.1 to 1.6 years for women, with all of these differences statistically significant. Adding an additional control for father's education reduces the differentials, but they are still large and significant—2.1 years for men and 1.3 years for women.

In summary, the data on educational attainment for the four postwar time periods indicate that American Jews have a substantially higher level of schooling, whether measured on average or as the proportion with 16 or more years of schooling, that this differential is greater among the men than among the women, and that the gap appears to have increased over time. Some of this higher level of schooling is attributable to Jews living predominantly in areas with higher schooling levels in general, and some is due to their greater parental education. Yet even after adjusting for these factors, the patterns remain (although the differences are reduced in magnitude). Indeed, even where other variables are the same, there has been an increase in the Jewish educational advantage from the fathers' to the sons' generation.

Labor Supply

The labor supply of a population is an important dimension of the economic characteristics of the group. A greater labor supply by men or women enhances family money income, on the one hand, thereby expanding the family's ability to purchase goods and services. On the other hand, a greater labor supply reduces the time available for engaging in "home production" and leisure-time activities. Home production activities include providing child care. Parental time—and for most families in practice this means predominantly mother's time—is an important "input" in children's developing a greater potential for success in schooling and, ultimately, in the labor market. Thus, greater female labor supply does not unambiguously enhance a group's economic situation. This depends instead on several factors, including the timing of this labor supply with respect to the number and age of children in the group.[10]

There are several dimensions of labor supply. This study focuses on the labor force participation rate, that is, the proportion of the adult (noninstitutionalized) members of a group who are either employed (i.e., wage, salary and self-employed persons) or are unemployed (i.e., looking for a job).

The labor force participation rates of adult "nonaged" men (25 to 54 years) are very high, vary but slightly across ethnic and religious groups, and have shown little change over time. Among younger men (aged 18–24), participation has declined over time as a result of increased college attendance, while among older men (aged 55 and over), earlier retirement has reduced participation.

The 1957 CPS data indicate that Jewish men aged 25 to 34 years had a participation rate of 97 percent, the same as for non-Jewish men (U.S. Bureau of the Census, no date, Table 11). Even for those aged 45 to 64 years there was little difference—

Table 3. Labor Force Participation Rates By Age Among Women
(Jews and Non-Jews) (percent)

	1957 CPS[a]		1970 Census[b]		GSS Respondents[c]	
Age	Jews	Non-Jews	Jews	Non-Jews	Jews	Non-Jews
14–17	NA	17.7	30.6	26.1	NA	NA
18–24	57.2	45.5	58.5	57.5	54.5	58.3
25–34	25.5	34.8	39.7	42.2	66.1	60.6
35–44	33.5	42.6	48.8	47.4	68.6	63.6
45–64	38.2	41.1	53.3	49.2	60.7	49.8
65 and over	8.5	11.5	19.7	10.7	26.2	9.8
All women	30.7	35.1	46.8	30.0	53.3	48.0

Sources: U.S. Bureau of the Census, "Tabulations of Data on the Social and Economic Characteristics of Major Religious Groups, 1957" mimeo, n.d., Table 11; U.S. Bureau of the Census, 1970 Census of Population, Public Use Sample, 1/100 sample (15 percent questionnaire); and National Opinion Research Center, *General Social Surveys, 1972–1987, Cumulative Data File* (Chicago: 1987).

Notes:
NA = Not available in source.
[a] Women aged 14 and over for Jews and all (Jews and non-Jews). Sample size: about 35,000 households.
[b] White women born in the United States with at least one foreign-born parent. Jews defined as those raised in a home in which Yiddish, Hebrew or Ladino was spoken instead of or in addition to English. Based on a 1/100 sample of the 1970 Census of Population (15 percent questionnaire).
[c] White women respondents. Sample size. 242 Jews and 9,228 non-Jews.

96 percent for the Jews, compared with 93 percent for non-Jews. The lower Jewish male labor supply among men aged 18 to 24 years (54 percent compared with 79 percent) is due to their higher college enrollment. The greater Jewish labor supply among men aged 65 and over (47 percent compared with 37 percent) is due to the greater proportion of Jews who are self-employed and in professional and other white-collar occupations.

Variations in labor supply are far more interesting among women. As shown in Table 3, labor force participation rates in the postwar period have increased for both Jewish and non-Jewish women in nearly every age group.[11] Except for the college-age population, the increase in labor supply was greater for the Jewish women. Although Jewish women had a lower participation rate in the 1957 CPS, the rate was higher among the 1980 GSS respondents. The greater increase in Jewish female participation rates may be attributed, in part, to the larger increase in their educational attainment and their lower fertility.[12]

Detailed analysis of the 1970 Census of Population reveals important differences between Jewish and non-Jewish women in the impact or effect of schooling and children on labor supply.[13] Jewish women's labor supply is more sensitive to the positive effect of schooling, thereby reinforcing the favorable effect on labor supply of the growth in the schooling differential. In addition, the labor supply of Jewish women is more sensitive to the presence of children in the home. That is, Jewish female labor supply declines relatively more than the non-Jewish female labor

Table 4. Female Labor Force Participation Rates for Married Women by Presence and Age of Children (Jews and non-Jews)

	1957 CPS[a]		1970 Census[b]	
	Jews	Non-Jews	Jews	Non-Jews
Total	27.8	29.6	51.7	46.8
No children under 18	30.0	35.6	55.4	50.2
With children 6–17, none under 6	28.6	36.7	49.2	44.7
With children under 6	11.8	17.0	25.1	31.1

Sources: U.S. Bureau of the Census, "Tabulations of Data on the Social and Economic Characteristics of Major Religious Groups, March 1957," n.d., Table 13. U.S. Bureau of the Census, 1970 Census of Population, Public Use Sample, 1/100 sample (15 percent questionnaire).
Notes:
[a] Women aged 18 and over for Jews and all (Jews and non-Jews).
[b] White women aged 25 to 64, second-generation Americans. Jews defined as in Table 3, footnote b.

supply when there are school-age and especially preschool children in the family (see Table 4). The decline in Jewish fertility has therefore increased the Jewish female labor supply by more than would a similar decline in non-Jewish fertility.

An analysis using the 1970 Census of differences in labor supply (holding constant age, schooling, other family income and location of residence), suggests a more "optimal" pattern of labor supply on the part of Jewish women. They are more likely to work before children are born and after the youngest attains age 18, and are less likely to work when the children are of preschool or school age. Among mothers with school-age children who work, the Jewish mothers are more likely to work part-year and part-time.

The greater labor supply of Jewish women is enhancing family income. The greater labor supply is also associated with low fertility, which eventually has implications for an aging Jewish population that is a smaller proportion of the total population. It is less clear what is happening to parental investments of time and other resources in the next generation of young Jews. If there is a decline in direct parental investments, and if high-quality alternatives (e.g., schooling) are not acquired, there may be negative implications for these children.

Occupational and Self-Employment Status

Occupational Status

A person's occupational status is one of the most commonly used measures of the level of economic attainment.[14] Occupation reflects skills previously acquired through schooling, apprenticeship programs and on-the-job training, as well as the myriad of unmeasured and more subtle characteristics that an individual brings to the labor market. It is a measure of the outcome of the labor market process.

Comparisons of achievement across time are facilitated by an examination of occupation, as distinct from earnings, since the latter are more sensitive to temporary or cyclical factors and need to be adjusted for changes in the overall price level.

Much of the analysis of occupational attainment will be presented in terms of the frequency distribution of workers by occupational status. Occupation is by definition a categorical variable—unlike age or earnings, which are quantitative and continuous variables. To convert the categorical occupational distribution into a quantitative variable, sociologists have developed occupational prestige scores. These scores reflect the evaluation by individuals as to how "good" a given occupation is, converted into an index number that is a linear combination of the average level of schooling and income of workers in the occupation.[15] The GSS includes the prestige scores for the occupational status of the respondents and for their fathers when the former were age 16. This permits an examination of a quantitative measure of occupation at the start and end of the interval under study.

Table 5 reports the occupational attainment for adult Jewish and non-Jewish men for the four time periods, using the three data sets. These data show a dramatic increase in the professionalization of the Jewish labor force. Professionals increased from 13.8 percent of the male Jewish labor force in the early post-Second World War period (GSS fathers) to 20.3 percent in 1957, 27.2 percent in 1970 and 43.0 percent in the 1980 period (GSS respondents). The increase was spread among a wide range of professional occupations, including medicine, law and academia.

This professionalization was counterbalanced by a decline in managerial employment from nearly half of the Jewish men in the early postwar period to a quarter in the more recent period. Blue-collar employment also declined. The proportion of Jews in craft, operative, transportation, laborer and service jobs declined continuously over the period, from 25 percent in the early postwar years to 22 percent in 1957, 18 percent in 1970 and 9 percent in the recent period. Farming was and remained a negligible occupation among the Jews.

In each of the time periods, there is a higher level of occupational attainment among the Jews than among the non-Jews, and although non-Jews have also experienced a rapid improvement in occupational status, the gap has widened. For example, in Table 5, the proportion of professionals among the Jews exceeded that of the non-Jews by 5.0 percentage points for the early postwar period: 10.4 percentage points in 1957, 11.8 percentage points in 1970 and 24.7 percentage points in the period around 1980. In contrast, blue-collar employment (craft, operative, laborer, transportation and service) declined much more sharply among the Jews, from 26 percent in the early postwar period to 9 percent around 1980, in contrast to 53 percent and 50 percent, respectively, among the non-Jews. (Among non-Jews, the farm owner and farm manager category declined from 15.6 percent to 3.1 percent.)

The occupational prestige scores in the GSS can also be used to document the higher level and greater improvement over time in occupational status among the Jews. Table 5 reports the frequency distribution of the occupational prestige scores of the male respondents and the fathers in the GSS separately for Jews and non-Jews. Typical occupations are listed for each of the prestige score categories to provide a better sense of the substantive interpretation of these values. About two-thirds of the Jewish male respondents had occupational prestige scores of 50 or

Table 5. Occupational Distribution and Self-Employment of Adult Men (Jews and Non-Jews) (percent)

	GSS Fathers[a] Jews	GSS Fathers[a] Non-Jews	1957 CPS[b] Jews	1957 CPS[b] Non-Jews	1970 Census[c] Jews	1970 Census[c] Non-Jews	GSS Respondents[d] Jews	GSS Respondents[d] Non-Jews
A) Occupation[e]								
Professional	13.8	8.8	20.3	9.9	27.2	15.4	43.0	18.3
Medicine (MDs, DDS)	2.5	0.9	NA	NA	6.1	1.4	8.3	0.8
Law	3.5	0.6	NA	NA	3.6	0.7	5.6	0.9
Col. & univ. teach.	1.1	0.4	NA	NA	1.3	0.6	4.9	1.0
Other P, T & K	6.7	6.9	NA	NA	16.2	12.7	24.2	15.6
Managers (nonfarm)	44.9	14.8	35.1	13.3	26.5	13.4	26.4	16.7
Sales	12.0	4.7	14.1	5.4	19.7	7.0	13.2	6.2
Clerical	3.9	3.6	8.0	6.9	8.3	8.1	8.3	5.8
Craft	13.1	24.6	8.9	20.0	8.4	23.5	4.2	24.0
Operatives (excl. transp.)	6.7	12.4	10.1	20.9	2.9	12.5	0.0	10.1
Transport	3.2	4.6	NA	NA	3.3	5.3	1.4	5.1
Laborers	1.1	7.1	0.8	10.2	1.1	5.4	0.0	5.3
Farm managers & farmers	0.0	15.6	0.1	7.3	0.2	2.3	0.0	3.1
Service	1.4	4.0	2.3	6.1	2.4	7.2	3.5	5.6
Total	100.0	100.0	100.0	100.0	100.0	100.0	100.0	100.0
B) Self-employed[f]	55.6	36.2	31.8	8.5	31.9	14.1	35.1	16.3

Sources: U.S. Bureau of the Census, "Tabulations of Data on the Social and Economic Characteristics of Major Religious Groups, 1957" mimeo, n.d., Table 15; U.S. Bureau of the Census, 1970 Census of Population, Public Use Sample, 1/100 sample (15 percent questionnaire); and National Opinion Research Center, *General Social Surveys, 1972–1987, Cumulative Data File* (Chicago: 1987).

Notes:
NA = Detail not available.
Figures may not add up to 100 percent because of rounding.

[a]Fathers of adult (aged 25 to 64) white male and female respondents, when respondent was age 16. Sample size: 283 Jews and 10,191 non-Jews.

[b]Employed males aged 18 and over for Jews and all (Jews and non-Jews). Sample size: about 35,000 households. Percent self-employed refers to self-employed managers (excluding farm) and professionals as percentage of all employed males. Self-employment not reported for other occupational groups. Operatives include transport workers.

[c]Adult (aged 25 to 64) white men not enrolled in school who worked in 1969 and were born in the United States with at least one foreign-born parent. Jews defined as those raised in a home in which Yiddish, Hebrew or Ladino was spoken instead of or in addition to English. Based on a 1/100 sample of the 1970 Census of Population (15 percent questionnaire).

[d]Adult (aged 25 to 64) white male respondents. Sample size: 144 Jews and 5,186 non-Jews.

[e]Professional refers to professional, technical and kindred workers; laborers includes farm laborers; service includes private household workers. Operatives excludes transportation workers except for the 1957 CPS.

[f]Percent self-employed is self-employed as a percentage of all workers except for 1957 CPS, where it is self-employed (and unpaid family workers) in professional and managerial occupations as a percentage of all workers.

more, in contrast to less than one-third of the non-Jews. Among the fathers, the proportions were more than half of the Jews and only one-fifth of non-Jews with scores of at least 50. Although the mean occupational prestige scores increased from fathers to sons from 40.5 to 41.9 among non-Jews, the increase was larger among the Jews, from 46.6 to 53.2.

It is known, however, that occupational status varies systematically with certain characteristics. On average, it increases with the level of education and is higher in urban rather than in rural areas. Both of these characteristics favor high Jewish occupational attainment. One of the releases from the 1957 CPS recomputes the occupational distribution for urban men by standardizing for the educational attainment of employed adult males (U.S. Bureau of the Census, no date, Table 15). That is, it shows what the occupational distribution of urban Jews would be if they had the same distribution of years of schooling as all urban men. When this is done, the proportion of Jewish professionals is below that for non-Jews, 10 percent compared with 12 percent (compare with Table 4, columns 3 and 4). The proportion of Jewish blue-collar workers increases under this experiment, becoming 30 percent compared with 59 percent for non-Jews. Jews still have a high proportion in the nonprofessional white-collar occupations (60 percent compared with 30 percent), especially as managers and sales workers. This exercise suggests that much of the Jewish occupational advantage in 1957 was attributable to their urban location and especially their higher level of schooling, but that with the exception of professionals they still had on average a higher occupational attainment.

Fortunately, far more can be done analyzing the occupational prestige scores for the respondents and fathers in the GSS, using as well such variables as age and marital status, education and place of residence.[16] Among the male workers in the early postwar period (the GSS fathers), the Jews had a statistically significant higher occupational prestige score, 46.6 versus 40.5, a difference of 6.1 points. Holding constant differences in their education, age and place of residence reduces this advantage to a statistically significant 3.1 points, or about half of the observed differential.

The observed difference in occupational prestige scores between Jewish and non-Jewish respondents in the GSS is a statistically significant 11.3 points. Controlling for the above-mentioned variables, the Jewish occupational prestige advantage is reduced, but Jews still have a statistically significant advantage of 3.8 points. Perhaps Jews do well because their fathers had a high occupational status, and occupational status is transmitted from father to son independent of schooling and other measured variables? After holding constant the father's occupational status, the result is only a small reduction in the Jewish occupational advantage, from 3.8 points to a still statistically significant 3.5 points.

The analysis indicates that, among employed adult males, Jews had a higher occupational status throughout the postwar period. Although diminished in value, this differential persists even after controlling for other readily measured variables such as age, schooling, urban residence and father's occupation. Moreover, there has been an increase in the relative Jewish occupational advantage over the period, even after controlling for other variables.

Self-Employment Status

There are three main occupational avenues for self-employment in the United States: as managers of nonfarm enterprises, as farm owners or as self-employed professionals. Most men working in agriculture in the United States are self-employed. For the United States as a whole, self-employment has decreased with the decline in the proportion of the agricultural labor force. Among the fathers in the GSS, 36 percent were self-employed, in contrast to the 16 percent self-employed among the respondents, reflecting the decline in the farm manager and farm owner occupational category from 16 percent to 3 percent.

In spite of the fact that a negligible number of American Jews are engaged in farming, Jews have a very high rate of self-employment—a rate that substantially exceeds that of non-Jews (Table 5). Jewish self-employment decreased from the early postwar period, when it was 56 percent, to 32 to 35 percent in the later time periods. These data mask more substantial movements in the nature of self-employment away from being a self-employed manager (primarily of a manufacturing or retail trade enterprise) to being a self-employed professional (doctor, lawyer, etc.).[17]

In the 1957 CPS data, self-employment status is reported only for those in professional and managerial occupations. Jews have substantially higher rates of self-employment in these two occupations. More than one-third of Jewish professionals were self-employed, twice the ratio for non-Jews. Among managers, more than two-thirds of the Jews were self-employed, in contrast to one-half among non-Jews.

Thus, the entrepreneurial spirit remains strong among Jews, although it is increasingly expressed in terms of self-employed professional activities rather than in the management of business enterprises.

Income

Income or earnings are a measure of both labor market performance and the ability to buy goods and services, that is, the command over resources. As a measure of the labor market outcome, income has the advantage of being a direct quantitative, continuous measure—as distinct from occupation, which is a categorical variable; or the occupational prestige score, which is a constructed value. However, two disadvantages of income are that nominal values may change over time merely because of inflation, and groups may differ in their trade-off between measured and unmeasured dimensions of full compensation. Furthermore, as would be expected, reporting difficulties prevented the collection of data on the income or earnings of the fathers in the GSS survey.

Table 6 reports the mean or median income or earnings among adult Jewish and non-Jewish men in the 1957 CPS, the 1970 Census and among the GSS respondents. In each of the three time periods, earned income is substantially higher among the Jews. In the 1957 CPS data, Jewish median income was 36 percent greater than that of non-Jews. The only standardization or statistical control shown

Table 6. Distribution of Occupational Prestige Scores
for General Social Survey Respondents and Fathers (Jews and Non-Jews)[a] (percent)

Score (Points)	Occupations	Fathers Jews	Fathers Non-Jews	Respondents Jews	Respondents Non-Jews
10–19	Construction laborers, baggage porters	3.9	7.4[b]	2.7	6.6
20–29	Sales clerks, taxi cab drivers	7.8	10.9	5.4	11.1
30–39	Restaurant managers, auto mechanics	15.9	24.6	10.9	26.1
40–49	Real estate agents, policemen	17.0	36.0	13.6	25.6
50–59	Librarians, bank tellers	44.5	14.1	36.1	18.8
60–69	Mechanical engineers	3.9	4.3	8.2	8.1
70–79	Lawyers, professors	5.7	2.0	18.4	3.4
80 and over	Physicians	1.4	0.5	4.8	0.3
Total		100.0	100.0	100.0	100.0
Mean score		46.6	40.5	53.2	41.9

Source: National Opinion Research Center, *General Social Surveys, 1972–1987, Cumulative Data File* (Chicago: 1987).
Notes:
Figures may not add up to 100 percent because of rounding.
[a]Respondent refers only to males, while the fathers are for male and female respondents.
[b]Includes one observation with a score less than 10 (bootblack).

in the released data is for urban residence and major occupational category. With these controls, the Jewish median income exceeds that of non-Jews by 6.7 percent (Table 7). That is, even within the same major occupational category, Jews had a higher level of income. Yet controlling in this way may result in "overadjusted" data, if the purpose of the exercise is to ascertain Jewish/non-Jewish income differences controlling for the skills the individual brings to the labor market. Although occupation is in part determined by age (labor market experience), schooling and other characteristics embodied in the person that are brought to the labor market, it is fundamentally a measure of the outcome of the labor market process.

The 1970 Census data on second-generation Americans show much higher mean earnings for Jews. The 55 percent greater earnings is reduced to 16 percent when a set of explanatory variables describing the skills and characteristics workers bring to the labor market is held constant.[18] That is, for the same readily measured inputs into the labor market, the Jews receive 16 percent higher incomes.[19]

The GSS respondent data also permit a comparative analysis of earnings. The observed earnings difference of nearly 40 percent is reduced to 15 percent when there is a statistical control for age (experience), schooling, marital status and place of residence. Within the nearly fifteen-year interval of the GSS data, there is no trend in the ratio of Jewish to non-Jewish earnings, other variables being the same.

Taken as a whole, these data suggest very high earnings for American Jews relative to non-Jews that are partly attributable to the difference in the skills (e.g.,

Table 7. Income or Earnings of Adult Men (Jews and Non-Jews)

Income or Earnings	1957 CPS (Median Income)[a]	1970 Census (Mean Earnings)[b]	GSS Respondents (Mean Earnings)[c]
Jews	4,900	16,176	27,322
Non-Jews	3,608	10,431	19,750
Ratio (1) to (2)			
Observed	1.36	1.55	1.38
Other variables held constant[d]	1.07	1.16	1.15

Sources: National Opinion Research Center, *General Social Surveys, 1972–1987, Cumulative Data File* (Chicago: 1987); U.S. Bureau of the Census, "Tabulations of Data on the Social and Economic Characteristics of Major Religious Groups, 1957" mimeo, n.d., Table 15; and U.S. Bureau of the Census, 1970 Census of Population, Public Use Sample, 1/100 sample (15 percent questionnaire).

Notes:

[a] Income in 1956 of males aged 14 and over with income for Jews and all (Jews and non-Jews). Sample size: about 35,000 households.

[b] Adult white men not enrolled in school who worked in 1969 and were born in the United States with at least one foreign-born parent. Jews defined as those raised in a home in which Yiddish, Hebrew, or Ladino was spoken instead of or in addition to English. Based on a 1/100 sample of the 1970 Census of Population (15 percent questionnaire).

[c] Earnings of adult (aged 25 to 64) white male respondents with earnings. Sample size: 124 Jews and 4,169 non-Jews.

[d] Statistical controls are for urban residence and occupational distribution for the 1957 CPS and for age (experience), schooling, location, marital status and weeks worked for white men in the 1970 Census (second-generation Americans) and the GSS.

schooling) and other characteristics (e.g., location) they bring to the labor market. Yet even after adjusting for these other characteristics, Jews have about 15 percent higher mean earnings. It is not obvious that there is a trend over time in this differential.[20] The earnings differential in favor of Jews appears to vary by level of schooling. It is small for those with very low levels of schooling and increases with schooling level.[21]

Summary and Conclusions

This paper has examined several dimensions of the economy of American Jews compared with white non-Jews in the postwar period by a study of census and survey data at four time periods.

American Jewish men had higher levels of schooling, occupational attainment and earnings in the 1950s than non-Jewish men. During the course of the postwar period, their levels of attainment increased sharply. For schooling and occupational status, the differential between Jews and non-Jews widened over this period. Even after holding constant several important determinants of attainment—such as age, place of residence, parental characteristics and, for occupation and earnings, also the person's level of education—Jews had more schooling (by about 2.1 years) and higher occupational status, and they earned more (by about 15 percent) than non-Jews.

There are interesting differences for women in some of these patterns. The Jewish educational attainment exceeds that of non-Jews by a smaller magnitude overall, and also when other variables are the same. For example, other variables being the same, Jewish women have only 1.3 years more schooling than non-Jews. The labor supply of Jewish women appears to have increased over time more rapidly than for non-Jewish women. This may be the result of the favorable effects of the higher level of education and smaller family size (lower fertility) of Jewish women. Furthermore, the pattern of labor supply with respect to age of the respondents appears to differ—Jewish women are less likely to work when there are young children at home, and they are more likely to work at other times. This suggests a greater sensitivity to the optimal allocation of parental time between child care and the labor market.

The entrepreneurial spirit remains strong among Jews. Throughout the period under study, Jews have had a much higher rate of self-employment, although its nature has changed. Jews are now less likely than previously to be self-employed managers and are more likely to be self-employed professionals. Within either occupational category, however, Jews have a much higher rate of self-employment than non-Jews.

There has been a concern that from generation to generation American Jews would "regress to the mean," that is, to the American norm. This concern appears to be without foundation. Jews retain a strong commitment to educational attainment and labor market advancement, and they continue to display a strong entrepreneurial spirit. The differentials in attainment in favor of Jews have not narrowed in the postwar period; in important instances, they even appear to have widened. Thus, although there are serious problems facing the American Jewish community, including issues of self-identity, intermarriage and an aging population, the American Jewish economy is doing well.

Notes

1. Arthur Ruppin, *The Jews of To-Day* (New York: 1913); Simon Kuznets, *Economic Structure of U.S. Jewry: Recent Trends* (Jerusalem: 1972); idem, "Immigration of Russian Jews to the United States: Background and Structure," *Perspectives in American History* 9 (1975), 35–126; Arcadius Kahan, *Essays in Jewish Social and Economic History* (Chicago: 1986).

2. Some additional notable exceptions include Barry R. Chiswick, "The Earnings and Human Capital of American Jews," *Journal of Human Resources* (Summer 1983), 313–336; idem, "The Labor Market Status of American Jews: Patterns and Determinants," *American Jewish Year Book 1985* (New York: 1984), 131–153; idem, "Labor Supply and Investment in Child Quality: A Study of Jewish and Non-Jewish Women," *Review of Economics and Statistics* (November 1986), 700–703; idem, "Jewish Immigrant Skill and Occupational Attainment at the Turn of the Century," *Explorations in Economic History* 28 (Jan. 1991), 64–86; idem, "The Skills and Economic Status of American Jewry: Trends Over the Last Half Century," in *A New Jewish World: Continuity and Change 1939-1989*, ed. Robert Wistrich (Jerusalem: forthcoming); Sidney Goldstein, "Socioeconomic Differentials Among

Religious Groups in the United States," *American Journal of Sociology* 74, no. 6 (May 1969), 612–631; William M. Kephart, "Position of Jewish Economy in the United States," *Social Forces* 28, no. 2 (Dec. 1949), 153–164; Thomas Kessner, *The Golden Door: Italian and Jewish Immigrant Mobility in New York City, 1880–1915* (New York: 1977); and Joel Perlmann, *Ethnic Differences: Schooling and Social Structure Among the Irish, Italians, Jews and Blacks in an American City, 1880–1935* (Cambridge: 1988). For studies that address the achievement of Jews in other diaspora countries, see Mordechai Altshuler, *Soviet Jewry Since the Second World War: Population and Social Structure* (New York: 1987); Daniel J. Elazar with Peter Medding, *Jewish Communities in Frontier Societies: Argentina, Australia and South Africa* (New York: 1983); and S. J. Prais and Marlena Schmool, "The Social-Class Structure of Anglo-Jewry, 1961," *Jewish Journal of Sociology* 16 (June 1975), 5–15.

3. In addition to the studies of Jews noted above, a notable exception is the analysis of "Euroethnics" in Stanley Lieberson and Mary C. Waters, *From Many Strands: Ethnic and Racial Groups in Contemporary America* (New York: 1988), and the U.S. Commission on Civil Rights, *The Economic Status of Americans of Southern and Eastern European Ancestry*, Clearinghouse Publication 89 (Washington, D.C.: Oct. 1986), both of which include analyses for those of Russian ancestry—a proxy for Jews.

4. These data, released in the U.S. Bureau of the Census, "Religion Reported by the Civilian Population of the United States: March 1957," *Current Population Reports, Population Characteristics*, Series P. 20, no. 79, 2 February 1958, and idem, "Tabulations of Data on the Social and Economic Characteristics of Major Religious Groups," mimeo (undated), have previously been studied by Chiswick, "Labor Market Status of American Jews"; Goldstein, "Socioeconomic Differentials"; and Kuznets, *Economic Structure of U.S. Jewry*.

5. See, e.g., Chiswick, "Earnings and Human Capital of American Jews"; Frances E. Kobrin, "National Data on American Jewry, 1970–71: A Comparative Evaluation of the Census Yiddish Mother Tongue Subpopulation and the National Jewish Population Survey," in *Papers in Jewish Demography, 1981*, ed. U. O. Schmelz, et al. (Jerusalem: 1983), 129–143; and Ira Rosenwaike, "The Utilization of Census Mother Tongue Data in American Jewish Population Analyses," *Jewish Social Studies* (April/July 1971), 141–159.

6. For a detailed technical analysis of Jewish/non-Jewish differences in economic characteristics using these data, see Chiswick, "Skills and Economic Status of American Jewry."

7. The apparently larger return from schooling for Jews than for non-Jews may reflect a higher quality of schooling or the unmeasured characteristics that enhance the productivity of schooling for Jews. See Barry R. Chiswick, "Differences in Education and Earnings Across Racial and Ethnic Groups: Tastes, Discrimination and Investment in Child Quality," *Quarterly Journal of Economics* (Aug. 1988), 571–597.

8. See, e.g., Leonard Dinnerstein, "Education and the Achievement of American Jews," in *American Education and European Immigration, 1840–1940*, ed. Bernard J. Weiss (Urbana: 1982).

9. For the technical detail, see Chiswick, "Skills and Economic Status of American Jewry." In addition, an examination of educational attainment within the time period (1972–1987) for the respondents' and fathers' samples reveals a significant relative improvement over time among the Jewish fathers, and a small, nonsignificant relative improvement among the Jewish respondents.

10. For the most comprehensive analysis of the economics of family formation and decision-making, see Gary S. Becker, *A Treatise on the Family* (Cambridge, Mass.: 1981).

11. Comparable data on the labor force participation of the mothers of Jewish respondents are not available in the GSS.

12. A lower labor supply for Jewish women, especially when there were children at home, appears to be emphasized by commentators at the turn of the century. See Nathan Glazer, *American Judaism* (Chicago: 1957), 80–81, and Gretchen A. Condran and Ellen A. Kramarow, "Child Mortality Among Jewish Immigrants to the United States," *Journal of Interdisciplinary History* 22, no. 2 (Autumn 1991), 223–254.

13. For the detailed analysis, see Chiswick, "Labor Supply and Investment in Child

Quality." Similar patterns emerge in an analysis of Jewish/non-Jewish differences in labor supply using data from Jewish communal surveys. For the United States, see Paul Ritterband, "Jewish Women in the Labor Force." Report prepared for the American Jewish Committee, March 1990; for Canada, see Byron G. Spencer, "Child Quality and Female Labor Supply: How Different Are Jewish Women?" (unpublished paper). Canadian Jewish women had a lower labor supply in the 1981 Census, similar to the 1957 CPS pattern.

14. See, e.g., Peter M. Blau and Otis Dudley Duncan, *The American Occupational Structure* (New York: 1967); David Featherman and Robert Hauser, *Opportunity and Change* (New York: 1978); and Albert J. Reiss with Otis Dudley Duncan, Paul K. Hatt and Cecil C. North, *Occupations and Social Status* (New York: 1961).

15. See Reiss, *Occupations and Social Status*, for further detail on the construction of the occupational-prestige scores.

16. See Chiswick, "Skills and Economic Status of American Jewry."

17. This shift has been less intense among non-Jews, as they have experienced a small increase in managerial employment from their previous low level (in contrast to the sharp decline for Jews), along with a less dramatic increase in professional occupations.

18. The Jews are older, have more schooling, are more likely to be currently married and are more likely to live in urban areas outside of the South. Each of these characteristics is associated with higher earnings among both Jews and non-Jews.

19. As a test, what happens if the broad occupational categories—in addition to the other explanatory variables—are held constant in the 1970 Census data? In this case, the Jewish earnings advantage falls to 10 percent. This is not very different from the 7 percent advantage in the 1957 CPS when the group differences in occupational structure are held constant.

20. The lower ratio in the 1957 CPS may arise from the statistical control for occupation, as well as from using medians rather than means if there is a greater "positive skewness" in the distribution of Jewish incomes.

21. In the 1970 Census data, for example, earnings increase by 8.0 percent per year of schooling for Jews and by 6.8 percent for non-Jews.

Investing in Themselves: The Harvard Case and the Origins of the Third American-Jewish Commercial Elite*
Henry L. Feingold

What some have seen as the Jewish penetration of the American economy and others simply an adaption to it occurred in two related patterns, one through business, the other through an enhancement of skills. In the former we can see how Jewish entrepreneurs gravitated toward new, unpreempted areas of the economy where they established new industries. They were as much "courageous enterprisers" in establishing the film industry during the twenties as they were in establishing the fur and Indian trades during the Colonial era.[1]

During the twenties, and to some extent in the decade before, a third strategy developed which played a major role in shaping the economic profile American Jewry would eventually assume. They invested in human capital through formal education and professional training. This was something new in the American Jewish experience. Relatively few members of the preceding Sephardic and German Jewish communities chose higher education as a path to achieve middle class status.[2]

The elevation of skills among Jews during the twenties was symbolized by the "invasion" of higher learning institutions of all kinds by Jewish students.[3] The increase in Jewish enrollment at Harvard was merely its most visible manifestation. Officials of

---

* A version of this article was originally delivered as the Elson Lecture at the 1987 National Conference of the American Jewish Historical Society and was entitled: "The Not-so-Lost Generation: American Jewry in the Twenties."
1 The term "courageous enterprisers" is used by Jacob Marcus to describe the pioneering commercial activity of colonial Jews. See Jacob R. Marcus, *Early American Jewry*, (Philadelphia: 1953), p. 530.
2 John Bodner, *The Transplanted: A History of Immigrants in Urban America* (Bloomington: 1985), p. 196.
3 The rise in Jewish enrollment actually began several years earlier. See Table, "Enrollment of Jewish Students in American Colleges and Universities in 1915–1916," *American Jewish Yearbook (AJYB)*, (5678) 19: 407–408. The term "Jewish invasion" was also employed then. See Nitza Rosovsky, *The Jewish Experience at Harvard and Radcliffe* (Boston: 1986), pp. 6–7. It is a recognizable pattern in the post-emancipation Jewries in the West, especially those of Germany, France and England, where, as in the United States, a disproportionate share of the "invasion" was composed of Jewish students from eastern Europe.

Originally published in *American Jewish History* (June 1988). Reprinted by permission of the American Jewish Historical Society.

Investing in Themselves

universities located near Jewish population concentrations in the large cities spoke of the "Jewish invasion" in alarmed tones. They felt it threatened the established conventions of American higher education, which sought as much to mold behavior as to develop minds. For good reasons Jews felt compelled to challenge that policy. Had it been allowed to stand, the new economic profile taking shape during this decade, which had at its core the enhancement of managerial, academic and other professional skills through university certification, would have been hampered. The significance of the Harvard case, which serves as the anchor of our examination of these developments, goes beyond merely another example of anti-Semitism. It threatened the mobility of the sons and daughters of the eastern European immigrants who were determined to better their position. It warrants a detailed examination.

* * *

The decade between 1919 and 1929 did not begin auspiciously for American Jewry. There was no reason to suspect that although the new immigration laws of 1921 and 1924 did not specifically mention Jews, the authors of the laws were convinced that the nation was about to be flooded by penniless Jews fleeing their war-devastated communities in eastern Europe. It was not much solace that the newly reorganized Ku Klux Klan had added Catholics as well as Jews to its familiar negrophobia. Jews understood that Henry Ford's publication of *The Protocols of the Elders of Zion* went beyond the denial of hotel accommodations at Saratoga Springs and even beyond the lynching of Leo Frank. Ford had, after all, become an American folk hero beloved by millions of ordinary Americans, and he possessed enormous financial resources to promote anti-Semitsm.

Nevertheless, that Jews established themselves economically during the twenties, despite such signs of hostility, is not as paradoxical as it might seem. Adversity, which in this period was coupled with opportunity, may have fueled the immigrant Jew's need for economic security. The twenties was a decade which possessed both. It was a prosperous period marked by the development of a new multiplier industry, the automobile, to replace the railroads and by an increase in productivity from newly developed electric power.[4] The result was a 40% increase in labor

---

[4] Multiplier industries are those which by virtue of their size and business volume stimulate the growth of related industries. They act as economic pump primers. Until World War I the railroad was such an industry, but its influence

productivity and a consequent 11% rise in real income. There would be more leisure time to spend such income as the work week declined by almost two hours. Some, looking at the 5,174 bank failures between 1921 and 1929 and the persistent malaise in the agricultural sector, would note later that it was a false prosperity, but that hardly concerned those who were prospering at the time.[5]

What was distinctive about the economic situation of American Jewry in the 1920s was not its great wealth or power but its configuration, "the curious . . . distribution in particular squares of the checkerboard."[6] Jews tended to congregate in nonpreempted areas of the economy or to pioneer in new ones like the film industry. They were frequently found, according to a *Fortune Magazine* study, where manufacturing and merchandizing converged or in areas like the clothing business where a Jewish presence had already been established.[7] Other such distinctly Jewish business areas were wholesale and retail merchandizing of tobacco products, the distillation and merchandizing of liquor, and auxiliaries of the clothing trade: hatmaking, furs, button retailing, and belts.

Jewish entrepreneurs were of course not exempt from the adverse effects of a rapidly changing economy, especially if they were an established part of the preexisting economic order. There was, for example, a net loss in Jewish banking, which after the death of Jacob Schiff in 1921 rapidly lost its Jewish character. They no longer fulfilled their management and capital needs from within the family and "crowd." With the possible exception of Goldman-Sachs, Jewish investment bankers made a good transition to the more complex regulated investment market of the thirties after the Glass-Steagal law was passed. But as early as 1911 Kuhn Loeb took on a non-Jewish partner, and Goldman-Sachs followed suit in 1915. In 1924 Lehman Brothers was no longer exclusively a family concern. The dejudaizing of the German Jewish banking nexus did not occasion a dechristianizing of non-Jewish banking houses. In 1936 the *Fortune* study reported

---

was on the wane. The automobile industry was a welcome new multiplier in the twenties.

5 Arthur S. Link, *American Epoch* (New York: 1955), pp. 300–306; William E. Leuchtenburg, *The Perils of Prosperity, 1914–1932* (Chicago: 1958), pp. 178–203.

6 Editors of Fortune, *Jews in America* (New York: 1936), p. 15.

7. The clothing business was dominated early by German Jews and continued to be 85 to 95% owned by Jews in the thirties. *Ibid.* p. 7.

that "there are practically no Jewish employees of any kind in the largest commercial banks."[8] August Belmont and Company was dissolved in 1930, and Seligman Company almost completely curtailed direct investment activity in June 1939. Others, like Kuhn Loeb and Lehman Brothers, also curtailed their business during the Depression. By the early twenties much of the German Jewish business establishment was still intact, but it had not kept pace with the expanding economy. By the thirties private investment banking, which had been a major economic asset of the preceding German Jewish community, was no longer in the Jewish arena. There was actually a moderate decline of prominent Jews in the top rungs of the economy. Of the 449 names listed in Henry Klein's *Dynamic America and Those Who Own It*, a popular survey published in 1921, only 33 of the 449 names were Jewish.[9] The Guggenheims were still listed among America's four richest families but no longer actively managed the mines. Well-known Jewish names like Straus, Schiff, Lewisohn, and Rosenwald, however, remained conspicuous in the second tier of fortunes of twenty million and less.[10] There was also some loss in an area where we would least expect it, large-scale retailing. Few of the new chains were Jewish owned, and many small Jewish retailers faced a challenge to remain in business.[11] Even the largest Jewish-owned retailing establishment, Sears Roebuck, fell upon bad times during the recession of 1921 and was only salvaged by the timely action of Julius Rosenwald, who invested a portion of his personal fortune to save the business.[12]

Sometimes anti-Semitic restriction played a role in shaping the Jewish economic profile. Jewish entrepreneurs displayed an uncanny ability to convert a handicap into an advantage. Few Jews were to be found on the boards of directors or in top management of America's major corporations. Yet Jews were not totally un-

---

8 *Ibid.* p.7; Vincent P. Carosso, "A Financial Elite: New York's German Jewish Investment Bankers," *American Jewish Historical Quarterly* (AJHQ) (September, 1976), 84–87.
9 *American Hebrew,* October 14, 1921, p. 597.
10 *Ibid.*
11 I. M. Rubinow, "The Economic and Industrial Status of American Jewry," in the *Proceedings of the National Conference of Jewish Social Service,"* Philadelphia, May 1932, p. 8 (typescript copy in folder "Jews in the United States, Economic Conditions, 1932–1957," Library of American Jewish Committee.)
12 Lawrence P. Bachman, "Julius Rosenwald," *AJHQ* 66 (September 1976), 96–97.

familiar with the manufacturing end of the automobile business.[13] The new industry followed the pattern of American basic industry, employing only three Jews in managerial positions and almost none on the boards of directors. Yet by 1927 Jews were already prominent in the automobile equipment market — tires, mirrors, headlights, etc. — and became conspicuous in the thriving used car market.[14] The business career of John D. Hertz is typical. A Czech Jew who had settled in Chicago, he founded the Yellow Cab Company in 1915, which went on to become number one in public transportation and car rentals.[15] Similarly, there were almost no Jews to be found in the steel industry with the exception of Inland Steel, which had some Jewish managers. But the scrap metal business, by 1924 capitalized at over $300 million, was, according to one study, 90% Jewish owned.[16]

In secondary industries and merchandizing, Jews were represented beyond their proportion of the population. They were making a name for themselves in industries such as real estate development and housing construction, printing, shoe manufacturing, Kosher foods, (based on a specific Jewish market), textile manufacturing, hotel keeping, the new film industry, and the general entertainment business.[17] Fairly early in using newly popular credit buying, Jewish merchants continued to establish large and small department stores, especially in middle-sized cities. Such stores capitalized on the established Jewish merchandizing grid, which had first developed during the Colonial period. In the twenties it was a phenomenon still largely confined to the east: Marshall Fields of Chicago and Prince, Scott and Company were not Jewish, nor were the big chain stores, such as Woolworth and Kress.

The breadth of Jewish *embourgeoisement*, especially through merchandizing, surpassed other groups. Jewish department store

---

13 Henry Citroen, for example, was called the Henry Ford of France. Ande Manners, *Poor Cousins* (New York: 1972), p. 298.
14 *Jews in America*, p. 9.
15 Manners, *Cousins*, 298.
16 *Jews in America*, p. 9. The figure is for 1924 and includes ferrous and nonferrous metals.
17 Rubinow, "Economic and Industrial Status," p. 6. Nathan Reich, "Economic Trends," in *The American Jew: A Composite Portrait*, ed. Oscar Janowsky (New York: 1942), pp. 167-169. The advent of processed foods triggered an expansion in the kosher food industry even while the percentage of kashrut observers decreased. In 1934 in New York City alone kosher food sales, not counting meat and poultry, amounted to $200 million. See Harold P. Gastwirt, *Fraud, Corruption and Holiness* (New York: 1974), pp. 7-9.

Investing in Themselves

ownership, for example, was merely the tip of the iceberg, the visible part of a merchandizing interest which reached into virtually every town in America. In many cases the Jewish merchant preceded the deveopment of the town or hamlet, which was organized around him. During the twenties it was often a successful small business which strengthened the back and shored up the pride of many a second-generation American Jew.[18]

Predictably where a new industry developed whose product consisted of words and images, such as advertising, publishing, radio, and film, the Jewish influence was more prevalent. The use of language and images is after all culturally close to home for Jews. The Jewish impact on the development of commercial radio is an especially interesting example since, together with Jewish influence in the film industry, it became the bugaboo of the anti-Semitic imagination. After the federal government lifted the ban on privately owned radio sets in 1919, the radio industry developed rapidly. By 1922 large scale manufacture of radio sets began and by 1929, 40% of American families owned radios. The first nationwide network, The National Broadcasting System, was organized by the Radio Corporation of America in 1924. The Columbia Broadcasting System followed suit in 1927. In both cases Jews played a prominent entrepreneurial role. But they did not supply the capital to build these networks and the local stations (there were 562 by 1924) which bought their programs, were characterized by a conspicuous absence of Jews.[19] The same was true of the printed media. There was an important Jewish representation in newspapers, for example in ownership of influential papers like the *Washington Post* and the *New York Times* but the large newspaper chains were overwhelmingly non-Jewish.[20] Similarly in the burgeoning advertising business six of the largest 200 agencies were owned by Jews, but few Jews were to be found in non-Jewish agencies and none in the lucrative position of accounts manager. Advertising was resistant to hiring Jews. Agency owners placed a high priority on looking and acting "American." Some Jews did of course "pass," which led to a favorite joke regarding such employees: "He used to be Jewish,

---

18 L. Harris, *Merchant Princes: An Intimate History of Jewish Families Who Built Great Department Stores* (New York: 1979), p. xv. For the negative image of the Jewish petty merchant in the thirties see Judd L. Teller, *Strangers and Natives* (New York: 1968), pp. 147–149.
19 *Jews in America*, p. 11; Link, *American Epoch*, pp. 310–311.
20 *Jews in America*, p. 10.

but he's allright now."[21] In publishing, there were virtually no large Jewish firms before 1915; by 1925 there were seven small, quality Jewish houses.[22] Clearly, when "mind" industries, such as radio and film, had a need for intellectual and entrepreneurial verve, Jews found their way to these new areas of the economy. In that way the film industry, a once marginal storefront business largely in the hands of Jewish nickelodeon owners, became a major business enterprise.[23] But even here it is difficult to detect a Jewish strategy to influence national perception or even a distinct Jewish sensibility, which can sometimes be noted after World War II. Despite the apprehension of anti-Semites, it was the lure of profit rather than the desire to influence public opinion which drew Jews to the "mind" industries.

* * *

Most observers would agree with Nathan Glazer's conclusion that the two decades between 1920 and 1940 served as a "great fulcrum," transforming American Jewry from a proletarianized immigrant group to a middle class one.[24] There is less agreement on whether the primary instrument for this transformation was intense education or small business. By the twenties both were being used simultaneously.[25] In many cases sons of immigrant workers were moving directly to higher education and the professions while the 70,000 new immigrants who arrived between 1921 and 1927 were, as often as not, compelled to start at the bottom of the economic ladder.

We move next to a closer examination of the factors which made up this process out of which grew the third commercial elite

---

21 Daniel Pope and William Toll, "We Tried Harder: Jews in American Advertising," *American Jewish History* (AJH), 72 (September, 1982), 45–46.
22 *Jews in America*, p. 13
23 *Ibid.*, p. 11; Larry May and Elaine May, "Why Jewish Movie Moguls: An Exploration in American Culture," *AJH*, 72 (September, 1982), 6–8. Harry Cohn (Columbia) had been a cobbler, trolley car conductor and vaudevillian; Jesse Lasky in the shoe business; Carl Laemmle (Universal) a clothing salesman; Louis Mayer (MGM) in the junk business; the Warner brothers cobblers and bicycle repairmen; Marcus Loew, the theater chain owner, a factory worker and an owner of nickelodeons; and Samuel Goldwyn a glovemaker.
24 Nathan Glazer, *American Judaism* (Chicago: 1972), p. 81.
25 Selma Berrol argues, for example, that education could not have been a primary mobility instrument for the first generation and for much of the second. The observations in this discussion apply to the twenties, when a change did in fact occur. See Selma Berrol, "Education and Economic Mobility: The Jewish Experience in New York City, 1880–1920," *AJHQ*, (March, 1976), 259–270.

Investing in Themselves

in the American Jewish experience. During the Colonial and early national periods Sephardic Jewry had produced a commercial elite based on ocean commerce, industrial secrets, and enterprises in undeveloped sections of the economy.[26] Similarly, the German Jews of the nineteenth century had produced a commercial elite which evolved primarily from merchandizing and eventually culminated in a Jewish commercial banking nexus popularly known as "our crowd." By the twenties the American economy had undergone considerable change from the openness of the pre-World War I decades. It was more consolidated and mature and broader in scope. To achieve place, the second generation of eastern European Jews had to employ a more varied strategy. This cohort was also numerically larger and more conspicuous than the former and required a broader spectrum of opportunities. Both external and internal factors were involved in its choice of education and certification to achieve middle class rank, eventually effecting thousands of Jewish families.

They climbed from the proletarianization of the immigrant generation to a modern educated urban middle class in barely three decades, one of which was marked by a severe economic depression, and they did so far earlier than other groups of the "new immigration."[27] Often they hardly had time to accustom themselves to their new position. They continued to speak with accents and use the hand gestures with which they were familiar. I mention this fact because we must be aware of the juxtaposition of accelerated mobility with only minimal acculturation to understand the adverse reaction in such institutions as Harvard. By the forties many second-generation Jews bore, in their economic if not social and cultural characteristics, a greater resemblance to the established Protestant groups than they did to their fellow immigrants. The intensive use of formal education and certification allowed them to bypass the roadblocks to which Jews were heir. This was the first group in American Jewish history to use a combination of professional training and traditional business enterprise.

---

26 The term "commercial" or "business" elite is used by Barry Supple to describe the "our crowd" phenomenon. "A Business Elite: German-Jewish Financiers in Nineteenth Century New York," *Business History Review*, 31 (Summer, 1957), 143–178.

27 Glazer and Moynihan, *Melting Pot*, p. lv; Thomas Kessner, *The Golden Door: Italian and Jewish Immigrant Mobility in New York City* (New York: 1977), pp. xi–xvii. See also Jacob Lestchinsky, "The Position of Jews in the Economic Life of America," in *Jews in a Gentile World*, I. Graeber & S.H. Britt, eds. (New York: 1942), pp. 402–416.

American Jewish History

To state that Jews were undergoing professionalization in the 1920's is to oversimplify. During the twenties the classification "professional" was not a precisely defined category since certification had not developed to the extent that we know it today.[28] Comparatively few Jews actually became professional, and it was not really a new phenomenon. Higher training had been occurring all along, even in the first generation. It may be more accurate to observe that in the twenties there occurred a general enhancement of skills through formal education and training and that attainment of professional status represented merely the tip of the iceberg.

How extensive was this movement? One survey based on 36 middle and small-sized cities in 1934 points out that the first phase of the movement between 1920 and 1950 was relatively slow, so that the number of Jews in the professional category varied anywhere from 7.4 to 12%.[29] Those figures are not far different from those for the Jews of Berlin or Vienna or other areas of large Jewish populations. American Jewry was following a typical post-emancipation urban pattern in its occupational distribution.

Since such enhancement involves intense education, we can get a better idea of the extent of it by viewing some figures on school attendance. Here the record is remarkable. Although Jews were less than 3.4% of the general population in 1934, they supplied 10% of the national student population and a far higher percentage in Jewish population centers. Moreover, the higher the educational level the more disproportionate the Jewish presence compared to other ethnic groups.[30] Jews simply attended

---

28 For the complexity of developing professionalism see Barton J. Bledstein, *The Culture of Professionalism: The Middle Class and the Development of Higher Education in America* (New York: 1976).

29 Nathan Goldberg, "Economic Trends Among American Jews," *Jewish Affairs*, (October 1, 1946), pp. 11–14, 17; Nathan Reich, "The Role of Jews in the American Economy," *YIVO Annual*, 5 (1950), 116. Simon Kuznets, "Economic Structure of U.S. Jewry: Recent Trends," (Jerusalem: 1972) (pamphlet in Economic Condition File, American Jewish Committee Library); Lestchinsky, "Position of Jews," pp. 406–410. A 1937 survey of 924,258 wage earners done for the Committee on Economic Adjustment sponsored by the American Jewish Committee gives the 7.4% figure for "professional" and finds that 13.5% were unemployed. See Ronald Bayor, "Italians, Jews and Ethnic Conflict," *International Migration Review*, 4 (Winter, 1972), 380.

30 Barry R. Chiswick, "The Earnings and Human Capital of American Jews," *The Journal of Human Resources*, 17 (Summer, 1983), 313–336. By 1957, 28.5% of Jews had graduated from college as compared to 10% for the general population. Kuznets, "Economic Structure," pp. 5–7. See also Glazer, *American Judaism*, p. 81, and N. Goldberg, "Economic Trends," p. 11.

31 Eli Ginzberg, "Jews in the American Economy: The Dynamics of Opportu-

Investing in Themselves

school longer and were more likely to graduate. In some cases the Depression actually reinforced the stay-in-school phenomenon: in 1935 Jews supplied almost three times as many students as their proportion of the population.

When the welfare state program of the New Deal created a much-expanded federal bureaucracy, newly minted Jewish professionals, lawyers, social workers, and economists were able to find their first positions with the government. Later, when the economy was placed on a war footing, they were again in an ideal position to use their elevated skills.[31] Unemployment in the Jewish community during the Depression did not vary much from that for non-Jews, but it might have been greater given the persistance of restrictive hiring practices and the fact that marginal small businesses, especially in the luxury fur and jewelry trades where Jews concentrated, were severely effected by the Depression. Moreover, employees with higher levels of education were in some measure more quickly reemployed and also were considered to have better potential for retraining.[32] Education paid off in the long run as well. Second generation Jews, according to one study, had a 16% higher earning capacity.[33] Small wonder that they grasped any opportunity for formal higher education.

In truth the Jewish investment in education, in human capital, proved to be a highly profitable one. Education and certification had, according to one researcher, a 20% higher rate of economic return even after controlling for occupation, region and time.[34] Most interesting for those Jews who argued so passionately about the real and imagined differences between Rumanian and Russian Jews or between Galizianer and Litvak is the fact that the Jewish rise in station was across the board. "There [were] no systematic differences among Jews by parent's country of birth," observed one economist.[35]

* * *

Modernizing societies are characterized by the development of

---

nity," in *Jewish Life in America*, Gladys Rosen, ed. (New York: 1978), p. 114; Reich, "Role of Jews," p. 170.

32 Irwin Rosen, "The Economic Position of Jewish Youth," American Jewish Committee Library, Jews in U.S. Economic Conditions, 1932–1936, mimeographed (1936). Barry R. Chiswick and June A. O'Neill, eds., *Human Resources and Income Distribution* (New York: 1977), pp. 91–93, 172–173.

33 Chiswick, "Earnings" pp. 313–314; Lestchinsky, "Position of Jews," pp. 313–314, 414.

34 Chiswick, "Earnings," p. 313.

35 *Ibid*.

Investing in Themselves

institutions of higher learning and formalized processes of certification. In their drive to move up during the twenties second generation Jews were compelled to gain access to these institutions. It is against this backdrop that Harvard's attempt to limit Jewish enrollment in 1922 is best viewed. It gives the historian a prism to understand what the Jewish drive for success in the twenties was all about. It reveals what happens when a mobility instrument, the university, believed by the aspiring group to be accessible because of its liberal philosophy, becomes suddenly unavailable. It can tell us how the custodians of the host university accommodated to the change of having among their students goal-directed, ambitious young Jews whose view of the use of a college experience was markedly at variance with the established culture of the university.

The problem began formally during the summer of 1922 when rumors circulated that Harvard intended to follow the practice already established at Columbia, Syracuse, Princeton, Rutgers and other major eastern universities of limiting Jewish enrollment. These universities had experienced an amazing rise in the registration of Jewish students.[36] By 1920 former bastions of Protestants like Hunter and City College in New York City had student populations which were 80% to 90% Jewish. Located in the city with the largest Jewish population and being free they stood little chance of resisting the flood of Jewish students. Indeed, CCNY would soon become known as "the College of the Circumcised Citizens of New York." Its atmosphere, according to Morris Raphael Cohen, its best known Jewish professor, had little of the gentility associated with American colleges. America had never seen anything like it. "The obvious crudeness of our youth, whose fine idealism had not yet been tempered by hard and cold realities, struck some of my colleagues as the chief evil which the colleges of the country needed to convert," observed Cohen.[37] But the officials of Harvard did not consider it their

---

36 In 1918 Columbia experienced a whopping 40% slightly lower than NYU's 42% which it lowered to 22% in two years by quietly imposing a quota. Syracuse registered 15% and Dartmouth and Princeton, not located near large Jewish population centers, a mere 7% and 9%. Stephen Steinberg, *The Academic Melting Pot: Catholics and Jews in American Higher Education* (New York: 1974), pp. 19–20. The fullest overall account is Marcia G. Synnot, *The Half-Open Door: Discrimination and Admissions at Harvard, Yale, and Princeton: 1900–1970* (Westport: 1979), pp. 11 ff.

37 Morris R. Cohen, *A Dreamer's Journey* (Boston: 1949), p. 151. See also Stephen Steinberg, "How Jewish Quotas Began," *Commentary*, 52 (September, 1971), 67–76.

Investing in Themselves

mission to convert raw Jewish students to civility.

The Jewish "inundation" of Harvard, while less marked, was no less keenly felt. In 1920 its Jewish enrollment was a mere 10%, but a year later it had risen to 15% and by 1922 it stood at 20%. The imminence of quotas at Harvard was known well before President Lowell, unlike the heads of other universities, decided to go public with his scheme to limit the admission of Jewish students. He was doing so, he proclaimed, not only for the protection of Harvard's integrity and character but to prevent the growth of anti-Semitism within the student body. "If their number should become 40% of the student body," he explained in a letter to Alfred Benesch, a prominent Jewish alumnus from Cleveland, "the race feeling would become intense. When on the other hand, the number of Jews was small, the race antagonism was also small."[38] Like Henry Ford, he was surprised at the uproar in the Jewish community. After all, he had not used the subterfuges employed at other large universities faced with a similar problem. Surely the Jews could see the necessity of the new policy.[39] We shall note later that some of them actually did see it Lowell's way.

We need not detail the development of the imbroglio which compelled Lowell to hand the case over to a special committee after the facuty refused to empower the admissions committee charged with implementing the new policy. Three of the faculty members on the committee were Jewish, and they and Julian Mack, the only Jewish member of Harvard's Board of Overseers, thwarted the scheme, at least temporarily. But here we are primarily interested in discovering the reason for American Jewry's intense reaction when in fact Harvard was among the last of the major universities to try to implement such a policy.

It was not Jewish students per se but a new kind of Jewish student which triggered the decision to implement quotas. Harvard experienced little difficulty in absorbing Jewish students before the turn of the century, when the Jewish applicants were primarily from established German Jewish families who in manners, dress and estate were hardly distinguishable from the non-Jewish majority. "But at the turn of the century," observes Samuel Eliot Morison, the historian of Harvard, "the bright Russian Jewish lads from the Boston public schools began to

---

38 Nathan C. Belth, *A Promise to Keep* (New York: 1979), p. 101–102.
39 *Ibid*. Harvard officials were convinced that Jews would agree to self-limitation and were astonished at the attitude of the Menorah group headed by Harry Starr. *American Hebrew*, September 22, 1922, p. 537.

arrive. There were enough of them in 1906 to form the Menorah Society, and in another fifteen years Harvard had her 'Jewish problem.'"[40] Many of them were "tram" students who lived at home. Those who lived on campus were segregated in two dorms, one of which, Walter Hastings Hall, was soon dubbed "little Jerusalem." They arrived with a different purpose from what Thorstein Veblen called the "cultivation of gentility" and the mastery of the "canons of genteel intercourse" preferred by the Protestant establishment.[41] They brought with them a distinctive eastern European Jewish style which took ideas seriously and gave high priority to what observant Jews call "lernen," a close study and mastery of text. When transmuted to modern secular values it came to mean a celebration of scholarship as reflected in academic performance. When a Jewish youth earned the highest marks on a standard battery of tests to measure character and psychic soundness given to entering freshmen, it was sufficient to rate the headline "Jewish Youth Attains Highest Rating in Psychological Tests in Colleges" in the *American Hebrew,* which regularly published scores of the New York State Regents scholarship examination and listed the percentage of Jewish winners.[42]

Lest we overdraw the image of a community drawn exclusively to what contemporary student culture contemptuously calls "nerdism," I hasten to add that such was hardly the case. American Jewish culture gave a high priority to academic achievement but also esteemed athletics. At least part of the complaint against Jewish students related to their supposed unwillingness to enter into the social life of the campus, most of which was dominated by national fraternities. But only some of that social isolation could fairly be attributed to a different set of values. They were as much excluded by others as self-excluded. Most fraternities did not welcome Jews and certainly not Jewish students who returned home or, worse, held jobs after classes.[43] Jewish students did form their own fraternities, but they never became the rage

---

40 Samuel Eliot Morison, *Three Centuries of Harvard* (Boston: 1936), p. 147, cited in Steinberg, *Melting Pot*, p. 5.
41 Steinberg, *Melting Pot*, p. 14. Of Norwegian stock, Veblen had little use for such criteria, but he appreciated the cultural sources of the Jewish academic performance. See "On the Intellectual Preeminence of the Jews," in *Essays in Our Changing Order,* ed. Leon Ardzrooni (New York: 1939). For the historic roots of the Protestant posture see E. Digby Baltzell, *The Protestant Establishment: Aristocracy and Caste in America* (New York: 1964).
42 *American Hebrew*, August 25, 1922, p. 352.
43 *Ibid.*, March 24, 1922, p. 497 (editorial). Jewish students did create their own fraternities, Zeta Beta Tau, Sigma Alpha Mu, Kappa Nu, and Tau Epsilon Phi.

Investing in Themselves

among the children of immigrants. When Harry B. Chambers, New York's Commissioner of the Board of Education, advocated the reinstatement of fraternities in the high schools in the spring of 1922, it created a considerable stir in the Jewish community. The *American Hebrew* opposed it because it interfered with the socialization of Jewish students and "led to self-complacent snobbery," recommending instead organizations like Arista, founded by Dr. William Felter, the Jewish principal of Girls High School in Brooklyn. Arista was "a society open to all who measured up to a high standard of character and scholarship . . . The one is open," Felter observed, "while the other is dark."[44]

Academic achievement was highly rated, but it never stood alone in the emerging Jewish constellation of values. When Vienna's champion Jewish soccer team visited the United States in 1927 a veritable craze of enthusiasm swept the Lower East Side, and when the baseball team of the almost all-Jewish Seward Park High School won the city championship, despite the fact that the team had no field on which to practice, the *American Hebrew* and the Yiddish dailies played the story to the hilt.[45] The names of Jewish students who had earned a letter for athletic performance as well as the records of Jewish boxers and stars in baseball and football were regularly published in the Anglo-Jewish press.

Scholarship also meant more than simply earning good grades, although that was its most obvious manifestation. At Columbia, where one-fifth of the students were Jewish, nearly half the students elected to Phi Beta Kappa in 1922 were Jews. Their preference for mental work was, however, not limited to study. The *Columbia Spectator* became one of the best college newspapers in the country when Jewish students took over editorship, and while the football team may have attracted few Jewish students for scrimmage, acting in a varsity play did. The cultural atmosphere of the university took on a tone of high excitement. Jewish students could generate a full student culture where athletics played merely one part and scholastic achievement was given high priority.[46] Meyer Shapiro, who would become the nation's

---

44 *American Hebrew*, March 24, 1922, p. 497.
45 *Ibid.*, July 8, 1921, p. 193 (editorial) and August 5, 1921, p. 273. See also Judd L. Teller, *Strangers and Natives*, p. 90. When the Hakoah Soccer team, wearing its blue and white colors, played at the Polo Grounds a holiday atmosphere prevailed in Jewish neighborhoods.
46 They didn't do too badly in campus sports either according to a special study made by Zeta Beta Tau, probably in response to the charge that Jewish students didn't go out for athletics. In the 1922 academic year in the 10 major

most distinguished art historian, was a member of the class of 1924; Lionel Trilling, perhaps its most noteworthy literary critic, graduated a year later; and Sidney Hook received his doctorate there in 1927. They were only the tip of the iceberg.[47]

Predictably, the emphasis on academic achievements did little to endear Jewish students to most of their Christian fellow students, who placed great value on learning the social graces which they believed were necessary for the positions they aspired to in business and society. One often notes in the reaction by Harvard students that, whether they admired Jews or despised them, they inevitably were aware of the change of emphasis a Jewish presence on campus caused. At times the reaction was a familiar anti-Semitism, reflected in this ditty popular at Harvard in 1910:

Oh, Harvard's run by millionaires
And Yale is run by booze,
Cornell is run by farmer's sons
Columbia's by Jews.

So give a cheer for Baxter Street
Another one for Pell
And when the little sheenies die,
Their souls will go to hell.[48]

At other times non-Jews felt a direct sense of proprietary loss, as reflected in this reaction of a Harvard undergraduate at the time of the crisis: "The Jews tend to overrun the College, to spoil it for the native born Anglo-Saxon young persons for whom it was built and whom it really wants."[49] Some felt that whether one chose to excel in scholarship or athletics was a matter of choice and neither preference deserved condemnation. "If the Jews have a complex on athletics," noted Professor Richard Cabot, who taught philosophy and ethics at Harvard, "our boys have one on the Phi Beta Kappa Society."[50] There could be no mistaking who he felt "our boys" were. Nor did all agree with Cabot's placement of academic achievement on a par with athletics. Morris R. Cohen quotes a military training instructor at

---

universities, excluding those three which practiced limitation, Jewish students earned 7% of the varsity letters awarded. Interestingly, in the category of honors for publications they earned 15.7%. *American Hebrew*, December 29, 1922, p. 207.

47 Alexander Bloom, *Prodigal Sons: The New York Intellectuals and Their World* (New York: 1986), pp. 29–30.
48 Steinberg, *Melting Pot*, p. 17.
49 William T. Ham, "Harvard Students on the Jewish Question," *American Hebrew*, September 15, 1922, p. 406.
50 *Ibid.*, September 22, 1922, p. 537.

Investing in Themselves

CCNY addressing his captive student audience: "If you want to be a he-man, go in for football, if you want to be a nut like Einstein, stick to the books."[51]

In the classroom the change of atmosphere was palpable. Jews broke the students' solidarity against their professors. Now the moment the professor posed a question there was no longer a stony resisting silence; instead, all the Jewish hands shot up, anxious to respond.[52] Unknowingly, such students violated the taboo against showy scholarship. The response was predictable. "History is full of examples where one race has displaced another by underliving and overworking," observed one student.[53] Another at Columbia School of Medicine noted that he now had to work much harder: "The Jews set the pace. They keep the scholastic standards high and make the rest of us work harder than we have ever worked before in order to keep up with them. Somehow or other they have an emotional intensity which drives them to study longer and harder than the average Christian."[54] Most preferred to attribute the superior performance of Jewish students to overzealousness.

According to the noted drama critic Walter P. Eaton, the problem was not based on the resentment of academic competition but "an instinct for self preservation. . . . In the last few years . . . a class of Jew has grown up, who by his innate cleverness and ambition and will-to-power, has reached our universities, but brings with him little or no cultural background, unpleasantly aggressive manners, and in general, an atmosphere disturbingly at variance with the spirit of the place he enters." Like many others, Eaton did not fear what he called Jewish cleverness. He observed that their mental equipment was actually modest. What he resented was their "rudeness of manners, lack of courtsey . . . and general vulgarity."[55] They did not accommodate to the rules of the college community; instead, they tried to change them. Jewish students were accused of wanting only to take from the university and giving little to it. That on daily walks they passed the Harvard Semitic Museum, donated by Jacob Schiff in 1902 and that Jewish alumni were more than generous to

---

51 Cohen, *Dreamer's Journey*, p. 224.
52 Steinberg, *Melting Pot*, pp. 12–13; Rosovsky, *Harvard and Radcliffe*, p. 7.
53 *Ibid.*, p. 13.
54 *American Hebrew*, September 29, 1922, p. 530.
55 Walter P. Eaton, "Jews in the American Theater," *American Hebrew*, September 22, 1922, p. 464.

their alma mater in which they took extraordinary pride, did not dissuade them.[56] They perceived the presence of an alien culture.

The Jewish perspective on the limitation policy was of course far different. They simply could not agree that it was their coarseness and insufficient standards of personal hygiene that had brought on the problem. Even if there was some truth in such complaints they could hardly serve as the criteria a liberal college like Harvard was bound to follow. Generally, Jews viewed scholastic merit as the most important criterion in university life, a belief in which many non-Jews concurred. That was the view expressed by a columnist in the *Harvard Graduates' Magazine*: "If some one racial group does gather to itself the virtues and excellences, mental and moral, so abundantly as to acquire of right a dominating representation in Harvard University, that right must be accorded it."[57] But most undoubtedly believed that if the possessions of such virtues were applied as standards of admission, Jewish representation would not be dominant, merely present.

Clearly something else was involved which was based on fear and resentment. Harry Starr, President of the Menorah Society and deeply involved in the limitations case, began by believing that the problem stemmed from the dislike of only certain Jews. But he soon learned differently. "We learned that it was *numbers* that mattered; bad or good, *too many* Jews were not liked. Rich or poor, brilliant or dull, polished or crude — *too many Jews*." He concluded that the policy had to be fought and it was up to Jews to remind Harvard of its tradition of complete equality and openness.[58]

That was the position taken by most Jews who refused to accept Lowell's contention that he was favoring limitation to prevent the rise of anti-Semitism at Harvard. They recalled that

---

56 Besides the Schiff donation, the Warburg family gave $200,000 for a new administration building in 1924, and the Lehman, Straus and Sachs families contributed $700,000 for the 1924 fund-raising campaign. *American Hebrew*, June 20, 1924, p. 200 and June 27, 1924, p. 214.
57 *American Hebrew*, October 6, 1922, pp. 551, 564, column, "From a Graduate's Window."
58 Harry Starr, "The Affair at Harvard: What Students Did," *Menorah Journal*, 8 (October, 1922), pp. 264–265. See also Belth, *Promise*, p. 5. Starr had surmised correctly. The figure which Lowell had in mind beyond which Harvard would no longer be able to absorb the "Menorah boys" was 15%. That is what he revealed in his now famous conversation with a Harvard alumnus on Christmas Eve aboard a delayed New York Central train. Victor A. Kramer, "What Lowell Said," *American Hebrew*, January 26, 1923, p. 391.

Investing in Themselves

Lowell had opposed the appointment of Brandeis to the Supreme Court in 1916 and that his advocacy of restrictionism at Harvard had been accompanied by a strong restrictionist position on immigration. But a small minority of "uptown" Jews did see merit in it. "One of the saddest features of the whole matter," wrote Louis Marshall to his brother-in-law Judah Magnes, "lies in the fact that some of our Jewish snobs are openly favoring a limitation which would exclude a large percentage of the Russian Jews who are seeking to get an education at Harvard and other institutions of like rank."[59] Often they were scions of the nineteenth century German-Jewish immigration who shared the notion that Jews were pushing too hard and sending their children to universities fully one generation ahead of the other groups who made up the "new immigration." The result was, according to one Harvard savant, that "there were in fact more dirty Jews and tactless Jews in college than dirty and tactless Italians, Armenians, or Slovaks."[60] A sermon at Temple Emanu-El in New York on September 22, 1922 sought to attribute the onerous characteristics of eagerness for money and material success to European rather than Jewish culture. The alleged "boisterousness and loudness" of Jews only seemed that way in contrast to the English and Americans of native stock, "who are generally cold and undemonstrative."[61] But Walter Lippmann, writing in the *American Hebrew*, was less inclined to make excuses:

> The rich and vulgar and pretentious Jews of our big American cities are perhaps the greatest misfortune that has ever befallen the Jewish people. . . . They undermine the natural liberalism of the American people. . . . I worry about upper Broadway on a Sunday afternoon where everything that is feverish and unventilated in the congestion of a city rises up as a warning that you can not build up a decent civilization among people who have lost their ancient piety and aquired no new convictions, among people who, when they are at last, after centuries of denial, free to go to the land and cleanse their bodies, now huddle together in a steam heated slum.[62]

For Lippmann, himself a Harvard graduate and the son of an established German Jewish family, it was all the fault of the Jews who seemed incapable of "moderate, clean and generous living." But on one point, "the loss of ancient piety," another

---

59 Charles Reznikoff, ed., *Louis Marshall: Champion of Liberty* (Philadelphia: 1945), v. 1, p. 268 (Marshall to J.L. Magnes, August 10, 1922).
60 Steinberg, *Melting Pot*, p. 11.
61 *American Hebrew*, September 22, 1922, p. 515.
62 Walter Lippman, "Public Opinion and the American Jew," *American Hebrew*, April 14, 1922, p. 575.

Harvard alumnus, Maurice Stern, agreed: "It is not the Jew who practices his Judaism who stirs up anti-Semitism, but the Jew who neglects it, besmirches and disgraces it."[63] Professor A. A. Goldenwasser, of the New School for Social Research, thought that Lowell was wrong but at least sincere. That was more than he could say for Nicholas Butler of Columbia and the other presidents of major universities who used subterfuge and concealment to impose such barriers. "Harvard," Goldenwasser insisted, was still the "most open minded," and "President Lowell is the least prejudiced of the heads of great American Universities."[64] Even Benesch, who was among the first Jewish alumni to confront Lowell, admitted in his letter that "Harvard probably has a problem with some of its Jewish students." But he attributed it not to their religion or race but to their poverty, their need to work, and the fact that they simply could not afford to live in the dorms.[65] Although Julian Morgenstern, President of Hebrew Union College, agreed that "noisy and assertive" Jews without an interest in athletics who thought only of earning a diploma were a problem, it was not a Jewish problem but a problem of the unacculturated foreign born. Jews were entering the university prematurely. He was convinced that quotas were not directed against Scandinavian or Italian-Americans because their children were not yet knocking at the university door. It was not a case of anti-Semitism but the problem of "the foreign born, un-American, or not-yet American Jew."[66]

The *American Hebrew,* conscious of the fact that Jewish enrollment in the universities reached well beyond the Jewish proportion of the population and that the universities, after all was said and done, were private institutions which voluntarily assumed a public responsibility, called for building up public colleges as a solution: "The nation . . . must provide the means to offer higher education to all her children who seek it. . . . The day of the state college and city university is dawning. State institutions will become the great depositories of American democracy." It was a prophetic cry.[67]

---

63 Stern was a Harvard graduate, class of 1922. His letter first appeared in Philadelphia's *Jewish Exponent* and then was mentioned in an editorial in the *American Hebrew,* July 28, 1922, p. 258.
64 *American Hebrew*, July 14, 1922, p. 447.
65 *American Hebrew,* June 23, 1922, p. 151.
66 Julian Morgenstern, "American Judaism Faces the Future," *American Hebrew,* September 22, 1922, p. 447.
67 *American Hebrew*, June 9, 1922, p. 109 (editorial). But for the next three years

Investing in Themselves

In fact, Jews like Lippmann were the exception rather than the rule. Jews confronted the Harvard limitations case with remarkable confidence. Marshall, the outspoken leader of the American Jewish Committee, identified Lowell as an "advocate of the higher anti-Semitism" and counseled against allowing him to put the burden on the Jews. "He has created the issue. He has insulted the intelligence of the American people. He has played with fire. . . . He has made his bed. Let him lie in it. We, as Jews, will not admit the soundness of his premises. We must insist upon the equality of right of treatment."[68] Horace Kallen, who learned of pluralism as an undergraduate at Harvard, also perceived that the *numerus clausis* did not stem from a failure of Jewish students but the sense of vulnerability felt by non-Jews when faced with the phenomenon of an ambitious minority anxious for place. "It is not the failure of the Jews to be assimilated into undergraduate society which troubles them," he wrote to a friend. "They do not want Jews to be assimilated. . . . What troubles them is the completeness with which Jews want to be and have been assimilated."[69]

Kallen may have gone too far. Student life at City College, where Jewish students were the majority in the twenties, as described by Morris Cohen and others, was distinctively different. It was characterized by a rough give-and-take at odds with the genteel intercourse of the Ivy League colleges. Even today discourse among the New York intellectuals, now three and four generations removed, is known for its passionate no-quarter-given quality.[70]

The Harvard case was special because of what it symbolized. That is why Jews made such a fuss about it while ignoring the

---

the idea of a Hebrew university, which had gained some support as a result of the Harvard affair, was rejected by the *American Hebrew* as an undesirable form of self-segregation. See, for example, the editorials of December 15, 1922, p. 163 and March 9, 1923, p. 521.

68 Reznikoff, *Marshall*, v. 1, p. 267 (Marshall to A. C. Ratshesky, June 17, 1922).
69 Steinberg, *Melting Pot*, p. 28
70 The work which captures the flavor of Jewish student life most completely is Cohen, *Dreamer's Journey*. See also Irving Howe, "The New York Intellectuals," in *Decline of the New* (New York: 1970) and *World of Our Fathers* (New York: 1976), pp. 280–286. Of the NYU downtown campus one observer noted "quickness of speech," casualness of dress, little interest in athletics and general extracurricular activities and little of the spirit generally associated with student life. See Felix Morrow, "Higher Learning on Washington Square: Some Notes on New York University," *The Menorah Journal*, (April, 1930), 346–357.

imposition of quotas at other universities. It was not only that arriviste Jewish students had a penchant for scholarship. From an immigrant Jewish perspective the intellectual atmosphere at Harvard may have appeared strange and cold; it was certainly a far cry from the exciting give-and-take which characterized Jewish intellectual discourse. Harvard aspired to being more than merely a finishing school for the well-born; its goal was to train an aristocracy based on ability, and that endeared it to Jews. If Harvard closed its doors that would serve as a signal for other American educational institutions to limit Jewish access. Had that occurred the Jews' rapid climb out of the working and lower middle class of their immigrant parents would have become more difficult. "Harvard is injecting into American College life an insiduous poison which may not be eliminated in decades," cried the *American Hebrew*.[71] Yet it had not raised a similar alarm over NYU's or Columbia's quotas because, as respected as these institutions were, they did not establish the norms for other institutions to follow. The second generation, concerned about establishing itself, understood that accessibility had something to do with keeping Harvard's doors open. They saw it in American terms. Limitation would be nothing less than "treason to America" because access to talent "is the American Ideal! . . . That has been a beacon of light to the Jews and the oppressed of all lands."[72] The victory, one newspaper editorial observed, "will carry its influence far beyond Cambridge. Like the shot first heard at Concord bridge it will be heard round the world."[73]

The solution imposed on Lowell was paradoxical. When the faculty committee reported back 10 months later it rejected the idea of quotas as running counter to Harvard's tradition of "equal opportunity for all regardless of race and religion." It fully supported the Jewish view that merit and academic achievement were the crucial criteria for admission to the University. It even ruled out "any novel process of screening which could be construed as a covert device" to limit enrollment of qualified students.[74] On the surface that meant that Jews had won their battle.

---

71 September 29, 1922, p. 529 (editorial).
72 James G. Heller, "Americanizing Our Universities," *American Hebrew*, October 10, 1922, p. 636.
73 *American Hebrew*, April 20, 1923, p. 745 (editorial).
74 The concern about "covert devices" undoubtly referred to the admissions application, which requested information on race, religion and family background and then inquired if there had been a family change of name. See *American Hebrew* editorials September 29, 1922, p. 529, and April 13, 1923, p. 744. See also Rosovsky, *Harvard and Radcliffe*, p. 20

Investing in Themselves

Harvard would remain in the ranks of the liberal universities. But the report also recommended that Harvard seek "a wider regional representation" through the "highest seventh" plan, which would encourage preparatory schools located west of the Mississippi to send capable students to Harvard.[75] At the same time the number of available spaces in the freshman class was limited to 1000. That proved sufficient to reduce the Jewish student population to 10% by 1931.[76] In a sense those favoring limitation had won after all. But nine years later James Conant redefined Harvard's mission along the lines of academic merit insisted upon by Jews all along. The proportion of Jews then rose to 25%.

* * *

From a Jewish perspective, the twenties served as the staging period for the remarkable achievement of contemporary American Jewry, which began in earnest after the interruption of the Depression and World War II. The extraordinary economic mobility of Jews has drawn the interest of historians. The decade of the twenties contains clues to the strategy Jews employed to achieve place. I have suggested here that it was achieved through a linkage of traditional small business activity and the enhancement of the skills of a portion of the second generation cohort. At the pinnacle of that enhancement was professionalization. In the post-World War II period the linkage of "shoe string capitalism" with skill enhancement produced American Jewry's third commercial elite, the one Daniel Moynihan and Nathan Glazer have called "egghead millionaires."[77] These were Jews who made their fortunes by the use of a professional or academic skill in combination with the traditional penchant for small business. In a word, rather than clothing or scrap metal, they sold their enhanced skill on the free market.

From a Jewish perspective what was different about the twenties was that Jews began to invest in themselves. They invested in

---

75 *American Hebrew*, April 13, 1923, p. 744; Synnot, *Half-Open Door*, p. 96 ff.
76 Rosovsky, *Harvard and Radcliffe*, p. 23; Belth, *Promise*, p. 108 ff.
77 The term "shoe string capitalism" was employed by Burton J. Hendricks in a series of anti-Semitic articles published in *World's Work* in December 1922 and January 1923. It is quoted in Max J. Kohler, "Reply to an Insidious Attack," *American Hebrew*, March 9, 1923, p. 522. Originally the term "egghead millionaires" referred to those Jews who started businesses in electronics and other highly technical areas where professional training was required. It was first used in "The Egghead Millionaires," *Fortune* (September, 1960), p. 172, ff. and then picked up by Nathan Glazer and Daniel P. Moynihan, *Beyond the Melting Pot* (Cambridge: 1963), p. 155.

human capital. Increased education and skills gave them better access to an increasingly complex economy which required such skills. While few Jews could be found in managerial positions in basic industries like transportation, mining or steel during the twenties, their presence increased in the newly established research laboratories and legal departments of major American corporations.[78] By the thirties Jews could also be found in the creative departments of the full service advertising agencies as the experts in marketing surveys, motivational research and the psychology of consumption. In the film industry Jewish movie moguls, who ultimately had to turn to Wall Street for financing, turned to Jews for screenwriting, adaptation of story lines, and sometimes for stars too. Jews could be increasingly found in the research and development departments of industry. The possession of some special skill — writing, script editing, accounting, design, research, engineering or legal knowledge — was becoming the ticket to finding place in industry, the expanding government bureaucracy, and the not-for-profit sector of the economy. Such skills were taught in professional and graduate schools and required certification or licensing. Hence the movement by Jewish young people to enroll in such schools.

When a major university like Harvard, recognized by all as playing a principal role in establishing the conventions of American society, threatened to curtail that development by limiting the enrollment of Jewish students, they resisted. Why there was such concern regarding Harvard's admission policy when other major universities subject to the "Jewish invasion" had earlier followed the same policy in more drastic and insidious form and aroused little outcry should not be a source of puzzlement. One major factor was the realization that what Harvard did would serve as a signal to universities that limitation of Jews was acceptable policy. We can also observe that the distaste for Jewish students focused on the ambitious sons of the eastern immigrants who, like all arrivistes, were more concerned with goals than with learning the social mores of the children of the well-to-do, including occasional descendants of established "uptown" Jewish families. The conflict was not only over the number of Jewish students

---

[78] Industrial research was formalized by the establishment of the Mellon Institute of Industrial Research in 1913. Three years later The National Academy of Science established the National Research Council. By 1927, 999 corporations were involved in either independent or cooperative research for product and cost improvement; Link, *American Epoch*, p. 306.

Investing in Themselves

at Harvard. Far more Jews were attending CCNY and NYU. It was about what the public announcement of such a policy meant. That is why the resolution of the Harvard case is so remarkable. Publicly the policy of limitation was rejected, but the enrollment of Jews was nevertheless limited by other, less public means. That, for the moment, served the needs of both sides.

In a sense the Harvard case marks the last stand of a social order which held that the right to station should be determined not by merit but by behavior and birth. Had it prevailed the impact would ultimately have been felt beyond the American Jewish community. It would have hampered the development of those crucial elites without which no modern complex society can function. During the twenties a generation of Jews, arguing the virtues of the merit system, was preparing itself to become part of those elites. There was of course an element of group self-interest in advocating open access based on academic merit. It would facilitate their climb to the highest rungs of the economic ladder. Yet by assuring a flow of competent professionals it also served the nation. The struggle against quotas at Harvard may have been one of those rare instances in history where doing good and doing well coincided.

The Impact of Feminism on American Jewish Life

by SYLVIA BARACK FISHMAN

Introduction

THE LIVES OF JEWS in the United States—like the lives of most Americans—have been radically transformed by 20 years of feminism. Some of these changes have been effected by the larger feminist movement and some by a specifically Jewish feminist effort. Thus, while many feminist celebrities, such as Betty Friedan and Bella Abzug, are Jews, the focus of their feminism has not been specifically Jewish in nature; they have profoundly changed the behavior and attitudes of American Jews as Americans and not as Jews. Pioneers of the contemporary Jewish feminist movement, on the other hand—women such as Rachel Adler, Paula Hyman, and Aviva Cantor—are primarily recognizable within the Jewish sphere. They and many other Jewish feminists have significantly altered the character of Jewish religious, intellectual, cultural, and communal life in the United States.

In the stormy late 1960s and early 1970s, when the rising stars of contemporary American feminism were publicly denounced from synagogue pulpits as aberrant and destructive, feminist attitudes and goals seemed revolutionary. Today, however, many general feminist and Jewish feminist attitudes and goals have been absorbed and domesticated within the public lives of mainstream American Jewry. Female rabbis and cantors have been trained, ordained, and graduated from Reform, Reconstructionist, and now Conservative seminaries, and are becoming accepted as part of the American Jewish religious scene. Life-cycle events for females, such as the *"Shalom Bat"* and Bat Mitzvah ceremonies, are commonplace. Women's organizations which a short time ago expressed ambivalence about the impact of feminism on their ranks now officially espouse feminist goals.[1]

---

[1] The Women's Division of the Council of Jewish Federations, for example, a group which seems to epitomize commitment to establishment values and communal survival, featured a number of feminist figures at its 1987 General Assembly in Miami. Enthusiastically calling themselves "feminists," officers of the Women's Division gave a platform to Amira Dotan, an Israeli female brigadier general; Alice Shalvi, founder of the Israel Women's Network; Susan Weidman Schneider, editor of *Lilith* magazine; and other highly identified feminists.

Originally published in *American Jewish Year Book* (1989). Reprinted by permission of the *American Jewish Year Book*.

In their private lives as well, American Jews demonstrate the impact of feminism. American Jewish women, historically a highly educated group, are even more highly educated today. Moreover, their educational achievements are by and large directed into occupational goals, rather than following the open-ended liberal arts and sciences mode that typified female higher education in the 1950s and 1960s. Partially because they are pursuing educational and career objectives, American Jewish women today marry later and bear children later than they did 25 years ago, and they are far more likely than married Jewish women in the past to continue working outside the home after they marry and bear children. The late-forming, dual-career family has become the norm in many American Jewish communities.

At the same time that feminism has become a mainstream phenomenon, important feminists have pulled back from the radicalism of their original positions. Most celebrated, perhaps, is Betty Friedan, who in *The Second Stage*[2] reevaluated family and voluntaristic activity as desirable goals for women. Many feminists have responded to the anti-Jewish bias of some strands of feminism not only with articulate denunciations but also with personal rediscovery of, and commitment to, more intensive Jewish experience, as Letty Cottin Pogrebin, editor of *Ms.* magazine testifies.[3] A number of recent appealing novels about strong, intelligent, accomplished—and yet passionate and vulnerable—Jewish women have also helped to deradicalize the face of Jewish feminism. Indeed, left-wing militant feminists have angrily denounced this mainstreaming of feminism with the claim that bourgeois hierarchies have coopted the movement.

The gap between establishment American Judaism and contemporary American feminism seems to have narrowed. A quasi-feminist stance appears to be *de rigueur* in large parts of the American Jewish community. However, the extent of substantive influence exerted by both general and Jewish feminism on American Jewish communal, organizational, religious, and familial life has yet to be examined. It is the purpose of this article to survey the impact of both types of feminism on key spheres of American Jewish life.

It is important to note at the outset that neither general nor Jewish feminism was created in a vacuum and neither exerts its influence in a vacuum; factors other than feminism have also been at work in effecting transformations. Feminist emphasis on career achievement and individual fulfillment is part of a general cultural focus on the individual, rather than on familial or communal values. Feminist critiques of religious texts, in-

---

[2]Betty Friedan, *The Second Stage* (New York, 1981).
[3]Letty Cottin Pogrebin, "Anti-Semitism in the Women's Movement: A Jewish Feminist's Disturbing Account," *Ms.*, June 1982, pp. 145–49.

cluding Jewish feminist critiques, are an outgrowth of earlier historical, political, economic, and psychological critiques of those texts by biblical and rabbinic scholars. Jewish feminist attempts to create new rituals and new prayers surely have been encouraged by the countercultural, hands-on approach to religious experience epitomized by the successive *Jewish Catalogs*, three compendia of "how-to" information about Judaism and Jewish living. Jewish feminist efforts to change Jewish law reflect a religious environment in which, except for traditional Conservative and Orthodox Jews—a small minority among Jews in the United States—Jewish legal systems are not regarded as sacred and immutable. Feminist attacks on voluntarism take place in a context in which the great majority of both men and women are disinclined to volunteer. Thus, while general and Jewish feminism have certainly contributed to the transformation of certain Jewish societal norms and values, they have done so as part of a larger constellation of cultural patterns. Therefore, this article will briefly indicate, where appropriate, additional movements and trends contributing to alterations on the American Jewish scene that are sometimes wrongly ascribed to feminism alone.

The primary focus in this article will be a discussion and assessment of the impact of both general American and Jewish feminism on demographic, religious, and organizational spheres of American Jewish life. Source materials used for these sections include: statistical data from population studies of several Jewish communities; published and unpublished studies on particular segments of the Jewish population; analytical works (both books and journal articles) that explore relevant aspects of American Jewish life; and articles in the popular press.[4]

In order to analyze the impact of feminism, feminist attitudes and goals must first be defined. We therefore begin with a brief review of the framework of contemporary American feminism and Jewish feminism.

---

[4]Much of the information in this study, both statistical data and literature, was gathered under the auspices of the Cohen Center for Modern Jewish Studies at Brandeis University. The author gratefully acknowledges both the Center facilities and the assistance of colleagues. The archival resources of the Center, made available through Prof. Marshall Sklare, were invaluable. Lawrence Sternberg, Center associate director, Prof. Gary Tobin, Center director, and Sylvia Fuks Fried, assistant director of Brandeis's Tauber Institute for the Study of European Jewry, reviewed the manuscript and made helpful suggestions; Dr. Mordecai Rimor, research associate, Gabriel Berger, research fellow, and Miriam Hertz, graduate student, helped gather statistical data; Dr. Paula Rhodes served as a student research assistant; and Sylvia Riese expedited the preparation of the manuscript. I am also grateful to several feminists and scholars whose generous assistance in discussing issues in this study was invaluable: Arlene Agus, Prof. Louis Dickstein, Rosalie Katchen, Prof. Debra Renee Kaufman, Prof. Egon Mayer, Prof. Jonathan Sarna, Prof. Nahum Sarna, Rabbi Sanford Seltzer, and Prof. Ellen Umansky.

CONTEMPORARY FEMINISM

The American Feminist Movement

Contemporary American feminism was born in an environment that nurtured utopian movements. Aiming to correct discrimination against women in both public and private realms, this feminism grew out of other protest movements in the 1960s: the civil rights movement, the antiwar movement, and the general antiestablishment, antimaterialistic spirit of the age. However, feminism was a reaction to, as well as an outgrowth of, other protest movements. Disillusioned with the misogyny rampant among many male leaders of the protest movements, women protest participants came to the conclusion that they too were an oppressed group, perhaps the most universally oppressed group of all.

Betty Friedan's *The Feminine Mystique*[5] became an early bible of the movement. Friedan's book faulted the American dream, which posited that every woman's ideal fulfillment came in the form of a nuclear family in the suburbs: working father, homemaker mother, several children, perhaps a pet or two, in a single-family house (complete with appliances) in a green residential area with a station wagon in the driveway. Such a life-style, charged Friedan, trapped women in a gilded but deadly cage in which they became unpaid household workers and chauffeurs, cut off from meaningful work, intellectual stimulation, and personal development.

Friedan argued that the "feminine mystique" was based on the assumption that women were emotionally and intellectually unsuited for the brutal environment of labor-force participation and independent life. Even when they studied in universities, women were geared toward personal refinements rather than career preparation. Deprived of occupational skills and confidence in their ability to live independently, Friedan suggested, women evaluated themselves primarily in terms of their physical beauty and their housekeeping and hostessing skills. Removed from the graduated evaluations of the marketplace, they measured themselves against a standard of absolute perfection, and always came up lacking. Thus, rather than insuring women a life of fulfillment and serenity, the "feminine mystique" guaranteed women a life of emptiness and frustration. Furthermore, the seemingly idyllic, normative American family unit could be disrupted without warning, through death or divorce, leaving the bereaved wife without necessary occupational skills and without the confidence to face the world as an independent adult.

For many feminists, the family—long women's *raison d'être*—became

---

[5]Betty Friedan, *The Feminine Mystique* (New York, 1963; 20th anniversary ed., 1983).

the enemy. The patriarchal family was pictured as a repressive cultural institution which served to restrict women to the domestic domain. As Gloria Steinem explained, the "demystified" origin and purpose of marriage was "to restrict the freedom of the mother—at least long enough to determine paternity." Men promoted religious and societal restrictions of female sexuality so that they might control "the most basic means of production—the means of reproduction."[6] Shulamith Firestone found even gestation and childbirth a barbarous process that served no useful purpose except to enslave women.[7]

Numerous articles and books explored contemporary feminist issues. A wide variety of organizational subgroups formed, with the purpose of translating feminist insights into social change. The largest, the National Organization of Women (NOW), concentrated on economic issues, such as promoting legislation to prevent discrimination against women in the marketplace through the Equal Rights Amendment (ERA). Other groups, such as Women Against Pornography, called attention to, and actively opposed, pornographic literature and films, which they characterized as hostile to women; they worked to reduce rape and other overt violence against women, sponsoring marches to "Take Back the Night." Smaller, more extreme groups, such as the Society for Cutting Up Men (SCUM) and No More Nice Girls, were openly antimale, recommending either independent or lesbian life-styles. Together, these feminist groups comprised a movement devoted to nothing less than the radical transformation of the position of women in the United States.

Jewish Feminism

In the late 1960s and early 1970s, a feminist movement with a specifically Jewish focus became distinct from generalized feminism. Jewish women began to examine the inequities and forms of oppression in Jewish life and, at the same time, to explore Judaism as a culture and religion from a feminist perspective. The critique of Judaism came from various quarters and focused on a range of issues. Some of these actually paralleled the broader feminist agenda; others addressed specific Jewish concerns. In the former category were attacks on Judaism for its part in relegating women to inferior status and to narrowly prescribed roles, at home and in the wider world. These attacks were often voiced by early activists in the general feminist movement, who also happened to be Jews. Thus, Vivian Gornick,

---

[6]Gloria Steinem, "Humanism and the Second Wave of Feminism," *The Humanist*, May/June 1987, pp. 11–15, 49.
[7]Shulamith Firestone, *The Dialectic of Sex* (New York, 1971).

in an article entitled "Woman as Outsider," characterized traditional Jewish relationships between the sexes as hateful and repressive, in a description that was fairly representative of certain strands within feminist thought:

> In the fierce unjoyousness of Hebraism, especially, woman is a living symbol of the obstacles God puts in man's way as man strives to make himself more godly and less manly. . . . These structures are not a thing of some barbaric past, they are a living part of the detail of many contemporary lives. Today, on the Lower East Side of New York, the streets are filled with darkly brooding men whose eyes are averted from the faces of passing women, and who walk three feet ahead of their bewigged and silent wives. If a woman should enter a rabbinical study on Grand Street today, her direct gaze would be met by lowered eyelids; she would stand before the holy man, the seeker of wisdom, the worshipper of the spirit, and she would have to say to herself:
>
> Why, in this room I am a pariah, a Yahoo. If the rabbi should but look upon my face, vile hot desire would enter his being and endanger the salvation of his sacred soul. . . . So he has made a bargain with God and constructed a religion in which I am all matter and *he* is all spirit. I am (yet!) the human sacrifice offered up for his salvation.[8]

Jewish family values were denounced, with the family depicted as a woman's prison, echoing views expressed in the general feminist movement. Jewish communal attitudes came under attack as well. The female volunteer, in particular, was denigrated as a mere pawn, an unpaid slave laborer who made it possible for paid male organizational employees to achieve their goals.[9] Not only did male communal professionals exploit the labor of female volunteers, feminists charged, but even male volunteers were culpable: male, but not female, volunteers had the opportunity to rise through the ranks to decision-making positions of prestige and power, while women were contained in low-ranking, powerless organizational ghettos.[10] Furthermore, those women who did enter Jewish communal work professionally were kept in the most subordinate, least lucrative slots, while male Jewish communal professionals rose into executive posts.

The religious realm gave rise to a number of specifically Jewish issues. Jewish divorce law, for example, and women's role in communal worship were two that received wide public attention. To Jewish feminists, they exemplified women's unequal status and cried out for immediate correction. Involvement with these pressing matters was accompanied by, and some-

---

[8]Vivian Gornick, "Woman as Outsider," *Women in Sexist Society: Studies in Power and Powerlessness*, ed. Vivian Gornick and Barbara K. Moran (New York, 1971), pp. 70–84.

[9]See, for example, Doris B. Gold, "Women and Voluntarism," in Gornick and Moran, eds., *Women in Sexist Society*, pp. 384–400; Paula Hyman, "The Volunteer Organizations: Vanguard or Rear Guard?" *Lilith*, no. 5, 1978, pp. 17–22; and Amy Stone, "The Locked Cabinet," *Lilith*, no. 2, Winter 1976–77, pp. 17–21.

[10]Aviva Cantor, "The Missing Ingredients—Power and Influence in the Jewish Community," *Present Tense*, Spring 1984, pp. 8–12.

times evolved into, deeper and broader consideration of women's place in Jewish history, law, and culture, past and present.

The growth of the Jewish feminist movement was aided by certain developments in the broader society.

The period of the late 1960s and early 1970s was one in which Jewish consciousness and pride were at a high in certain circles—particularly on college campuses—and in which challenges to authority were the norm among American middle-class young adults, especially among Jewish youth. Educated young Jews were actively exploring and challenging their heritage—but Jewish women found that their particular concerns were not being adequately addressed. Articles began to appear by women who were fluent in Jewish source materials, addressing specifically Jewish problems from a feminist perspective. Two early articles that sparked Jewish feminist thought were Trude Weiss-Rosmarin's "The Unfreedom of Jewish Women,"[11] which focused on the "unfairness of Jewish marriage laws to divorced and abandoned women," and Rachel Adler's "The Jew Who Wasn't There,"[12] which contrasted male and female models of traditional Jewish piety. Adler's article appeared in a special issue of *Davka* magazine—a counterculture publication—that included a variety of feminist articles.

By late 1971, Jewish women's prayer and study groups were being formed. Women from the New York Havurah (one of the new coed, communal worship-and-study groups that developed on college campuses) joined together with like-minded friends to explore the status of women in Jewish law. Eventually this group evolved into Ezrat Nashim (a double-entendre that refers to the area in the synagogue traditionally reserved for women but that also means, literally, "the help of women"), a particularly influential, albeit small, organization. Committed to equality for women within Judaism, Ezrat Nashim comprised primarily Conservative women, many of whom had attended the Hebrew-speaking Conservative Ramah camps. Their appearance at the convention of the Conservative Rabbinical Assembly in 1972—the same year that the Reform movement voted to admit women to its rabbinical program—was an important initiating step in the process of influencing Conservative leaders to consider admitting women to the Conservative rabbinical program.[13] Jewish feminism went from a small, localized effort to a broader, more diverse operation at the first national Jewish women's conference in 1973, organized by the North Amer-

---

[11]Trude Weiss-Rosmarin, "The Unfreedom of Jewish Women," *Jewish Spectator,* Oct. 1970, pp. 2–6.
[12]Rachel Adler, "The Jew Who Wasn't There," *Davka*, Summer 1971, pp. 6–11.
[13]Steven Martin Cohen, "American Jewish Feminism: A Study in Conflicts and Compromises," *American Behavioral Scientist,* Mar.-Apr. 1980, pp. 519–58.

ican Jewish Students' Network. Drawing more than 500 women of varied educational levels and religious backgrounds from throughout North America, the conference spawned new groups, regional and local conferences, and a National Women's Speakers' Bureau.[14]

The ideas and issues percolating within the formative Jewish feminist movement were published and widely circulated in a special issue of *Response* magazine, called *The Jewish Woman: An Anthology*.[15] Edited by Elizabeth Koltun, the 192-page issue included 30 articles and a bibliography. Many of the authors contributing to this issue became key figures in Jewish feminism: Judith Hauptman (Talmud), Paula Hyman and Judith Plaskow Goldenberg (women in rabbinic literature and law), Martha Ackelsberg (religious and social change), Aviva Cantor Zuckoff and Jacqueline K. Levine (communal issues), Marcia Falk (biblical poetics), Charlotte Baum (American Jewish history), Rachel Adler (women in Jewish law and culture), and others. The work was later revised for book publication by Schocken Books, and included additional articles by other Jewish feminist thinkers, among them Arlene Agus (women's rituals), Blu Greenberg (feminist exploration within a traditional context), and Sonya Michel (American Jewish literature).[16]

A second National Conference on Jewish Women and Men in 1974 also drew hundreds of participants and gave birth to the Jewish Feminist Organization (JFO), which was committed to promoting the equality of Jewish women in all areas of Jewish life. The JFO survived only a short time, however, and was succeeded by a more limited New York Jewish Women's Center, which was active from approximately 1975 to 1977.

The autumn of 1974 also saw the publication of a special issue of *Conservative Judaism*, which explored topics connected to "Women and Change in Jewish Law." Among the articles was one that became a hallmark of Jewish antifeminism. In it, psychiatrist Mortimer Ostow characterized Jewish feminism as an attempt to obliterate "the visible differences between men and women" and a possible encouragement of "trans-sexual fantasies." Even if this were not a conscious or unconscious aim of Jewish feminists, Ostow warned, the end result of fully empowering women within public Judaism would be to emasculate Jewish men, producing a society where women dominated the synagogue but suffered frustration in the bedroom as a result.[17] Ostow's article evoked a flood of profeminist responses from

---

[14]Martha Ackelsberg, "Introduction," in *The Jewish Woman: An Anthology*, ed. Elizabeth Koltun, special issue of *Response* magazine, 1973, pp. 7–9.
[15]Ibid.
[16]Elizabeth Koltun, ed., *The Jewish Woman: New Perspectives* (New York, 1976).
[17]Mortimer Ostow, "Women and Change in Jewish Law," *Conservative Judaism,* Fall 1974, pp. 5–12.

both men and women, which were gathered together in a second special issue of *Conservative Judaism*, titled "Women and Change in Jewish Law: Responses to the Fall 1974 Symposium." In a detailed statement leading off the collection, Arthur Green answered Ostow's objections to Jewish feminism point by point, noting that "the gentleness of a loving mother-God might serve as a good counter-balance to the sometimes overbearing austerity of God as father, king and judge. Mother Rachel, Mother Zion, and widowed Jerusalem have done much to add to the warmth of our spiritual heritage."[18]

Although Reform Judaism had no theological barriers to the ordination of women, it was not until 1972 that the first female Reform rabbi, Sally Priesand, was ordained. It would be another decade before the first female Conservative rabbi, Amy Eilberg, would be ordained at the Jewish Theological Seminary (in 1985) and two women would be named to tenured positions in Judaica: Paula Hyman to a chair in Jewish Studies at Yale, and Judith Hauptman as associate professor of Talmud at JTS (both in 1986).

The development and growth of Jewish feminism in the interim have been documented in a variety of publications. One striking piece of evidence for the legitimation of Jewish feminism by the Jewish intellectual and organization establishments was the appearance in the 1977 *American Jewish Year Book* of a special article, "The Movement for Equal Rights for Women in American Jewry." In this piece, Anne Lapidus Lerner captured the atmosphere of hopeful ferment that pervaded many Jewish religious and communal arenas.

A unique product of Jewish feminism is a glossy magazine, *Lilith*, which was created to explore religious, political, communal, and personal aspects of Jewish life through the eyes of Jewish feminism. The premier issue, published in 1976, featured a photograph of a woman wearing *tefillin* and an interview with Betty Friedan. Although *Lilith*, which operates on a shoestring, has appeared on a somewhat irregular basis, each issue has a wide readership, especially among highly identified Jewish women. In addition, many books and anthologies have gathered and disseminated Jewish feminist thought. Among the most comprehensive, Baum, Hyman, and Michel's *The Jewish Woman in America* [19] utilizes historical, sociological, and literary sources to trace the odyssey of Jewish women in American Jewish life. Susannah Heschel's anthology *On Being a Jewish Feminist*[20] explores and updates these issues, with a special emphasis on "creating a

---

[18] Arthur Green, "Women and Change in Jewish Law: Responses to the Fall 1974 Symposium," *Conservative Judaism*, Spring 1975, pp. 35–56.
[19] Charlotte Baum, Paula Hyman, and Sonya Michel, *The Jewish Woman in America* (New York, 1976).
[20] Susannah Heschel, ed., *On Being a Jewish Feminist: A Reader* (New York, 1983).

feminist theology of Judaism." The Biblio Press has published several extensive bibliographies listing materials relating to Jewish feminism,[21] and Susan Weidman Schneider, editor of *Lilith*, compiled a broad-based practical compendium of Jewish feminist resource materials, including hundreds of names and addresses, as well as useful summaries and discussions, in *Jewish and Female*.[22]

The growth of Jewish feminism was helped, ironically, by the presence of anti-Semitism within the ranks of the general feminist movement. The anti-Semitism emerged on several fronts. The first was political and came as a tidal wave of anti-Israel criticism at a series of international women's conferences. Listening with horror to the repeated condemnation of "Zionist oppression," Jewish participants learned that even among women they could feel like outsiders.[23]

On the religious front, some Christian feminist theologians asserted that Christianity had been ruined by Judaism, with Jewish patriarchalism sullying what would otherwise have been a purely egalitarian Christianity. Just as Protestant thinkers once blamed the Old Testament for infusing values of vengeance and carnality into Christianity, feminist theologians managed to ascribe the strikingly misogynist and antisexual attitudes of some of the Gospels to "a concession to Judaism" or "an unavoidable contamination" by "the sexism of first century Palestinian Judaism." Consequently, Jewish feminist scholars sometimes felt chastened in their approach to classical Jewish texts, in the apprehension that their critiques might "be misunderstood or even misappropriated as providing further proof to Christian feminists for their negation of Judaism."[24]

A third form of anti-Semitism sought to deny Jewish women their own sense of group identity. A professor of American history and women's studies recalls that at a conference on women's issues, which included talks on the black female experience, the Hispanic female experience, and the Irish Catholic female experience, the conference organizer insisted, "Jewish women are just white middle class women. There is nothing that differentiates them from the ruling majority. There is no reason to treat them as a specialized minority or to devoté any of our time to their particular experi-

---

[21]Biblio Press, Fresh Meadows, New York.

[22]Susan Weidman Schneider, *Jewish and Female: Choices and Changes in Our Lives Today* (New York, 1984).

[23]See, for example, Friedan, *The Second Stage*, pp. 162–66; Pogrebin, "Anti-Semitism in the Women's Movement"; and Annette Daum, "Anti-Semitism in the Women's Movement," *Pioneer Woman*, Sept.–Oct. 1983, pp. 11–13, 22–24.

[24]Susannah Heschel, "Current Issues in Jewish Feminist Theology," *Christian-Jewish Relations* 19, no. 2, 1986, pp. 23–32. See also Judith Plaskow, "Blaming Jews for Inventing Patriarchy," and Annette Daum, "Blaming Jews for the Death of the Goddess," *Lilith*, no. 7, 1980, pp. 11–12, 12–13.

ence." As Ellen Umansky comments, "By the early 1970s, it seemed to many that they were embraced as women but scorned as Jews." In reaction to the pressure that they either repudiate their Judaism or at least keep silent about it, Umansky notes that "many Jewish feminists, especially secular feminists, began to assert their Jewishness, vigorously, forcefully, and with pride." Jewish feminism, Umansky adds, "emerged as a means of asserting both *Jewish* visibility within the feminist movement and *feminist* consciousness within the U.S. Jewish community."[25]

The goals of Jewish feminism—as distinct from general feminism—as Cohen[26] points out, can be divided roughly into "communal" and "spiritual" areas. Although communally oriented Jewish feminists have been most interested in gaining access to seats of decision making and power, the spiritualists have worked for development in the areas of ritual, law, liturgy, and religious education. However, it should be noted that the division between religious and communal feminist agendas is not always clear, and in fact the two areas often impinge upon and affect each other.

Similarly, while the themes of contemporary American feminism and Jewish feminism are distinct, within the lives of American Jews they often overlap. Thus, a particular Jewish woman, sensitized by the ubiquitousness of feminist values in society, may work toward both occupational development and fuller participation in public Jewish prayer and ritual. Within her life, these enterprises may be linked emotionally and intellectually. The particular blend of feminism and Jewish feminism found in the United States today is a unique American hybrid, which does not exist in exactly the same form among any other contemporary Jewish population.

Feminism and Family

Probably no single aspect of feminism has aroused as much anxiety and debate as its possible impact on "the Jewish family," long regarded as the foundation of Jewish continuity and strength. Even within the Jewish feminist world, lines have been sharply drawn over this issue. At one end of the ideological spectrum, Martha Ackelsberg asserts that "the nuclear family as we know it is not, in itself, central to the continuity of Judaism: it is instead, simply one possible set of relationships through which young people may be born, nurtured, and prepared for membership in the Jewish community, and adults may find opportunities for companionship and intimacy. Once we realize that there are other means to achieve those same

---

[25]Ellen M. Umansky, "Females, Feminists, and Feminism: A Review of Recent Literature on Jewish Feminism and a Creation of a Feminist Judaism," *Feminist Studies* 14, Summer 1988, pp. 349–65.
[26]Cohen, "American Jewish Feminism," p. 529.

ends, and that even 'undermining the family' need not necessarily threaten Jewish survival, the path is open to think about alternatives to the nuclear family."[27] Ackelsberg urges the Jewish community to accept and encourage a number of alternative household styles. Individuals can contribute to the survival of the Jewish community through many pathways, she maintains, not only by having children. "Heterosexual nuclear families are not the only contexts in which people can or do covenant, nor are they the only units in or through which people may express love, or long-term care and commitment," Ackelsberg insists.[28]

In an exchange with Ackelsberg in *Sh'ma*, Susan Handelman disputes the claim that Jewish vitality is separable from traditional normative Jewish family life. Reaching back to Genesis, with its poignant preoccupation with matchmaking, marriage, and procreation, Handelman posits that the Jewish family was the primary and most enduring institution of Judaism. The family not only educated the young and supported Jewish institutions, it was the embodiment of Jewish values. To speak of Judaism without the primacy of the traditional Jewish family, Handelman suggests, is to commit an irreparable violence upon both the religion and the culture.[29]

Other female Jewish intellectuals are wary of feminist agendas, especially as they seem to endanger Jewish values. Thus, Marie Syrkin states that Jewish women who eschew motherhood are maiming themselves and the Jewish community. She feels they should revise their values and recognize that, on a personal level, "some forms of achievement can be gained only through the loss of a vital aspect of womanhood." On a communal level, she warns that the feminist agenda may directly conflict with the survival of the Jewish people: "Insofar as feminism liberates women from traditional roles and encourages life-styles antithetical to procreation and the fostering of the family, feminist ideology affects the Jewish future."[30]

Lucy Dawidowicz states her case against the "new Amazons . . . of women's liberation" even more firmly. She dismisses most strands of Jewish feminism as "a kind of ideological *sh'atnez*, the mixture of wool and linen prohibited in Jewish law." Unlike "Jewish women of achievement" in the past, who were "animated as much by passion to Jewish commitment as by personal ambition," she argues, most contemporary Jewish feminists "are merely an adjunct of the worldwide feminist movement." Indeed, according

---

[27]Martha A. Ackelsberg, "Families and the Jewish Community: A Feminist Perspective," *Response* 14, no. 4, Spring 1985, pp. 5–19, 18.
[28]Martha A. Ackelsberg, "Family or Community? A Response," *Sh'ma*, Mar. 20, 1987.
[29]Susan Handelman, "Family: A Religiously Mandated Ideal," ibid.
[30]Marie Syrkin, "Does Feminism Clash with Jewish National Need?" *Midstream*, June/July 1985, pp. 8–12.

to Dawidowicz, "only the most Jewishly committed feminists seem even to be aware of the incompatibilities between some objectives of the feminist movement and the Jewish communal need for stability, security, and survival."[31]

The normative Jewish family may indeed be a threatened institution, but it is not threatened exclusively by feminism. Other, equally important factors include: a cultural ethos that stresses individual achievement and pleasure; materialistic expectations that elevate the perceived standard of what a "middle-class" life-style comprises; a tightening economic market requiring dual incomes to maintain middle-class life-styles; the sexual revolution; and patterns of chronological polarization that split families by sending adolescents to far-off university campuses and grandparents to the Sunbelt.

Attitudinal Change

Whether the forecasts of doom concerning the Jewish family have merit or not, only future historians will be able to assess. What is clear at this point is that, in keeping with their general well-documented tendency to hold liberal social attitudes, Jews have warmly embraced the feminist idea. In a 1985 study of Jewish and non-Jewish women, conducted by Sid Groeneman for B'nai B'rith Women, non-Jewish and Jewish women were compared on a composite scale that measured attitudes toward "feminism, or . . . the modern version of women's roles and rights." Nearly half of Jewish women surveyed scored "high" on this scale, compared to only 16 percent of non-Jewish women. Several attitudes displayed by Jewish women can be construed as indicating a major change from traditional Jewish attitudes toward the family. Thus, 60 percent or more of Jewish women disagreed with the following statements: (1) "A marriage without any children will normally be incomplete and less satisfying"; (2) "When both parents work, the children are more likely to get into trouble"; (3) "Most women are happiest when making a home and caring for children." An overwhelming 91 percent of Jewish women—compared to 56 percent of non-Jewish women—agreed that "every woman who wants an abortion ought to be able to have one."[32]

Furthermore, the goals that these Jewish women had for their daughters indicated that feminist values were being passed to the next generation.

---

[31]Lucy S. Dawidowicz, "Does Judaism Need Feminism?" *Midstream*, Apr. 1986, pp. 39–40.

[32]Sid Groeneman, "Beliefs and Values of American Jewish Women," a report by Market Facts, Inc., presented to the International Organization of B'nai B'rith Women, 1985, pp. 30–31. The data were drawn from 956 questionnaires roughly divided between Jewish and non-Jewish informants. Ages of the women who completed the questionnaires were 59 percent ages 25 to 44, 41 percent ages 45 to 64. The study presents dramatic documentation of the transformation of values among American Jewish women under age 45.

Only 22 percent of Jewish women had family-oriented goals for their daughters, such as wanting their daughters to "have a good family, husband, marriage, children," or being "loving, caring, good parents." In contrast, 69 percent of Jewish women wanted their daughters to have qualities that would help them function successfully in the world, such as being "independent, self-reliant, self-sufficient, self-supportive, determined, ambitious, intelligent, knowledgeable, talented, skillful and creative."[33]

The study also found its sample of Jewish women to be far more liberal than non-Jewish women in attitudes toward premarital and extramarital sex. More than three-quarters of Jewish women said that sex before marriage was acceptable, while fewer than half of non-Jewish women approved of premarital sex. Perhaps even more startling, given Jewish religious and cultural prohibitions against adultery, 28 percent of Jewish women said they "could envision situations when sex with someone other than one's spouse is not wrong," compared to only 12 percent of the non-Jewish sample.[34]

Lesbianism remains a force in the Jewish feminist movement, as in the general feminist movement. Anne Lerner notes "the degree to which lesbianism, in particular, has become an accepted fact of life" at the Reconstructionist Rabbinical College.[35] Evelyn Torton Beck, in her anthology *Nice Jewish Girls*, describes the painful encounters of Jewish lesbians with anti-Semitism among lesbian feminists, but also offers testimony to the creative force and Jewish pride of some lesbian Jewish women.[36]

DEMOGRAPHIC CHANGES IN THE LIVES OF AMERICAN JEWISH WOMEN

The true impact of feminism and related social forces can be seen in the daily lives of American Jewish women, men, and children. During the past 20 years, dramatic changes have taken place in patterns of American Jewish family formation and in the educational and occupational profile of American Jews. Areas of change in the lives of American Jewish women that have been substantively influenced by feminism include later marriage and childbirth, higher levels of education and occupational achievement, and changed patterns in labor-force participation.

---

[33]Ibid., pp. 38–40.
[34]Ibid., pp. 23–24.
[35]Anne Lapidus Lerner, "Judaism and Feminism: The Unfinished Agenda," *Judaism*, Spring 1987, pp. 167–73.
[36]Evelyn Torton Beck, *Nice Jewish Girls: A Lesbian Anthology* (New York, 1982). See also Batya Bauman, "Women-identified Women in Male-identified Judaism," in Heschel, ed., *On Being a Jewish Feminist*, pp. 88–95.

THE IMPACT OF FEMINISM / 17

Changes in Life-Cycle Patterns[37]

Few statistics more strikingly illustrate cultural change than the figures on marital status among American Jews (table 1). Twenty years ago the National Jewish Population Study found that four out of five American Jewish households consisted of married couples, the great majority of whom either had or expected to have two or more children. At that time, the percentage of Jewish singles was far below the percentage of singles in the general U.S. population: only 6 percent of American Jewish adults had never been married, compared to 16 percent singles in the 1970 U.S. Census data. In contrast, in the 1980s, the proportion of Jewish singles equals or exceeds that of the general population in many cities: about one-fifth of Jewish adults in most U.S. cities have never been married. Furthermore, the

---

[37] All nationwide figures for the American Jewish population in 1970 are derived from the National Jewish Population Study. Data from individual city studies are drawn from the following city studies completed in the 1980s, including: Gary A. Tobin, *A Demographic Study of the Jewish Community of Atlantic County* (Jan.1986); Gary A. Tobin, *Jewish Population Study of Greater Baltimore* (July 1986); Sherry Israel, *Boston's Jewish Community: The 1985 CJP Demographic Study* (May 1987); Policy Research Corporation, *Chicago Jewish Population Study* (1982); Population Research Committee, *Survey of Cleveland's Jewish Population, 1981* (1981); Allied Jewish Federation of Denver, *The Denver Jewish Population Study* (1981); Gary A. Tobin, Robert C. Levy, and Samuel H. Asher, *A Demographic Study of the Jewish Community of Greater Kansas City* (Summer 1986); Bruce A. Phillips, *Los Angeles Jewish Community Survey Overview for Regional Planning* (1980); Michael Rappeport and Gary A. Tobin, *A Population Study of the Jewish Community of MetroWest, New Jersey* (1986); Ira M. Sheskin, *Population Study of the Greater Miami Jewish Community* (1982); Bruce A. Phillips, *The Milwaukee Jewish Population Study* (1984); Lois Geer, *The Jewish Community of Greater Minneapolis 1981 Population Study* (1981); Paul Ritterband and Steven M. Cohen, *The 1981 Greater New York Jewish Population Survey* (1981); William L. Yancey and Ira Goldstein, *The Jewish Population of the Greater Philadelphia Area* (Philadelphia: Institute for Public Policy Studies, Social Science Data Library, Temple University, 1984); Bruce A. Phillips and William S. Aron, *The Greater Phoenix Jewish Population Study* (1983-1984); Jane Berkey and Saul Weisberg, United Federation of Greater Pittsburgh, *Survey of Greater Pittsburgh's Jewish Population* (1984); Gary A. Tobin and Sylvia Barack Fishman, *A Population Study of the Jewish Community of Rochester, New York* (forthcoming); Lois Geer, *1981 Population Study of the St. Paul Jewish Community* (1981); Gary A. Tobin and Sharon Sassler, *San Francisco Bay Area Population Study* (1988); Gary A. Tobin, *A Demographic and Attitudinal Study of the Jewish Community of St. Louis* (1982); Gary A. Tobin, Joseph Waksberg, and Janet Greenblatt, *A Demographic Study of the Jewish Community of Greater Washington D.C.* (1984); Gary A. Tobin and Sylvia Barack Fishman, *A Population Study of the Jewish Community of Worcester* (Sept. 1987). Percentages in this paper have been rounded from .5 to the next highest number. Data were collected through a variety of sampling methodologies to reach both affiliated and nonaffiliated Jews, with a strong emphasis on random-digit-dialing telephone interviews. Much of the data presented here is taken from published studies; in these cases the studies are cited. Some information has been taken directly from complete data files from Jewish population studies made available to the Cohen Center for Modern Jewish Studies. References to this data simply refer to the particular community.

271

percentage of divorced Jewish households has risen from 6 percent in 1970 to double or triple that figure in some cities. Even though the Jewish divorce rate is not higher than the national average, it is far higher than the previous Jewish divorce rate: in Boston, for example, the 5-percent divorce rate of 1985 is five times higher than the 1965 divorce rate of 1 percent. The percentage of American Jewish households consisting of married couples has dropped to two-thirds, as has the overall married-couple rate in the 1980 census data.

American Jewish women are marrying later and beginning their families later. Often, the age at which the first child is born is substantially later than the age of first marriage. In a common scenario, a woman who marries at age 28 may postpone bearing her first child until age 34 in order to finish her professional training and establish her career. In Baltimore, among the 87 percent of Jewish women ages 45 to 64 who had children, one-third gave birth to their first child before age 22 and another one-half gave birth between ages 23 and 29. Thus, for mothers ages 45 to 64, four out of five had given birth to their first child before they reached age 30. In contrast, for women currently ages 25 to 34, only half had ever given birth. While some analysts are sanguine about the effect of delayed childbirth on Jewish population growth,[38] others warn that postponing childbearing will, on average, mean smaller American Jewish families.[39]

There are several reasons why families may not achieve their expected

---

[38]Calvin Goldscheider is the foremost proponent of the idea that expected family size, rather than the current number of children per family, reveals the actual completed family size that will be achieved by a given cohort. According to this view, delayed marriage and childbirth among a group can mean they have very few children during a certain period but will bear them later and fulfill their family-size expectations. Goldscheider states: "Expected fertility measures show a very high aggregate prediction for actual fertility. That has been the case particularly for Jews . . . who plan and attain their family size desires with extreme accuracy." Calvin Goldscheider, *Jewish Continuity and Change: Emerging Patterns in America* (Bloomington, Ind., 1986), pp. 92–94.

[39]U.O. Schmelz and S. DellaPergola argue strongly against the so-called optimistic position. See "Demographic Consequences of U.S. Population Trends," AJYB 1983, vol. 83, pp.148–59, 154. As noted in Gary A. Tobin and Alvin Chenkin, "Recent Jewish Community Population Studies: A Roundup," AJYB 1985, vol. 85, pp. 154–78, 162–63, the most striking evidence of the lowered Jewish fertility rate is the declining number of young people in the American Jewish population. Nearly one-third of the Jewish population was under 20 years old in the 1970 National Jewish Population Study, but in the post-1980 individual city studies only between one-fifth and one-quarter of American Jews were 19 years of age or younger. The figures for individual cities are as follows: New York—23 percent age 19 and under; Washington, D.C.—23 percent age 17 and under; St. Paul—21 percent age 19 and under; Minneapolis—27 percent age 19 and under; Milwaukee—24 percent age 17 and under; Rochester—24 percent age 19 and under; Pittsburgh—22 percent age 19 and under; Phoenix—25 percent age 17 and under; Philadelphia—17 percent age 15 and under; Nashville—28 percent age 19 and under; Miami—20 percent age 19 and under; Denver—21 percent age 17 and under; Los Angeles—20 percent age 17 and under.

TABLE 1. MARITAL STATUS OF CONTEMPORARY JEWISH POPULATIONS IN U. S. CITIES, COMPARED TO 1980 U.S. CENSUS, 1970 NJPS, AND 1970 U.S. CENSUS (PERCENT)

Location	Year Study Completed	Married	Single	Widowed	Divorced
Atlantic City	1985	67	13	13	6
Boston	1985	61	29	4	5
Baltimore	1985	68	19	9	5
Chicago	1982	65	23	6	6
Cleveland	1981	69	11	13	8
Denver	1981	64	23	4	9
Kansas City	1985	70	17	7	5
Los Angeles	1979	57	17	12	14
Miami	1982	61	7	23	8
Milwaukee	1983	67	14	9	10
Minneapolis	1981	66	22	7	5
Nashville	1982	70	17	8	5
New York	1981	65	15	11	9
Phoenix	1983	63	18	9	10
Richmond	1983	67	14	12	7
Rochester	1987	68	23	6	3
St. Louis	1982	68	9	17	6
St. Paul	1981	66	20	11	3
San Francisco	1988	69	19	4	7
Washington, D.C.	1983	61	27	4	7
Worcester	1987	69	14	—18—	
U.S. Census	1980	67	19	8	6
NJPS	1970	78	6	10	5
U.S. Census	1970	72	16	9	3

Source: See text footnote 37.

family size. First, where family size expectations are maintained, biological problems such as infertility are far more frequent as the age of the primipara (first-time mother) rises. Furthermore, the rate of fetal abnormalities rises along with age of the mother, sometimes further discouraging later childbirth. In addition, as numerous older first-time mothers have testified, the disruptive effect of children on an established dual-career household can serve as an effective motivation for limiting family size; sometimes expected family size is revised downward in response to the emotional and logistical difficulties that follow the birth of a first child. Finally, some employers actively discourage the birth of more than one child.

In addition to its effect on population size, the postponement of marriage and family formation may have a deleterious effect on synagogue and Jewish organizational affiliation. As part of a long-standing pattern of American Jewish life, the great majority of Jews do not join synagogues and organizations until they have married and had children. This life-cycle effect, in addition to the time constraints suffered by dual-career couples, seems to be one reason for diminished proportions of American Jewish women being actively involved in Jewish institutions.

Feminist goals may also lead to stress within marriage, and thus to divorce. Noticing that a surprisingly high proportion of divorced women in the general population had master's degrees, researchers analyzed the relationship between higher education and marital history. They found that women who obtained their master's degrees before marriage were not more likely than average to be divorced, whereas women who obtained their master's degrees after marriage were far more likely than average to be divorced. The researchers hypothesized that marriages which from their inception included a woman already in a professional role were psychologically adjusted to weather the pressures of two careers far better than those which began with more conventionally divided gender roles, and later switched course.[40]

No study has been published analyzing Jewish populations in this way, but data on the relationship between educational levels and marital status among Jewish women indicate that there may be a correlation between educational achievement and divorce. Among Jewish women in Baltimore, 32 percent of divorced women had master's degrees, compared to 7 percent of singles, 15 percent of married women with children at home, and 22 percent of married women with grown children. In Boston, among women ages 35 to 45, 9 percent of married women had master's degrees compared to 26 percent of divorced women in that age group. Unfortunately, the population studies do not reveal the date of degree completion, so we do not know what proportion of the divorced women's M.A.s were obtained before, during, or after their marriages. It is not possible, therefore, to establish a causal relationship between the educational achievement of Jewish women and divorce.

---

[40]Sharon K. Houseknecht, Suzanne Vaughan, and Anne S. Macke, "Marital Disruption Among Professional Women: The Timing of Career and Family Events," *Social Problems,* Feb. 1984, pp. 273–83.

Educational and Occupational Achievement

Another area of American Jewish life clearly influenced by feminism is the freedom of educational and occupational opportunity that American Jewish women now enjoy. Jewish women ages 25 through 34 are far more likely than women over age 55 to complete their bachelor's degrees and to obtain postgraduate degrees, as shown in table 2, which uses data from MetroWest (Essex and Morris counties), New Jersey. However, while MetroWest Jewish women ages 25 to 34 are about as likely as men to complete bachelor's degrees and to obtain master's degrees, men are still over three times as likely as women to complete medical, dental, legal, and doctoral degrees.

Impressionistic evidence indicates that Jewish women are currently enrolling in large numbers in professional programs, and data on the career plans of Jewish college women also show that the aspirations of young Jewish females have changed. Charles Silberman reports that a "1980 national survey of first-year college students taken by the American Council on Education found that 9 percent of Jewish women were planning to be lawyers—up from 2 percent in 1969. The proportion planning a career in business management increased by the same amount, and the number planning to be doctors tripled, from 2 percent to 6 percent. In this same period the number of Jewish women planning to be elementary school teachers dropped . . . from 18 percent in 1969 to six percent in 1980; those choosing secondary school teaching plummeted from 12 percent to only one per-

TABLE 2. SECULAR EDUCATION OF JEWS IN METROWEST, N.J.,[a] BY SEX AND AGE (PERCENT)

Education Completed	25–34 F/M	35–44 F/M	45–54 F/M	55–64 F/M	65+ F/M
H.S. or less	16/15	15/10	24/14	42/18	63/39
B.A.	56/50	53/38	50/42	37/45	27/37
M.A.	24/23	27/26	23/23	18/21	7/15
D.D.S., M.D., Atty.	3/11	3/18	[b]/12	1/10	2/ 6
Ph.D.	1/ 2	2/10	3/ 9	2/ 6	2/ 3
Total %	100/101	100/102	100/100	100/100	101/100

Source: See text footnote 37.
[a]MetroWest data from Essex and Morris counties, New Jersey.
[b]Indicates less than 1%.
(N = 1,477 males, 1,623 females)
Totals above or below 100% due to rounding of numbers.

cent."[41] Data collected during the next decade will indicate whether the gap between male and female completion of professional degrees will continue to narrow.

Just as educational data show that Jewish women are achieving more than in the past, occupational data on American Jewish women show some areas of movement. Table 3, reporting the occupations of currently employed Jewish men and women in MetroWest, New Jersey, illustrates the advancement of women into medicine, law, engineering, and science, as well as into executive positions. Still, while women in the younger groups are twice as likely to be employed in those fields as women in the older groups, Jewish men are still far more likely than Jewish women to be doctors, lawyers, or engineers.

Jewish women ages 35 to 44 are twice as likely to be physicians or attorneys as are women ages 55 to 64—but Jewish men ages 35 to 44 are more than four times as likely as Jewish women to be practicing those professions. Women have increasingly been moving into engineering and the sciences, going from 2 percent in the 45 to 54 age group to 4 percent in the 25 to 34 age group, while men engineers and scientists from ages 25 to 54 have remained at a stable 8 percent.

Jewish women ages 35 to 64 are outnumbered by men three to one in managerial positions; however, women ages 25 to 34 almost equal men in these positions. Younger Jewish women are far more likely to be executives and far less likely to be clerical or administrative support workers. The percentage of managers and administrators doubles in the younger group: 22 percent of women ages 25 to 34, compared to 11 percent of the women ages 35 to 54. Seventeen percent of women ages 25 to 34 are employed as clerical workers, compared to 28 percent of women ages 45 to 54 and 38 percent of women ages 55 to 64.

Data from Washington, D.C. (see table 4) illustrate the occupational shifts that are most pronounced in those communities offering broad employment possibilities to women. In Washington, Jewish women ages 25 to 34 show a strong shift toward law as a professional career choice. However, while the percentage of Washington Jewish women practicing law has increased tenfold from the oldest to the youngest groups, Jewish men are still more than twice as likely to practice law, even in the youngest group.[42] (While Washington is unique in its atypically large demand for attorneys

---

[41]Charles Silberman, *A Certain People: American Jews and Their Lives Today* (New York, 1985), p.123.

[42]Nine percent of women ages 25 to 34 are attorneys, compared to 1 percent of women ages 45 to 54. It should be noted that the practice of law among younger Jewish men has increased substantially also: 23 percent of men ages 25 to 34 are lawyers or judges, compared to 13 percent ages 45 to 54.

TABLE 3. OCCUPATIONS OF CURRENTLY EMPLOYED JEWS IN METROWEST, N.J.,[a] BY SEX AND AGE (PERCENT)

Occupations	25–34 F/M	35–44 F/M	45–54 F/M	55–64 F/M
M.D., D.D.S., etc.	1/ 6	2/ 9	1/ 8	1/ 8
Atty., judge	2/ 7	2/11	b/ 8	b/ 4
Engineer, scientist	4/ 8	4/ 8	2/ 8	1/10
Teacher, soc. worker	14/ 1	30/ 4	19/ 4	20/ 3
College prof.	b/ 1	1/ 3	2/ 1	1/ 1
Writer, artist	5/ 4	3/ 1	7/ 1	2/ 3
Allied health	9/ 4	6/ 1	7/ 2	7/ 2
Manager, admin.	22/25	11/30	11/33	9/29
Technical, sales	22/27	19/24	21/26	16/29
Clerical	17/ 3	20/ 2	28/ b	38/ 2
Service	4/14	2/ 7	2/ 6	3/ 9
Total %	100/100	100/100	100/97	98/100

Source: See text footnote 37.
[a]MetroWest data from Essex and Morris counties, New Jersey.
[b]Indicates less than 1%.
(N = 1,388 males, 1,427 females)
Totals above or below 100% due to rounding of numbers.

in government-related positions, the growth of law as the career of choice for Jewish women has been noted in many law schools and many Jewish communities.)

The practice of medicine, college teaching, writing, and artistic work is highest among women ages 35 to 44. While the data cited by Silberman indicate that teaching and social work are losing their appeal for young Jewish women, this is not the case in Washington. The percentage in these traditionally "female" fields climbs from older to younger working women, with 18 percent of Washington Jewish women ages 35 to 44 working as teachers or social workers. The percentage of Washington Jewish women involved in clerical work has diminished, but not radically: about one-fifth of Washington Jewish women ages 25 to 34 are clerical or administrative support staff.

As a city which offers broad occupational opportunities for women, Washington may dramatize some new trends in career movement. In the large metropolitan areas, especially on either coast, Jewish women are edging away from professional fields that are relatively weak in terms of

TABLE 4. OCCUPATIONS OF CURRENTLY EMPLOYED JEWS IN WASHINGTON, D.C., BY SEX AND AGE (PERCENT)

Occupations	25–34 F/M	35–44 F/M	45–54 F/M	55–64 F/M
M.D., D.D.S., etc.	2/ 7	4/ 8	1/ 7	3/ 4
Atty., judge	9/23	4/24	1/13	1/ 8
Engineer, scientist	3/11	4/12	2/21	5/16
Teacher, soc. worker	16/ 3	18/ 2	18/ 2	13/ 4
College prof.	3/ 4	3/ 5	2/ 8	3/ 4
Writer, artist	8/ 7	9/ 4	4/ 4	4/ 3
Allied health	8/ 2	4/ 1	3/ 4	3/ 1
Manager, admin.	20/16	19/28	24/28	20/31
Technical, sales	10/16	9/10	17/ 9	14/20
Clerical	16/ 6	20/ 2	24/ 2	29/ 2
Service	4/ 5	5/ 4	4/ 4	4/ 5
Total %	99/100	99/100	100/102	99/98

Source: See text footnote 37.
(N = 1,159 males, 998 females)
Totals above or below 100% due to rounding of numbers.

financial and status rewards and into fields that offer larger salaries. In most Midwestern and smaller cities, on the other hand, these new career trends among Jewish women have not yet had much statistical impact; in those areas, Jewish female professionals still cluster in the lowest paid fields—teaching and social work. Thus, among working Jewish women in Pittsburgh, 21 percent are social workers or teachers, while 4 percent are physicians, dentists, attorneys, or engineers. In Minneapolis, 16 percent of working Jewish women are social workers or teachers—more than five times the percentage in more lucrative professions. Denver has a relatively high proportion—almost 12 percent—of female doctors, lawyers, and engineers, partially because of the exceptionally high percentage of female engineers (8 percent, compared to 9 percent male engineers). In contrast, in Minneapolis, only 3 percent of Jewish women are doctors, lawyers, or engineers, compared to 17 percent of Jewish men; in Pittsburgh, the ratio is 4 percent women to 20 percent men; and in St. Louis, the ratio is 2 percent women to 17 percent men.

Labor-Force Participation

In 1957, only 12 percent of Jewish women with children under six worked outside the home, compared to 18 percent of white Protestants. As recently as 15 years ago it was still true that Jewish women were likely to work until they became pregnant with their first child, and then to drop out of the labor force until their youngest child was about junior-high-school age. Barry Chiswick has suggested that the high occupational achievement level of Jewish men may owe a great deal to Jewish women who provided an environment of family stability.[43]

The labor-force participation of Jewish women today departs radically from patterns of the recent past. In most cities the majority of Jewish mothers continue to work, at least part-time, even when their children are quite young. This phenomenon can be examined in two ways: by looking at age group and by looking at family type. An examination of changes among age groups is useful, because it permits comparison with earlier data. Thus, in the 1975 Boston study, the labor-force participation of Jewish women dipped lower than that of any other white ethnic group during the childbearing years. Among women ages 30 to 39, the number of working Boston Jewish women in 1975 fell to 42 percent, compared to about half of white Protestant, Irish Catholic, and Italian Catholic mothers. Past age 40, the percentage of Boston Jewish women at work soared higher than that of any other subgroup, with almost three-quarters of Jewish women in the labor force.[44]

Data from the 1985 demographic study of the Boston Jewish population show a very different picture, as seen in table 5. The majority of Jewish women in every age group except for those over 65 are working, and the younger the age group the more likely they are to be employed. Only about one-third of Boston Jewish women in the two age groups most likely to have young or school-age families—ages 30 to 39 and 40 to 49—are not employed.

If we examine the working-mother phenomenon from a life-cycle vantage point, the present high rate of labor-force participation by Jewish mothers with even the youngest children emerges unequivocally. Table 6 compares the employment patterns of mothers of preschool children in ten cities. In Boston, Baltimore, San Francisco, and Washington, three out of every five Jewish mothers of preschool children are employed.

Perceived economic need is probably the single most significant factor affecting the proportion of Jewish women who work outside the home. As

---

[43]Barry R. Chiswick, "The Labor Market Status of American Jews: Patterns and Determinants," AJYB 1985, vol. 85, pp. 131–53.
[44]Goldscheider, *Jewish Continuity and Change*, pp. 125–34.

TABLE 5. EMPLOYMENT STATUS OF BOSTON JEWISH WOMEN, 1985, BY AGE (PERCENT)

Ages	Not Employed	Employed Full-Time	Employed Part-Time
18–29	15	65	19
30–39	28	38	34
40–49	35	45	19
50–64	43	33	25
65+	94	3	2

Source: Adapted from *1985 CJP Demographic Study,* p. 25.

has been widely demonstrated among the general American population, for middle-class families today, two incomes are often needed in order to attain and maintain a middle-class standard of living: that is, purchase of a single-family home in a desirable location, relatively new automobiles and major

TABLE 6. LABOR-FORCE PARTICIPATION OF JEWISH MOTHERS OF CHILDREN UNDER 6, COMPARED TO 1986 U.S. CENSUS (PERCENT)

Cities	Full-Time	Part-Time	Homemaker	Other
Boston	29	36	33	2
Baltimore	27	38	35	1
Kansas City	28	21	44	7
MetroWest	22	26	49	4
Milwaukee	18	32	36	14
Philadelphia	23	14	59	3
Pittsburgh	29	25	42	4
Phoenix	26	21	50	3
Rochester	22	32	42	4
San Francisco	36	25	31	8
Washington	34	30	30	6
Worcester	15	34	51	1
U.S. Census	—54—			

Source: Adapted from Gabriel Berger and Lawrence Sternberg, *Jewish Child-Care: A Challenge and an Opportunity* (Cohen Center for Modern Jewish Studies, Brandeis University, *Research Report* No. 3, Nov. 1988), p. 20.

appliances, and attractive educational options for one's children, including college and possibly private school and/or graduate school. It is also true that perceptions of what constitutes a middle-class life-style have been significantly revised upward, so that more income is needed by "middle-class" families. These factors are especially significant for American Jewish families, which have traditionally had a strong ethic of providing their children with "everything."[45]

However, in addition to economic need, employment opportunities, job preparation, and social pressure are equally important factors in the labor-force participation of Jewish women. Younger Jewish women are more likely than their mothers to have used their schooling to prepare for specific careers, and they are often less willing to let those careers lie fallow while they become full-time homemakers. Younger women are also more likely to be surrounded by peers who urge them to work, rather than to become homemakers. By and large, women over 50 received their schooling at a time when most Jewish women did not work after marriage unless there was dire financial need. Consequently, even women who completed college often had no specific career preparation; the liberal arts degree was used as a kind of intellectual finishing school. Moreover, a wife's working might indicate that her husband was an inadequate provider; therefore even women who were trained as teachers or librarians sometimes hesitated to return to the job market. Furthermore, according to David Reisman, 20 years ago a woman who successfully combined career and family life was likely to be greeted with "shrewish and vindictive" envy by her peers, rather than admiration or a spirit of live and let live.[46]

The great majority of middle-aged and older Jewish women, therefore, have worked only part-time or not at all for many years. Their daughters, on the other hand, have matured with an ethos that is more likely to make the homemaker feel defensive. Among women 40 and under, especially those who live in cities with a strongly career-oriented atmosphere, even women with young children often complain that they are made to feel inadequate if they are not pursuing careers at the same time that they are raising their families.

---

[45]Marshall Sklare states the matter well: " . . . [H]e offers the child what are sometimes termed the 'advantages' or, in common American-Jewish parlance 'everything,' as in the expression: 'they gave their son everything.' 'Everything' means the best of everything from the necessities to the luxuries: it includes clothing, medical attention, entertainment, vacations, schools, and myriad other items." Marshall Sklare, *America's Jews* (New York, 1971), p. 88.
[46]David Reisman, "Two Generations," *Daedalus*, Spring 1984, 711-35.

Personal and Communal Implications of Demographic Change

As we have seen, substantial proportions of today's American Jewish households no longer fit the classic pattern of a working, highly educated husband living with a nonemployed, somewhat less educated wife and their several mutual children. Better education and career aspirations for women, later marriage and later childbirth, smaller families, rising rates of divorce, and widespread labor-force participation of Jewish mothers have changed the demographic profile of the American Jewish family. These changes have serious implications for individuals, who are confronted by difficult lifestyle decisions. They have also challenged the organized Jewish community to evaluate and make adjustments to new demographic realities.

It should be noted that although this discussion places the concept of "working mother" in a contemporary feminist context, the attempt at fusion of the two roles has long historical antecedents in the Jewish family. European and immigrant Jewish women often had a "characteristic aggressiveness and marketplace activism"[47] which they saw as an intrinsic part of their commitment to family and to society at large. Jewish women worked long hours at the sewing machine; they took in boarders; they ran grocery stores to help support their families. They also took active and often dangerous roles in union organizations because they believed that they could help better society. At the same time, connections between work and family were the norm in many traditional Jewish families.

For Jewish couples who married before the impact of women's liberation, there was almost always a commitment to the primacy of the family. They did not wonder whether or not to have children, and postponement of the first child was likely to depend on the father's career—as many couples waited until the conclusion of a residency or other professional training—rather than the mother's. Today, however, there are no *a priori* commitments to marriage and family, or to traditional gender roles. A 1985 survey found that only one-third of Jewish women believe that home-centered women make better mothers than women who work outside the home; while close to one-half of non-Jewish women think that employed women are less effective mothers and that children are more likely to get into trouble when both parents work.[48]

Couples now deciding to have children face an entirely different set of psychological barriers from those in the past. Rather than worrying about family or communal disapproval if working mothers decide to continue working, many are anxious about employer and peer-group disapproval if

---

[47]Hasia Diner, "Jewish Immigrant Women in Urban America," unpublished paper for the Mary I. Bunting Institute, Radcliffe College.

[48]Groeneman, "Beliefs and Values of American Jewish Women."

they curtail their working hours and career advancement to make time for child care. Contemporary values, which emphasize holding a stimulating job, personal development and growth, and experiencing the pleasures of an open and vital society, make the decision to have children a difficult one.

Young women who have devoted many years to higher education and professional training and then to establishing careers are torn by conflicting desires. As they edge into their 30s and beyond, many long for a child but worry that the limitations imposed by pregnancies and maternity leaves will stunt their professional growth. Most are less willing than earlier working women to fall back temporarily to part-time or free-lance work and to risk jeopardizing career advancement.[49] In Baltimore, for example, more than half of the married women who haven't yet had children are professionals, compared to one-third of the women with children at home and fewer than one-quarter of women with grown children.

Again, it is important to remember that women alone are not responsible for these decisions: many potential fathers too are concerned that children will change a very pleasant dual-career life-style by limiting their freedoms, diminishing their financial status, and imposing on them a portion of child-care and family-related household tasks.[50]

The changes that have taken place in attitudes and life-style have certainly not met with universal acceptance. Some critics warn that feminism has introduced attitudes and behaviors that may be destructive, in both the short and the long run, to the survival of the Jewish people in the United States. Others regard feminist agendas as a litany of immature demands. If Jewish women want to work and have children, claim these critics, they are making the decision and ought to be willing to shoulder the responsibilities themselves.

Blu Greenberg, a modern Orthodox feminist, is torn between desire for feminist advancement and fears for the physical survival of the Jewish community. Although she has written and spoken widely on behalf of feminist agendas, especially within traditional religious realms, she points out that "by delaying childbirth from the 20s to the 30s, we lose an entire generation every three decades. Career counseling with the Jewish people's needs in mind," she suggests, "would temper feminist claims with Jewish ones; it would enable couples to consider more seriously the option of having children first and then moving on to dual careers."[51]

---

[49]Fertility decisions by career couples have been a favorite topic for the media. Among many articles, see Darrell Sifford, "Couples Agonize Over Parenthood," *Boston Globe*, Apr. 24, 1980; Nan Robertson, "Job VS Baby: A Dilemma Persists," *New York Times*, Nov. 18, 1982.

[50]Nadine Brozan, "New Marriage Roles Make Men Ambivalent About Fatherhood," *New York Times*, May 30, 1980.

[51]Blu Greenberg, "Feminism and Jewish Survival," in *On Women and Judaism: A View from Tradition* (Philadelphia, 1981), pp. 151–69, 164.

Both Midge Decter and Ruth Wisse see the conflict between career and family as basically an individual, rather than a communal problem. They assert that individual women can deal with career/family conflicts through strength of character and good planning. Decter portrays "the liberated woman" as a spoiled child of the sixties, who does not have enough common sense and self-discipline to know "that marriage is not a psychic relationship but a transaction, in which a man forgoes the operations of his blind boyhood lust, and agrees to undertake the support and protection of a family, and receives in exchange the ease and comforts of home." Decter notes wryly that "if a woman opts to have both marriage and a career, she will put herself in the way of certain inevitable practical difficulties, the managing of which will on the other hand also widen her options for gratification."[52]

Wisse shares Decter's jaundiced view of the *angst* that some feminists report when they think about juggling career and familial responsibilities. She tells modern mothers to be more firm in urging their daughters to marry and have children at the biologically appropriate time. If daughters speak of careers, perhaps mothers should answer as Wisse's mother did: "*Bay yidn zaynen nishto kayn nones*"—"We Jews have no nuns." Furthermore, she has nothing but scorn for women who do not appreciate the blessings of the conventional marriage: "Happy is the woman whose husband is prepared to carry the economic burden of the family during at least her child-rearing years, and those who have enjoyed such protective blessings are nothing short of wicked when, explicitly or implicitly, they contrive to destroy the fragile contract that promotes them."[53]

On the other side of the spectrum are Jewish communal leaders and thinkers who either approve of the feminist agenda and think it should be supported in Jewish life, and/or who take a pragmatic approach to the landscape of American Jewish family life as it exists today. Paula Hyman castigates Jewish community leaders who seem to value women more for their reproductive value than for the contribution which they *as individuals* can make to the Jewish community.[54]

In reality, while some women reject traditional family life in the single-minded pursuit of a career, many Jewish women today do indeed feel their familial and professional interests to be organically related. It is these women who are most likely to state that their traditional orientation helps them to balance dual responsibilities. Sheila Kamerman points out that in the past even working women "shaped and fitted their work around their

---

[52]Midge Decter, *The Liberated Woman and Other Americans* (New York, 1971), p. 94.
[53]Ruth Wisse, "Living with Women's Lib," *Commentary*, Aug. 1988, pp. 40–46.
[54]Ben Gallob, "Leader Flays Appeal for Larger Families," *Jewish Advocate* (Boston), Sept. 20, 1979, quoting recent issue of *Sh'ma*.

families and their family responsibilities while men have shaped and fitted their families around their work and job demands. Some of the tensions now emerging are a consequence of some women adopting men's attitudes and behavior, while others are insisting that some modification is required of both men and women if the goal is for individual, family and child well-being."[55]

Some observers feel that regardless of one's approval or disapproval of feminism, it is incumbent on Jewish communal organizations to work to accommodate new life-styles, rather than to judge them, to exhort against them, or to hope they will go away. Gladys Rosen points out that the near-demise of the extended family opens the way for communal involvement in support for dual-career families: "There is a desperate need for universal Jewish day care for preschoolers and expanded opportunities for day school education which would enable mothers to work while offering enriched Jewish education to their children."[56] Rela Geffen Monson notes that in terms of support, the relationship of Jewish institutions and the Jewish family has actually been reversed: the family is becoming "the recipient of community services rather than their support." This reordering offers Jewish communal organizations and institutions the opportunity to assist in transmission of values to the children of the new American Jewish family, she urges.[57]

Shirley Frank suggests that a number of broad attitudinal and practical changes by the Jewish community are needed to support Jewish families. Jewish community leaders who say they want larger Jewish families ought to champion expanded after-school Jewish programs which incorporate Hebrew school curricula with recreational programming, she says. They ought to make sure that every community has attractive Jewish day-care programs. Every synagogue service, every adult educational program, every Jewish social event ought to automatically offer good child-care provisions. Children should be seen as a welcome part of Jewish life by the very people who urge women to have more children—and then "openly discriminate against" or "ostracize" families with "restless small children or wailing infants."[58]

---

[55]Sheila B. Kamerman, *Being Jewish and Being American: A Family Policy Perspective on the U.S. Social Policy Agenda and the Jewish Communal Policy Agenda*, a paper prepared for the American Jewish Committee's Task Force on Family Policy, Feb. 1981, p. 23.

[56]Gladys Rosen, "The Impact of the Women's Movement on the Jewish Family," *Judaism*, Spring 1979, p. 167.

[57]Rela Geffen Monson, "Implications of Changing Roles of Men and Women for the Delivery of Services," *Journal of Jewish Communal Service* 63, no. 4, Summer 1987, pp. 302–10.

[58]Shirley Frank, "The Population Panic: Why Jewish Leaders Want Jewish Women to Be Fruitful and Multiply," *Lilith*, no. 4, Fall/Winter 1977/78, pp. 13–17, 17.

Despite the problems associated with balancing the demands of family and career, many of those who are doing it find that the blend leads to general feelings of happiness, satisfaction, and fulfillment. The great majority of Jewish career women with large families in Kuzmack and Salomon's study (Washington, D.C., 1980) were pleased with their lives on both a personal and a professional level. Almost 85 percent felt they were "successful" or "very successful" at child rearing; three-quarters described themselves as personally "extremely satisfied" or "very much satisfied"; and over 80 percent said they were "successful" or "very successful" at work.[59]

When considering the challenges faced by dual-career Jewish families and the Jewish communities they live in, it is important to note that feminism is often practically combined with deep emotional ties to Jewish values. While some have attempted to identify the dual-career couple with an assimilationist, "egalitarian" family model,[60] many of the women who aspire to combine work and motherhood are more committed Jewishly than either men or stay-at-home mothers.[61] Dual-career couples are an important, even predominant, group among young and middle-aged cohorts in every Jewish denomination. Kuzmack and Salomon's study showed that the great majority of such women are deeply committed to Jewish life. All but six of the women belonged to synagogues, three-quarters sent their children to religious schools, and more than half marked the Sabbath with some form of observance.

Although the Washington women said that their Jewish values and lifestyles enhanced familial devotion, stability, and structure, and increased the family's ability to weather dual-career stresses and strains, they felt that the local Jewish community was sadly failing Jewish dual-career families. They voiced the complaint that "the Jewish community is urging us to have more children, but it isn't willing to help us meet the cost." The area of largest dissatisfaction was that of day care and Jewish education. "Mothers of young children . . . complained bitterly about the lack of Jewish day care centers. 'Children should be raised in a Jewish environment, and day-care is part of that,' " said one. Others complained that Hebrew schools, day schools, and Jewish camps were unwilling to lower tuition fees for large Jewish families unless their income was very low. Jewish organizations, they felt, retained the attitude that Jewish women should have more children

---

[59]Linda Gordon Kuzmack and George Salomon, *Working and Mothering: A Study of 97 Jewish Career Women with Three or More Children*, National Jewish Family Center, American Jewish Committee, 1980, p. 23.

[60]Norman Linzer, *The Jewish Family: Authority and Tradition in Modern Perspective* (New York, 1984).

[61]Abraham D. Lavendar, "Jewish College Women: Future Leaders of the Jewish Community," *Journal of Ethnic Studies* 52, Summer 1976, pp. 81–90.

and that Jewish women should bear the financial and psychological burden of raising those children.[62]

While Jewish women were taught for centuries that the home was their proper sphere of influence, American Jewish women today energetically pursue educational and occupational accomplishment as well. At the same time, many American Jewish women reject the notion that they are uniquely responsible for the well-being of their households; rather, they seek to share responsibility for that sphere with husbands, paid household help, and family-support institutions.

Despite the skepticism of both male and female critics of the feminist agenda, the influence of feminism on the educational and occupational lives of American Jewish women seems to be growing, rather than weakening. As a result, feminism is having a major impact not only on the family but on another cornerstone of Jewish society as well—Jewish communal organizations.

CHANGES IN COMMUNAL LIFE AND ORGANIZATIONAL BEHAVIOR

The Feminist Critique of Voluntarism

Jewish communal and organizational life, like other spheres of Jewish life in America, has been strikingly affected by feminism. Women have penetrated former male bastions of power as volunteers in Jewish organizations and have worked for equity as professional Jewish communal workers. Not least, Jewish organizations have become more aware of the needs of contemporary American Jewish women, men, and children in changing households. Voluntarism fit well into the lives of American Jewish women, especially in the years after World War II. In the 1950s, the typical American Jewish woman was better educated and more leisured than her Gentile counterpart. Jewish women had two or three children as compared to a rate of three to four children for non-Jews, and they spaced their children carefully, beginning childbearing later and finishing earlier than non-Jewish women. The majority of American Jewish children were in school by the time their mothers reached their late thirties.

Articulate and well educated, many Jewish women poured their energies into communal work. Volunteer communal work earned familial and communal approval. It was seen as an extension of the role of the nurturing Jewish mother and drew on the long tradition of the Jewish

---

[62]Ibid., pp. 19–21.

woman as a giver of charity and a doer of good deeds. Jewish women and the organizations they served thrived together: voluntarism gave women the opportunity to use their intelligence, organizational ability, and talents in challenging projects; communal organizations on local, national, and international levels were enabled to complete major projects because Jewish women treated volunteer work with dedication and seriousness.

However, in the 1960s and 1970s female voluntarism came under the critical scrutiny of the feminist movement. To feminist critics, voluntarism was a subterfuge, an escape from the emptiness of the homemaker's existence. Doris Gold, for one, lambasted a system that exploited "more than 13 million volunteers who 'work' for no pay at all—a virtual underground of antlike burrowers in our social welfare institutions." Calling female voluntarism "pseudowork," Gold wondered "why have trained, educated, 'aware' women opted for voluntarism, instead of structured work or creativity, during or after childrearing years?"[63]

In "The Sheltered Workshop," Aviva Cantor asserted that Jewish organizational work was nothing more than "a placebo," or "a distorted form of occupational therapy," designed to keep Jewish women "busy with trivia and involved with a lot of time-consuming social activities."[64]

For many Jewish feminists, the issue is not so much that the volunteers are not paid—male volunteers, after all, are unpaid as well—as that female volunteers have been systematically cut off from opportunities for decision making and power. One vivid symbol of institutional resistance to change is the UJA's policy of sexual exclusiveness in its local leadership cabinets and its prestigious National Young Leadership Cabinet, which grooms future leaders of federations. Because only men are allowed in many local cabinets and in the national cabinet, feminists charge that they serve the function of perpetuating an anti-egalitarian bias. UJA leaders cite "intense male camaraderie" as a primary reason for excluding women from the cabinet: it has been claimed that men in leadership positions bond together in intense personal and idealistic relationships, and that women would disrupt male bonding; and it has been feared that the presence of women in the pressured and deeply involved atmosphere of weekend retreats and working weekends would entice men into extramarital relationships. The national UJA leadership has so far withstood pressure to change its policy and to admit women to its most effective structure for molding future leaders.[65]

Jewish women who have attained positions of power in Jewish organiza-

---

[63]Gold, "Women and Voluntarism," pp. 384–400.
[64]Aviva Cantor, "The Sheltered Workshop," *Lilith*, no. 5, 1978, pp. 20–21.
[65]Stone, "The Locked Cabinet," pp. 17–21.

tions have joined in the critique. Although, unlike many feminist critics, they do not find organizational activities worthless per se, they say that women have been consciously excluded from opportunities for power. One of the first to voice distress publicly over inequities in the Jewish communal world was Jacqueline Levine, then vice-president of the Council of Jewish Federations and Welfare Funds (CJF). Stating that she had frequently been included as "the only—and therefore the token—female representative" in Jewish communal leadership settings, Levine cited leadership figures as they existed in 1972: in three of the top ten cities, 13 percent of the combined boards of directors and 16 percent of the persons serving on federation committees were women. The percentages of women involved were somewhat larger in the medium-size and smaller cities.[66]

From a feminist standpoint, the situation has improved in the past decade and a half, but is still far from equitable. Women now comprise between one-quarter to one-fifth of federation board members, executive committee members, and campaign cabinet members. Women have been federation presidents in Baltimore, Boston, Dallas, Houston, Los Angeles, Milwaukee, New York, Omaha, Toledo, and San Jose. Shoshana Cardin has served as the first female president of CJF. The percentage of women on the boards of federations and federation-funded agencies rose from 14 percent in 1972 to 40 percent in the mid-1980s.[67] According to a 1987 JWB study, women comprise one-third of all Jewish community-center board members.[68] Ironically, perhaps, as Chaim Waxman observes, among Jewish women's organizations, where it might be expected that all chief executive officers would be women, a substantial number of male directors are to be found.[69]

The Contemporary Jewish Female Volunteer

The Jewish population studies conducted in more than 20 U.S. cities since 1980 give us figures on the current percentage of American Jewish women who volunteer for Jewish causes. Testimony by Jewish communal leaders, organizational records, and anecdotal evidence indicate that 25 years ago the percentage of American Jewish women who volunteered for Jewish causes was much higher. However, we lack sufficient comparable data from the past to state this as a firm fact.

---

[66]Jacqueline K. Levine, "The Changing Role of Women in the Jewish Community," *Response*, Summer 1973, pp. 59–65. This is an edited text of an address to the 1972 General Assembly of the Council of Jewish Federations and Welfare Funds.
[67]Reena Sigman Friedman, "The Volunteer Sphere," *Lilith*, no. 14, Winter/Spring 1985–86, p. 9.
[68]Edward Kagen, *A Profile of JCC Leadership* (New York, 1987).
[69]Chaim I. Waxman, "The Impact of Feminism on American Jewish Communal Institutions," *Journal of Jewish Communal Service*, Fall 1980, pp. 73–79.

Jewish women are more likely than non-Jewish women to volunteer for certain kinds of organizations. According to one targeted study, Jewish women are ten times more likely than non-Jewish women to volunteer for ethnic causes, such as B'nai B'rith (compared to NAACP and Polish Women's Alliance, among non-Jewish populations), by a margin of 39 percent to 3 percent. Although Jewish women are substantially less likely to volunteer for a church or synagogue group than are non-Jewish women (59 percent of Jewish women compared to 69 percent of non-Jewish women), the synagogue group remains the single activity most likely to attract Jewish women. Among nonsectarian causes that attract Jewish women, high on the list are business and professional activities, which draw the membership of 28 percent of Jewish women but only 16 percent of non-Jewish women. This may be related to the relatively high rate of careerism among Jewish women. Jewish women are also far more likely to volunteer time for cultural activities, civic and public affairs, and feminist causes.[70]

No research has yet been published analyzing the Jewish organizational behavior of a large sample of American Jewish women. However, several studies both of the general population and of Jewish women have focused on specific groups of active volunteers. These studies give some indication of the demographic factors that correlate most closely with a propensity to volunteer.

The factors motivating Jewish women to volunteer may be somewhat different from those motivating women in the general population. Among the latter, research indicates an inverse correlation between careerism and voluntarism. A study of a Midwestern population found that women who were highly educated but were married to men who disapproved of their working outside the home were the group most likely to participate in volunteer work. The portrait of the typical volunteer in this nonsectarian study revealed a woman younger than 45, well educated, and satisfied with her traditional marriage.[71] In contrast, several leadership studies of active Jewish women volunteers suggest that many Jewish women who volunteer are labor-force participants. The "Council of Jewish Federations Women's Division Leadership Survey,"[72] a 1987 profile of CJF Women's Division

---

[70]Groeneman, "Beliefs and Values of American Jewish Women," pp. 11–12.

[71]Vicki R. Schram and Marilyn M. Dunsing, "Influences on Married Women's Volunteer Work Participation," *Journal of Consumer Research* 7, Mar. 1981, pp. 372–79. Data from this study are part of the Quality of Life Survey 1976–77. The data are drawn from interviews with 228 homemakers in Champaign-Urbana, Illinois, originally contacted through random sampling in the 1970–71 Survey of Life Styles of Families. Only married women under age 65 with children and husbands were included in this study.

[72]Gary A. Tobin and Sylvia Barack Fishman, "CJF Women's Division Leadership Survey Executive Summary," Cohen Center for Modern Jewish Studies, Brandeis University. The data for this study were gathered from 130 completed questionnaires, which were distributed

activists, showed that well over half of those with school-age children, ages 6 to 17, worked outside the home.

Household income seems to be positively related to volunteer activity, especially in leadership positions. Annual household income among the CJF Women's Division leaders in the sample was $135,000 for women ages 35 to 44 and $171,000 for women ages 45 to 64. Both average incomes are approximately two to three times higher than average incomes for Jewish families in those age brackets.

Ninety-four percent of the Women's Division leadership sample were currently married. Like most American Jewish women, they were highly educated: 62 percent of the respondents had B.A.s, 24 percent M.A.s, and 3 percent doctorates, medical, dentistry, or law degrees.

The Women's Division volunteers in the sample tended to be more traditional than other American Jewish women, both in terms of family formation patterns and in terms of religious observance. Respondents in the study averaged about three children each in their households, compared to about two children typical of all American Jewish households. Likewise, respondents were far more likely to mark the Sabbath and Jewish holidays with some observance.

Similarly, a study of Jewish women volunteers in Dallas[73] revealed a group of affluent, highly educated, fairly traditional women. The group was far more likely than average to maintain Jewish observances such as lighting Sabbath candles, fasting on Yom Kippur, eating only matzah and no bread on Passover, and to belong to a synagogue. Like the Women's Division leadership, the annual household income of Dallas Jewish leadership is relatively high: over one-third of the group enjoyed a household income of over $100,000 and another one-quarter had a household income of between $75,000 and $100,000.

The Dallas study seems to illustrate a disparity between behaviors and attitudes toward feminism that may be peculiar to Southern Jewish populations, which are more likely to be influenced by cultural prescriptions of traditional feminine roles. While more than half of the group worked outside the home, almost two-thirds said they perceived themselves as "home-

---

to Women's Division leaders during and after the 1986 CJF General Assembly. Respondents represented a diverse group from federations throughout the United States.

[73]The Dallas study of Jewish leadership was conducted during the spring of 1981 by mailing survey questionnaires to board officers and committee heads in Jewish organizations. Ninety-three women responded; they included leaders in the Federation, Jewish Family Services, Jewish Vocational Counseling Service, Jewish Community Center, Home for Jewish Aged, American Jewish Committee, American Jewish Congress, B'nai B'rith Anti-Defamation League, and all temples and synagogues. Jeffrey Becker Schwamm, "Recruitment of the Best: A Study of Why Dallas Jewish Women Leaders Volunteer," *Journal of Jewish Communal Service* 60, no. 3, Spring 1984, pp. 214–21.

makers," 40 percent said they perceived themselves as "career women," and only 36 percent said they perceived themselves as "feminists." Despite this reluctance to identify themselves as feminists, when asked about incentives to volunteer in Jewish communal organizations, two-thirds of the Dallas volunteers said that "dealing with problems which are challenging" was "very important." More than half named "intellectual stimulation" and "self-actualization and personal growth" as "very important." Thus, even in some highly traditional Jewish environments where women are loathe to identify themselves as feminists, mainstream Jewish women have tended to internalize feminist perspectives.

Volunteers, Employed Women, and Jewish Communal Responses

Money is a factor in voluntarism for obvious reasons, but also for some that are not so obvious. The authors of the Dallas study comment that "transportation, convenience of meeting location, and alternative child-care arrangements represent no problem to almost all the respondents." Many less affluent Jewish women who combine careers and motherhood, however, have indicated that transportation, convenience of location, and alternative child-care arrangements are crucial issues indeed. A university professor participating in a panel discussion on "American Jewish Women and the World of Work" described her difficulties in chauffeuring her six-year-old from Jewish nursery school in the morning to nonsectarian day care in the afternoon. "After a day of working and driving back and forth," she commented, "I can't imagine a Jewish communal cause which would be interesting or important enough to drag me out of the house to start driving around for more child care."[74]

Conflict between labor-force participants and homemakers adds another, troubled dimension to the impact of feminism on the Jewish communal realm. Jewish mothers who do not work outside the home sometimes express hurt that the contemporary Jewish community does not assign them adequate status. Homemakers may feel that career women expect them to carry an unfair share of volunteer work, yet look down on them because of their apparent lack of ambition and skills. Still, Zena Smith Blau points out that although fewer Jewish women today are willing to throw themselves heart and soul into the many Jewish communal organizations that have flourished on the free talents, intelligence, and time of Jewish wives, volunteerism among Jewish women remains significantly higher than among high-status Protestant and nonreligious women. Blau speculates that the traditional emphasis on community work in Jewish families may have

---

[74]Ileana Gans, panelist commenting at the Conference on Jewish Culture in the South: Past, Present, and Future, Asheville, North Carolina, Apr. 1988.

contributed to Jewish marital stability: the optional social interactions and ego-gratification derived from communal work refreshed the marital bond and relieved stress.[75]

Some women use their volunteer work as a basis for vocational retraining after their children are grown and become career women after all.[76] However, others find that their volunteer activities and "life experience" do not gain them much ground in the job market, and that they must retrain themselves to gain occupational skills and credentials.[77] Other Jewish homemakers devote considerable time and energy to self-development, enrolling in classes of all kinds, partially in an effort to demonstrate to themselves that they are just as accomplished as their salaried sisters. These women also may be less willing than women in the past to volunteer, because they perceive the call to voluntarism as a form of exploitation of their nonemployed status.

It cannot be stressed enough that feminism has affected the voluntaristic activity of Jewish men as well as Jewish women. This is especially true in dual-career families. For couples who are under intense pressure during the working hours, evenings and weekends become a haven not easily abandoned for communal causes. Furthermore, when dual-career couples decide to have children, they are often extremely "professional" about the concept of "quality time" with their children. Volunteer activities which cut into these times are sometimes perceived as diminishing, rather than enhancing, the social aspects of their lives. This new generation of Jewish parents is often repelled, rather than attracted, by the segregated structure of synagogue brotherhoods and sisterhoods and federation women's divisions and leadership cabinets.

The Professional Jewish Communal Worker

Feminism has affected Jewish communal life not only through its volunteers but through its professionals as well. Jewish communal service is a field increasingly populated by women; the 1988 enrollment of the Hornstein Program in Jewish Communal Service at Brandeis University, for example, consisted of 26 women and 11 men. Still, despite the presence of qualified women in the field, many of whom hold graduate degrees and many of whom have more seniority than the men they work with, very few

---

[75]Zena Smith Blau, "A Comparative Study of Jewish and Non-Jewish Families in the Context of Changing American Family Life," prepared for the American Jewish Committee Consultation on the Jewish Family and Jewish Identity, 1972.
[76]John Corry, "Mrs. Lieberman of Baltimore: The Life and Times of an Organization Lady," *Harper's*, Feb. 1971, pp. 92-95.
[77]Schneider, *Jewish and Female*, pp. 482-84.

women are promoted to executive positions. One recent article noted that "a 1981 survey of over 2000 professional staff in 273 agencies, conducted by the Conference of Jewish Communal Service (CJCS), indicated that although women constituted over half (58 percent) of the total staff, they made up only 8 percent of executive directors and assistant directors. A great majority of professional women (92 percent) were in the two lower job categories: 32 percent as supervisors and 60 percent line staff."[78]

Those who do achieve executive positions frequently earn salaries far lower than those of their male colleagues. Thus, a report by the Jewish Welfare Board in 1984 noted that 112 men were employed as executive directors, compared with 4 women, and that the average male director earned $51,500 while the average female director earned $44,250. In a similar 1984 CJF report, among the 80 male executive directors, the average salary was $53,179, while among the 8 female executive directors the average salary was $25,294.[79] Some of the reasons cited for not promoting women are the same as those given in the nonsectarian world: women are reluctant to relocate; women get married and pregnant and are therefore unreliable employees. Other reasons are peculiar to the world of Jewish communal service. It is a constant struggle to find high-caliber persons interested in the field, therefore attention cannot be "wasted" on efforts for equal opportunities for women; if women flood the executive strata of Jewish communal service, salaries in the field will automatically be depressed.[80]

Few wealthy female volunteers who have risen to power have worked to substantively improve the situation for female professionals in Jewish communal service. Moreover, some powerful female professionals have been loathe to rock the boat in order to benefit the female line workers below. Jacqueline Levine asserts that "too often those who have been accepted, or co-opted, or have 'made it,' don't look any farther than their own inclusion."[81] Many Jewish agencies have published statements and formed commissions to promote affirmative action, including the American Jewish Committee, the American Jewish Congress, the Anti-Defamation League of B'nai B'rith, the National Jewish Community Relations Advisory Council, the Council of Jewish Federations on a national level, as well as many on local levels. However, as many observers have commented, acknowledging and studying the problems have not always led to equity even within those organizations themselves.

---

[78]Reena Sigman Friedman, "The Professional Sphere," *Lilith*, no. 14, Fall/Winter 1985–86, p. 11.
[79]Debby Friss, "Room at the Top?" *Hadassah Magazine*, Jan. 1987, pp. 20–23.
[80]Ibid.
[81]Levine, "Changing Role," p. 60.

THE IMPACT OF FEMINISM / 41

Interestingly, both men and women in power have indicated that feminist goals in the Jewish communal world will be achieved when women learn to be more aggressive in furthering their own cause. Thus, Irving Bernstein, former UJA executive, discussing the underrepresentation of women on the National Executive Committee and Campaign Cabinet of the national UJA, states that women's progress is impeded by women's discomfort with the idea that they must forcefully assert themselves and their views, even in the face of opposition.[82] Naomi Levine, former executive director of the American Jewish Congress, urges women to study job descriptions, salaries, and promotions, and to take legal action where necessary to eliminate discrimination.[83] Anne Wolfe, who served as national staff director of the American Jewish Committee's committee on the role of women, says that "nice conferences" change little; "a much more revolutionary push by women" is needed to achieve feminist goals.[84]

Despite feminist progress in many areas—and despite the apparent mainstreaming of feminist attitudes within many national Jewish organizations—the relationship between Jewish communal life and feminist goals is still troubled. Feminism has brought new conflicts into Jewish communal life and has exacerbated older ones. However, it also presents the Jewish communal world with the opportunity to utilize more fully the skills of American Jewish women, both as volunteers and as professional workers for the Jewish community.

FEMINISM AND JEWISH RELIGIOUS MOVEMENTS

The Feminist Critique of Judaism

More than in any previous period of Jewish history, women today have made themselves central to the public functioning of religious life. This has led to sharp conflict, with opponents arguing that feminist efforts in this area will undermine normative Judaism. The evidence is, however, that feminist interest in Jewish prayer, study, ritual, and life-cycle celebrations has been marked by high creativity, and that as feminists have explored Jewish religious life, they have often demonstrated a renewed commitment to Judaism. Feminists argue that they have involved Jewish women in their Judaic heritage on an egalitarian basis for the first time in Jewish history:

---

[82]Steven M. Cohen, Susan Dessel, Michael Pelavin, "The Changing (?) Role of Women in Jewish Communal Affairs," in Koltun, ed., *The Jewish Woman*, pp. 193–200.
[83]Cantor, "The Missing Ingredients," p. 12.
[84]Ibid.

that they have empowered Jewish women to acquire the intellectual tools needed to deal competently with Jewish source materials and texts, as well as the liturgical skills which make them equal partners with men in prayer; that they have examined Jewish source materials from a female-centered, rather than a male-centered perspective; and that they have created rituals and midrashim which deal specifically with the feminine experience of Jewish life cycles, history, and culture. According to feminists, Jewish women are at last gaining the opportunity to explore their own spirituality.

Some aspects of this creative renewal—such as Jewish life-cycle celebrations for females—affect huge numbers of American Jewish women; other aspects—such as female ordination and the practice by women of traditionally male-focused rituals—directly affect only highly committed and involved women. However, even women who are not directly involved in the more intensive forms of Jewish feminist spirituality may be indirectly shaped by an environment in which women have increasingly become public Jews.

It is of course ironic that at a time when most American Jewish men seem to be drawing away from Jewish ritual, and few men worship regularly with *tallit* and *tefillin*, some Jewish women have been exploring these and other traditionally male modes of religious expression. While fewer Jewish men are attracted to the rabbinate, partially because restrictive codes barring them from other professions have almost disappeared, increasing numbers of Jewish women have been entering the field, first in the Reform (1972) and Reconstructionist (1975) branches and later in the Conservative (1985) denomination. Among the masses of American Jewish boys and girls, the education of Jewish females has drawn close to approximating the education of Jewish males.

For most of Jewish history, the role of women within Judaism was shaped by rabbinic law (Halakhah). Although this body of law prescribed behavior for Jewish women, they were not involved in the formal discussion or decision-making processes—they were passive recipients of a nonrepresentative system.[85]

---

[85]Blu Greenberg summarizes the laws and concepts which most determined a Jewish woman's role thus: "Talmudic law spelled out every facet of the law as it applied to the woman. She was exempt from those positive commandments that must be performed at specific times, such as wearing the *tzitzit* and *tefillin*, reciting the *Shema*, and the three complete daily prayer services (Kiddushin 29a; Eruvin 96b; Berakhot 20a-b; Menahot 43a). She was exempt also from certain commandments that were not time specific (Eruvin 96b). In various communal or group events, she could be a participant-observer but had no equal status in performance of ritual. This held true for the mitzvah of *sukkah*, the celebration of *simhat bet ha-sho'evah*, the redemption of the firstborn, inclusion in the minyan for grace after meals, and reading the Torah at the communal prayer service (Sukkah 2:18, 53a; Kiddushin 34a; Megillah 47b, 23a)." Greenberg, *On Women and Judaism*, pp. 62–63.

According to some Jewish feminist scholars, such as Rachel Biale, the Halakhah has not excluded Jewish women nearly as much as the folk cultures that have surrounded it. It was folk culture, not postbiblical Jewish law, for example, that perpetuated the notion of menstrual contamination and made menstruating women feel unwelcome in synagogues in certain European Jewish communities. Contrary to popular opinion, Biale suggests, "the law may have preceded common practice in what to the contemporary eye are liberal, compassionate attitudes toward women."[86] Most feminist scholars of Judaism, however, would be inclined to agree with Judith Plaskow's view[87] that the Halakhah contains much that is objectionable because it has been male-centered from its inception. Even at Mount Sinai, she points out, Moses addresses the community as though it were composed exclusively of men. This exclusion is deeply troubling to feminists because biblical memory is an active force in the spiritual lives of Jews. Plaskow maintains that the issue of female exclusion extends into, and is exacerbated by, later developments in Halakhah, as expounded through the Talmud, its commentators, and the responsa literature. Because "Halakhah is formulated by men in a patriarchal culture," she asserts, it defines the normative Jewish experience as the experience of men. According to Plaskow, "Feminism questions any definition of 'normative' Judaism that excludes women's experience."

Jewish feminists involved with religious issues can be divided between those who feel bound by Jewish law and those who do not. The former have been careful to maintain all ritual requirements incumbent upon Orthodox women, while working to effect change within the law itself. The latter feel that rabbinic law can be treated as a flexible guide to practice rather than as a rigid set of demands. They have worked for behavioral change within Jewish religious life, urging women to take on religious duties and roles previously proscribed to women, even if those duties and roles are prohibited by traditional law. Both types of Jewish feminists have sought to revitalize traditional modes of religious expression for women, as well as to create new rituals and liturgies.

American Jewish Life-Cycle Celebrations

In the past, ritual responses to the birth of a girl were pallid. The father was one of several men in the synagogue called to make a blessing on the

---

[86]Rachel Biale, *Women and Jewish Law: An Exploration of Women's Issues in Halakhic Sources* (New York, 1984), p. 7.
[87]Judith Plaskow, "Standing Again at Sinai: Jewish Memory from a Feminist Perspective," *Tikkun* 1, no. 2, 1987, pp. 28–34; idem, "Halakhah as a Feminist Issue," *Melton Journal*, Fall 1987, pp. 3–5.

Torah, and there he would recite a prayer for the health of mother and child and name his daughter. Some families would also mark the occasion by serving simple refreshments after Sabbath services, but no talk was given and no songs were sung, nor was the infant herself brought to the synagogue. As recently as 25 years ago, a lavish *kiddush* for a girl could arouse sarcastic commentary: "You're doing all this for a girl?" Today, however, an elaborate *kiddush* is expected for the birth of a daughter, even in strictly Orthodox circles. Moreover, neglected customs have been revived and new customs have arisen to give both mother and daughter the opportunity to mark these momentous events. In some synagogues, women who have just given birth recite *birkat hagomel* aloud during the Torah-reading portion of the Sabbath service, thanking God for the deliverance from danger, rather than leaving such thanksgiving to the father's proxy recital. The once unknown ceremony of "*Shalom Bat*," welcoming a daughter, has become ubiquitous in Jewishly knowledgeable communities. In the home or synagogue, with mother and daughter present, friends gather to listen to talks, eat, sing, and celebrate together. Some parents compose new prayers for the occasion; others make use of printed materials that have been written and disseminated in liberal Orthodox, Conservative, Reform, and Reconstructionist circles.[88]

Reconstructionist founder Mordecai Kaplan, who was also closely associated for many years with the Jewish Theological Seminary, may have been the first to suggest the concept of Bat Mitzvah,[89] and Conservative Judaism made popular the actual celebration of this event. At first, few families chose to celebrate the Bat Mitzvah,[90] and many Conservative synagogues limited the celebration to less problematic Friday-night services, when the Torah is not read. By the late 1980s, however, most Conservative and almost all Reform congregations had made Bat Mitzvah and Bar Mitzvah ceremonies virtually identical, including calling girls to the Torah.

For women who missed having a Bat Mitzvah in their youth, such a celebration at a later stage in life provides the opportunity for both a renewed commitment to Judaism and a feminist assertion of personhood. One recent adult Bat Mitzvah states, "In the midst of our Jewish lives, there was a void—something that was not quite okay for us. One of us said she wanted to stand where her husband and four children stood and read a *haftarah* from the same bimah. Two of us are making up for being denied

---

[88]For a listing of printed materials on *Shalom Bat* ceremonies, see Schneider, *Jewish and Female*, pp. 121-29.

[89]Carole Kessner, "Kaplan on Women in Jewish Life," *Reconstructionist*, July-Aug. 1981, pp. 38-44.

[90]Marshall Sklare, *Conservative Judaism: An American Religious Movement* (New York, 1972), pp.154-55.

this chance years ago when we were told in our shuls there was no such thing as girls being bat mitzvah."[91] These ceremonies involve women ranging in age from young adulthood to old age and are a regular feature in many Conservative and Reform congregations.

Orthodox practitioners have slowly responded to the pressure to celebrate a girl's religious majority. Some congregations have established a format for celebrating Bat Mitzvah on Sunday morning or Shabbat afternoon at a special *se'udah sh'lishit*, the traditional festive "third meal." At these occasions the girl typically delivers a *d'var torah*, a homiletic address illustrating her familiarity with biblical texts, marking the seriousness of the occasion. Other congregations leave the mode of celebration up to the discretion of the child and her parents. These celebrations have become commonplace in many Orthodox circles, with families sometimes traveling great distances to be at a Bat Mitzvah, just as they would for a Bar Mitzvah. Much feminist commentary on this phenomenon has tended to concentrate on the disparity between limited Orthodox forms of Bat Mitzvah, on the one hand, and egalitarian Conservative and Reform modes of Bat Mitzvah, on the other. This, however, misses the point that Orthodoxy has in fact traveled a farther road than the Conservative, Reform, and Reconstructionist branches in breaking away from previously prevailing norms.

Synagogue Participation and Ritual Observance by Women

The diversity of congregational attitudes toward female participation in synagogue services is illustrated in a 1978 study that evaluated questionnaires filled out by the rabbis of 470 congregations of different sizes, drawn from different branches of the American Jewish religious community and distributed among the several geographic areas of the United States.[92] Investigators Daniel Elazar and Rela Monson found that mixed seating and women leading the congregation in English readings were almost universal among Reform and Conservative congregations. Almost all Reform congregations counted women toward a *minyan* (required prayer quorum) and allowed them to chant the service; slightly less than half the Conservative congregations did so; and none of the Orthodox. Nearly all Reform congregations and about half of Conservative congregations honored women with *aliyot* to the Torah, while none of the Orthodox congregations did. Women gave sermons in almost all Reform congregations, more than three-quarters of Conservative congregations, and 7 percent of Orthodox congregations.

---

[91]Susan Gilman, "Bat Mitzvah Ceremonies Not Just Kid Stuff," *Queens Jewish Week* (New York), May 27, 1988.
[92]Daniel J. Elazar and Rela Geffen Monson, *The Evolving Role of Women in the Ritual of the American Synagogue* (Philadelphia and Jerusalem, 1978).

Most Reform congregations and almost two-thirds of Conservative congregations had women opening the ark and chanting *kiddush* and *havdalah*, but only 2 percent of Orthodox congregations did similarly. As these data were gathered in the late 1970s, and before the Conservative movement's landmark decision to ordain female rabbis, we can safely assume that considerable movement has taken place in most Conservative congregations to increase egalitarian practices.

Egalitarian attitudes toward prayer become especially important to women who wish to say *kaddish* daily for departed loved ones. Traditional synagogues are the most likely to have daily prayers—and they are also the most likely to be unwilling to count women for a *minyan*, posing a serious problem for the would-be female *kaddish* reciter. Greta Weiner recalls entering one Conservative synagogue, only to be pushed to the back of the chapel by a man who insisted that her presence would be "disruptive to the men trying to pray." Refusing to count her and her teenage daughter for the *minyan*, the congregation that evening had only nine men and did not include the *kaddish* in its prayers.[93]

The egalitarian prayer model is championed outside established synagogues in many *havurot*. *Havurot*—prayer and study groups which often involve relatively small numbers of fairly knowledgeable and/or committed Jews—have a participatory and egalitarian ethos. They have been the locus of much creative ferment in the American Jewish community, ferment which has often filtered out and eventually influenced more established synagogues and temples. Because *havurot* have no rabbis, cantors, or other professionals to lead services, read from the Torah, deliver sermons, and teach classes, and rely on group members to undertake these responsibilities, they have been pioneers in providing opportunities to women in these areas.

The expansion of female participation in worship takes place not only in an egalitarian context but in an all-female setting as well. In all-female prayer groups, women have the opportunity to lead prayers and read the Torah, and in general to be active participants in a ritual sphere in which for millennia they were nonessential auxiliaries. Even in all-female groups, however, conflicts arise between Orthodox and non-Orthodox women. While some non-Orthodox women welcome the all-female context so that they can read, lead, and pray without the potentially intimidating presence of men, Orthodox women need the all-female format because they will only perform in this way if men are not present. Furthermore, many Orthodox women will not recite the approximately 20 percent of the prayer service reserved for a quorum of ten men unless they receive permission to do so from a recognized male rabbinical *posek* (person recognized as a competent

---

[93]Greta Weiner, "The Mourning Minyan," *Lilith*, no. 7, 1980, pp. 27–28.

formulator of Jewish law). As Steven Cohen notes, feminist religious styles "are predominantly determined by differences in approach to Jewish life rather than by differences in approach to feminism."[94]

Prayer is far from a new concept for women in the Orthodox Jewish world. According to Maimonides and other classical rabbinical commentators, women are required to pray daily, although they are excused from the time restrictions for prayer and are not counted as part of a *minyan*. Consequently, in the past, numerous Orthodox European women prayed daily in their homes, as do many contemporary Orthodox American women. Nor is group prayer by women per se controversial, as it is a regular occurrence in many Orthodox girls' yeshivahs. Two new phenomena have infuriated some Orthodox rabbis, however: women choosing to pray separately, rather than being relegated to separation by men; and women carrying and reading from Torah scrolls.

In the words of one participant, Rivkeh Haut, "Reading from a *sefer torah* is at the heart of every women's prayer service. The Torah is carried about the room, so that every woman present may reach out and kiss it. The entire Torah portion for that week is read. This Torah reading is the basic innovation of women's *tefillah* [prayer] groups."[95] Orthodox Jewish women of all ages have reported being moved to tears the first time they looked into a Torah scroll as part of a women's prayer group. "I never realized how much I was excluded from—or how much it meant to me," said one Boston grandmother.

Despite the cautious respect with which Orthodox women approached this activity, some Orthodox leaders launched vigorous campaigns against female group prayer. Thus, in 1985 Rabbi Louis Bernstein, then president of the Rabbinical Council of America, invited five Yeshiva University Talmud professors to issue a responsum on the appropriateness of female *minyanim*, this despite the fact that the prayer groups scrupulously avoided identifying themselves as such. The resulting one-page responsum prohibited women's *minyanim* as a "falsification of Torah," a "deviation," and a product of the "licentiousness" of feminism. The responsum, condemned by more moderate modern Orthodox figures for its startling, undocumented brevity and blatant lack of halakhic objectivity,[96] was followed by a more scholarly but no less inflammatory 17-page article by Rabbi Hershel Schacter.[97] When some of the rabbis involved were interviewed by the popular Jewish press, their remarks underscored the personal and political

---

[94]Cohen, "American Jewish Feminism," pp. 530–31.
[95]Rivkeh Haut, "From Women: Piety Not Rebellion," *Sh'ma*, May 17, 1985, pp. 110–12.
[96]See, for example, David Singer, "A Failure of Halachic 'Objectivity,'" *Sh'ma*, May 17, 1985, pp. 108–10.
[97]See Michael Chernick, "In Support of Women's Prayer Groups," *Sh'ma*, May 17, 1985, pp. 105–08, for a discussion of Schacter's article in Yeshiva University's journal *Beit Yitzhak*, Mar. 1985.

nature of their "halakhic" ruling. "What are they doing it for? A psychological lift? It has no halakhic meaning. If they want to get their kicks there are other ways to get it," said one, under cover of anonymity. Bernstein dismissed the importance of Orthodox women's spiritual explorations by stating, "They [the rabbis] don't owe the women anything."[98]

Despite the negative reaction among key elements of Orthodox leadership, women's prayer groups continue to flourish in many cities. Even in areas where women's prayer groups do not meet on a regular basis, they meet for special occasions, such as Simhat Torah. They have become a popular locus for Orthodox Bat Mitzvahs, since they offer girls the opportunity to read from the Torah and recite the *haftarah*, the reading from Prophets.

The impact of feminism on Orthodox women's observance can be seen in other phenomena as well, such as the pressure that exists in many communities to construct an *eruv*. The *eruv*, a Sabbath boundary marker, transforms a given area from a public realm to a private realm, according to talmudic law, thus making it halakhically acceptable to carry objects on the Sabbath—and to push a baby carriage as well. Prof. Nahum Sarna suggests that when Orthodox communities assumed that young women would simply remain home with their children until they could walk to the synagogue, few communities went to the trouble of setting up and maintaining an *eruv*. Today, however, far larger proportions of Orthodox women assume that their proper place is in the synagogue on the Sabbath morning, even after they have attained the life-cycle stage of motherhood. Consequently, notes Sarna, construction of an *eruv* has become a high communal priority in areas where large numbers of young Orthodox couples have settled.[99]

Jewish Education

It is difficult to overestimate the importance of Jewish education in helping women to advance significantly within the religious sphere. In Judaism, no activity is more revered than study; study confers status on the individual and makes possible the mastery of the basic Jewish sources. For most of Jewish history, study was an activity available to women only on the rudimentary level and in informal contexts. Widespread formal Jewish education for women is a relatively recent phenomenon.[100]

---

[98]Larry Cohler, "Orthodox Rabbis' Responsa Condemns Women's Prayer Groups," *Long Island Jewish World*, Feb. 15–21, 1985.

[99]Nahum Sarna, personal conversation, Sept. 1988.

[100]Deborah R. Weissman, "Education of Jewish Women," *Encyclopedia Judaica Year Book, 1988* (Jerusalem, 1988), pp. 29–36.

The slow, cumulative growth of Jewish education for women is linked to the process of Emancipation and acculturation to Western society. In Germany, where the Jewish community was profoundly affected by the ideals of the Haskalah (Jewish Enlightenment), both the burgeoning Reform movement and the enlightened neo-Orthodox movement of Samson Raphael Hirsch sponsored formal Jewish education for girls. In Eastern Europe, where the Jewish community proved more resistant to Westernization, such schooling came somewhat later. After World War I, some secular Jewish schools, both Yiddishist and Hebraist, provided formal education for girls. Most importantly, Sara Schnirer[101] established the Bais Yaakov movement, which revolutionized Jewish education for girls in the Orthodox world. Schnirer's educational work won the support of such leading Orthodox figures as the Hafetz Hayyim and the Belzer Rebbe, who pointed out that women receiving sophisticated secular education but rudimentary Jewish education were likely to abandon Orthodoxy. Today, intensive Jewish education of girls is widely accepted by all Orthodox elements as an absolute necessity. In day schools ranging from Satmar's Bais Rochel system, which eliminates the 12th grade to make sure its graduates cannot attend college, to coeducational Orthodox schools such as Ramaz in New York and Maimonides in Boston, which provide outstanding secular education and teach both boys and girls Talmud, a rigorous Jewish education for girls has become an undisputed Orthodox communal priority. During the past decade, it has also become increasingly popular for Orthodox young women to spend a year of religious study in an Israeli yeshivah between high school and college.

Young American Jewish women today are far more likely than their grandmothers were to receive some formal Jewish education (see table 7).[102] In MetroWest, New Jersey (Essex and Morris counties), only 56 percent of women over age 65 had received some formal Jewish education, compared to 80 percent of girls ages 14 to 17. Additionally, data *not* included in table 7 show that among American Jewish women over age 55, the Orthodox women are the most likely to have received some formal Jewish education

---

[101]The daughter of a Belzer Hassid, Sarah Schnirer was born in 1883 and received minimal Jewish education as a child, but pursued her education on her own and later with neo-Orthodox teachers in Vienna. She returned to Krakow determined to "rescue Judaism for the new generation" by providing intensive Jewish education for girls in an Orthodox setting. In 1917 she opened a school with 25 girls; the school expanded rapidly and new branches were established. In 1937-1938, 35,585 girls were enrolled in 248 Bais Yaakov schools in Poland alone. See Menachem M. Brayer, *The Jewish Woman in Rabbinic Literature*, vol. 2 (Hoboken, N.J.: Ktav, 1986), pp. 79-80.

[102]This discussion draws upon Sylvia Barack Fishman, *Learning About Learning: Insights on Contemporary Jewish Education from Jewish Population Studies*, Cohen Center for Modern Jewish Studies, Brandeis University, 1987, pp. 25-29.

and the nonobservant and the "just Jewish" the least likely.[103] Sunday School education for girls is most frequent in the Reform movement, while Orthodox girls are most likely to be exposed to day schools, private tutors, Yiddish schools, and the like.

Ordination

In 1972, Hebrew Union College, the Reform seminary, ordained Sally Priesand as the first female rabbi. Since then, the school has ordained well over 100 women. Over one-third of the entering rabbinic class in 1986 was female. Still, most Reform congregations continue to express a preference for a male primary rabbi; women rabbis are far more likely to find employment as assistant rabbis, chaplains, and Hillel directors.[104]

Now that the earliest female Reform rabbis have attained some seniority within the movement, it remains to be seen if they will also attain rabbinical posts with the prestige and salaries commensurate with their status.

Female Reform cantors have found much more widespread acceptance and have obtained employment in many prestigious congregations. In 1986 the entire entering class of cantors at Hebrew Union College was composed of women. Halakhically, women cantors pose as many problems as women rabbis (although the problems are somewhat different), and there is no halakhic difference between a primary rabbi and an assistant rabbi. Therefore, the bias against women primary rabbis but in favor of women cantors and assistant rabbis would appear to be cultural. Clearly, despite assumptions of full egalitarianism, a substantial number of Reform congregants seem content to relegate female clergy to subordinate positions.

The struggle within the Jewish Theological Seminary in moving toward Conservative ordination of women provides a well-documented case study of the evolution of women's role within American Judaism. The way toward considering such an idea was opened by the votes first to give women *aliyot* (1955) and later to count women for a *minyan* (1973) by the Rabbinical Assembly's Committee on Jewish Law and Standards. During the late 1970s, there was strong pressure within the Conservative movement to change the Seminary's policy and to begin to ordain women as Conservative rabbis. Seminary chancellor Gerson D. Cohen and Rabbi Wolfe Kelman,

---

[103]"Just Jewish" refers to respondents in the Jewish population studies who did not define themselves by any wing of Judaism, i.e., Orthodox, Conservative, Reform, Reconstructionist, or Traditional, but said instead that they were "just Jewish." In addition, some population studies categorize people by the number of Jewish rituals they observe, independent of their denominational identification, as "highly observant," "moderately observant," "low-observant," and "nonobservant." "Other" (generally a very small percentile) refers to people who do not currently define themselves as Jewish.

[104]I am grateful to Rabbi Sanford Seltzer for a conversation clarifying many of these issues.

TABLE 7. FORMAL JEWISH EDUCATION OF JEWS IN METROWEST, N.J.,[a] BY AGE, SEX, AND DENOMINATION (PERCENT)

Age and Sex

	0–5 M/F	6–13 M/F	14–17 M/F	18–24 M/F	25–34 M/F	35–44 M/F	45–54 M/F	55–64 M/F	65–74 M/F	75+ M/F
Total ever received Jewish education	33/39	85/80	88/80	89/79	82/64	89/63	89/63	87/55	85/56	90/58
Total received no Jewish education	65/58	13/18	12/20	11/20	18/33	10/35	9/34	11/43	13/39	8/41

Denomination and Sex

	Orthodox All M F	Conservative All M F	Reform All M F	Just Jewish All M F	Other All M F
Total ever received formal Jewish education	81 89 73	78 88 69	75 84 66	51 63 39	61 74 48
Total received no Jewish education	18 10 26	19 10 28	24 15 33	48 36 59	35 25 47

Source: Sylvia Barack Fishman, *Learning About Learning: Insights on Contemporary Jewish Education from Jewish Population Studies* (Cohen Center for Modern Jewish Studies, Brandeis University, 1987), pp. 26, 27.
[a]MetroWest data from Essex and Morris counties, New Jersey.

executive vice-president of the Rabbinical Assembly, were strongly in favor of the change, as were many younger pulpit rabbis. At the annual convention of the Rabbinical Assembly in May 1977, the majority of rabbis voted to ask for the formation of an interdisciplinary commission "to study all aspects of the role of women as spiritual leaders in the Conservative Movement." The final report of the commission, presented in 1979, minimized both halakhic difficulties and the strength of feeling of dissenting rabbis. It stated that it would be morally wrong for the Conservative movement to continue to deny ordination to qualified women. A majority of Conservative congregations, said the commission, were ready to accept female rabbis, as were three-quarters of current rabbinical students. The commission strongly recommended "that the Rabbinical School of The Jewish Theological Seminary of America revise its admission procedures to allow for applications from female candidates and the processing thereof for the purpose of admission to the ordination program on a basis equal to that maintained heretofore only for males," and that the Seminary "educate the community" properly "so as to insure as smooth and as harmonious an adjustment to the new policy as possible."[105]

The commission's premises and recommendations were opposed by several older and senior Seminary professors who themselves had studied at Orthodox yeshivahs and were committed to traditional halakhic Judaism. At the Seminary chapel, for example, men and women were seated separately, despite the long-standing and accepted Conservative custom of mixed pews, and despite the majority opinion of the Rabbinical Assembly's Law Committee permitting the counting of women as part of the *minyan* for public worship, issued in 1973. The ordination of women was also opposed by a substantial group of Conservative pulpit rabbis.

Shortly after the commission report appeared, Charles Liebman, then a visiting professor at the Jewish Theological Seminary, and Saul Shapiro, an active Conservative layman and a senior planner with IBM, prepared *A Survey of the Conservative Movement and Some of Its Religious Attitudes*,[106] for the Biennial Convention of the United Synagogue of America in November 1979. Liebman and Shapiro divided the Conservative laity into a large group that had little if any commitment to the halakhic process and a small, loyal core that took Halakhah seriously. Liebman and Shapiro suggested

---

[105]*Final Report of the Commission for the Study of the Ordination of Women as Rabbis*, Jan. 30, 1979. Signed by Gerson D. Cohen, Victor Goodhill, Marion Siner Gordon, Rivkah Harris, Milton Himmelfarb, Francine Klagsbrun, Fishel A. Perlmutter, Harry M. Plotkin, Norman Redlich, Seymour Siegel, and Gordon Tucker.

[106]Charles S. Liebman and Saul Shapiro, *A Survey of the Conservative Movement and Some of Its Religious Attitudes*, sponsored by the Jewish Theological Seminary of America in cooperation with the United Synagogue of America, Sept. 1979.

that the traditional minority might well represent Conservative Judaism's best chance for a viable and vital future, but warned that it could be alienated from the Conservative movement if female rabbis were ordained by the Jewish Theological Seminary.

Liebman and Shapiro's view did not deflect the agenda of the pro-ordination factions. A group of women who wanted to become Conservative rabbis were already studying at the Jewish Theological Seminary. On December 6, 1979, they sent a letter to members of the faculty, in which they said:

....We are seriously committed to Jewish scholarship and to the study of Jewish texts. Although some of our specific practices vary, we are all observant women who are committed to the halachic system.

We wish to serve the Jewish community as professionals in a variety of educational and leadership capacities. We are interested in teaching, writing, organizing, counseling and leading congregations. Although we realize that these tasks can be performed by people who are not rabbis, we desire to receive rabbinical training, and the title "rabbi," because we feel that with this authority we can be most effective in the Jewish community. We believe that our efforts are sorely needed and that there are many communities where we would be fully accepted and could accomplish much towards furthering a greater commitment to Jewish life.

We are fully aware that there are a number of complicated halachic issues related to Jewish women. We feel that these issues should be addressed carefully, directly and within the scope of the halachic process. This process, however, should not delay the admission of women to the Rabbinic School. We wish above all to learn and to serve God through our work in the Jewish community.[107]

In December 1979, the faculty senate of JTS voted 25 to 18 to table the question of ordination. In the spring of 1980, Gerson Cohen announced the initiation of a new academic program for women, which would be parallel to the rabbinic program but would sidestep the emotional issue of ordination. In May 1980, however, the Rabbinical Assembly voted 156 to 115 supporting women's ordination. Although the entire senior faculty of the Seminary's department of Talmud continued to oppose ordination, as did a large minority of pulpit rabbis, in October 1983, the Seminary faculty voted 34 to 8 to admit women to the rabbinical program. The first women entered the rabbinical school in September 1984; the class included 18 women and 21 men. Amy Eilberg, already an advanced student, was the first woman to receive Conservative ordination, graduating in 1985.

The Orthodox movement could hardly remain untouched by all this, despite the denunciations of leading Orthodox figures. Indeed, a few Orthodox rabbis responded positively to feminist ferment within the Conservative movement, suggesting that something similar might eventually happen in

---

[107]Signed by Debra S. Cantor, Nina Beth Cardin, Stephanie Dickstein, Nina Bieber Feinstein, Sharon Fliss, Carol Glass, and Beth Polebaum.

the Orthodox community. Rabbi Avraham Weiss stated: "There are aspects of the rabbinate such as public testimony, involvement in a bet din and leading a public liturgical service that women may not, according to Jewish law, be involved in. However there are aspects of the rabbinate—the teaching of Torah and counseling—in which women can fully participate on the same level as men. . . .a new title must be created for women to serve this purpose."[108] Blu Greenberg went one step further. In an article entitled "Will There Be Orthodox Women Rabbis?" she answered in the affirmative:

> Will it happen in my lifetime? I am optimistic. At this moment in history, I am well aware that the Orthodox community would not accept a woman as a rabbi. Yet we are moving towards a unique moment in history. More than any other, the Orthodox community has widely educated its women in Torah studies. Thus, though it rejects the formal entry of women into rabbinic studies, *de facto,* through the broad sweep of day school, yeshiva high school education and beyond, it has ushered them, as a whole community, into the learning enterprise. At the very same moment in time, Reform, Reconstructionist, and Conservative Judaism are providing us with models of women as rabbis. At some point in the not-too-distant future, I believe, the two will intersect: more learned women in the Orthodox community and the model of women in leadership positions in the other denominations. When that happens, history will take us where it takes us. That holds much promise for the likes of me.[109]

Feminist Ritual, Midrash, and Liturgy

Jewish feminists concerned with religious issues have urged the inclusion of female experience and female images of the divine in Jewish ritual, midrash, and liturgy.

At the radical end of the spectrum are those who seek to discover and recreate "goddess spirituality." The popular Jewish press reported that a student at the Reconstructionist Rabbinical College, Jane Litman, was building small goddesses and ostensibly worshiping them. Litman denied this, saying that the goddess episode was misinterpreted by "name-callers who seek to halt the forward march of social justice." She stated that "most liberal Jews accept that images of God are psycho-social symbols, not descriptions of any tangible reality," and insisted that "women's images of the Deity must be given the same credence as men's." Several other feminists came to Litman's defense, including novelist E. M. Broner, who argued that goddess worship was a way of gaining access to a deity which

---

[108]Quoted in "First Woman Set for Conservative Ordination Looks to Future," *Jewish Week* (New York), Mar. 1, 1985.
[109]Blu Greenberg, "Will There Be Orthodox Women Rabbis?" *Judaism,* Winter 1984, pp. 23–33.

THE IMPACT OF FEMINISM / 55

"Judaism had expunged." Such creative exploration, said Broner, put "women on the cutting edge of Judaism, making us stretch."[110]

Most Jewish feminists seeking to develop female-oriented rituals recoil from incorporating goddesses into Judaism. Ellen Umansky, for one, urges exploration that is mindful of both Jewish tradition and the spiritual needs of Jewish women.[111] Arlene Agus states bluntly, "Worship of other deities is simply not a legitimate route for Jews to take." Agus notes that there are several "continuums" in Jewish feminist thinking, and that most seek to build and expand, rather than to totally transform, normative Judaism.[112]

Many Jewish feminists are interested in revisions of the liturgy that incorporate feminine attributes of the godhead and references to the matriarchs. Traditional Jewish prayers, Umansky points out, refer repeatedly to God in male imagery and continually recall the interaction of God with male biblical figures. She argues that if "Jewish women are not subordinate and if their relationship with God is every bit as intimate as the relationship of men, then let us change the liturgy to reflect this awareness." She goes on:

> How many times can I praise God as the Shield of Abraham or the Shield of Our Fathers without feeling that if He left out our mothers, surely He must be leaving out me. . . . The image that dances before me is of a male God who blesses His sons, those human beings (our fathers) who were truly created in His image. To Jewish medieval mystics, God was not simply a King and a Father but also Shechinah, She-Who-Dwells-Within. The Shechinah represented the feminine element of the Divine. It was She who went into exile with the people of Israel, She who wept over their sorrows, She they yearned to embrace. The Kabbalists, then, knew God as Mother and Father, Queen and King. Might we not incorporate these insights into our worship service?[113]

Jewish feminists have also worked to create rituals which express women's spirituality within the context of Jewish tradition. Agus[114] describes the Jewish feminist attraction to the celebration of Rosh Hodesh, the festival of the New Moon, which "traditionally held unique significance for women perhaps dating back as far as the Biblical period." The Rosh Hodesh celebration is appealing to tradition-minded yet creative feminists, says Agus, precisely because "it offers unlimited opportunities for exploration of feminine spiritual qualities and experimentation with ritual, all within the

---

[110]"Can a Reconstructionist Rabbi Go Too Far?" *Baltimore Jewish Times*, Mar. 27, 1988. Jane R. Litman, "Can Judaism Respond to Feminist Criticism?" *Baltimore Jewish Times*, Apr. 24, 1987.
[111]Prof. Ellen Umansky, telephone conversation, Sept. 1988.
[112]Arlene Agus, telephone conversation, Sept. 1988.
[113]Ellen Umansky, "(Re)Imaging the Divine," *Response*, no. 13, Fall/Winter 1982, pp. 110–19.
[114]Arlene Agus, "This Month Is for You: Observing Rosh Hodesh as a Woman's Holiday," in Koltun, ed., *The Jewish Woman*, pp. 84–93.

framework of an ancient tradition which has survived up to the present day." In the Rosh Hodesh ceremonies suggested by Agus, women wear new clothes, give charity, recite prayers, poems, and a special *kiddush*, recite *sheheheyanu* (thanksgiving prayer) at the eating of new fruits, have a festive meal featuring round and egg-based foods, and include the prayers said on festivals, *shir hama'alot* and *ya'aleh veyavo,* in the grace after meals.

The Passover Seder has provided another opportunity for creative feminist spirituality. In describing the evolution of the first of her feminist Haggadahs, Aviva Cantor deals with both the strengths and the limitations of feminist transformations of Jewish ritual. She states:

> I rewrote the Haggadah, first taking care of the minor changes: making God "ruler of the universe" instead of "king," adding the names of Jacob's wives to the Exodus narrative, and changing "four sons" to "four daughters." The major change was to utilize the four-cups ritual and to dedicate each cup of wine to the struggle of Jewish women in a particular period. The Haggadah's aim was to provide connecting links between Jewish women of the past and us here in the present. A great deal of material came from Jewish legends and historical sources, some only recently discovered.

Although the feminist Seder experience was quite enjoyable for the participants, Cantor reports, she missed the heterogeneity of the traditional ceremony:

> As much as I loved a Seder with my sisters, what gnawed at me was the memory of the Seders I had at home, in my parents' house, Seders of men and women of several generations, with children running underfoot and spilling the wine. The Seder has always been a family celebration and, for me, a Seder just for women seems incomplete.

At the ideal Seder, Cantor concludes, "women would be as 'visible' as men, but neither men nor women would be the entire focus of the Seder."[115]

One ritual in which women are indisputably the entire focus is the traditional immersion in the *mikveh*, the ritual bath, related to the laws of family purity. Orthodox Jewish law requires married women to bathe thoroughly and then to immerse themselves in the *mikveh* prior to resuming sexual activity, following menstruation and seven "white" days. In some non-Orthodox communities, brides visit the *mikveh* before their weddings, even if they do not intend to maintain the family purity laws after marriage. Much to the surprise of older American Jews, many of whom regarded the *mikveh*—when they thought of it at all—as a quaint relic of outmoded attitudes and life-styles, interest in the *mikveh* has enjoyed a renaissance of sorts in certain circles. A key factor was Rachel Adler's positive discussion

---

[115]Aviva Cantor, "Jewish Women's Haggadah," in Koltun, ed., *The Jewish Woman*, pp. 94–102. See also "An Egalitarian Hagada," *Lilith*, no. 9, Spring/Summer 1982, p. 9.

in the first *Jewish Catalog*.[116] Feminists exploring Jewish women's spirituality and religious expression, together with well-educated younger generations of Orthodox women who take religious obligations seriously, and newly observant women who seek the structured environment and sexual limits of Orthodoxy, have revitalized *mikvehs* in many communities. Positive articles about *mikvehs* have appeared in several publications, including the *Reconstructionist* and *Hadassah Magazine*. Two students at the Reconstructionist Rabbinical College explain how *mikveh* ties in to their search for Jewish feminist spirituality:

> It appeals to the individual on the many levels of her spiritual existence and relationships. First, it addresses her relationship with her future husband—that intimate, binding relationship of two people who at times fuse in body and soul. Next, it addresses her relationship with other Jewish women, who have ancient and current ties to her through water. Finally, it addresses her relationship with all Jews, through Torah and its folkways.[117]

Their "Ceremony for Immersion" includes prayers and blessings in Hebrew and English, some drawn from traditional sources and some newly composed.

Traditional Women and the Ba'alot Teshuvah

Ironically, the feminist striving for liberalization of the role of Jewish women has produced at least two species of backlash: right-wing emphasis on the intensification of woman's traditional role and increasing numbers of women who retreat from the sexual and social pressures of contemporary American life into highly structured Orthodoxy, within the *ba'al teshuvah* (religious renewal) movement.

During the past few years the *New York Times* has run attractive full-page advertisements, paid for by the Lubavitch movement, showing a Jewish mother and daughter blessing the Sabbath candles. The texts of the advertisements speak of the importance of tradition in the lives of American Jewish women, and the importance of women in preserving Judaism. In their own way, these Lubavitch advertisements are a vivid testimonial to the new prominence and visibility of women in contemporary American Jewish life.

Davidman[118] and Kaufman[119] have documented the surprisingly feminist

---

[116]Rachel Adler, "Tumah and Taharah—Mikveh," in *The Jewish Catalog*, comp. and ed. Richard Siegel, Michael Strassfeld, and Sharon Strassfeld (Philadelphia, 1973), pp. 167–71.

[117]Barbara Rosman Penzer and Amy Zweiback-Levenson, "Spiritual Cleansing: A Mikveh Ritual for Brides," *Reconstructionist*, Sept. 1986, pp. 25–29.

[118]Lynn Davidman, "Strength of Tradition in a Chaotic World: Women Turn to Orthodox Judaism" (doctoral diss., Brandeis University, 1986).

[119]Debra Kaufman, "Coming Home to Jewish Orthodoxy: Reactionary or Radical

mentality that motivates some women to seek an Orthodox setting, in which they feel women are less harassed and more respected than in the outside world. Some of Davidman's Orthodox informants stated that Orthodox Judaism offers integrity for women in a way that contemporary society does not:

> ... [I]t also has to do with not being seen as a sexual object, which I think is a totally pro-woman attitude. You have to love me for what I am and not for what you can get off me, and that's the laws of *tum'ah* (ritual impurity) and *taharah* (ritual purity) in Judaism. ... Take a look at what's going on out there, how women have been objectified. On the one hand you can say it's keeping women down on the farm by keeping their heads covered. On the other hand, you could say, hey, it's by maintaining a certain attitude towards women which is not to objectify them as a sexual object.

However, for some women seeking Orthodoxy, it is precisely the retreat from the pressures of feminism that is appealing. Women such as these often seek out Hassidic settings, where gender roles are most clearly defined—women are expected to be loving and pious wives and mothers. As one of Davidson's informants put it:

> ... [F]or many women, to relearn devotion, to replace narcissism with devotion, is really a very natural thing because it's more feminine to be devotional than to be narcissistic ... just the way our bodies are built, a woman is, by nature, going to give of herself. ... So when you teach a woman about devotion and marriage and selflessness and altruism, what you're really telling her is to be herself. ... The biological function is consistent with the rest of her so that the way her body behaves is also the way the mind behaves and it's also the way the soul behaves.

In her study of modern Orthodox, Agudah-affiliated, and ultra-Orthodox women, Sarah Bunim[120] shows that many "have internalized the value system of the secular world." They are often highly educated and committed to careers, and they are also often agitated by what they perceive as inadequate religious roles for women in Orthodox Judaism—leading them to place even greater emphasis on the satisfactions of career achievement. Even among the most Orthodox *kollel* groups which Bunim studied, in which contact with secular values is kept to a minimum and women occupy a clearly subservient position as enablers of husbands who devote themselves to full-time study, feminism has had a curious impact: the status of the husband in the community is influenced by the money and prestige of his wife's job.

Women?" *Tikkun* 2, no. 3, July-Aug. 1987, pp. 60–63; idem, "Women Who Return to Orthodox Judaism: A Feminist Analysis," *Journal of Marriage and the Family,* Aug. 1985, pp. 541–55.

[120]Sarah Silver Bunim, "Religious and Secular Factors of Role Strain in Orthodox Jewish Mothers" (doctoral diss., Wurzweiler School of Social Work, Yeshiva University, 1986).

"Get": The Unsolved Problem

A long-standing problem for Jewish women, one that has resisted solution, is in the area of Jewish marriage and divorce law. It is a problem that affects not just Orthodox and Conservative Jews, who follow Halakhah in this area, but any woman who wishes to marry or remarry in a Jewish religious framework.

According to traditional Jewish law, when a couple divorces, the man must place a *get*, a divorce contract, into the hands of his wife, indicating that she is no longer his wife. Without a *get*, the woman remains his wife in the eyes of Jewish law. If she then marries another man without receiving a *get*, she is legally an adulteress and children resulting from the new union are illegitimate, *mamzerim*. *Mamzerim* are not allowed to marry other Jews; they can only marry other *mamzerim*. Under certain circumstances, however, the husband can legally marry again even without a *get*.

Because women have far more to lose than men do if no *get* is obtained, some men have used this as a means to blackmail their wives during divorce proceedings. For example, they threaten not to give their wives a *get* unless they receive custody of the children, or unless their wives relinquish court-ordered financial settlements or alimony payments. Both feminists and concerned rabbis have worked for methods to prevent such extortion, either through use of a prenuptial agreement or through a religious annulment of the marriage. Several Orthodox lay leaders have banded together to form an organization to deal with the problem, appropriately named G.E.T., Getting Equitable Treatment. However, according to Honey Rackman, they have made little headway:

> Despite the attention *get* blackmail has been given in the Jewish media and the waste of young women spending their childbearing years in ugly and often vicious conflict with recalcitrant husbands, the Orthodox establishment has not responded. Ostrich-like, some Orthodox rabbis have even suggested that there is no problem. They maintain that they are dealing satisfactorily with the individual cases that come before them. With their best handwringing gesture, they gently shoo from their presence "feminist" troublemakers, with condescending assurances that they too are deeply troubled and suffer sleepless nights but cannot change the law.[121]

Rackman, for one, is convinced that the "patient is curable if only the qualified doctors would administer the medicine at their disposal."

It is not inconceivable that resistance to punishing men who will not comply with the *get* is related to general hostility to feminist goals, particularly in the Orthodox community. The rising rate of divorce among Jews is often attributed to the female independence, both emotional and occupa-

---

[121] Honey Rackman, "Getting a *Get*," *Moment*, May 1988, pp. 34–41, 58–59.

tional, fostered by feminism. Jewish women who divorce their husbands, like Jewish women who put on *tefillin* or study the Talmud, can be profoundly unsettling to a community long accustomed to the principle that women are ideally domestic, rather than public, beings.

In Israel, the *get* issue is of pressing concern to all women, since matters of marriage and divorce are controlled entirely by Orthodox rabbinic authorities. American Jewish feminists have been instrumental in supporting the Israel Women's Network—through the New Israel Fund—which has as one of its main goals the reform of the rabbinical courts.[122]

CONCLUSION

In tandem with other factors making for change in American society, feminism has had a powerful impact on the American Jewish community. Increasing numbers of American Jewish women pursue career-oriented educational programs and the careers which follow. Partially as a result, they are marrying later and having fewer children than Jewish women 25 years ago. Moreover, a majority of today's American Jewish women, in contrast to the pattern of the past, continue to work even when they are the mothers of young and school-age children.

These demographic changes have affected the Jewish community in several important areas. First, they have created a large population of single adults, including never-married and divorced persons, who are far less likely to affiliate with the Jewish community in conventional ways. Second, they have produced a population of beginning families who are, as a group, older and more focused than beginning families 25 years ago. Third, they have fostered a dual-paycheck work ethic among Jewish parents, which makes both men and women disinclined to volunteer time for Jewish organizations. Fourth, they have resulted in a client population of Jewish children who are in need of child-care provision from birth onward, and a corresponding parental population demanding that the Jewish community provide Jewish-sponsored child care for children of varying ages.

Jewish religious life and Jewish culture have been profoundly transformed by Jewish feminism in all its guises. From birth onward, American Jewish girls today are more likely than ever before in Jewish history to be treated in a manner closely resembling the treatment of boys vis à vis their religious orientation and training. Increasing numbers of Jewish girls are welcomed into the Jewish world with joyous ceremonies, just as their brothers become official Jews with the ceremony of *Brit Milah.* American Jewish

---

[122]*New Israel Fund Annual Report*, 1988, p. 23.

schoolgirls receive some sort of formal Jewish education in almost the same numbers as their brothers. Bat Mitzvah has become an accepted rite in the American Jewish life cycle in all wings of Judaism, with the exception of the ultra-Orthodox.

Jewish women are counted for *minyanim* and receive *aliyot*, in all Reform and a majority of Conservative synagogues. Despite vehement attacks by some Orthodox rabbis, women's prayer groups around the country give Jewish women of every denomination the opportunity to participate in communal worship and Torah reading. College-age and adult Jewish women take advantage of greater access to higher Jewish education, with increasing numbers of women augmenting their knowledge of traditional Jewish texts. Reform, Reconstructionist, and Conservative female rabbis and cantors have been graduated and serve the Jewish community in pulpits and in other positions. Women hold tenured positions in Judaica in universities—including the Ivy League—and rabbinical seminaries. In addition, many women find meaning in traditional and innovative Jewish feminist liturgy and rituals. Through Jewish women's resource centers, networks, and publications of all types, Jewish feminists communicate with each other and increase communal understanding of Jewish feminist goals.

In the Jewish communal world, women assertively pursue both professional and volunteer leadership positions in local and national Jewish organizations. During the past 15 years, the number of women in such leadership positions has increased substantially, although neither the number of female executives nor the status and salary level of most of their positions comes close to matching that of male executives. Similarly, female representation on communal boards has improved in the past decade but does not come close to equaling that of men. Jewish women who express a desire for a more equal distribution of communal power have been advised by communal leaders that they must be prepared to fight aggressively for that power, including litigation, where necessary.

Despite the mainstreaming of feminist and Jewish feminist goals within the American Jewish community, the relationship between feminism and Judaism remains troubled. Some elements in rabbinical and communal leadership have a "knee-jerk" antifeminist response to any and all items on the Jewish feminist agenda. On the Jewish feminist side, there often exists a kind of tunnel vision which puts feminist agendas ahead of Jewish communal well-being and survival. In truth, there are certain areas in which the goals of feminism and the goals of Judaism are at odds with each other. In their "Orthodox response" to "Women's Liberation," Chana Poupko and Devora Wohlgelernter point up these differences:

> It is here that we come to the question of priorities. Of the 36 capital crimes of the Torah, 18 deal with crimes which undermine the family unit: homosexuality,

incest, etc. The other 18 are things which ensure the preservation of *Klal Yisrael.*
. . . It seems clear that the priority is survival and for the sake of survival much must be sacrificed. . . . The concept of sacrifice is alien to the modern feminist movement. But, sacrifice is inherent in Jewish thought. The Midrash says that Yitzchak was blind after the *Akedah.* Perhaps what the Midrash is telling us is that when there is a priority involved, one never gets away as a whole person. The point of the *Akedah* is that every Jew is a sacrifice on the altar. The feminist notion of "self-fulfillment" is likewise foreign to Jewish thought and attempts at translation result in the derogatory expression, *sipuk atzmi,* which has a selfish connotation. . . . It seems that our Sages saw self-fulfillment in terms of the nation's preservation.[123]

Personal agendas, family agendas, and communal agendas—as we have seen in the preceding analysis—are often in conflict in the lives of contemporary American Jewish men and women. Personal fulfillment often conflicts directly or indirectly with optimum family life, and both personal and familial goals may diverge from communal goals. In resolving these conflicts, the American Jewish community is faced with an extraordinary challenge, one, Jewish feminists point out, that should not be perceived as a challenge facing women alone.

To strong proponents of feminism, the multifaceted flowering of American Jewish women overshadows any communal difficulties which may result. Jewish feminists argue that the personal needs of female individuals are as significant as the personal needs of male individuals. If those needs must be sacrificed for the sake of the family, the community, or *klal yisrael,* they contend, women should not bear the burden alone. Women will no longer consent to be the "sacrifice" that guarantees the well-being of a male-centered community.

Remembering that women comprise, after all, at least one-half of the Jewish people, it seems appropriate for Jewish survivalists of all denominations to reconsider the validity of feminist goals case by case and to search for constructive ways in which to reconcile Jewish feminism with the goals of Jewish survival. It is hard to imagine what communal good could be served by religious and communal leaders rigidly adhering to an automatic antifeminist stance. On the other hand, it seems appropriate for Jewish feminists, to the extent that they are serious about Jewish survival, to weigh carefully the repercussions of proposed changes and to consider their responsibility to the community as a whole. Indeed, it is one of the achievements of American Jewish feminism that women are now in a position to examine these issues—and to make choices.

---

[123]Chana K. Poupko and Devora L. Wohlgelernter, "Women's Liberation—An Orthodox Response," *Tradition,* Spring 1976, pp. 45–52.

Rage and Representation:
Jewish Gender Stereotypes in American Culture

RIV-ELLEN PRELL

Jewish mothers, for more than fifty years, and Jewish princesses for the last decade, are well-known and pervasive stereotypes of Jewish women held by Jews, as well as by many other Americans. In combination, the two stereotypes provide opposing, if related, images of women who overwhelm men, respectively, by excessive nurturance or acquisitiveness.

According to these stereotypes, Jewish mothers give too much, whether it is food or demands for success. They suffer and induce guilt in their ever disloyal children, particularly sons. They behave like martyrs and constantly deny their own needs and wishes. The Jewish mother's character is captured well by the ethnic variant on the light bulb jokes of the 1970s.

How many Jewish mothers does it take to change a light bulb?
None, "I'll sit in the dark."[1]

Martyred, willing to sacrifice, yet miffed at those who neglect her and forget her sacrifices, the stereotypical Jewish mother exaggerates all forms of maternal nurturing only to invert them by her demand to be compensated through the constant love and attention she will never directly request.

By contrast, Jewish American Princesses (JAPs) require everything and give nothing. In jokes about them, they are completely focused on themselves and their overwhelming needs. They do not nurture, but require others to meet their constant demands. They do not take responsibility, or cook, or clean for their families. They are particularly obsessed with their physical attractiveness, although not in the interest of sexual pleasure. A widely circulating joke about JAPs conjures up the stereotype.

"How do you get a JAP to stop having sex? Marry her."

In this paper I examine pervasive Jewish gender stereotypes held by Jewish men about Jewish women. They appear in popular, widely circulated jokes,

Originally published in *Uncertain Terms: Negotiating Gender in American Culture*, edited by Faye Ginsburg and Anna Lowenhaupt Tsing, 1990. Reprinted by permission of Beacon Press.

as well as in canonized literature written by American Jewish men. These gender stereotypes are changing. Jewish mothers are yielding to Jewish American Princesses, and a male stereotyped persona, the Jewish American Prince, is appearing on the scene for the first time. Stereotypes, then, change because they are sensitive to changing issues of relations between ethnic and majority groups. I will argue that the changing humor and stereotypes reveal the conflicts experienced by Jewish men as they negotiate their difference from and continuity with American culture.

These stereotypes certainly reveal a particular form taken by Jewish men's ideas and anxieties about women. What is less apparent is that the women of these jokes may also symbolize many facets of American Jewish life for men. The culture that gave rise to and nurtured these widely known gender images communicated powerful constructions of what constituted success, Americanization, loyalty, and Jewishness. Gender and ethnicity are linked in this humor because how Jewish men think about Jewish women may well reveal how they think about themselves as Americans and Jews.

Scholars of ethnicity, normally committed to the study of boundaries and differences, in this case between Jews and Christians, systematically overlook the *intra*-group differentiation between men and women who share an ethnic group. Gender and ethnicity are rarely, and only recently considered together. Men and women, for example, may be joined by ethnic ties, but they often experience the consequences and meaning of their ethnicity differently. Feminist anthropologists, historians, and sociologists have demonstrated the significance of these differences in a variety of cultures and historical periods.

Gender is significant not only because it forms the basis of social relationships within ethnic groups, but also because it frequently symbolizes the ethnic group for its members, as well as outsiders. Long suffering, nurturing mothers and distant fathers are each gender-coded symbols, which may represent an entire ethnic group in the mass media and to its members. Interpreting these stereotypes provides clues for understanding what links gender to ethnicity and how that link operates to establish both differentiation from outsiders and within groups.

Gender can be made to represent ethnic experience because it is so closely associated with relationships—self and other, child and parent—that quite explicitly portray one's place in a group. Gender, then, can be linked to intimacy or outsiderhood, or versions of both, and is a powerful symbolic vehicle for constructing, and reconstructing, the significance of ethnicity for minority men and women within a dominant culture.

Stereotyping is inevitable when groups, differentiated by a variety of factors, meet within a single social system. Stereotypes simplify and concretize difference. Sometimes humans admire others from afar, creating positive stereotypes, but more often stereotypes denigrate and differentiate groups to the advantage of those who hold these ideas. In neither positive nor negative cases are stereotypes accurate depictions of reality. Rather, they are representations of others, sometimes created out of limited shared experiences, and sometimes out of fears projected on others one may know well. Gender stereotypes are more likely the latter. In combination with ethnicity, gender stereotypes may be decoded to understand how difference is expressed not only between groups, but within them, as well.

Jewish stereotypes, like all other cultural stereotypes, rely on broad social categories. For example, both European and American Jewish humor have employed culturally significant categorical differences, such as social class, region of origin, and level of religious and secular education. Contemporary American Jewish humor, however, particularly since the 1960s, seems singularly focused on gender. The Jewish mother is the most prominent figure of contemporary Jewish humor[2] and jokes about her began before the Second World War. Jokes about Jewish American Princesses developed in the 1960s and flowered in the 1980s. As a result, the joke repertoire about Jewish women includes wives and potential marriage partners, as well as mothers. As Susan Schnur wrote about students, Jewish and non-Jewish, whom she taught at Colgate University in 1987, "I had been raised on moron jokes; *they* had been raised on JAP jokes."[3] Jokes about Jewish women have become a common coin of American life, as well as the central province of American Jewish humor. The subjects and numbers of jokes about women are expanding, but the images are redundant. The Jewish mother and princess reflect one another. The jokes often rest on simple inversions of characterizations thought to be ridiculous.[4]

Gendered jokes have dominated American Jewish humor, but women rather than men are consistently the subjects of these jokes. There are no Jewish father jokes, and the Jewish American Prince is just developing as a stereotype, not yet the subject of a series of jokes. Both the prominence of women in the humor and the absence of men from it require explanation as much as the roles (mother and princess) that are featured, to the exclusion of any other type of woman. Gender stereotypes, and the humor that makes use of them, seem neither random nor idiosyncratic. They depend on a narrowed, yet consistent set of messages and ideas. Jewish women are, for example, associated with a number of roles and activities, as well as social movements that range beyond mother and potential wife. The presence of Jewish women in unions, Socialist movements, and contemporary politics from feminism to anti-war activism conceivably could have yielded a stereotype of a political activist. Many Jewish women have, like their middle- and upper-class counterparts in the larger society, been active participants in voluntary and charitable associations, but no stereotype of a "society lady" has emerged. Linking Jewish women to men through these two stereotypes is an issue to be understood rather than assumed.

Marilyn Strathern, an anthropologist who writes about New Guinea, has put the problem of gender stereotypes well by differentiating between "the ideal" and the "actual,"[5] urging us never to read from stereotype to behavior, or idealized images to actual social relations, because representations are not actualities. Gender stereotypes are symbolic representations of the sexes, underpinning formal relations of authority or power. While typifications may tell us about many features of a society, how women and men actually function in a particular social system cannot be predicted by the stereotype alone. In Strathern's research among New Guinea Hageners, men and women may well be associated with either gender stereotype. Stereotypes must be "read" for cultural notions and then interpreted in light of how men and women behave. The inevitable inconsistencies can aid our understanding of cultural prescriptions, as well as the realities of social existence.

In a pluralistic and literate society the matter of stereotypes is more complex. Stereotypes are often written into literature, which is then read by members of the subculture, as well as by those outside of it. Inscribed in print, these stereotypes take on reality for people inside and outside a subculture. At the same time, male and female stereotypes may stand as cultural symbols for a series of relationships between opposites. They may also symbolize intra-psychic conflicts about belonging and rejection, associating women, for example, with negative ethnic group qualities, such as aggression, and distancing males from these associations. All of these possibilities only underscore Strathern's caution, that gender stereotypes cannot be read literally but must be understood in a series of contexts.

Strathern's insight is crucial for understanding American Jewish gender stereotypes. The popular and scholarly studies of these stereotypes consistently discuss whether or not they are "true" or "provable." While Jews have long been engaged in combatting anti-Semitic stereotypes, their encounter with gender stereotypes is of a different order. Jewish gender stereotypes are largely held among and generated by Jews themselves. They tend, then, to articulate internally held constructions. Yet, they bristle with the hostility and degradation that are associated with anti-Semitism. To read the stereotypes as actualities moves us away from the task of understanding what they mean.

Some argue that the stereotypes are untrue, others that they are true, and others still that they are both true and untrue.[6] Those that argue they are untrue claim, by way of sociological and quantifiable studies that, for example, Jewish mothers are not measurably more protective than others, or that Jewish college aged women are not different from their peers.[7] They claim, particularly in the cases where these stereotypes are also held in the wider society, that these caricatures are codes for anti-Semitic accusations masked by gender.[8] And indeed, some suggest that gender slurs seem to function to overshadow the transparent anti-Semitism.[9]

Nevertheless, there are those who argue that the stereotypes are based on accurate descriptions of behavior, and link their "truth" to cultural and historical developments. They explain that a history of uncertainty and oppression creates a preoccupation with safety, hence the Jewish mother with her suffocating behavior.[10] Others argue that a long religious tradition of sexual repression leads to certain attitudes toward the body and pleasure, hence the Jewish woman characterized as the frigid Jewish princess.[11] Or, as folklorist Alan Dundes suggests, more recent Jewish American Princess stereotypes suggest a rejection of middle-class norms that idealize complicit women devoted to denying their own needs in order to satisfy those of their families.[12]

Finally, there are those who write that the stereotypes are *both* true and untrue. For example, several writers who have looked at the stereotypes of Jewish women's sexuality suggest that Jewish men may denigrate women's sexuality out of their fear of inadequately competing with gentile men.[13] Others argue that these stereotypes constitute a Jewish internalization of anti-Semitism expressed by the larger culture. This more profoundly psychological analysis recognizes the complex process by which minorities represent themselves to themselves as outsiders in a majority culture. These typifications involve internalized negative stereotypes held by others about one's own group. The very popularity of the JAP jokes with some non-Jews may well support this point. The implicit anti-Semitism of JAP jokes means one thing within the Jewish community and another outside of it, but both associate Jews with an unfair and undeserved affluence.[14] Indeed, the JAP humor of the late 1980s is more hostile and, by implication, violent than previous decades.

What is the difference between a JAP and a vulture?
Painted Nails.
What do you call 48 JAPs floating face down in a river?
A start.[15]

Jokes, such as these, wish the death of people who are both women and Jews. The graffiti about JAPs reported on college campuses suggests that these stereotypes share much in common with racist ones. The line between "self-hate" and anti-Semitism is becoming harder to draw.

My point is not to support or deny these analyses of stereotypes. Rather, it is to suggest that virtually all approaches to the study of Jewish gender stereotypes invoke an unexpectedly positivist base that assumes they are capable of being accurate reflections of reality, or at least partially true, or generated from seekers of truth. What is missing in this conversation is some sense of these gender stereotypes as symbolic representations of American Jewish experience, and any inquiry into why relations between men and women are a medium for constructing Jews' relationships to other Jews and to American culture.

The humor, as I read it, suggests a fundamental incompatibility at the core of American Jewish culture. To be an American and a Jew necessitates relinquishing one or another of those identities. Social class, career aspirations, styles of interaction and sexuality—separately and together—are codes for and symbols of how one is American. I suggest that the stereotypical suffocating mother or whiny and withholding wife express ideas about how Jewish men understand their own place in American society. These stereotypical women represent the anxiety, anger, and pain of Jewish men as they negotiate an American Jewish identity. Jewish women, in these stereotypes, symbolize elements of "Jewishness" and "Americanness" to be rejected. Jewish women represent these features precisely because of their link to Jewish men, whom they do and do not resemble. Like a distorted mirror, Jewish men see Jewish women as inaccurately reflecting themselves. These stereotypes suggest that women may be represented as "too Jewish" or "too American," through their pattern of sexuality, nurturance, and consumption. Because gender and ethnicity are about sameness and difference, these stereotypes associate certain features of American and Jewish life with women that Jewish men fear and wish to abandon.

AMERICAN CULTURE AND THE JEWISH AMERICAN PRINCESS

No one is certain where this stereotype began, but a princess-like character appears in Herman Wouk's novel *Marjorie Morningstar*,[16] and the character of Brenda Patimkin in Philip Roth's short story "Goodbye Columbus" some years later.[17] Both works of fiction were made into popular films. This stereotyped young woman is a figure of post-war American Jewish affluence, whose key features concern consumption and sexuality, activities that figure as structural opposites in the humor and stereotype. The JAP is as rapacious and eager a consumer as she is unwilling to engage with her husband in an animated and mutually satisfying sexual relationship. When she is sexually active it is as a lure to entrapment.

The JAP can be both a wife and a daughter in the humor, and both relations make possible her insatiable desire to consume through acquiring expensive things and going to expensive places. Perhaps the most often told "consumption joke" asks, "What is a JAPs' favorite wine?" The punch line ranges from, "Take me to Florida" to "Buy me a mink." The answer not only may interchange various luxury consumer items for one another, but can vary depending on the person to whom it is directed. Some versions specifically include "Daddy, take me to..." in the joke. Such jokes use consumption to link a woman to her husband and her father as vehicles for achieving her desire. JAP jokes about sexuality only link husband and wife and assume her to be withholding and uninterested, or portray the JAP as sexually active because she is an unmarried woman. One JAP joke makes the complex links disturbingly clear. "How do you give a JAP an orgasm? Scream 'Charge it to Daddy'."[18] There is no mutuality in any of these relations. The JAP takes but does not give. She takes because she is dependent and may give only to create dependence.

What is particularly striking about the humor as Jewish humor is how it portrays the butt of the jokes. Jewish humor in Europe and America typically has been iconoclastic. It is anti-authoritarian, mocking all authorities, including God. Jews have often used their sharp humor to puncture the authorities within and without their community, who could not otherwise be criticized. Little people tended to emerge triumphant by the punch line of the joke.[19] This humor often ridicules the grandiose as offending a fundamentally democratic spirit. By contrast, the JAP, almost always the butt of the joke, is a whiner and a consumer, but she is neither powerful nor authoritative. Paradoxically, she, not the males who support her, is open to ridicule. As American Jewish humor focuses on gender, its sharp edge is directed at a relatively powerless figure. If the JAP is grandiose, the others in her world of affluence are free of ridicule and not the butt of the joke.

JAP jokes are atypical Jewish humor for a second reason. They are unmarked by any specific Jewish characteristics. There is no Yiddish in the jokes, or even dialects, both of which have been essential features of many generations of American Jewish jokes. The JAP has few qualities in common with other Jewish characters in Jewish humor. She is neither the fool, nor a clever deceiver. There is only a small measure of parody in the humor and some irony. If there is one humorous device it is, of course, exaggeration, but little else.

JAP jokes are constructed around completely American figures in American settings, behaving like Americans, in other words: consumers. Indeed, even the name of the stereotype, the JAP, is interesting because of the position of "American" in it. "Jewish mothers," or "German Jews," or "rabbis," or "schnorrers" (hangers on), never carried a cultural designation specific to the United States. The JAP stereotype is overwhelmingly marked by the American experience; the post-war American experience, in particular. Although there is evidence in earlier immigrant novels of vulgar bourgeois women, in Yezierska's *Bread Givers*[20] and Gold's *Jews Without Money*,[21] they were neither young, nor on the verge of marriage. Even married JAPs do not have children. Brenda Patimkin's mother in Roth's "Goodbye Columbus" was a woman of the suburbs, but she was not a princess, for all her wealth and attractiveness. The JAP, then, has no accent, and no history marred by suffering, hunger, or want, all typical of immigrant experiences. She is not only fully American, but epitomizes American success; she is affluent.

THE CONSTRUCTION OF THE JAP STEREOTYPE

The JAP is in every way American, and yet she is the butt of contemporary Jewish humor. What, then, is funny about the Americanness of the JAP? The answer lies in part in understanding from whose perspective the JAP is constructed. The JAP is a different type of Jew and American than the teller of the joke. Folklorist Alan Dundes' analysis of the JAP implies that Jewish women have created the image as a protest. He writes, "For women, the JAP joke cycle pinpoints what's wrong with the traditional roles women were expected to accept cheerfully in the American upwardly mobile, middle-class."[22] However, these jokes are not told from the point of view of women. They are always told *about* women. Women are the butt of the jokes.²³ Although women may tell these jokes, they tend to tell them about others. Although some women may call themselves "JAPs," or wear gold necklaces that say "JAP," they are typifying themselves from another's point of view.

Dundes draws a peculiar conclusion about the JAP joke from the point of view of women when he insists that the disinclination of women to engage in oral sex is because it "presumably give(s) primary pleasure to males."²⁴ Nowhere do the jokes suggest that any form of sex is pleasant for women. And Dundes also argues that the humor portrays autonomous women because the JAP is free to shop and beautify herself. This conclusion is hardly convincing if we are to believe that this joke cycle appeals to middle-class women as an expression of protest against their lack of autonomy and self-expression.

In JAP jokes women are passive, except for engaging in those activities done for the purpose of making themselves attractive—shopping, staying thin, and beautifying themselves—which depend on leisure and affluence. A greeting card that consists of JAP jokes portrays a JAP: She is standing, dressed in tennis whites. She wears high heeled shoes, drapes a mink coat over her shoulder, wears a long strand of pearls at her neck, and a Diet Pepsi with a straw stands before her. The diet beverage and tennis attire suggest a preoccupation with staying thin, but the portrayal of her as a physically active or competent woman, even for leisure, is undermined by the presence of jewelry, mink coat and, above all, high heeled shoes. Affluence and consumption undermine her physical vigor.

These stereotyped women are emulating culturally prescribed standards of beauty associated with the highest social strata. Whether this form of beauty—obsessively thin and highly styled—is directed toward men may be debatable. Nevertheless, this appearance depends on affluence and leisure, the combination of which is most likely acquired through marriage.

The jokes and images present women as non-sexual and narcissistic. More to the point, they make men victims of prey of women because men finance consumption but get nothing in return. In the jokes JAPs withhold sex and victimize men. These jokes, their images, their anger, and exaggeration are constructed by males about women. The perspective of the joke teller and the butt are quite straightforwardly differentiated by gender. What appears to be funny about the jokes, what constitutes a "protest" in the humor, is that men saddled with demands for producing economically to finance consumption reveal their true oppressors. The message of the humor is that Jewish wives or potential wives are slave drivers and ridiculous in their unceasing consumption. For all of their apparent beauty JAPs are frauds, sexless and childish. Men tell these jokes as an apparent protest against their fate with these women.

Paul Cowan's memoir about his journey to become a Jew articulates a related perspective.²⁵ He wrote about events that occurred decades before he became committed to feminism and Judaism. Consequently, we must read this passage about his relationship to Jewish women as a young man in light of his "new" consciousness. In the memoir he describes why he avoided young Jewish women after reading *Marjorie Morningstar*. In this novel he discovered "Shirleys," stereotyped Jewish women feared by the novel's initially appealing male character, Noel Airman, who wants a career in theater. For Wouk and Cowan the "Shirley"—a predecessor of the JAP— had the potential to ruin a man's life. Cowan writes:

I feared that Jewish women would imprison me. It left me feeling scared that my idealized version of my adult self as a latter day James Agee or John Dos Passos would be stifled by some Shirley who outwardly encouraged me to adventure, but who privately planned to trap me in a stifling suburban home. By contrast, the blondes to whom I was attracted were golden girls who would help me act out my journalist's version of the frontiersman's dream. They would provide me with protective coloration....[26]

Cowan makes explicit that the JAP stereotype is a gender stereotype held by Jewish men about Jewish women. It is constructed by a Jewish man in opposition to his immediate world. He does not want to exist within his family's expectations. He does not want to be forced to work or live like his father, who achieved affluence for the family. He does not want to be constrained by the expectations or narrowed vistas of American Jews hurtling themselves toward suburban success.

Precisely as the Jewish male rejects the Jewish American Princess as the embodiment of middle-class Jewish life, he does so with another woman and another life in mind. I would argue that JAPs are always constructed in contrast to a concealed stereotyped Christian woman who Lenny Bruce called "the shiksa goddess," or Philip Roth portrayed as "the monkey" in *Portnoy's Complaint*.[27] If Jewish women consume, then there is an unnamed stereotyped woman who does not. If the JAP avoids oral sex, as in the single minded preoccupation of JAP jokes, there is a stereotyped woman who apparently delights in it. Cowan implies this general opposition between Jewish and Gentile women when he writes of the "protective coloration" of the "golden girl," who is decisively not Jewish. If the JAP is accessible and the expected partner of the Jewish man, the Shiksa may be interesting in part because she, like many aspects of American culture, may not be attainable.

In the published text of a performance piece, "The Last Jew in America," Susan Mogul reflects Cowan's and Wouk's construction of Jewish men's attitudes toward Jewish women by dramatizing a Jewish woman's view of this relationship in the following monologue:

My mother said, "You know, Susan, you could be the last Jew in America, with the way all your brothers and sisters are intermarrying." I thought I owed it to my research, at least to try to go after a Jewish guy and see what it's like. Who knows?

Anyway, I went out to the Beverly Hills singles bars one night, and I had absolutely no luck. Christian guys would come up and we talked, but no Jewish action whatsoever. So I called up my friend Carol Mike on the phone and I said, "You know, Jewish men just don't want to date Jewish women, I'm convinced of it. We'll conduct a scientific experiment. I'll prove I'm right."

I went down to Woolworth's and I picked up this cross for $5.95, and of course, I scratched the words "not really" on the back to protect myself from the wrath of my father and of God as well. (She hangs the cross around her neck.)

Well! You would not believe the action. You think I'm exaggerating, but really. I'd never gotten so much attention from Jewish men *in my life*, or from men at all.[28]

Cowan and Mogul both reveal a construction of Jewish gender relations in which Jewish men reject Jewish women. A woman is not essentially attractive or unattractive. What makes a woman attractive to a Jewish man is that she is identifiably non-Jewish. As a non-Jew she will not be focused on consumption, her husband's productivity, and success, either because she already has it or because she is so poor and undemanding she cannot imagine it.

The asymmetry of the identifiers "American" (desirable) and "Jewish" (undesirable) reflects a second asymmetry between male and female. What is constructed in these male generated Jewish gender stereotypes is not a simple, more familiar mirror image. We do not find oppositions, such as male is to female as strong is to weak or aggressive is to passive. Rather, we find a triangulated relationship. Jewish men are to Jewish women are to Christian women as successful is to demanding is to acquiescent, or as sexual potency is to frigidity is to sexual desire. The third term is ever present but always invisible. It is the JAP's Jewishness and its relationship to her Americanness that the stereotype and humor feature. Jewishness is what she shares with the constructor of the stereotype. As he seeks his counterpart, he must construct two females, one like him and one unlike him, rejecting the Jewish woman and their shared qualities in favor of the American woman. Frederic Cople Jaher argues that in American Jewish fiction, Jewish protagonists are inevitably punished for their liaisons with gentile women. He writes that "Jewish boys who forsake Jehovah and virtuous women of their own faith for Dionysius and gentile temptresses inevitably get punished."[29] Jewish gendered humor, as well as the stereotype itself, demonstrates that Jewish men also perceive themselves as punished for liaisons with "virtuous women of their own faith." The punishment results from associating Jewish women with the American economic success that deprives men of the sexual rights associated with Gentile women.

CONSUMERS AND CONSUMED:
THE REFIGURING OF AMERICAN AFFLUENCE

The JAP stereotype describes married, but apparently childless women, or women in search of a marriage partner at the age of marriageability.

Like the princess of fairy tales, the JAP always stands on the threshold of womanhood. The JAP's link to marriage is the most salient feature in her portrait as entrapper. Middle-class American Jewish men, not unlike most American men in the middle-class, see adult status, ambition, career, and marriage as linked. Mainstream American Jewish culture has successfully encouraged its young adults to make choices that lead to careers that guarantee, at minimum, a middle-class life. The American Jewish family has made this career pattern for men its highest priority since immigration, certainly emphasizing education and success over religious observance and Jewish education. Not only are American Jews economically successful ethnics, they have achieved their success through education leading to a limited number of professional and career choices. They do so with remarkable loyalty to their ethnic group, demonstrated by their choice to live among Jews and maintain Jewish friendships. This pattern is particularly true of second and subsequent generations of men who have been in the work force for a longer time than Jewish women and whose careers are determinative of family social class status.[30] Although, as a group Jewish women are well-educated, until recently they stayed at home with their children and entered the labor force much later, if at all.[31] These Jewish patterns are, of course, shared with the white middle-class. Major demographic studies of New York, Boston, and Rhode Island demonstrate that Jewish success and Jewish identification, although not religious adherence, have been achieved.[32]

In American culture, success is associated with and symbolized by consumption, particularly since the Second World War. Jokes centering on JAPs' preoccupation with consumption, T-shirts that proclaim "I live to shop," and all the caricatures of spending to excess are the products of this pervasive American pattern. Warren Susman[33] and William H. Whyte,[34] among others, have written about the transformation of American society to a consumption rather than production oriented culture. Nothing characterizes the suburban family more completely than shared consumption. And Elaine May's recent book on the post-war family maintains that consumption was a critical element in maintaining families against divorce in the 1950s.[35] Indeed, her discussion of the Nixon-Kruschev debates in the 1950s demonstrates that even global policy was argued on the grounds of who had better consumer items and would be likely to maintain them over time.

The JAP stereotype, then, articulates the epitome of middle-class life and family oriented consumption, whether owning the proper designer labels, spending a great deal of time in restaurants, or redecorating a home. The humor moves back and forth in its portrayal of the JAP as American (focused on consumption) and Jewish (narcissistic, sexually withholding, and manipulative). The jokes in no overt sense differentiate Jewish and American, but the humor depends on identifying against the JAP. The ironic juxtaposition of consumption and frigidity make clear that the JAP is the consummate consumer who cannot herself be consumed. A series of jokes, in fact, juxtapose shopping and sex.

How does a JAP fake an orgasm? She thinks of going shopping.
What's a JAP's favorite position? Bending over credit cards.
What's a JAP's favorite position? Facing Neiman-Marcus (or Bloomingdale's).[36]

All that has been achieved by American success has been showered on the JAP, who inexplicably resists the sexual relationship that assures her continued affluence. This stereotype-driven humor, of course, does not *describe* Jews' social class, women's shopping habits, or sexual relations. Rather, it *represents* Jewish men's distress about becoming American men. Jewish women are portrayed as a barrier to adult male life because they withhold sex and demand production. Men are victimized by both demands and refusals. What appears to be the normal steps to adult life—education, career, marriage—in jokes and stereotypes are perilous steps on the way to disaster because of who waits in the wings as the appropriate marriage partner. Marriage will not ensure sexuality, and will lead to a career that will drive one toward giving and receiving nothing in return. JAP jokes are only peripherally about women. Rather, women's demands and refusals symbolize what will become of men as they enter adulthood, only to be deprived of their dreams.

LINKS AND SPACES BETWEEN JEWISH MOTHERS AND JEWISH AMERICAN PRINCESSES

To understand these key elements of the stereotype—consumption and the refusal to be consumed—requires reconsidering the older, more conventional female gender stereotype of the Jewish mother. Dundes' discussion of this stereotype attempts to generate the new acronym JAM, Jewish American Mother, but it is his invention and has not yet caught on in the culture. The Jewish mother has no geographic specificity. Novak and Waldoks, in their *Big Book of Jewish Humor*, suggest that the humorous figure of the Jewish mother appears only after migration to America.[37] This view is only partially correct. There has always been a Jewish mother or "Yiddishe mama," but she was not a butt of humor until the second generation of immigrant society. Henry Roth's *Call It Sleep*[38] and Michael Gold's *Jews Without Money* both enshrine a perfect mother. She is present everywhere in the immigrant experience, from music to theater and film to novels. But she is the representation of the lost world, the fantasy perfect mother, who is characterized above all by total and complete self-sacrifice for others, particularly her sons. Indeed, Novak and Waldoks argue that it is the Jewish mother's changing economic role that is responsible for her becoming a figure of ridicule. In Europe, she was a productive member of the family. In America, she no longer actively contributed to its economic survival. Rather, her inactivity became a sign of the financial success of her husband.[39]

These changes may well contribute to the stereotype. Nevertheless, it is not her financial dependency but her preoccupation with her children and concern for them, the very aspects of the once romanticized Jewish mother, which are the subjects for ridicule. Her characteristics change less than the perceptions of them held by her sons. By the second generation, she became the butt of humor because Jewish men were now the products of families focused on acculturation and these sons rendered self-sacrifice as suffocation. Jewish men did not want to sacrifice and could not bear the sacrifices apparently implied by their mother's behavior. The all-giving mother was revealed as the all-demanding mother.

Ironically, for all of their differences, mother and princess present the same dangers to Jewish males. The Jewish mother cannot give her children enough food. The classic JAP joke about her ability to nurture states that what she makes best for dinner is "reservations." Over a period of a mere two decades the stereotype of the Jewish woman became two stereotypes; a nurturer and a person unable to cook, feed, or care for her family, particularly her husband. Jewish mothers were separated from Jewish wives. The Jewish mother, however, bears a partial resemblance to the "shiksa" who gives all and asks nothing. The difference between "shiksa" and "mother" is that there are hidden demands in the mother's gift, and that the mother is not Gentile, American, or mainstream. Shiksas are not associated with food and they are less nurturant than undemanding. Ultimately, then, what unites the Jewish mother and the Jewish princess is that each is a threat to the Jewish male; son and potential husband. These women are entrappers and seducers. Neither will give without asking for something in return. They are also bound to one another by their relationships to men.

Are Jewish mothers represented as having special alliances with Jewish princesses? Are these gender representations linked? I would suggest not. In literature, humor and folklore Jewish mothers are primarily tied to their sons. Jewish princesses seem to be made by their fathers in the humor I have reviewed. In all types of literature, humor, and folklore there is an ever present sexual antagonism between men and women of the same generation, and an over attachment across generations. What cannot or will not be expressed between men and women of the same generation is played out between parents and opposite sex children as intimacy without a sexual component. Mothers indulge their sons and fathers indulge their daughters. Mothers hold out high aspirations for their sons, apparently expecting them to be different from the men they married. Fathers withdraw from their wives, and delight in creating a royal daughter, despite the fact that they are never portrayed as kings.[40] The father-daughter link portrayed in JAP humor and stereotypes reflects the sudden affluence of many Jews following a major economic depression and World War Two.[41]

ACCULTURATION AND ITS COSTS

In these gender stereotypes we see at work both the representations of profound contradictions in American Jewish life, and the process of transmitting those very contradictions. In these stereotypes one finds consumption and success bought at the price of lost sexuality. We see women who demand and never reciprocate, leaving men successful yet betrayed. We see men feeling themselves under constant threat of annihilation, either in the person of the suffocating mother or the parasitic wife. The success that makes consumption possible satisfies the mother but does not provide the avenue for adult sexuality or mutuality. The promises of American culture pay off only in liaisons with the other, the shiksa or Gentile, who then makes it impossible to continue Jewish life.[42]

The cultural costs and implications of an economic system in which men produce and women consume is well-documented. From Thorsten Veblen to feminist Barbara Ehrenreich, social critics have noted the inevitability of men's resentment and women's portrayal as parasites built into this division of labor.[43] Elisa New's analysis of a recent book about the trial of a husband who murdered his wife because she was a "Jewish princess" effectively argues that Jews have collapsed American Jewish culture with American success, to such an extent that they have become indistinguishable.[44] Female representations among Jews—mother and princess—then clearly share much in common with other middle-class representations of women as narcissistic and sexually withholding.

These analyses do not, however, address other implications for male-female opposition within the family. In the case of American Jews the Jewish family is associated with the continuation of the Jewish people. To marry a Jewish partner is increasingly seen as the most certain insurance for transmitting a culture and history. Sociologists have documented thoroughly the fact that when they form families American Jewish adults become synagogue members and ritual participants. The center of Jewish life has moved from community to family to the individual. The individual is the center of gravity for Judaism. The choices leading to economic success and endogamous marriage are the most powerful promise for a continuing Jewish people.

The individualism of the American Jew, however, is rather different from the individualism of American culture, which idealizes the freedom to move anywhere, unfettered by any past. Unlike the quintessential American communities of the 1970s described by Frances FitzGerald, American Jews do not make up their lives free of a history.[45] The American Jew is, of course, no longer closely tied to a community bound by shared religious obligations and a single status hierarchy, as was the case for many centuries for Jews throughout the world. American Jews do not deny one another a place in their communities if they desecrate the Sabbath or violate various laws of purity. Nevertheless, neither are they free of a past nor do strongly identified Jews hope that their children will set out in search of an uncharted future. American Jews' persistent identification with Judaism despite their non-observance of Jewish religious practice makes clear to their children that they should continue to be Jews. Individuals are autonomous and free to make their own choices. But these choices include the proper marriage partners, having children who understand that they are Jews, and being successful. These choices are expected, even overdetermined. They seem to be the minimum requirement for remaining within the normative Jewish community. Approval, love, and acceptance, qualities often associated with Jewish families, are typically withdrawn when individuals exercise their "autonomy" to make the wrong choices. Undeniably, American Jewish families emphasize these issues as they raise their children, and it is these cultural demands that are represented in the humor.

To be free of JAPs is to assert one's freedom from obligation, responsibility, and productivity, but it is also to negate the Jewish people, the family, and hence the self. To be linked to a JAP is to undermine the self linked to community. The Jewish mother who nurtures, protects, and rewards makes one Jewish and successful. The JAP takes and withholds and is constructed as the poisoned reward for success. This terrible dilemma is normally associated with the "wrong" choices made by Jewish men who are attracted to the forbidden outsider, the shiksa, who symbolizes an unambiguous Americanization. Intermarriage, however, implies abandoning one's own family and people. The stereotypes that are increasingly apparent in the 1980s suggest that Jewish men construct Jewish women as representations of a vision of American success associated with their parents' dreams for them. In this sense, the JAP is another version of the Jewish mother, bent on blocking access to unfettered autonomy precisely because she represents American expectations for consumption and success. This culturally acceptable union continues the Jewish people both by promoting the achievement of success and producing another generation. Obviously, men share these cultural norms or the choice would not entail such conflict and agony. Marriage, women, and gender relations all symbolize this generationally transmitted conflict between the Jewish man's wish to enter adulthood and reproduce the Jewish people, and a fear of that course as destroying his development as an autonomous male.

Jewish gender images, then, represent the tension between reproducing Judaism, maturing and assuming responsibility, and pursuing one's destiny. That men were trained for careers and women for marriage was one common pattern for success that appears to evoke this inevitable tension. However, stereotypes are not sociological road maps for describing how American Jews became who they are. Rather, they symbolize, through one gender's perspective, the association of sexuality, acculturation, family, and consumption, the key themes of American Judaism in the post-war period. These could not be European or immigrant stereotypes because they assume affluence; they reflect and construct choices and possibilities unavailable until the period of increasing assimilation. Indeed, Jewish intermarriage skyrocketed in the 1960s when these stereotypes were just taking shape.[46] They speak most centrally to the association of Judaism and suburban success, and the projection of that desire for success onto women. Americanization as a middle-class aspiration appears to be feared by men, who associate Americanization with Jewish women. The other, the Gentile woman, remains a counterbalance fantasy partner for freedom from this connection, but at the cost of a future.

ARE THERE PRINCES IN THE ROYAL FAMILY?

I have emphasized female stereotypes in this chapter. I emphasize the perspective of the stereotype because it provides the key to understanding why these gender representations appear when they do and in the form that they do. There are stereotypes about Jewish men, but few are named. There is no Jewish father, for example, although there is the pervasive stereotype of the Jewish male as passive. Only recently has a defined stereotype of the Jewish prince emerged. The writer Nora Ephron describes him in her book *Heartburn*. He wants attention and service lavished upon him. She writes,

You know what a Jewish prince is, don't you? If you don't, there's an easy way to recognize one. A simple sentence, "Where's the butter?" Okay. We all know where the butter is, don't we? The butter is in the refrigerator . . . But the Jewish prince doesn't mean "Where's the butter?" He means "Get me the butter." He's too clever to say "Get me" so he says "Where's." And if you say to him (shouting) "in the refrigerator" and he goes to look, an interesting thing happens, a medical phenomenon that has not been sufficiently remarked upon. The effect of the refrigerator light on the male cornea. Blindness. "I don't see it anywhere." . . . I've always believed that the concept of the Jewish princess was invented by a Jewish prince who couldn't get his wife to fetch him the butter.[47]

The Jewish prince is simply the son of the Jewish mother. He has become the butt of the joke and stereotype. The presence of this stereotype simply inverts the mirroring images of one male and two women, one Christian and one Jewish, for one woman and two males.

These direct inversions—prince and princess—emerge as stereotypical parallel figures as Jewish mother and father did not. The culture generated a marked Jewish mother and left Jewish males entirely unmarked. Perhaps the newest gender stereotypes speak to a change in family relations, in part created by the fact that both men and women are likely to be employed. Changing family relations are unlikely, however, to be the sole explanation for these stereotypes. Gender representations continue to express the tensions and conflicts surrounding assimilation, acculturation, and success which continue to be associated with one's family of origin and choice of marriage partner.

I have argued that Jewish gender stereotypes are a strategic site for the analysis of American Jewish culture. I suggest that the focus of American Jewish humor on gender relations requires that we understand why these relations effectively symbolize how Jews attempt to remain Jews and live in the American mainstream. Understanding that the point of view of the stereotype is male, I have argued that Jewish women are associated with the desire for prestige, consumption, the continuity of the Jewish people, and the absence of erotic desire. Gender stereotypes are a rich vein to be mined for understanding American culture and the ways in which social class, ethnicity, gender and culture guide the construction of American lives.

These stereotypes suggest that Jewish men and women do not experience their Judaism in precisely the same way. Both are clearly affected by the association of Judaism with social class, but women, until recently, were dependent on husbands' and fathers' successes to achieve Americanization and mobility. Men reacted to that dependence in the portraits they made of wives and mothers as demanding and suffocating. The link of class and ethnicity is a close one for American Jews, who seek success without assimilation. Since cultural uniqueness is guaranteed by marriage choice, it should not be surprising that the dangers and enticements of assimilation are expressed in representations of Jewish women, both young and mature, as dependent, insatiable consumers with devastating power.

NOTES

I appreciate the helpful, often witty, always insightful comments of Howard Eilberg-Schwartz, Sara Evans, Steven Foldes, Amy Kaminsky, Elaine Tyler May, Cheri Register, Anna Tsing, and Barbara Tomlinson on a previous draft of this chapter.

1. William Novak and Moshe Waldoks, *The Big Book of Jewish Humor* (New York: Harper and Row, 1981).
2. William Novak and Moshe Waldoks, *The Big Book of Jewish Humor* (New York: Harper and Row, 1981).
3. Susan Schnur, "When a J.A.P. is not a Yuppie? Blazes of Truth," *Lilith: The Jewish Women's Magazine* 17 (1987): 10–11.
4. Alan Dundes "The J.A.P. and the J.A.M. in American Jokelore," *Journal of American Folklore* 98 (1985): 456–475. Dundes has also noted the link between these two stereotypes; as I note, our approaches differ on several points.
5. Marilyn Strathern, "Self Interest and the Social Good: Some Implications of Hagen Gender Imagery," in *Sexual Meanings; the Cultural Construction of Gender and Sexuality*, Sherry Ortner and Harriet Whitehead, eds. (Cambridge: Cambridge University Press, 1981), 166–91.
6. Dundes, 466–68, addresses these issues of Jewish women's stereotypes and some of the literature on the stereotypes.
7. See Zena Smith Blau, "In Defense of the Jewish Mother," *Midstream* 13 (2): 42–49 and Sherry Chyat, "JAP-Baiting on the College Scene," *Lilith: The Jewish Women's Magazine* 17 (1987): 42–49.
8. Chyat, 7.
9. Francine Klagsburn, "JAP: The New Anti-Semitic Code Words," *Lilith: The Jewish Women's Magazine* 17 (1987): 11.
10. Charlotte Baum, Paula Hyman and Sonya Michel, *The Jewish Woman in America* (New York: Plume, 1975), 242.
11. Susan Weidman Schneider, "In a Coma! I Thought She Was Jewish!: Some Truths and Some Speculations About Jewish Women and Sex," *Lilith: The Jewish Women's Magazine* (1979): 5–8.

12. Dundes, 470.
13. Schneider.
14. Jewish gender stereotypes have captured some interest of late. Graffiti was found in 1986 at Syracuse University throughout the library slurring Jewish American Princesses. These incidents have been discussed by Chayat 1987, Schnur 1987, and Judith Allen Rubenstein, "The Graffiti Wars," *Lilith: The Jewish Women's Magazine* 17 (1987): 8–9.
15. Cited in *Lilith* 17 (1987).
16. Herman Wouk, *Marjorie Morningstar* (Garden City, N.Y.: Doubleday, 1965).
17. Philip Roth, *Goodbye Columbus* (New York: Houghton Mifflin, 1959).
18. From Noble Works Greeting Card.
19. Novak and Waldoks, xx–xxi.
20. Anzia Yezierska, *Bread Givers: A Struggle between a Father of the Old World and a Daughter of the New* (New York: Pera Press, 1975). Originally published in 1925.
21. Michael Gold, *Jews Without Money* (New York: Avon Books, 1965). Originally published in 1930.
22. Dundes, 470.
23. The significance of gender for the perspective of the joke is also noted by Gladys Rothbell, "The Jewish Mother: Social Construction of a Popular Image," in *The Jewish Family: Myths and Reality,* Steven Cohen and Paula Hyman, eds. (New York: Holmes and Meir, 1986), and E. Fuchs, "Humor and Sexism," in *Jewish Humor,* Avner Ziv, ed. (Tel Aviv: Papyrus Publishing House, 1986).
24. Dundes, 470.
25. Paul Cowan, *An Orphan in History: Retrieving a Jewish Legacy* (Garden City, New York: Doubleday, 1982).
26. Cowan, 112.
27. Philip Roth, *Portnoy's Complaint* (New York: Random House, 1969).
28. Susan Mogul and Sandy Nelson, "The Last Jew in America: A Performance by Susan Mogul," *Images and Issues* 4 (1984): 22–24.
29. Frederic Cople Jaher, "The Quest for the Ultimate Shiksa," *American Quarterly* 35 (1983): 529.
30. See Steven M. Cohen, *American Assimilation or Jewish Revival?* (Bloomington: Indiana University Press, 1988) and Calvin Goldscheider and Alan S. Zuckerman, *The Transformation of the Jews* (Chicago: University of Chicago Press, 1984).
31. Sidney Goldstein and Calvin Goldscheider, *Jewish Americans: Three Generations in a Jewish Community* (Englewood Cliffs, N.J.: Prentice-Hall, 1966).
32. See Steven M. Cohen, *American Modernity and Jewish Identity* (New York: Tavistock, 1983), Cohen, and Goldstein and Goldscheider.
33. Warren I. Susman, *Culture as History: The Transformation of American Society in the Twentieth Century* (New York: Pantheon Books, 1984).
34. William H. Whyte, *The Organization Man* (Garden City, NY: Doubleday, 1956).
35. Elaine Tyler May, *Homeward Bound: American Families in the Cold War Era* (New York: Basic, 1988).
36. Dundes, 464. In the third joke, an obvious reference is made to Jews facing east when they pray in remembrance of their allegiance to ancient Israel

and Jerusalem, which was the center of worship. In the joke shopping is associated with prayer and sex is stimulated by facing a substitute sacred center.

37. Novak and Waldoks, 268.

38. Henry Roth, *Call It Sleep* (New York: Avon, 1976). Originally published in 1934.

39. Novak and Waldoks, 268.

40. Patricia Erens' study of the portrayal of Jews in American films demonstrates that in the 1920s the patriarchal father was the source of power and villainy in films. He grows weaker and virtually disappears from films as the mother grows more powerful and suffocating. See *The Jew in American Cinema* (Indiana University Press: Bloomington, 1984), 256–257.

41. Writers about eastern European Jewish life have emphasized the very powerful link between sons and mothers. Some have suggested a link between daughters and fathers as well, but in general the father is characterized as remote. Both the mother-son attachment and son-mother-in-law hostility are articulated in folklore, but far less exists around the daughter-father tie. See Marc Zborowski and Elizabeth Herzog, *Life is With People: The Culture of the Shtetl*, 8th ed. (New York: Schocken Books, 1971).

42. In a related argument regarding Roth's *Portnoy's Complaint,* Alan Segal notes that Portnoy can only escape his condition by "shedding" a Jewish identity which dominates and controls him. His means of escape is "sex with the goyim" or "shikses" on "a compulsive scale which both emancipates and imprisons him because its pleasure derives from it being forbidden." Segal does not focus on Roth's female contemporaries, but only the Jewish mother. Alan Segal, "Portnoy's Complaint and the Sociology of Literature," *British Journal of Sociology,* xxii (1971): 267.

43. *The Hearts of Men: American Dreams and the Flight From Commitment* (New York: Doubleday, 1983).

44. "Killing the Princess: The Offense of A Bad Defense," *Tikkun* 2 (1989): 17.

45. Frances FitzGerald, *Cities on a Hill: A Journey Through American Cultures* (New York: Simon and Schuster, 1986).

46. Cohen, *American Assimilation.*

47. Nora Ephron, *Heartburn* (New York: Knopf, 1983).

Value Added: Jews in Postwar American Culture

Stephen J. Whitfield

(BRANDEIS UNIVERSITY)

Americans are "descended from the same ancestors, speaking the same language, professing the same religion, attached to the same principles of government, very similar in their manners and customs," John Jay wrote in *The Federalist* No. 2, in defense of the new Constitution.[1] At least he got the politics right: All the basic political institutions of the United States had been created by the end of the eighteenth century, and none since then. But the Framers could scarcely have imagined how the culture would keep shifting into new configurations. Regional and ethnic customs would vary widely, new languages would get injected (at least for one or two generations) and religious pluralism would become legitimated, largely because Americans increasingly did *not* have the same ancestors.

In this kaleidoscope, virtually no minority has been more colorful than the Jews, whose integration into a culture that they themselves have helped to transform has been especially conspicuous in the postwar era. The argument of this essay is entangled in paradox, however, for the distinctiveness of the Jewish impact—which has extended the contours of American culture over the past half century—has also weakened the sense of difference that has historically defined Jewish identity itself. The value system of the majority has become so open and variegated that the Jews themselves are now less conscious of their own beleaguered status as a minority. So successfully have they become included in American society, so impressively have they contributed to its democratic spirit, that it has become problematic what remains of their own subculture, what still separates the Jews as a singular people, an *'am eḥad*.

One of their ancestors, Benedict Spinoza, was the first Western thinker to uncouple church and state and thus divide the sphere of values from the apparatus of power, in his *Tractatus Theologico-Politicus* (1670). More than a decade earlier, twenty-three Dutch Jews—they could not quite be classified as his "coreligionists"—became the first to disembark in what became the United States, where his principles would be pushed to their furthest point even as its citizenry continued to think of itself as pious. By certain indices, the Americans are more devout than any Western nation other than the Irish; and yet the American public culture has now become almost

Originally published in *Studies in Contemporary Jewry* 8 (1992). Reprinted by permission of Oxford University Press.

completely secularized, even surpassing the imagination of seventeenth-century skepticism. So complete is this triumph, for example, that Irving Berlin's "God Bless America" (1918, rev. 1938) could never conceivably replace "The Star Spangled Banner" as the national anthem, despite the fact that it is easy to sing and remember. The principle of separation of church and state is simply too much of an obstacle.[2]

Until the early 1960s, however, the full implications of secularization as well as pluralism were unrealized. Although the election of a Roman Catholic to the presidency has not recurred, John F. Kennedy's victory in 1960 meant that it was no longer necessary for the holder of the nation's highest office to be a Protestant. Two years later, another symbolic defeat was inflicted on the traditions of religious conformity with the landmark U.S. Supreme Court decision of *Engel* v. *Vitale*. Though Protestantism had long unofficially dominated public education in most of the country, the Supreme Court banned the recitation of prayer after the parents of five New York children challenged its compulsory feature. (One of these sixth-graders was eleven-year-old Joe Roth, the son of two Jewish Communists. Until his graduation, he later recalled, some of his classmates would cross themselves in fear before talking to him.) The shock waves caused by the ruling reverberated beyond Long Island and across the country. About 80 percent of the citizenry disagreed with the Supreme Court's ruling, and liberal as well as conservative clergy expressed their outrage. Two years later, the Republican candidate for the presidency doubted whether 1964 was "the time for our Federal government to ban Almighty God from our school rooms"; and a conservative Catholic, William F. Buckley, Jr., warned of increasing antisemitism if the Jews weren't "careful."[3]

Nonetheless, the *Engel* decision remained in force, and the pluralist ideal was thus not only vindicated but was also widely applied in practice. No single faith—not even Christianity itself—achieved a privileged status in the public culture, antisemitism continued to decline dramatically, and society became increasingly accommodating to minorities. Roth himself, who also survived "the theological reverence of Communism in my house," became a Hollywood film director and then head of the Twentieth Century Fox studios,[4] as though personally warranting President Richard M. Nixon's contempt for "the arts," as he told an aide in 1972, because "you know—they're Jews, they're left-wing—in other words, stay away!"[5]

Such antisemitic outbursts, especially when originating with intelligent people, can illuminate the impact of the Jews in American life, and in this sense they deserve at least as much scholarly attention as the claims of communal defense agencies. The florid exaggerations must be discounted, of course, but even the rancid complaint of Henry Adams, who was the grandson and great-grandson of earlier U.S. presidents, should not be dismissed: "We are in the hands of the Jews," he wrote in 1896. "They can do what they please with our values." Nearly two decades later, Adams amplified his sense of a cultural shift:

> The atmosphere really has become a Jew atmosphere. It is curious and evidently good for some people, but it isolates me. I do not know the language, and my friends are as ignorant as I. We are still in power, after a fashion. Our sway over what we call society

is undisputed. We keep Jews far away, and the anti-Jew feeling is quite rabid. . . . Yet we somehow seem to be more Jewish every day.[6]

Such anxieties were ugly, but they were not utterly misplaced. Indeed, they corresponded to the rise of an inescapable new system for the creation, packaging and marketing of the popular arts in which Jews were intimately involved. A revised edition of H. L. Mencken's *The American Language* noted, for instance, that "the most fruitful sources of Yiddish loans [into English] are the media of mass communications—journalism, radio and television."[7] Yet that lowly "jargon," which Henry Adams had found so "weird" when he heard it "snarled,"[8] is well-known to two recent American Nobel Prize laureates in literature: Isaac Bashevis Singer and one of his translators, Saul Bellow. In the family of a third laureate, Joseph Brodsky, Yiddish had already evaporated (though he was born in Russia itself, in 1940). But it is the mother tongue of still another writer holding U.S. citizenship to have won a Nobel Prize: Elie Wiesel. In Hollywood, meanwhile, newspapermen-turned-scenarists such as Ben Hecht (an urbane cynic whose Jewish nationalism became so ardent in the Second World War era that the Irgun later named an illegal immigrant ship after him) and Herman Mankiewicz (an atheist who kept a kosher home) helped make American movies in the 1930s and 1940s talk at a frenetic, witty pace. Hollywood's off-screen talk is still subject to ethnic fields of force. In a recent David Mamet play about movie deal makers, for example, "hiding the *afikomen*" is the double entendre for sexual "scoring" with the blonde secretary, whose own phoniness   Madonna played her on Broadway—one seedy character contrasts unfavorably with the Baal Shem Tov.[9] And when a new film monthly listed the most powerful figures in Hollywood, the first thirteen names already included enough for a minyan. Among them was Steven Spielberg, who is as rich as a brace of Bronfmans. The most successful director in history has *mezuzot* on the doorposts of his own ministudio.[10]

At one time Jews also headed all three private television networks, whose programs were noted in the most widely read magazine to be invented in the postwar era: *TV Guide*. From 1953 until 1989, its publisher was Walter H. Annenberg, the chief legatee of a family that savored a spectacular comeback from the New Deal era. (His father, who published the *Racing Form* and the *Inquirer*, had become so embroiled in anti-Roosevelt politics that the president growled to his secretary of the treasury: "I want Moe Annenberg for dinner." The cabinet officer's reply was reassuring: "You're going to have him for breakfast—fried." The publisher was convicted of income tax evasion and was jailed from 1940 until 1942, when he died of a heart attack. In 1969, Moe Annenberg's son got the satisfaction of becoming ambassador to the Court of St. James—a post to which John Jay had earlier been accredited.)[11]

And even Christian religious festivities have not been immune to Jewish influence, what with Irving Berlin strutting at the head of "The Easter Parade" (1933) and "Dreaming of a White Christmas"—the hit from *Holiday Inn* (1942) that may be the best-selling song ever. No wonder that an immigrant born with the name of Israel Baline grew up invoking the Deity to bless America.

Not only was the Jewish romance with America lavishly expressed in the postwar era; perhaps more importantly, it was reciprocated. Scholarly histories on the Jewish condition in the United States, though their titles may refer to "unease," very rarely draw divisions as do books about "Germans" and "Jews" (as though Jews could not *really* be Germans).[12] Or consider another contrast. A classic history of racism in the American colonies and early republic, Winthrop D. Jordan's *White over Black* (1968), is curiously subtitled "American Attitudes Toward the Negro" (when the author clearly means *white* attitudes). But the equivalent error that has assumed "American" to be synonymous with "gentile" is uncommon. Though the birth certificate of modern Jews is written in German, they were, in Solomon Liptzin's phrase, never more than "Germany's stepchildren." The "world of our fathers," however, for all of its poignant confusions and ferocious tensions, has become thoroughly implanted in America, where the children and grandchildren of Jewish immigrants have felt very much at home.

Millennia of martyrdom do not weigh heavily on the shoulders of most American Jews, who seem to bear no special historical burden of suffering and exhibit little sense of living in *galut*. At the dawn of the postwar era, Diana Trilling praised Isaac Rosenfeld's autobiographical novel *Passage from Home* for "its ability to use its Jewish background as a natural rather than a forced human environment." Rosenfeld had managed, she wrote as early as 1946, to "avoid the well-established emotions of Jewish separateness—the emotions of specialness, embattledness, social overdeterminism, self-pity and self-punishment." *Passage from Home* would thus help revise a paradigm that, to Trilling, had become a familiar minority sensibility:

> Unable to believe that his environment really belongs to him, the Jewish novelist cannot envision a valid personal drama of development within it. At best he writes a fiction of dignified resistance or acceptance, at worst a fiction of fierce personal aggression and of the individual effort to rise above the restrictions of Jewish birth.

But Rosenfeld, she felt, had managed to handle "the fact of being Jewish . . . as simply another facet of the already sufficiently complicated business of being a human being."[13]

The naturalness of the American environment was shown in an oddity associated with the historical understanding of the 1960s, the decade that most severely tested the national attachment to John Jay's "same principles of government." The most influential analyst of Lyndon B. Johnson's political failure in Vietnam was David Halberstam (*The Best and the Brightest* [1972]), and LBJ's preeminent biographer has been Robert A. Caro (*The Years of Lyndon Johnson* [1982, 1990]). Their huge and important books on Johnson's policies and career betray no special Jewish sensibility or angle of vision, though Halberstam is a descendant of Rabbi Meir Katzenellenbogen, a famed halakhic authority in sixteenth-century Padua, and Caro is a probable descendant of Yosef Karo, the sixteenth-century codifier of the Shulḥan Arukh.[14] In their effort to fathom the complications of modern American history, such writers have typified the indifference of most of their fellow Jews to the further complexities and demands of their ancient heritage.

A formal Jewish culture in America is thin, and except for some immigrant intellectuals, has added little to the rejuvenation of Judaic thought. No native-born Americans have become canonical figures in the evolution of the Jews' religious and moral ideas.[15] Although all the great works of Judaism were composed in exile (except for the Bible itself), none has been written by an American. A cohesive and internally consistent Jewish culture in the United States now consists mostly of memories that are fading, its husk battered in the transmission to succeeding generations, its custodians and most sophisticated legatees generally found in academe and in museums.

The postwar reference points of Jewish culture have not been indigenous to the United States but have been defined instead by the two events that have irrevocably altered Jewish history itself: the extermination of two-thirds of European Jewry and the rebirth of Israel. The significance of the Holocaust and of Zionism has dwarfed whatever has happened in the United States. But the Jews who were so enmeshed in American culture nevertheless had to come to terms with that catastrophe and that hope, however vicariously, and in doing so enlarged and transformed the boundaries of that very culture. How those two events were absorbed and accommodated merits illustration.

The most poetically effective of all subjects, Edgar Allan Poe once theorized, is the death of a beautiful woman.[16] Yet even this morbid seer did not consider for literary purposes a more haunting and terrible death, the sort that brutally forecloses a natural emergence into maturity. Nor did any nineteenth-century writer, no matter how darkly penetrating, foresee that such a violent denial of life would be multiplied, under conditions of maximal suffering, by six million. That is a statistic too numbing to contemplate, too staggering for the ordinary moral intelligence to confront without flinching. But the fate of Anne Frank brought the pain inside.

The diary of her adolescence in the secret annex in Amsterdam was written in Dutch and published in abbreviated form in Holland only two years after she died in Bergen-Belsen. In 1950, translations of *Het Achterhuis* appeared in both French and German, but to little effect. The posthumous power of her words to give concreteness to the Holocaust began only with the publication of *The Diary of a Young Girl* in the United States in 1952.

The catalyst was Meyer Levin, an American novelist who first read the French translation. But he was told by Otto Frank, the only survivor among the eight Jews who had hidden at 263 Prinsengracht, that several distinguished American and British publishers had already rejected his daughter's diary: "Unfortunately, they all said, the subject was too heartrending; the public would resist, the book would not sell." Levin persisted: "I sent the Diary to a half dozen editors whom I knew. The reactions were uniform: they were personally touched, but professionally they were convinced that the public shied away from such material." Then, in the annual literary issue of the American Jewish *Congress Weekly,* Levin urged publication and was eventually persuasive. *Commentary* serialized it, and Levin designated it a classic on the front page of the *New York Times Book Review* after Doubleday published it. Brandished with Eleanor Roosevelt's introduction, *The Diary of a Young Girl* has been translated into fifty-one languages and has sold more than sixty million copies.[17]

Levin went on to write a theatrical version of the diary, even though producer Herman Shumlin warned him: "It's impossible. You simply can't expect an audience to come to the theater to watch on the stage people they know to have ended up in the crematorium. It would be too painful. They won't come."[18] A play other than Levin's, written by Albert Hackett and Frances Goodrich, opened on Broadway in 1955. It won a Pulitzer Prize but also provoked a court battle, initiated by Levin, concerning alleged distortions of the original work.[19] The stage adaptation led to the republication of the *Diary* in German and, according to one historian, "caught the imagination of the German reading public." Attending a performance of the *Diary* in West Berlin in 1956, the British critic Kenneth Tynan recorded "the most drastic emotional experience the theatre has ever given me. It had little to do with art, for the play was not a great one; yet its effect, in Berlin, at that moment of history, transcended anything that art has yet learned to achieve." After it was over,

> the house-lights went up on an audience that sat drained and ashen, some staring straight ahead, others staring at the ground, for a full half-minute. Then, as if awakening from a nightmare, they rose and filed out in total silence, not looking at each other, avoiding even the customary nods of recognition with which friend greets friend. There was no applause, and there were no curtain-calls.

Tynan acknowledged that his report was "not drama criticism. In the shadow of an event so desperate and traumatic, criticism would be an irrelevance. It can only record an emotion that I felt, would not have missed, and pray never to feel again."[20]

Though the Broadway production had, in his opinion, "smacked of exploitation," the emotional force of the New York version was also overwhelming. Pivotal to its effect was director Garson Kanin, who also directed films. (Indeed, when he visited Anne's tiny cubicle in Amsterdam, Kanin quickly noticed a Dutch movie poster on the wall above her bed, among the photos of Hollywood stars that she had collected. The poster announced: "*Tom, Dick and Harry*—starring Ginger Rogers, directed by Garson Kanin.") Among the ten actors Kanin picked for the New York production was Joseph Schildkraut, an Academy Award winner for his portrayal of Captain Dreyfus in Warner Brothers' *The Life of Emile Zola* (1937). Schildkraut's 1,068 performances as Otto Frank, over the course of three years,

> were probably the most important and decisive of my whole life. Because I did not merely act a part, but had to live as Otto Frank through the whole terrible and shattering experience of an era which can never be erased from the memory of my generation.... It was, I believe firmly, not accidental that *The Diary of Anne Frank* became the culmination of my professional life.

Himself the son of a leading stage actor who had come from the Balkans to revive for German audiences a love of their own classics, Schildkraut had "never before . . . felt such an intimate relationship to a play, never such an identification with a part." For Anne Frank's diary "actually wrote the epitaph to a whole period of the history of Europe, the history of Germany, [and] the tragedy of the Jews."[21]

The play next became a George Stevens film (1959), in which Schildkraut also starred as Otto Frank, and has gone through other permutations as well. At one Bonds for Israel rally in New York's Madison Square Garden in New York, for example, a torch was brought from the new state and used to light a menorah on stage. Schildkraut lit it and said the prayer just as he had done in the final scene in

Act I on Broadway. "Thirty thousand people filled the arena, a sea of humanity," he recalled. "And like powerful waves the murmurs, sighs, prayers of that mass rose up to me, engulfed me, carried me away. I felt sorrow and exultation. My eyes burned, my heart ached in pride and grief." And in a March 1990 UNICEF benefit concern in New York, Michael Tilson Thomas conducted the New World Symphony in a concert piece he wrote entitled "From the Diary of Anne Frank." (As the grandson of the Yiddish theatrical pioneer Boris Thomashefsky, Thomas was a living link to the culture that the Nazis destroyed.) No wonder that Anne Frank's biographer could claim that "her voice was preserved out of the millions that were silenced, this voice no louder than a child's whisper. It has outlasted the shouts of the murderers and has soared above the voice of time."[22]

The last sentence in her diary was written only three days before the murderers came, and that whisper could not be unmediated. In the United States, her words could only be heard resonating inside a culture not known for its appreciation of the tragic—or of the suffering for which no grief or retribution is sufficient, the kind of loss with which no vengeance or restitution is commensurate. In an era when not even the term "Holocaust" was in use, when not even a name was available to summarize the evil of the Third Reich, when neither knowledge of nor interest in the Nazi genocide was conspicuous, morally serious artistic impulses were frustrated. It was exceedingly difficult to make sense of the senseless, to make mass murder intelligible to a mass audience. Some American moviegoers found *The Diary of Anne Frank* baffling, apparently not realizing that the film was based on one family's actual experience and assuming that what they were viewing was fictional. One early cut of the film ended at Bergen-Belsen, which so vexed a preview audience that it was changed, as in the Broadway play, to conclude on the more optimistic note of Anne's proclamation that "in spite of everything, I still believe that people are really good at heart." Otto Frank himself realized that audiences responded as much to the pathos of adolescent yearning as to the horror outside the secret annex.[23]

But what generated the greatest controversy was the evasion of the distinctively Jewish character of the family's ordeal. Meyer Levin himself blamed the playwrights Hackett and Goodrich, a husband-and-wife team of scenarists who had previously won an Oscar for *Seven Brides for Seven Brothers*. They were not Jewish, though the head of production at M-G-M assured Levin that, in researching the Hanukah scene, the team had "gone to the most prominent Reform rabbi in Hollywood."[24] Their distortions, which Levin also attributed to the editorial influence of playwright Lillian Hellman, had provoked his lawsuit. But the failure to underscore the uniquely Jewish dimension to the *Diary* was also cultural. In the early 1950s, audiences were still uneasy with particularism and peoplehood, with facing the lethal implications of diaspora history. The awful terminus of the Holocaust, it was widely assumed, had to be shown instead under the auspices of universalism: what happened to Anne Frank might have happened to anyone.

For example, the diarist herself wondered:

> Who has made us Jews different from all other people? Who has allowed us to suffer so terribly up till now? It is God who has made us as we are, but it will be God, too, who will raise us up again. If we bear all this suffering and if there are still Jews left, when it

is over, then Jews, instead of being doomed, will be held up as an example. Who knows, it might even be our religion from which the world and all peoples learn good, and for that reason and that reason only do we have to suffer now. We can never become just Netherlanders, or just English, or just . . . representatives of any other country for that matter, we will always remain Jews, but we want to, too.

This echo of the covenant is posthumously twisted into something quite different in both the play and the film. "We're not the only people that've had to suffer," Anne is made to say. "There've always been people that've had to . . . Sometimes one race . . . Sometimes another."25

Meyer Levin therefore asked:

Why had her Jewish avowal been censored on the stage? It is an essential statement, epitomizing the entire mystery of God and the Six Million, a pure and perfect expression of the search for meaning in the Holocaust, for all humanity, Jewish or not. Nowhere in the substitute drama is this touched upon. This brazen example of the inversion of a dead author's words epitomizes the programmatic, politicalized [sic] dilution of the Jewish tragedy. Millions of spectators the world over were unaware they were subjected to idea-censorship.26

Nor were the actors in the Hanukkah scene to sing in Hebrew because, as the playwrights explained to Otto Frank, "it would set the characters in the play apart from the people watching them . . . for the majority of our audience is not Jewish. And the thing that we have striven for . . . is to make the audience understand and identify themselves. . . ." According to *Het Achterhuis*, Anne's sister Margot wanted to be a nurse in Palestine if she had survived the war, but neither on stage nor on screen is her Zionist sentiment mentioned.27 And although Susan Strasberg had drawn raves for her Broadway portrayal of Anne Frank, Twentieth Century Fox honored earlier Hollywood custom by casting a non-Jewish actress named Millie Perkins instead.

It is interesting to contrast the reception of the *Diary* with that of Elie Wiesel's *La Nuit* (1958), which did not appear in an English translation until 1960 (after twenty publishers had already rejected it), but it is doubtful that the mass audience would have been prepared for his unsparingly bleak memoir of the camps—before which the *Diary* of course stops short. As Peter Novick has pointed out, American culture in the 1950s was not yet ready for Wiesel, who was born a year before Anne Frank. He was East European, poor, observant and unassimilated. She had been Western, middle-class, of Reform background, so assimilated that she was pleased that in December 1943 Hanukkah occurred so close to Saint Nicholas's Day and Christmas.28 Anne Frank was therefore a more endearing icon of violated innocence. For most American Jews as well as non-Jews, identification was thus made easier, reinforcing an interpretation of the Holocaust that generalized it into the signature event of universal suffering.

Though Anne had dreamed of visiting the holy places in Eretz Israel, what she really wanted to do was to travel all over the world and become a writer.29 That is the very sort of life that Philip Roth has led. In his novella *The Ghost Writer*, the twenty-three-year-old deutero-Roth named Nathan Zuckerman visits an older and more austere Jewish writer and imagines that Amy Bellette, a young researcher who is also staying in the house, has survived Bergen-Belsen and is really Anne Frank. Roth's tale is both a gesture of imaginative resistance to the Holocaust—wondering, as many undoubtedly have, whether something so unbearable and incomprehensible might just possibly not have been so truly awful as it was—as well as a melancholy acceptance of its finality. Amy Bellette is only herself. For "when the sleeve of her coat fell back," Zuckerman "of course saw that there was no scar on her forearm. No scar; [and therefore] no book" after all.[30]

For Anne Frank could *not* still be alive, and hers are only the words of a ghost writer. She can "live" only in memory, only in representation. In the United States she can also live as a fragile symbol of Jewish identification, as an inspiration to sustain *ahavat yisrael*. Zuckerman, for example, stands accused of disgracing the Jewry of New Jersey with his scandalous fiction. But redemption is still possible, according to Judge Leonard Wapter, a distant family friend. "If you have not yet seen the Broadway production of *The Diary of Anne Frank*," Wapter writes the errant young novelist, "I strongly advise that you do so. Mrs. Wapter and I were in the audience on opening night; we wish that Nathan Zuckerman could have been with us to benefit from the unforgettable experience."

Zuckerman refuses to reply, and tells his father:

> "Nothing I could write Wapter would convince him of anything. Or his wife."
> "You could tell him you went to see *The Diary of Anne Frank*. You could at least do that."
> "I didn't see it. I read the book. *Everybody* read the book."
> "But you liked it, didn't you?"
> "That's not the issue. How can you *dis*like it?"[31]

And in fact her diary eludes such categories of judgment. Though its theatrical and cinematic distortions must be set in the context of the 1950s, when a vigorous and various pluralism was still subdued to a consensus that emphasized social stability, the *Diary* was virtually unique in the attentiveness to the Holocaust that it commanded. In American thought and expression, that subject was at first only slowly and rarely broached. In films, for example, even Stanley Kramer's moralistic *Judgment at Nuremberg* (1961) managed to depict the evil of Nazism without including any major or even minor Jewish characters. Not until Sidney Lumet's *The Pawnbroker* (1965) did Hollywood directly tackle the subject of the Holocaust again;[32] and even then the protagonist, a Jewish survivor named Sol Nazerman (Rod Steiger), was presented as a Christ figure, bearing stigmata. But the trickle of films soon became a flood that has helped shape the sensibility of American Jews—and of many of their neighbors.

While still struggling to restore Anne Frank's authentic voice, Meyer Levin did some research on the history of the Yishuv in Palestine, considering the possibility of giving the topic fictional treatment. Then he saw the galleys for "a novel of Israel" that Doubleday was about to publish, and realized that he would have to pursue another theme. The novel was *Exodus*.

Its author was Leon Uris, a former high school dropout from Baltimore, where he had flunked English three times before joining the U.S. Marines at the age of seventeen. *Exodus* proved to be one of the publishing sensations of the era. For more than a year it remained on the *New York Times* best-seller list (including nineteen weeks perched at the top) and was a Book-of-the-Month Club alternate selection. The hardcover edition has never gone out of print, having sold to date more than half a million copies in some forty printings; the Bantam paperback was quickly reordered at a rate of two thousand per month, reaching almost seven million copies after sixty-three printings. Although propaganda novels have occasionally punctuated the history of U.S. mass taste, *Exodus* was unprecedented. For it was not intended to arouse indignation over a domestic issue, such as the moral horror of slavery (*Uncle Tom's Cabin*), the ugliness of urban working conditions (*The Jungle*) or the plight of migrant farmers (*The Grapes of Wrath*). *Exodus* was published when American Jewish interest in Israel was slight and levels of philanthropy and tourism were—by later standards—low,[33] and when ethnicity was suppressed or disdained as an embarrassing residue of the immigrant past. It was therefore astonishing that an American could write a Zionist epic that would virtually fly off the shelves of American bookstores. The year that it was published, ex–Prime Minister David Ben-Gurion asserted: "As a piece of propaganda, it's the greatest thing ever written about Israel."[34]

Though no political repercussions were immediately discernible, the political value of *Exodus* was unmistakable. Its popularity was not only a tribute to the expanding hospitality of the majority culture, however. It was also evidence that the Jewish people was now permitted to view their own experience through American mythology, to think of themselves not only as virtuous but as courageous, tough and triumphant. Uris pulled off such a feat by outflanking or evading the customary concerns of the ethnic novel—the tension between Old World authority and tradition versus New World promise and freedom. Ignoring such conventional issues as the peril posed to the family or the crises of belief, he drew heavily on the exploits of Yehudah Arazi, a Mossad agent who operated illegal Zionist ships in the Mediterranean under the British Mandate and who had drawn considerable press attention to the plight of Jewish refugees.[35] Uris transposed to the Middle East the adventure formulas that middlebrow American readers already expected. In making Jewish characters into heroes skillful with weapons, the ex-marine who had scripted the Western film *The Gunfight at the O.K. Corral* (1957) knew how to keep the action flowing. Indeed, the scene in Chapter 16, in which the Haganah frees Irgun prisoners from the British, might have been called "the gunfight at the Akko jail."

The critic Leslie Fiedler therefore felt compelled to lodge a protest against "stereotype-inversion . . . [which] merely substitutes falsification for falsification, sentimentality for sentimentality."[36] The courage of Uris's Israelis seemed designed to contradict General George S. Patton's denigrating remark (made after he slapped a couple of hospitalized U.S. soldiers in 1943) that "there's no such thing as shell shock. It's an invention of the Jews."[37] In Uris's novel, "the Jewish military heroes are presented as Jews already become, or in the process of becoming, Israelis." The book thus represented "a disguised form of assimilation, the attempt of certain Jews to be accepted by the bourgeois, Philistine gentile community on the grounds that, though they are not Christians, they are even more bourgeois and philistine."[38]

This interpretation now seems mistaken, however. *Exodus* tapped a subterranean

Jewish nationalism when the path toward full assimilation seemed utterly unobstructed, and represented an unexpected detour for countless readers. "I have received thousands of letters in the last quarter of a century telling me that *Exodus* has substantially changed their lives," the author claimed, "particularly in regard to young people finding pride in their Jewishness. Older people find similar pride in the portrait of fighting Jews in contrast to the classical characterization as weakspined, brilliant intellects and businessmen."[39]

Exodus was Doubleday's third "Jewish" blockbuster in six years (after *Diary of a Young Girl* and Herman Wouk's *Marjorie Morningstar*) and won the National Jewish Book Award, a year before the same National Jewish Welfare Board gave its award to Roth for *Goodbye, Columbus* (1959). With its very different stereotypes, *Exodus* was thus wedged between the two novels that established the image of "the Jewish American princess"—a stereotype that eventually superseded "the Jewish mother" that Roth himself so giddily pilloried a decade later in *Portnoy's Complaint* (1969).

The romance between a *sabra* and a gentile nurse (the only important American character in the novel) was in the foreground of this sage of the genesis of the Third Jewish Commonwealth. The love story seemed to reiterate the staples of earlier popular works, stretching back to Israel Zangwill's *The Melting-Pot* (1908) in imagining how interethnic or interreligious love might surmount the primordial hatreds that history had nurtured. But *Exodus* shattered that convention when the nurse, the incarnation of the American majority culture, casts her lot at the end with the Jewish independence fighters; and the enormous appeal of the novel suggested a certain deceleration of the assimilationist impulses that previous American Jewish fiction had registered. (The effect on Otto Preminger, who adapted the novel to the screen in 1960, was admittedly less impressive. While on location in Israel, the director wanted to marry an Episcopalian. Because the Weizmann Institute's Meyer Weisgal, who was cast in a brief scene, was willing to testify to the rabbinate that the bride was Jewish, the couple was married in Haifa rather than in Cyprus.)[40]

The popularity of Preminger's movie was unaffected by the picket lines of neo-Nazi George Lincoln Rockwell and his followers in eastern cities. From the film score, crooner Pat Boone quarried a hit song notable for its egocentric arrogance ("This land is mine/God gave this land to me"), undoubtedly boosting a successful packaged tour organized in 1960 that traced the route of events in Uris's novel. The following year, El Al airlines announced a sixteen-day tour that would cover the very places where Preminger and his crew had shot scenes for *Exodus*.[41] Jewish ethnicity became a segment of the market.

The breadth of the appeal of *Exodus* was revealed in its impact upon a versatile black teacher and writer named Julius Lester. The son of a Methodist minister, he recalled that, while attending all-Negro Fisk University in Nashville, Tennessee, a classmate thrust the novel at him. Its effect "on me was so extraordinary that I wanted to go and fight for Israel, even die, if need be, for Israel." Lester added that "Israel spoke to the need I had as a young black man for a place where I could be free of being an object of hatred. I did not wish I were Jewish, but was glad that Jews had a land of their own, even if blacks didn't."[42] By the late 1980s Lester had become a Jew and even a cantor in a Conservative shul in western Massachusetts.

Though the passions that he felt and enacted were rarely as spectacular among his new coreligionists, one sociologist claimed it was "virtually impossible to find a Reform home in the 1950s without a copy of Leon Uris's *Exodus.*" His novel undoubtedly awakened pride in the fulfillment of a dream that was both democratic and humane as well as nationalist.[43]

Though literary critics ignored *Exodus* (except to spray it with buckshot), it has appeared in more than fifty translations (most importantly, Russian);[44] and even hostile reviewers might be hard put to challenge Uris's assertion that "it has been among the most influential novels in history."[45] Uris himself insisted on a standard of aesthetic judgment that would privilege psychic health and affirmation. In an interview in the *New York Post*, he denounced

> a whole school of American Jewish writers who spend their time damning their fathers, hating their mothers, wringing their hands and wondering why they were born. This isn't art or literature. It's psychiatry. These writers are professional apologists. Every year you find one of their works on the best-seller list. Their work is obnoxious and makes me sick to my stomach. I wrote *Exodus* because I was just sick of apologizing— or feeling that it was necessary to apologize.[46]

When Uris added that, contrary to the diaspora stereotype, "we have been fighters," Roth was provoked to retort, "So bald, stupid, and uninformed is the statement that it is not even worth disputing." Having published a hilarious short story about quite unheroic Jews in military uniform, "Defender of the Faith" (1959), Roth saw little "value in swapping one simplification for the other." Saul Bellow's judgment was more measured:

> It may appear that the survivors of Hitler's terror in Europe and Israel will benefit more from good publicity than from realistic representation, or that posters are needed more urgently than masterpieces. Admittedly, some people say, *Exodus* was not much of a novel, but it was extraordinarily effective as a document and we need such documents now. We do not need stories like those of Philip Roth which expose unpleasant Jewish traits. . . . [But] in literature we cannot accept a political standard. We can only have a literary one.[47]

Politics could not be easily excluded, however, especially when novelists themselves incorporated large historical and political themes in their work. Uris's subsequent *Mila 18* (1961), which was number four among best-sellers that year, counterposed an episode of desperate heroism—the Warsaw ghetto uprising—to the passive victimization that the *Diary of a Young Girl* represented. And in one of his most complex fictions to date, *The Counterlife* (1986), Roth rewrote *Exodus* as ambivalence, putting Nathan Zuckerman, the sort of assimilated novelist whose real-life counterparts Uris had attacked, in the Holy Land. There Nathan confronts his brother Henry, a dentist from suburban New Jersey, now Hanoch, who has chosen to relive on the West Bank the vigilant and embattled Zionism that Ari Ben-Canaan had projected. It is as though the safely suburban professional man whom Marjorie Morningstar had married at the end of Wouk's novel was suddenly thrust, in *The Counterlife*, into a condition of radical insecurity, falling under the sway of the brilliant, fanatically right-wing Mordecai Lippman. *The Counterlife* may be the most dramatic and sophisticated novel that an American has yet written on the moral and political dilemmas facing Israel and of Israel's meaning for American Jewry.

With the news that Roth's *Portnoy's Complaint* would become the first foreign novel translated into Czech under a post-Communist regime,[48] the story of the Jewish impact upon American culture was elevated into a different and even mysterious dimension. The multiple ironies associated with minority life in America could no longer be confined to the United States. For if Czech readers could find engrossing the struggles between Alex and Sophie Portnoy, then even Jewish particularism had lost its specificity, its hermetic pungency, its implosive force. Thus the distinctly postwar phase of the Jewish involvement in American culture—especially mass culture—may be over.

This has been a story that might begin with *The Jolson Story* (1946), starring Larry Parks, a Kansan playing a Jew who was famous for singing in blackface. This cinematic envoi to vaudeville was released when the unrivaled power of the film industry was about to yield to television. The coda of that story might be a videocassette made in 1984 of a one-woman Broadway show, *Whoopi Goldberg*, written by and starring a black comedienne—who was raised as a Roman Catholic but who has given herself a Jewish surname—playing (among other roles) a black, streetwise junkie who visits the Anne Frank House in Amsterdam, and then breaks down and cries while meditating on vulnerability. The supervisor of the Broadway production was Mike Nichols, born Michael Igor Peschkowsky in Berlin in 1931, who had arrived in New York in 1939 knowing two English sentences: "I don't speak English" and "Please don't kiss me."[49] Yet the Jewish embrace of America was about to be fully consummated—and reciprocated.

The romantic tales that Broadway, Hollywood and publishers' row once chose to narrate tended to locate impediments to love in ethnicity, religion and "race"— though, except for race itself, these were hurdles that could be overcome. After the Second World War, the credibility of such impediments crumbled in an increasingly tolerant and diverse America. Hollywood's leading men in its golden age of the 1930s and 1940s tended to be handsome WASPs (Cary Grant, Gary Cooper, Clark Gable, John Wayne) and, somewhat later, their occasional Jewish facsimiles such as John Garfield (né Julius Garfinkle), Tony Curtis (né Bernard Schwartz) and the half-Jew Paul Newman. But while Jewish actresses (unless named Barbra Streisand) are still expected to conform to Anglo-Saxon conventions of what a good profile is, the requirement has now been waived for Jewish actors. The seismic shift in sexual attractiveness can be discerned in *Play It Again, Sam* (1972), when a businessman guesses that his wife (Diane Keaton) must be having an affair with "some stud." The camera suddenly focuses on his guilty, self-conscious best friend (Woody Allen),[50] whose imaginary romantic adviser is Humphrey Bogart. Instead of ridiculing himself as a *nebbish* (as in earlier Woody Allen comedies), he proves himself capable of winning Keaton (off-screen, too).

Director Woody Allen can of course give Actor Woody Allen his pick of women, whether played by Keaton, Charlotte Rampling, or Mia Farrow; but it is noteworthy that audiences have not rebelled. Nor is there widespread puzzlement—much less disapproval—when short, nasal Dustin Hoffman wins Katherine Ross (in *The Graduate* [1967]) and then Jessica Lange (in *Tootsie* [1982]), or when Hoffman, like Allen himself in *Manhattan* (1979), plays the former husband of the ethereal Meryl Streep (in *Kramer vs. Kramer* [1979]). Art Garfunkel (rather than Jack Nicholson) marries Candice Bergen in *Carnal Knowledge* (1971), Jeff Goldblum gets to keep Michelle Pfeiffer as well as a bundle of cash in *Into the Night* (1985), Ron Liebman attracts Sally Field in *Norma Rae* (1979), and Billy Crystal gets to be more than friends with Meg Ryan in *When Harry Met Sally . . .* (1989). If unprepossessing and even unglamorous Jews can play romantic leads without the novelty of such casting attracting notice—or popular resistance—then Jews and gentiles may have become so comfortable with one another in American society that the historic distinction between them matters less than ever.

Because Jewish values and images have nicked the nation's postwar culture, making it less monochromatic and more variegated, the critical detachment that this marginal people once felt has largely dissipated, and the case for pronounced Jewish separation has been decisively weakened. Thanks to the disproportionate Jewish contribution to the popular arts, the traditional bifurcation between "them" and "us" is blurring into irrelevance. In so benign a setting, where neighbors are more accessible than ancestors, what "we" have left to defend and cultivate cannot be articulated with the same confidence as in the past. The explanation for assimilation that is herein proposed is therefore paradoxical: The very Jewish enlargement and invigoration of American culture that has enabled Jews to identify so fully with it has made Jewish identity under such conditions problematic. That national culture is not so much a distant threat as a distorted mirror, but the Jewish faces that it reveals are coming to resemble everyone else's.

Notes

1. Alexander Hamilton, John Jay and James Madison, *The Federalist: A Commentary on the Constitution of the United States*, ed. Edward Mead Earle (New York: 1937 [1788]), 9.

2. Margaret Carlson, "Oh, Say, Can You Sing It?," *Time* 135 (12 Feb. 1990), 27. "If winning were everything," Carlson claims, "'God Bless America' might carry the day. Anyone can belt out a respectable version."

3. Stanley I. Kutler, *The School Prayer Controversy in America: Constitutionalism, Symbolism, and Pluralism* (Tel-Aviv: 1984), 12–17; Aljean Harmetz, "Has Joe Roth Got the Key to Success at Fox?" *New York Times*, 4 March 1990.

4. Harmetz, "Has Joe Roth Got the Key."

5. "Newly Released Tapes," in Staff of the *Washington Post*, *The Fall of a President* (New York: 1974), 222.

6. Henry Adams to Charles Milnes Gaskell, 31 July 1896 and 19 February 1914, quoted in *The Jew in the Modern World: A Documentary History*, eds. Paul R. Mendes-Flohr and Jehuda Reinharz (New York: 1980), 370.

7. H. L. Mencken, *The American Language: An Inquiry into the Development of English in the United States*, rev. ed., ed. Raven L. McDavid and David W. Maurer (New York: 1963 [1919]), 253–256, 260–264.

8. Henry Adams, *The Education of Henry Adams*, rev. ed., ed. Ernest Samuels (Boston: 1973 [1918]), 238.

9. Pauline Kael, "Raising Kane," in *idem*, Herman J. Mankiewicz and Orson Welles, *The Citizen Kane Book* (Boston: 1971), 17–20, 51; David Mamet, *Speed-the-Plow* (New York: 1987), 34, 72.

10. "The Most Powerful People in Hollywood," *Premiere* 3 (May 1990), 63-65; "Maker of Hit After Hit, Steven Spielberg is Also a Conglomerate," *Wall Street Journal*, 9 Feb. 1987.

11. Henry Morgenthau Diaries, 10 April 1939, quoted in Ted Morgan, *FDR: A Biography* (New York: 1985), 555-556; John Cooney, *The Annenbergs* (New York: 1982), 20, 125-138.

12. Consider Leonard Dinnerstein's *Uneasy at Home: Antisemitism and the American Jewish Experience* (New York: 1987) and Arthur Hertzberg's *The Jews in America: Four Centuries of an Uneasy Encounter* (New York: 1989), as well as Jacob Neusner's *Stranger at Home: "The Holocaust," Zionism, and American Judaism* (Chicago: 1981).

13. Diana Trilling, *Reviewing the Forties* (New York: 1978), 167-168.

14. Neil Rosenstein, *The Unbroken Chain: Sketches and the Genealogy of Illustrious Jewish Families from the 15th-20th Century* (New York: 1976), 312; Israel Shenker, "Now, Jewish Roots," *New York Times Magazine* (20 March 1977), 42-44; Fred A. Bernstein, "In an Explosive Biography, Robert Caro Portrays L.B.J.'s Path to Power as the Low Road," *People* 19 (17 Jan. 1983), 31-32.

15. Stephen J. Whitfield, *American Space, Jewish Time* (Hamden, Conn.: 1988), 60-64.

16. Edgar Allan Poe, "The Philosophy of Composition" (1846), in *The Portable Poe*, ed. Philip Van Doren Stern (New York: 1945), 557.

17. Sander L. Gilman, *Jewish Self-Hatred: Anti-Semitism and the Hidden Language of the Jews* (Baltimore: 1986), 345; Meyer Levin, *The Obsession* (New York: 1973), 34; Harry Mulisch, "Death and the Maiden," *New York Review of Books* 33 (17 July 1986), 7.

18. Quoted in Levin, *Obsession*, 36.

19. A full account of the legal battle is given in Levin, *Obsession*.

20. Gilman, *Jewish Self-Hatred*, 345; Kenneth Tynan, *Curtains* (New York: 1961), 450-451.

21. Joseph Schildkraut (as told to Leo Lania), *My Father and I* (New York: 1959), 2-3, 233, 236, 237.

22. *Ibid.*, 237-238; Ernst Schnabel, *Anne Frank: A Portrait in Courage* (New York: 1958), 192.

23. Judith E. Doneson, *The Holocaust in American Film* (Philadelphia: 1987), 69, 76, 80-81; Anne Frank, *The Diary of a Young Girl*, trans. B. M. Mooyaart-Doubleday (Garden City, N.Y.: 1952, paperback ed. 1953), 237.

24. Levin, *Obsession*, 152; Doneson, *Holocaust in American Film*, 74.

25. Frank, *Diary of a Young Girl*, 186-187; Frances Goodrich and Albert Hackett, *The Diary of Anne Frank* (New York: 1956), 168; Levin, *Obsession*, 29-30; Doneson, *Holocaust in American Film*, 69-70, 82.

26. Levin, *Obsession*, 30.

27. Quoted in Doneson, *Holocaust in American Film*, 70; Levin, *Obsession*, 126.

28. Frank, *Diary of a Young Girl*, 108-113; Gilman, *Jewish Self-Hatred*, 349.

29. *Diary of a Young Girl*, 177, 206, 210; Levin, *Obsession*, 121.

30. Philip Roth, *The Ghost Writer* (New York: 1980), 207.

31. *Ibid.*, 128, 135.

32. Stephen J. Whitfield, *Voices of Jacob, Hands of Esau: Jews in American Life and Thought* (Hamden, Conn.: 1984), 30-41; Annette Insdorf, *Indelible Shadows: Film and the Holocaust* (New York: 1983), 6-10, 23-28.

33. David Biale, *Power and Powerlessness in Jewish History* (New York: 1986), 184.

34. Quoted in Edwin McDowell, "*Exodus* in Samizdat: Still Popular and Still Subversive," *New York Times Book Review*, 26 April 1987, 13.

35. Herbert Agar, *The Saving Remnant: An Account of Jewish Survival* (New York: 1960), 204-215.

36. Leslie A. Fiedler, *Waiting for the End: The American Literary Scene from Hemingway to Baldwin* (New York: 1964), 91.

37. Phillip Knightley, *The First Casualty: The War Correspondent as Hero, Propagandist, and Myth Maker* (New York: 1975), 320.

38. Fiedler, *Waiting for the End*, 91.

39. Leon Uris, letter to author, 16 April 1985.
40. Otto Preminger, *Preminger: An Autobiography* (New York: 1978), 225–226; Meyer Weisgal, . . . *So Far: An Autobiography* (New York: 1971), 313–315.
41. Patricia Erens, *The Jew in American Cinema* (Bloomington: 1985), 217, 219; David H. Bennett, *The Party of Fear: From Nativist Movements to the New Right in American History* (Chapel Hill: 1988), 325; Daniel J. Boorstin, *The Image, or What Happened to the American Dream* (New York: 1962), 107.
42. Julius Lester, "All God's Children," in *Jewish Possibilities: The Best of Moment Magazine*, ed. Leonard Fein (Northvale, N.J.: 1987), 28; idem, *Lovesong: Becoming a Jew* (New York: 1988), 29–30.
43. Norman Mirsky, "Nathan Glazer's *American Judaism* after 30 Years: A Reform Opinion," *American Jewish History* 77 (December 1987), 237; William A. Novak, "Twenty Important Jewish Books Written Since 1950," *The Jewish Almanac*, ed. Richard Siegel and Carl Rheins (New York: 1980), 425.
44. Even the enormous impact of the novel in America was overshadowed by its Russian version, *Ishkod*, circulating illegally in the Soviet Union. An Israeli embassy official stationed there from 1959 until 1962 has disclosed that he and other staffers gave away numerous copies of the Bantam (U.S.) edition, which had arrived through the diplomatic pouch. The former official, who remains anonymous, recalled that "the book went from hand to hand. Remember, this was before the Six-Day War, when the Russian people were told Jews were bad, Jews were cowards. The book allowed them to identify with the Jewish national movement." The 599 pages of the Bantam paperback were translated and then typed page by page, using as many legible carbon copies as possible in a nation where "private" citizens were denied access to Xerox machines. Four different translations were done by groups of people who were unaware that others were also producing a *samizdat Exodus*. A unit of "ideological Zionists" did some censorship of its own by eliminating the love affair between Ari Ben-Canaan and Kitty Fremont—the very convention that made it formulaic for American readers. As Jerry Goodman, the executive director of the National Conference on Soviet Jewry, explained: "They couldn't see a Jew having an affair with a non-Jew" (McDowell, "*Exodus* in Samizdat," 13). "There were dozens of such translations done in every city in Russia with Jews and by prisoners in the Gulag," the novelist later claimed. "Many of these translations had eight or ten translators working on them, and other times a family would read it aloud during one entire night so that they could pass it along" (Leon Uris, letter to author, 16 April 1985).

Here was a novel that was to change lives—such as Eliahu Essas's. In 1966 the mathematician read a seventy-page digest of *Ishkod*, of which roughly sixty pages consisted of historical background. "But the other ten were involved with the personalities, and they were digested so well that the hero became our hero." Four years later, Essas received in Moscow a two-volume translation that Aliyah Library in Israel also produced. "I read it once, then again the next year, and I participated with many others making typewritten copies" (McDowell, "*Exodus* in Samizdat," 13; Martin Gilbert, *The Jews of Hope* [New York: 1985], 169–173). Natan Sharansky's autobiography records how the appeal of Zionism grew stronger while he was still a student: "Friends began giving me books about Israel, including the novel *Exodus*, which was circulated in *samizdat* form and had an enormous influence on Jews of my generation" (Natan Sharansky, *Fear No Evil*, trans. Stefani Hoffman [New York: 1988], xv). Though it was a work of fiction uninfected by any explicitly anti-Soviet propaganda, the distribution of *Ishkod* was manifestly illegal (see McDowell, "*Exodus* in Samizdat," 13). At the trial of Leonid (Ari) Volvovsky in 1985, evidence was presented that he had given Uris's novel to a woman who was asked to pass it on to others. The computer expert was charged, among other crimes, with distributing "anti-Soviet propaganda." A few months earlier, a similar accusation had been brought against Yakov Levin, a Hebrew teacher in Odessa; he too was sentenced to three years in prison for slander. Both he and Volvovsky were released early in 1987. A year later, at an emotional Action for Soviet Jewry benefit in Boston, Volvovsky met Uris for the first time, along with Senator Edward M. Kennedy.

"When my wife Jill was photographing in a reception center in Israel," Uris has recalled, "people came up and showed her letters saying that, when they started reading *Exodus*, that was the first step for applying for a visa to come out of Russia." In a transfer center for Soviet Jews in Vienna, he met a woman who was among the typists of *Ishkod*. In the fall of 1989, Uris went to Moscow, where he accepted a twenty-six-year-old, first-edition *samizdat* of *Exodus*. Weeping, he responded: "This means more to me than a Nobel Prize. I thank you all in this hall tonight, and I thank B'nai B'rith for bringing me here." During Simhat Torah services in the synagogue, the worshipers roared and applauded loudly upon hearing the announcement from the *bimah* that Uris was there. The Muscovites mobbed the author when he carried a Torah scroll through the sanctuary, kissing the Torah cover—and Uris as well (Michael Neiditch, "Uris in the USSR," *Jewish Monthly* 104 [Jan. 1990], 35–37).

No Jewish book was ever more cherished in the U.S.S.R. than *Ishkod*. "For Soviet Jewish activists," Jerry Goodman asserted, "it was probably more meaningful than even the Bible. Most of the Jewish activists in the late 1960s and early 1970s always cited to me the importance of the book. They didn't treat it as a literary experience; it was history—the only knowledge they had of the Jewish experience." "Its impact was enormous," Essas explained after settling in Israel in 1986, thirteen years after his first application for an exit visa. "It was our first encounter with Jewish history. It gave us inspiration, and turned almost everybody who read it into more or less convinced Zionists." He added: "It gave us hope and pride when we needed it. It was the first book to teach us about the Jewish tradition, which is very different from what the Government said it was" (McDowell, "*Exodus* in Samizdat," 13).

45. Leon Uris, letter to author, 16 April 1985.

46. Quoted in Philip Roth, "Some New Jewish Stereotypes" (1961), in *Reading Myself and Others* (New York: 1975), 138.

47. Roth, "Some New Jewish Stereotypes," 138; Saul Bellow, Introduction to *Great Jewish Short Stories* (New York: 1963), 14.

48. *New York Review of Books*, 37 (12 April 1990), 2.

49. Cathleen McGuigan, "The 'Whoopie' Comedy Show," *Newsweek*, 103 (5 March 1984), 63; Steve Erickson, "Whoopi Goldberg," *Rolling Stone* (8 May 1986), 39–42, 90, 92, 94; Rex Reed, *Do You Sleep in the Nude?* (New York: 1969), 61.

50. *Woody Allen's Play It Again, Sam*, ed. Richard J. Anobile (New York: 1977), 162.

Index

Abzug, Bella
  and the impact of feminism on Jewish life, 257
Achterhuis, Het, 341
Ackelsberg, Martha
  and the impact of feminism on Jewish life, 267, 268
  and *The Jewish Woman: An Anthology,* 264
Adams, Henry
  and Jews in postwar American culture, 338, 339
Adler, Cyrus
  and New York Sephardim, 91
Adler, Rachel
  and Jewish feminism, 257
  and *The Jewish Woman: An Anthology,* 264
  "The Jew Who Wasn't There," 263
  "Tumah and Taharah—Mikveh," 310
Adventure in Freedom (Handlin), 27
Advertising industry
  in the 1920s, 238
Age of Anxiety (Bernstein), 26
Agriculture schools
  percentage of Jews in, 192
Agus, Arlene
  and the impact of feminism on Jewish religious life, 309, 310
  The Jewish Woman: An Anthology, 264
Ahavah (Diamond), 26
Ahavath Shalom Society of Monastir
  and New York Sephardim, 91, 93
Alcalay, Isaac
  and New York Sephardim, 98
Aleph Zadik Aleph (AZA)
  and American Jewish occupational patterns in the 1920s, 161–62, 163, 164
  and Jewish occupational patterns, 172, 174, 175, 185

Allen, Woody
  and Jews in postwar American culture, 349
America, La, 87, 89, 92, 94, 95, 107
American Hebrew, 245, 246, 250, 251
American Jew, A Zionist Analysis, The (Halpern), 30
American Jewish Committee
  and affirmative action, 294
  and impact of Holocaust survivors on American society, 72
  and Jewish/communist stereotype, 29
  and postwar Jewish migration to Los Angeles, 44
  and Joseph Proskauer, 19
American Jewish Conference
  and Jewish/communist stereotype, 29
American Jewish Congress
  and Commission on Law and Social Action, 21
American Jewish Women and the World of Work, 292
American Jewish Yearbook, 9, 26, 265
  and American Jewish occupational patterns at turn of the century, 144
American Language, The (Mencken), 339
American Sephardi, The, 108
Angel, Marc D.
  essay by, 75–136
Annenberg, Moe
  and Jews in postwar American culture, 339
Annenberg, Walter H.
  TV Guide, 339
Anti-Defamation League
  and affirmative action, 294
  and Red Scare, 29
Arazi, Yehudah
  and Jews in postwar American culture, 346
Aroghetti, Jacob
  and Levantine Sephardim, 83

INDEX

Ashkenazi, American
    Ashkenazi-Sephardi intermarriage, 124–28
    compared with American Sephardi, 75–134
Athletics
    Jews in, 246, 247
Atlanta, Georgia
    Sephardi community in, 106, 129–34
Aufbau, 53, 54, 56
August Belmont and Company
    and Jewish banking in the 1920s, 236
Automobile industry
    Jews in (1920s), 237

Baline, Israel
    and Jews in postwar American culture, 339
Baltimore, Maryland
    American-born Jewish occupational patterns in, 187
    Jewish occupational patterns in, 150
Bankers
    Jews as percentage of, 177, 179, 235–36
Bardin, Shlomo
    and Brandeis Camp Institute, 44
Barkey, Jack
    and New York Sephardim, 101
Barocas, David
    and American Sephardim, 109
Baron, Salo W.
    and Committee of 300, 25
Baruch, Bernard
    support of Zionism by, 19
Bat, Luba
    and impact of Holocaust survivors on American society, 63
Baum, Charlotte
    and Jewish feminism, 265
    and *The Jewish Woman: An Anthology*, 264
Beck, Evelyn Torton
    Nice Jewish Girls, 270
Behar, Leon
    and Seattle Sephardim, 108
Behar, Nissim
    and Levantine Sephardim, 78
Belkin, Samuel
    and American Sephardim, 108
    and Committee of 300, 25
Bellette, Amy
    and Jews in postwar American culture, 344

Bellow, Saul
    and Jews in postwar American culture, 339, 348
Ben-Canaan, Ari
    and Jews in postwar American culture, 348
Ben-Gurion, David
    case for a Jewish state brought before United Nations by, 20
    and Jews in postwar American culture, 346
Benjamin, Judah P.
    and tercentenary, 26
Benyunes, Joseph A. de
    and New York Sephardim, 103, 104
Bergen, Candice
    and Jews in postwar American culture, 350
Berlin, Irving
    and Jews in postwar American culture, 338, 339
Bernardete, Maír José, 76, 91
    Hispanic Culture and Character of the Sephardic Jews, 76, 109
Bernstein, David
    and tercentenary, 28
Bernstein, Irving
    and the impact of feminism on Jewish religious life, 295
Bernstein, Leonard
    Age of Anxiety, 26
Bernstein, Louis
    and the impact of feminism on Jewish religious life, 301, 302
Best and Brightest, The (Halberstam), 340
Biale, Rachel
    and the impact of feminism on Jewish religious life, 297
Biblioteca Universal Sefardi, 109
Big Book of Jewish Humor (Novak and Waldoks), 328
Billings, John
    and American Jewish occupational patterns at turn of the century, 141–42
Biltmore Conference
    on a Jewish commonwealth, 20
Blau, Zena Smith
    and the impact of feminism on Jewish life, 292
Blaustein, Jacob
    on political loyalties of American Jews, 22
Bloch, Ernest
    Israel Symphony, 26

INDEX

B'nai B'rith Hillel Foundation
  educational sponsorships to refugees by, 65
Bogart, Humphrey
  and Jews in postwar American culture, 349
Boone, Pat
  and Jews in postwar American culture, 347
Boorstein, Daniel
  The Genius of American Politics, 26
Boston, Massachusetts
  friction between Jews and Irish in, 6
  Jewish occupational patterns in, 155
Boulakia, Jean
  and North African Sephardim, 111
Boz del Pueblo, La, 107
Brandeis, Louis D., 250
Brandeis Camp Institute
  and Shlomo Bardin, 44
Bread Givers (Yezierska), 323
Brodsky, Joseph
  and Jews in postwar American culture, 339
Broner, E. M.
  and the impact of feminism on Jewish religious life, 308
Brooklyn Polytechnic, 191
Brown, Charles
  on effects of postwar Jewish migration, 44
Buckley, William F., Jr.
  and Jews in postwar American culture, 338
Buffalo, New York
  Jewish occupational patterns in, 155
  Jewish socioeconomic status in, 176
  percentage of Jewish professionals in, 195
Bunim, Sarah
  and Jews in postwar American culture, 312
Business schools
  percentage of Jews in, 192

Cabot, Richard
  anti-Semitism of, 247
Call It Sleep (Roth), 328
Cantor, Aviva
  and the impact of feminism on Jewish life, 288
  and Jewish feminism, 257
  "The Sheltered Workshop," 310
Cardin, Shoshana
  and the impact of feminism on Jewish life, 289
Cardozo, David Jessurun
  and New York Sephardim, 97

Carnal Knowledge, 350
Caro, Robert A.
  The Years of Lyndon Johnson, 340
Castro, Federico
  on Sephardi feelings toward Spain, 122
Central Sephardic Jewish Community of America
  and New York Sephardim, 98
Chambers, Harry B.
  and fraternities in high schools, 246
Chicago, Illinois
  Jewish occupational patterns in, 139–40, 150, 155
  1930s occupational patterns in, 168
Chiswick, Barry
  on high occupational achievement of Jewish men, 279
Cincinnati, Ohio
  American-born Jewish occupational patterns in, 187
  Sephardi community in, 106
City College of New York City, 190
  1920s Jewish enrollment at, 243
Cleveland, Ohio
  Jewish occupational patterns in, 155
Clothing industry
  Jews in 1920s, 235
Cohen, Benjamin V.
  and Commitee of 300, 25
Cohen, Gerson D.
  and the impact of feminism on Jewish religious life, 304
Cohen, Hayyim
  and Syrian Sephardim, 110
Cohen, Morris Raphael, 247, 252
  on Jewish enrollment at City College of New York, 243
Cohen, Steven M.
  and the impact of feminism on Jewish religious life, 301
  and impact of Holocaust survivors on American society, 68
Colleges
  and American-born Jewish occupational patterns, 190–96
Colonial America
  Sephardi community in, 80
Columbia Broadcasting System
  in the 1920s, 238
Columbia Spectator, 246

357

INDEX

Columbia University, 190, 191
    reactions to increased Jewish enrollment at, 247–48
    1920s quotas on Jewish enrollment at, 243
Commentary, 69, 341
Commission on Law and Social Action
    creation of, 21
Committee of 300
    and tercentenary, 24–28
Communism, anti-
    and Jewish/communist stereotype, 28–30
Congregation Shearith Israel
    Sephardi settlement in Latin America encouraged by, 88
Congress Weekly, 29, 341
Conservative Judaism, 264, 265
Conservative Judaism
    postwar efforts for social justice by, 21
    in the 1930s, 8
Construction industry
    Jews in (1920s), 237
Coughlin, Charles E.
    anti-Semitic broadcasts of, 5
Council of Jewish Federations
    and affirmative action, 294
"Council of Jewish Federations Women's Division Leadership Survey," 290–91
Counterlife, The (Roth), 348
Cowan, Paul
    and the Jewish American Princess stereotype, 324, 325, 326
Crystal, Billy
    and Jews in postwar American culture, 350
Current Population Survey (CPS)
    and postwar American Jewish economy, 216, 220, 225, 226
Curtis, Tony
    and Jews in postwar American culture, 349

Dallas, Texas
    postwar Jewish migration to, 36
Dalven, Joseph
    Sephardic Home News, 108
Davka, 263
Dawidowicz, Lucy
    and the impact of feminism on Jewish life, 268, 269
    on postwar period, 17

Decter, Midge
    and the impact of feminism on Jewish life, 284
Defender of the Faith (Roth), 348
Dentistry schools
    percentage of Jews in, 192
Detroit, Michigan
    American Jewish occupational patterns in, 197
    Jewish occupational patterns in, 164–65
    1930s occupational patterns in, 168, 170
Diamond, David
    Ahavah, 26
Diary and World-Wide Directory of Sephardic Congregations, 107
Diary of Anne Frank, The (Frank), 343, 345
Diary of a Young Girl, The (Frank), 341, 342, 343, 344, 345, 347, 348
Dobrinsky, Herbert C.
    and American Sephardim, 108
Dreifus, 108
Dundes, Alan
    and the Jewish American Princess stereotype, 321, 323, 324, 328
Dynamic America and Those Who Own It (Klein), 236

Easton, New York
    Jewish occupational patterns in, 165
Eaton, Walter P.
    stereotypical views on Jews in higher education by, 248
Economics
    American Jewish socioeconomic status, 174–76, 200
    American Jewish success in, 137–58
    postwar American Jewish economy, 215–32
    role of Jews in American economy, 177–79
    schools of, 192
    1920s American Jewish economy, 234–39
    See also Occupational patterns, American Jewish
Editorial Gredos, 109
Education
    and American-born Jewish occupational patterns, 190–96
    and athletics, 246, 247
    educational attainment, 217–20
    and percentage of Jews in professional schools, 192–96

public, 252–55
reactions to increased Jewish enrollment at universities, 233–56
and women, 275–78, 302–4
and 1920s quotas on Jewish enrollment at universities, 239–56
Educational attainment
and postwar American Jewish economy, 217–20
Ehrenreich, Barbara
and the Jewish American Princess stereotype, 330
Eilberg, Amy
and the impact of feminism on Jewish religious life, 307
and Jewish feminism, 265
ordination of, 265
Eisenhower, Dwight D.
and Commitee of 300, 25
and tercentenary, 26
Elazar, Daniel
and the impact of feminism on Jewish religious life, 299
Emigrante, El, 107
Engineering schools
percentage of Jews in, 192, 195
Ephron, Nora
Heartburn, 332
Epstein, Helen
and impact of Holocaust survivors on American society, 72
Equal Rights Amendment (ERA)
and American feminist movement, 261
Ermanado, El, 108
European Jewry
American Jewish community's support of, 19
Exodus (Uris), 345, 346, 347, 348
Ezrat Nashim
and Jewish feminism, 263

Falk, Marcia
and *The Jewish Woman: An Anthology,* 264
Farrow, Mia
and Jews in postwar American culture, 349
Federalist, The (Jay), 337
Federation of Jewish Philanthropies/United Jewish Appeal
and impact of Holocaust survivors on American society, 68

Federation of Oriental Jews
and New York Sephardim, 95
Feingold, Henry L.
essay by, 215–32
Felter, William
and Arista, 246
Feminine Mystique, The (Friedan), 260–61
Feminism, 257–59
American feminist movement, 260–61
and changes in life-cycle patterns of women, 271–74
and communal and organizational life, 282–86
and educational improvements for women, 275–78, 302–4
and family, 267–70
Jewish feminism, 261–66
and Jewish religious life, 295–316
and occupational improvements for women, 275–81, 293–94
and voluntarism, 287–92
Fiedler, Leslie
and Jews in postwar American culture, 346
Field, Sally
and Jews in postwar American culture, 350
Film industry
Jews in (1920s), 237, 238
Finkelstein, Barbara
and impact of Holocaust survivors on American society, 72
Finkelstein, Louis
and Commitee of 300, 25
Firestone, Shulamith
and American feminist movement, 261
Fishman, Sylvia Barack
essay by, 257–316
Fitzgerald, Frances
and the Jewish American Princess stereotype, 330
Ford, Henry
The Protocols of the Elders of Zion, 234, 244
Forestry schools
percentage of Jews in, 192
Fortune, 235
study of American Jewish occupational patterns by, 177
Foster, Arnold
and Jewish/communist stereotype, 29

359

Foundation for the Advancement of Sephardic Studies and Culture
and American Sephardim, 109
Frank, Anne
Diary of Anne Frank, The, 343, 345
Diary of a Young Girl, The, 341, 342, 343, 344, 345, 347, 348
Frank, Otto
and Anne Frank, 341, 342, 343, 344
See also Frank, Anne
Frank, Shirley
and the impact of feminism on Jewish life, 285
Frankfurter, Felix
support of Zionism by, 19
Franks, Jacob
and American Sephardim, 79
Fraternities, high school
Jewish opposition to, 246
Fraternities, Jewish, 245–46
Friedan, Betty, 260
The Feminine Mystique, 260–61
and the impact of feminism on Jewish life, 257
The Second Stage, 265
Friedman, Howard
on effects of postwar Jewish migration, 44
From the Diary of Anne Frank (Thomas), 343
Frontiers of Faith, 26

Gadol, M. S.
and American Sephardim, 89
A New Chapter of Sephardi History in America, 89, 107
and New York Sephardim, 94, 95, 99, 101
Gaon, Solomon
and American Sephardim, 108
Garfield, John
and Jews in postwar American culture, 349
Garfunkel, Art
and Jews in postwar American culture, 350
Gartner, Lloyd P.
essay by, 1–16
Gedelecia, Joseph
and New York Sephardim, 92
Gejdenson, Sam
and impact of Holocaust survivors on American society, 74
Gender stereotypes, Jewish
in American culture, 317–33

General Social Survey (GSS)
and postwar American Jewish economy, 217–27
Genius of American Politics, The (Boorstein), 26
Getting Equitable Treatment (GET), 313
Ghost Writer, The (Roth), 344
Glass-Steagal law
and Jewish banking in the 1920s, 235
Glazer, Nathan, 239
and impact of Holocaust survivors on American society, 69
Gold, Doris
and the impact of feminism on Jewish life, 288
Gold, Michael
Jews Without Money, 323, 328
Goldberg, Nathan
essays by, 137–58, 159–84, 185–214
Goldblum, Jeff
and Jews in postwar American culture, 350
Goldenberg, Judith Plaskow
and *The Jewish Woman: An Anthology,* 264
Goldenwasser, A. A.
on Harvard's treatment of Jews, 251
Goldman-Sachs
and Jewish banking in the 1920s, 235
Goldstein, Bernard
on migration to Los Angeles, 38
Goldstein, Israel
and Commitee of 300, 25
Goldstein, Sidney
postwar Jewish migration, 39
Gomez, Moses
and American Sephardim, 79
Goodbye Columbus (Roth), 322, 347
Goodman, Edward
and impact of Holocaust survivors on American society, 66
Goodrich, Frances
Seven Brides for Seven Brothers, 343
Gordis, Robert
Judaism, 29
Goren, Arthur A.
essay by, 17–34
Gornick, Vivian
and Jewish feminism, 262
"Woman as Outsider," 261–62
Graduate, The, 349
Grapes of Wrath, The (Steinbeck), 346

Green, Arthur
and "Women and Change in Jewish Law: Responses to the Fall 1974 Symposium," 265
Greenberg, Blu
and the impact of feminism on Jewish religious life, 308
and *The Jewish Woman: An Anthology,* 264
Will There Be Orthodox Women Rabbis?, 283
Greenberg, Simon
and University of Judaism, 44
Groeneman, Sid
and the impact of feminism on Jewish life, 269
Gunfight at the O.K. Corral, The, 346

Hacker, Louis
and New York Sephardim, 89, 90, 91, 93, 96, 105
Hackett, Albert
and Jews in postwar American culture, 342
Hadassah Magazine, 311
Halberstam, David
The Best and Brightest, 340
Halpern, Ben
The American Jew, A Zionist Analysis, 30, 31
Hananiah, Jack David
and New York Sephardim, 92
Handelman, Susan
and the impact of feminism on Jewish life, 268
Handlin, Oscar
Adventure in Freedom, 27, 36
on postwar migrations, 35–36
The Uprooted, 27
Hapgood, Hutchins
The Spirit of the Ghetto, 215
Harvard Graduates' Magazine, 249
Harvard University, 190, 191
and 1920s quotas on Jewish enrollment, 233–56
Hauptman, Judith
and Jewish feminism, 265
and *The Jewish Woman: An Anthology,* 264
Hayyim, Hafetz
and the impact of feminism on Jewish religious life, 303

Heartburn (Ephron), 332
Hebrew Immigrant Aid Society (HIAS)
and refugee resettlement, 63
travel fare advances to Jewish refugees by, 63
Hebrew Immigrant Shelter and Aid Society (HISAS)
on Levantine Sephardim in United States, 84, 85
Hebrew Union College
ordination of women at, 304
Hecht, Ben
and Jews in postwar American culture, 339
Held, Adolph
and Commitee of 300, 25
Hellman, Lillian
and Jews in postwar American culture, 343
Helmreich, William B.
essay by, 61–74
Hendricks, Henry S.
and New York Sephardim, 105
Herskovits, Willie
and impact of Holocaust survivors on American society, 63
Hertz, John D.
and Yellow Cab Company, 237
Heschel, Susannah
On Being a Jewish Feminist, 265
Hexter, Maurice
and Cincinnati Sephardim, 106
and New York Sephardim, 91
Hillman, Bessie
and impact of Holocaust survivors on American society, 63
Hillman, Sidney
and impact of Holocaust survivors on American society, 63
Hirsch, Samson Raphael
and the impact of feminism on Jewish religious life, 303
Hispanic Culture and Character of the Sephardic Jews (Benardete), 76, 109
Hoffman, Dustin
and Jews in postwar American culture, 349
Holiday Inn, 339
Holocaust rescue
late efforts for, 11–12
Holocaust survivors
impact on American society from, 61–74

Hook, Sidney, 247
 and Columbia University, 247
Hotel keeping industry
 Jews in 1920s, 237
Houston, Texas
 Jewish migration to, 36
Hunter College (New York City)
 1920s Jewish enrollment at, 243
Hyman, Paula
 and impact of feminism on Jewish life, 257, 284
 and Jewish feminism, 265
 and *The Jewish Woman: An Anthology,* 264

Income, Jewish
 and postwar American Jewish economy, 226–28
 in the 1920s, 235
Indianapolis, Indiana
 Sephardi community in, 106
Inquirer, 339
Instituto Arias Montana de Estudios Hebraicos
 Sephardi studies at, 109
Instituto Ibn Tibbón
 Sephardi studies at, 109
Into the Night, 350
Inventory of American Jewish History, 26
Island of Rhodes
 Sephardi community in, 106
Israel, Edward L.
 and American Jewish occupational patterns in the 1920s, 161
"Israel and the American Jewish Community" (Sherman), 23
Israel Symphony (Bloch), 26
It Can't Happen Here (Lewis), 5

Jacobson, Israel
 and American Sephardim, 81
Jaher, Frederic Cople
 and the Jewish American Princess stereotype, 326
Jay, John
 The Federalist, 337
Jewish Agency
 and Joseph Proskauer, 19
Jewish American Princess (JAP)
 and gender stereotypes in American culture, 317–33
Jewish and Female (Schneider), 266

Jewish Catalogs, 259, 311
Jewish Colonization Association
 aid to refugee farmers by, 65
Jewish Feminist Organization (JFO)
 origins of, 264
Jewish National Fund
 and Great Depression, 9
Jewish Poultry Farmer's Association (JPFA)
 and impact of Holocaust survivors on American society, 69
Jewish Way, The, 54
Jewish Woman: An Anthology, The (Koltun), 264
Jewish Woman in America, The (Baum, Hyman, and Michel), 265
Jewry, American
 from 1929 to 1945, 1–16
 from 1945 to 1955, 17–32
Jews Without Money (Gold), 323, 328
"Jew Who Wasn't There, The" (Adler), 263
Jew Within American Society, The (Sherman), 24
Johns Hopkins University, 191
Johnson, Lyndon B.
 and Jews in postwar American culture, 340
Joint Distribution Committee
 and Great Depression, 9
Jolson Story, The, 349
Jordan, Withrop
 White Over Black, 340
Joseph, the Righteous, and his Brothers, 108
Judaism (Gordis), 29
Judgment at Nuremberg (Kramer), 345
Jungle, The, 346

Kallen, Horace
 on Jews in higher education, 252
 "The Tercentenary, Yomtov or Yahrzeit," 29–30
Kamerman, Sheila
 and the impact of feminism on Jewish life, 284
Kanin, Garson
 and Jews in postwar American culture, 342
Kaplan, Mordecai M.
 and Conservative Judaism, 8
 and the impact of feminism on Jewish religious life, 298
 Bezalel C. Sherman on, 24
 and tercentenary, 30

INDEX

Karo, Yosef
and Jews in postwar American culture, 340
Karpeles, John
and New York Sephardim, 98
Katzanellenbogen, Meir, 340
Kazin, Alfred
on life in the Depression, 4
Keaton, Diane
and Jews in postwar American culture, 349
Kelman, Wolfe
and the impact of feminism on Jewish religious life, 304
Kennedy, John F.
and Jews in postwar American culture, 338
Klein, Henry
Dynamic America and Those Who Own It, 236
Klutznik, Philip
political career of, 21
Kohn, Eugene, 29
Koltun, Elizabeth
The Jewish Woman: An Anthology, 264
Kosher foods industry
Jews in 1920s, 237
Kramer, Stanley
Judgment at Nuremberg, 345
Kramer vs. Kramer, 350
Kuhn, Loeb
and Jewish banking in the 1920s, 235, 236
Ku Klux Klan
in the 1920s, 234

Labor Zionist Organization
and "Israel and the American Jewish Community," 23
La Guardia, Fiorello H.
and friction between Jews and Irish, 6
support of Franklin D. Roosevelt by, 7
LaHana, Victor
and New York Sephardim, 101
Lange, Jessica
and Jews in postwar American culture, 349
Lantos, Tom
and impact of Holocaust survivors on American society, 74
Last Jew in America, The (Mogul), 325
Law schools
percentage of Jews in, 192
Lehman, Herbert H.
Anti-Defamation League's honor of, 29
support of Franklin D. Roosevelt by, 7
support of Zionism by, 19
Lehman Brothers
and Jewish banking in the 1920s, 235, 236
Lehrman, Irving
and Miami Beach Jewish Center, 43
Lemann, Nicholas
Texas Monthly, 37
Lerner, Anne Lapidus
and the impact of feminism on Jewish life, 270
and Jewish feminism, 265
Lester, Julius
and Jews in postwar American culture, 347
Leuchtenburg, William
on Franklin D. Roosevelt, 6
Levin, Meyer
and Jews in postwar American culture, 341, 342, 343, 344, 345
Levine, Jacqueline K.
and the impact of feminism on Jewish life, 289, 294
and *The Jewish Woman: An Anthology,* 264
Levine, Naomi
and the impact of feminism on Jewish religious life, 295
Levy, Albert
La Vara, 107, 108
Levy, John H.
and New York Sephardim, 101
Levy, Louis N.
and American Sephardim, 109
Lewis, Sinclair
It Can't Happen Here, 5
Liebman, Charles
on dual identity of American Jews, 17
and the impact of feminism on Jewish religious life, 306, 307
Life of Emile Zola, The, 342
Lilith (Schneider), 265, 266
Lippmann, Walter, 252
on affluent Jews, 250
Liptzin, Solomon
and Jews in postwar American culture, 340
Litman, Jane
and the impact of feminism on Jewish religious life, 308
Lopez, Aaron
and Western Sephardim, 76

INDEX

Los Angeles, California
  postwar migration to, 35–46
  Sephardi community in, 106
  1930s occupational patterns in, 168
Lowell, A. Lawrence
  and quotas on Jewish enrollment, 244, 249–52
Lowenstein, Steven M.
  essay by, 51–60
Lumet, Sidney
  The Pawnbroker, 345
Luz, La, 107
Luzero Sephardi, El, 107

Maeso, David Gonzalo
  and American Sephardim, 109
Magid, Jacques
  and Levantine Sephardim, 85
Magnes, Judah L.
  and New York Sephardim, 95
Magnin, Edgar
  on new ethnicity from Jewish migration, 45
Mamet, David
  and Jews in postwar American culture, 339
Manhattan, 350
Mankiewicz, Herman
  and Jews in postwar American culture, 339
Manner, Ande
  Poor Cousins, 215
Man's Opportunities and Responsibilities Under Freedom, 27, 32
Marcus, Jacob Rader
  and American Sephardim, 81
Marjorie Morningstar (Wouk), 322, 325, 347
Markens, Isaac
  on economic success of American Jews, 137
Marshall, Louis, 10
  death of, 1
  on A. Lawrence Lowell, 252
  on reaction to Russian Jews in higher education, 250
May, Elaine
  and the Jewish American Princess stereotype, 327
McCarthy, Joseph
  and Red Scare, 28, 29
Me'am Lo'ez, 109
Medical schools
  percentage of Jews in, 192, 193–94

Melting-Pot, The (Zangwill), 347
Mencken, H. L.
  The American Language, 339
Menken, Mortimer
  and New York Sephardim, 102
Merchandizing industry
  Jews in 1920s, 237–38
Miami, Florida
  postwar migration to, 35–46
Miami Beach Jewish Center
  and Irving Lehrman, 43
Michel, Sonya
  and Jewish feminism, 265
  and *The Jewish Woman: An Anthology*, 264
Michigan
  Jewish occupational patterns in, 160
Migration, postwar
  and Los Angeles, 35–46
  and Miami, 35–46
Mila 18 (Uris), 348
Milwaukee, Wisconsin
  Jewish occupational patterns in, 155, 160
Minnesota
  Jewish occupational patterns in, 160
Mogul, Susan, 326
  The Last Jew in America, 325
Monsky, Henry
  and Omaha Friendship Club of Los Angeles, 42
Monson, Rela Gaffen
  and the impact of feminism on Jewish life, 285, 299
Moore, Deborah Dash
  essay by, 35–50
Morgenstern, Julian
  on Jews in higher education, 251
Morgenthau, Henry, Jr.
  and "Report to the Secretary on the Acquiescence of this Government in the Murder of Jews," 11
  and United Jewish Appeal, 19
Morison, Samuel Eliot
  on Russian Jews in higher education, 244–45
"Movement for Equal Rights for Women in American Jewry, The," 265
Ms., 258

National Broadcasting System
  in the 1920s, 238

National Conference on Jewish Women and
    Men (1974)
  and Jewish Feminist Organization (JFO), 264
National Jewish Community Relations
    Advisory Council
  and affirmative action, 294
National Organization for Women (NOW)
  and American feminist movement, 261
Neighborhood Settlement House
  and New York Sephardim, 102–5
New, Elisa
  and the Jewish American Princess
    stereotype, 330
*New Chapter of Sephardi History in America,
    A* (Gadol), 89
New Deal
  and American Jewry, 6–7, 9
New Lives (Rabinowitz), 67
New London, Connecticut
  American-born Jewish occupational patterns
    in, 189
  1930s American Jewish occupational
    patterns in, 195
  1930s occupational patterns in, 171
Newman, Paul
  and Jews in postwar American culture, 349
New Orleans, Louisiana
  American Jewish occupational patterns in,
    197
  1930s occupational patterns in, 170
Newspaper industry
  Jews in 1920s, 238
New York City
  American Jewish occupational patterns in,
    187, 197
  friction between Jews and Irish in, 6
  German-Jewish community in Washington
    Heights, 51–60
  Jewish occupational patterns in, 137–40,
    141, 150, 160
  Jewish socioeconomic status in, 175
  Sephardi community in, 79, 81, 88, 89–106,
    129–34
  1930s occupational patterns in, 168, 170
New York Jewish Women's Center, 264
New York Post, 348
New York Sun
  on economic success of American Jews,
    137–38

New York Times, 238, 311, 346
New York Times Book Review, 341
New York University, 191
Nice Jewish Girls (Beck), 270
Nichols, Mike, 349
Nicholson, Jack
  and Jews in postwar American culture, 350
Niger, Samuel
  and Commitee of 300, 25
Niles, David
  support of Zionism by, 19
Nixon, Richard M., 327, 338
No More Nice Girls
  and American feminist movement, 261
Norma Rae, 350
North Africa
  Sephardi community in, 111–12
Novick, Peter
  and Jews in postwar American culture, 344
Nuit, La (Wiesel), 344

Occupational patterns, American Jewish
  among American-born Jews, 185–213
  and postwar economy, 215–31
  at the turn of the century, 137–58
  in the 1920s, 159–83
  in the 1930s, 167–79
Ohio
  percentage of Jewish professionals in, 196
  See also Cincinnati, Ohio
Omaha, Nebraska
  Jewish occupational patterns in, 165–66
  postwar Jewish migration to, 438
Omaha Friendship Club of Los Angeles
  and Henry Monsky, 42
On Being a Jewish Feminist (Heschel), 265
Oriental Committee of Congregation Mikveh
    Israel
  Sephardi settlement in Latin American
    encouraged by, 88
Oriental Committee of the Sisterhood
  and New York Sephardim, 94
Orthodox Rabbinical Council of America
  postwar efforts of, 21
Ostow, Mortimer
  and "Women and Change on Jewish Law,"
    264
Ovadia, Mazal
  and New York Sephardim, 98

Ovadia, Nissim J.
  and New York Sephardim, 97

Palestine Foundation Fund
  and Great Depression, 9
Paley, William S.
  and Commitee of 300, 25
Papo, Joseph M.
  and New York Sephardim, 98
Parks, Larry
  and Jews in postwar American culture, 349
Passage from Home (Rosenfeld), 340
Patton, George S.
  and Jews in postwar American culture, 346
Pawnbroker, The (Lumet), 345
Pennsylvania
  Jewish occupational patterns in, 160
Perkins, Millie
  and Jews in postwar American culture, 344
Perlmutter, Nathan
  on migration and a sense of Jewish community, 39
Pfeiffer, Michelle
  and Jews in postwar American culture, 350
Pharmacy schools
  percentage of Jews in, 192, 193
Philadelphia, Pennsylvania
  Jewish occupational patterns in, 139–40, 150, 155
  1930s occupational patterns in, 168
Pittsfield, Massachusetts
  Jewish occupational patterns in, 165–66
Plaskow, Judith
  and the impact of feminism on Jewish religious life, 297
Play It Again, Sam, 349
Poe, Edgar Allan
  and Jews in postwar American culture, 341
Pogrebrin, Letty Cottin
  and *Ms.*, 258
Pool, David de Sola
  and American Sephardim, 88
  and New York Sephardim, 89, 90, 92, 96, 100, 101, 102
  Sephardi settlement in Latin America encouraged by, 88
Poor Cousins (Manner), 215
Portland, Oregon
  Sephardi community in, 129–34

Portnoy's Complaint (Roth), 325, 347
Potofsky, Jacob S.
  and Commitee of 300, 25
Poupko, Chana
  and the impact of feminism on Jewish religious life, 315
Precious Heritage, A, 26
Prell, Riv-Ellen
  essay by, 317–36
Preminger, Otto
  and Jews in postwar American culture, 347
Priesand, Sally
  and the impact of feminism on Jewish religious life, 304
  ordination of, 265, 304
Princeton University
  1920s quotas on Jewish enrollment at, 243
Printing industry
  Jews in 1920s, 237
Professionalism, Jewish
  origins of, 239–56
  percentage of Jews in professional schools, 192–96. *See also* Education
Progress, The, 108
Progresso, El, 107
Proskauer, Joseph
  and Jewish Agency, 19
Protocols of the Elders of Zion, The (Ford), 234
Publishing industry
  Jews in 1920s, 238, 239
Pyle, Ernie
  and impact of Holocaust survivors on American society, 63

Rabin, Leon
  on migration experience, 36
Rabinowitz, Dorothy
  New Lives, 67
Racing Reform, 339
Rackman, Honey
  and the impact of feminism on Jewish religious life, 313
Radio Corporation of America
  in the 1920s, 238
Radio industry
  Jews in 1920s, 238
Rampling, Charlotte
  and Jews in postwar American culture, 349

Real estate development industry
  Jews in 1920s, 237
Rebbe, Belzer
  and the impact of feminism on Jewish religious life, 303
Reconstructionist, The, 29, 311
Red Scare
  and Jewish/communist stereotype, 28–30
Reform Judaism
  postwar efforts for social justice by, 21
  in the 1930s, 8
Reisman, David
  on working women, 281
"Report to the Secretary on the Acquiescence of this Government in the Murder of Jews," 11
Response, 264
Rifkind, Simon
  and Committee of 300, 25
Rishkin, Steven
  and impact of Holocaust survivors on American society, 72
Ritterband, Paul
  and impact of Holocaust survivors on American society, 68
Rochester, New York
  Sephardi community in, 106
Rockwell, George Lincoln
  and Jews in postwar American culture, 347
Rogers, Ginger
  and Jews in postwar American culture, 342
Roosevelt, Eleanor
  and Jews in postwar American culture, 341
Roosevelt, Franklin Delano
  inclusiveness of, 6–7
  and State Department's anti-Semitic activities, 11
Rosen, Gladys
  and the impact of feminism on Jewish life, 285
Rosenberg, Ethel
  arrest of, 28–29
Rosenberg, Julius
  arrest of, 28–29
Rosenfeld, Isaac
  Passage from Home, 340
Rosenman, Samuel
  and Commitee of 300, 25
  support of Zionism by, 19

Rosenwald, Julius
  rescue of Sears, Roebuck by, 236
Ross, Katherine
  and Jews in postwar American culture, 349
Roth, Henry
  Call It Sleep, 328
Roth, Joe
  and Jews in postwar American culture, 338
Roth, Philip
  The Counterlife, 348
  Defender of the Faith, 348
  The Ghost Writer, 344
  Goodbye Columbus, 322, 347
  Portnoy's Complaint, 325, 347, 349
Ruppin, Arthur, 215
Rutgers University
  1920s quotas on Jewish enrollment at, 243
Ryan, Meg
  and Jews in postwar American culture, 350

Samuel, Ralph E.
  and Commitee of 300, 24–25
Sandberg, Neil
  on effects of postwar Jewish migration, 44, 45
San Francisco, California
  Jewish socioeconomic status in, 176
  percentage of Jewish professionals in, 195
Sarna, Nahum
  and the impact of feminism on Jewish religious life, 302
Sarnoff, David
  and Commitee of 300, 25
Schacter, Hershel
  and the impact of feminism on Jewish religious life, 301
Schiff, Jacob
  and Jewish banking in the 1920s, 235, 236
Schildkraut, Joseph
  and Jews in postwar American culture, 342
Schneider, Susan Weidman
  Jewish and Female, 266
  Lilith, 265, 266
Schnirer, Sara
  and the impact of feminism on Jewish religious life, 303
Schnur, Susan
  and Jewish gender stereotypes in American culture, 319

Schoenfeld, Eugene
    and impact of Holocaust survivors on American society, 65
Sears, Roebuck
    Julius Rosenwald's rescue of, 236
Seattle, Washington
    Sephardi community in, 106, 129–34
Second Stage, The (Friedan), 258
Sefarad, 109
Seixas, Mendes
    and American Sephardim, 81
Self-employment status
    and postwar American Jewish economy, 222–26
Seligman Company
    and Jewish banking in the 1920s, 236
Sephardi, The, 98
Sephardic Bulletin, The, 108
Sephardic Home News (Dalven), 108
Sephardic World, 109
Sephardim, American
    cultural activities of, 155–57
    and Latin American settlement, 88
    and Levantine Sephardim, 125–26, 130–33
    New York City communities, 137–54
    and North African Sephardim, 111–12
    population distribution of, 133–37
    Sephardi-Ashkenazi intermarriage, 124–28
    survey of, 160–82
    and Syrian Sephardim, 110–11
    and Western Sephardim, 124–25
Seven Brides for Seven Brothers (Hackett and Goodrich), 343
Shamah, Mosheh
    and Syrian Sephardim, 111
Shapiro, Meyer
    and Columbia University, 246–47
Shapiro, Saul
    and the impact of feminism on Jewish religious life, 306, 307
Shearith Israel Bulletin, 82, 100
"Sheltered Workshop, The" (Cantor), 288
Sherman, C. Bezalel
    Israel and the American Jewish Community, 24
    The Jew Within American Society, 23
Sh'ma, 268
Shoe manufacturing industry
    Jews in 1920s, 237

Shumlin, Herman
    and Jews in postwar American culture, 341
Silberman, Charles
    and educational improvements for Jewish women, 275, 277
Silver, Abba Hillel
    case for a Jewish state brought before United Nations by, 20
    leadership of, 10
Singer, Isaac Bashevis
    and Jews in postwar American culture, 339
Sisterhood of Shearith Israel
    and New York Sephardim, 100–105
Society for Cutting Up Men (SCUM)
    and American feminist movement, 261
Socioeconomic status, American Jewish, 174–76
    See also Economics
Spanish and Portuguese Synagogue
    and New York Sephardim, 94, 99–100
Spinoza, Benedict
    Tractatus Theologico-Politicus, 337
Spirit of the Ghetto, The (Hapgood), 215
Stamford, Connecticut
    American Jewish occupational patterns in, 197
    1930s occupational patterns in, 170
Starr, Harry, 249
State Department
    anti-Semitism of (1930s), 11–12
Staten Island, New York
    American-born Jewish occupational patterns in, 189
Steinem, Gloria
    on marriage, 261
Stern, Maurice
    criticism of "non-pious" Jews by, 251
Stevens, George
    and Jews in postwar American culture, 342
Stiles, Ezra
    and Western Sephardim, 76
Strasberg, Susan
    and Jews in postwar American culture, 344
Strathern, Marilyn
    and Jewish gender stereotypes in American culture, 319, 320
Streep, Meryl
    and Jews in postwar American culture, 350
Streisand, Barbra
    and Jews in postwar American culture, 349

Survey of the Conservative Movement and Some of Its Religious Attitudes, A, 306
Susman, Warren
and the Jewish American Princess stereotype, 327
Syracuse University
1920s quotas on Jewish enrollment at, 243
Syria
Sephardi community in, 110–11
Syrkin, Marie
and the impact of feminism on Jewish life, 268

Tercentenary, 24–30
"Tercentenary, Yomtov or Yahrzeit, The" (Kallen), 29–30
Texas Monthly (Lemann), 37
Textile industry
Jews in 1920s, 237
Thomas, Michael Tilson
From the Diary of Anne Frank, 343
Toch, Ernst
and tercentenary, 26
Toledo, Ohio
postwar Jewish migration to, 438
Tom, Dick and Harry, 342
Tootsie, 349
Touriel, Acher
and New York Sephardim, 98
Tractatus Theologico-Politicus (Spinoza), 337
Trenton, New Jersey
percentage of Jewish professionals in, 195
Trilling, Diana
and Jews in postwar American culture, 340
Trilling, Lionel
and Columbia University, 247
Truman, Harry
loyalty program of, 28
Tucson, Arizona
Jewish migration to, 36
TV Guide (Annenberg), 339
Tynan, Kenneth
and Jews in postwar American culture, 342

Umansky, Ellen
and the impact of feminism on Jewish life, 267, 309
Uncle Tom's Cabin, 346
"Unfreedom of Jewish Women, The" (Weiss-Rosmarin), 263

Union Peace Society
and New York Sephardim, 91, 93
United Palestine Appeal
formation of, 9
United States Immigration Commission
and American Jewish occupational patterns at turn of the century, 144
Universities
and American-born Jewish occupational patterns, 190–96
1920s quotas on Jewish enrollment at, 243–54
University of Judaism
and Moshe David, 44
Uprooted, The (Handlin), 27
Uris, Leon
Exodus, 345, 346, 347, 348
Mila 18, 348

Valensi, Edward
and New York Sephardim, 101
Vara, La (Levy), 107, 108
Veblen, Thorsten
and the Jewish American Princess stereotype, 330

Wagner, Robert F.
support of Franklin D. Roosevelt by, 7
Wapter, Leonard
and Jews in postwar American culture, 345
War Refugee Board
and late rescue efforts, 11–12
Washington Heights, New York City
German-Jewish community in, 51–60
Washington Post, 238
Waxman, Chaim
and the impact of feminism on Jewish life, 289
Weiner, Greta
and the impact of feminism on Jewish religious life, 300
Weisgal, Meyer
and Jews in postwar American culture, 347
Weiss, Avraham
and the impact of feminism on Jewish religious life, 308
Weiss-Rosmarin, Trude
"The Unfreedom of Jewish Women," 263
When Harry Met Sally, 350

INDEX

White Over Black (Jordan), 340
Whitfield, Stephen
  essay by, 337–53
Whoopi Goldberg, 349
Whyte, William H.
  and the Jewish American Princess stereotype, 327, 330
Wiesel, Elie
  La Nuit, 344
"Will There Be Orthodox Women Rabbis?" (Greenberg), 308
Wise, Stephen S.
  and Great Depression, 10
Wisse, Ruth
  and the impact of feminism on Jewish life, 284
Wohlgelernter, Devora
  and the impact of feminism on Jewish religious life, 315
Wolfe, Anne
  and the impact of feminism on Jewish religious life, 295
"Woman as Outsider" (Gornick), 261–62
Women, Jewish
  changes in life-cycle of, 271–74
  educational improvements for, 275–78, 302–4
  and family, 267–70, 282–86
  and Jewish religious life, 295–316
  occupational improvements for, 275–78, 293–94
  and voluntarism, 287–92
  See also Feminism
Women Against Pornography
  and American feminist movement, 261
"Women and Change in Jewish Law"
  and *Conservative Judaism,* 264
"Women and Change in Jewish Law: Responses to the Fall 1974 Symposium"
  Conservative Judaism, 265
Worcester, Massachusetts
  American Jewish occupational patterns in, 197
  percentage of Jewish professionals in, 195–96
  1930s occupational patterns in, 170
World Sephardi Institute
  and American Sephardim, 109
World War II
  and American Jewry, 10–12
  American Jewry following, 17
  Jewish migration to Miami and Los Angeles following, 35–46
  Jewish migration to southern and western cities during, 36–37
Wouk, Herman
  Marjorie Morningstar, 322, 325, 328, 347

Years of Lyndon Johnson, The (Caro), 340
Yellow Cab Company
  and John D. Hertz, 237
Yiddish literature, 23
Yiddishe Farmer, Der, 70

Zangwill, Israel
  The Melting-Pot, 347
Zuckerman, Nathan
  and Jews in postwar American culture, 344, 345, 348
Zuckoff, Aviva Cantor
  and *The Jewish Woman: An Anthology,* 264